Theopolitical Figures

Edinburgh Studies in Comparative Political Theory & Intellectual History
Series Editor: Vasileios Syros

Edinburgh Studies in Comparative Political Theory & Intellectual History welcomes scholars interested in the comparative study of intellectual history/political ideas in diverse cultural contexts and periods of human history and Comparative Political Theory (CPT).

The series addresses the core concerns of CPT by placing texts from various political, cultural and geographical contexts in conversation. It calls for substantial reflection on the methodological principles of comparative intellectual history in order to rethink of some of the conceptual categories and tools used in the comparative exploration of political ideas. The series seeks original, high-quality monographs and edited volumes that challenge and expand the canon of readings used in teaching intellectual history and CPT in Western universities. It will showcase innovative and interdisciplinary work focusing on the comparative examination of sources, political ideas and concepts from diverse traditions.

Available Titles:
Simon Kennedy, *Reforming the Law of Nature: The Secularisation of Political Thought, 1532–1689*

Lee Ward, *Recovering Classical Liberal Political Economy: Natural Rights and the Harmony of Interests*

Evert van der Zweerde, *Russian Political Philosophy: Anarchy, Authority, Autocracy*

Haig Patapan, *Modern Philosopher Kings: Wisdom and Power in Politics*

Montserrat Herrero, *Theopolitical Figures: Scripture, Prophecy, Oath, Charisma, Hospitality*

Forthcoming:
Leandro Losada, *Machiavelli in Argentina and Hispanic America, 1880–1940: Liberal and Anti-Liberal Political Thought in Comparative Perspective*

Filippo Marsili and Eugenio Menegon, *Translation as Practice: Intercultural Encounters between Europe and China and the Creation of Global Modernities*

Vassilis Molos, *The Russian Mediterranean: Shaping Sovereignty and Selfhood on the Island of Paros, 1768–1789*

Miguel Vatter, *Machiavelli and the Religion of the Ancients: Platonism and Radical Republicanism*

Theopolitical Figures

Scripture, Prophecy, Oath, Charisma, Hospitality

MONTSERRAT HERRERO

EDINBURGH
University Press

To my father

Edinburgh University Press is one of the leading university presses in the UK. We publish academic books and journals in our selected subject areas across the humanities and social sciences, combining cutting-edge scholarship with high editorial and production values to produce academic works of lasting importance. For more information visit our website: edinburghuniversitypress.com

© Montserrat Herrero, 2023, 2025

Edinburgh University Press Ltd
13 Infirmary Street
Edinburgh EH1 1LT

First published in hardback by Edinburgh University Press 2023

Typeset in 11/15 Adobe Sabon
by Manila Typesetting Company

A CIP record for this book is available from the British Library

ISBN 978-1-3995-2291-5 (hardback)
ISBN 978-1-3995-2289-2 (paperback)
ISBN 978-1-3995-2288-5 (webready PDF)
ISBN 978-1-3995-2256-4 (epub)

The right of Montserrat Herrero to be identified as the author of this work has been asserted in accordance with the Copyright, Designs and Patents Act 1988, and the Copyright and Related Rights Regulations 2003 (SI No. 2498).

Contents

Acknowledgements	vi
Introduction: The Theological Turn in Political Philosophy	1
1. Scripture or the Unconditional Character of Justice	39
2. Prophecy or the Deconstruction of Historical Expectation	73
3. Oath or the Given Word	117
4. *Charisma* or the Power as Gift	157
5. Hospitality or the Limits of the Political Community	206
Epilogue	239
Bibliography	251
Index	280

Acknowledgements

This book, like any form of scripture, traces a biographical trajectory and owes much to the dialogue with a number of colleagues. First and foremost, I would like to thank the members of my research group Religion and Civil Society, at the Institute for Culture and Society of the University of Navarra, for the incalculable hours we have spent over the years sharing and discussing ideas. I am particularly grateful to the medievalist Jaume Aurell, with whom I have been working for years in the field of political theology. I would also like to thank all the colleagues with whom I have been able to discuss in one way or another the ideas expressed in the book for their invaluable help in different forums. I am thinking of Rafael Alvira, Martin Aurell, Antonio Bento, Arthur Bradley, Philippe Buc, Emmanuel Cattin, Antonio Cerella, Mitchell Dean, William Franke, Andrea Mura, Henning Ottmann, Luisa Simonutti, Elettra Stimilli, Miguel Vatter, Carmelo Vigna and Robert Yelle. In a special way my gratitude also goes to Vasileios Syros. Together with Ersev Ersoy, he facilitated the reception of the manuscript of this book at Edinburgh University Press.

Special thanks are due to Philip Muller and his son, Philip Muller Aguirre, proofreaders of the manuscript. For someone like me, whose mother tongue is not English, their labour was of great value. The combination of a veteran philologist and a young philosopher, at the time my doctoral student, happened to work wonderfully.

I am also grateful to those at the Institute for Culture and Society who spend their time in securing material resources so that we can devote more time to research, in particular Jaime García del Barrio and Alex Hansen.

Finally, I would like to dedicate this book to my father, José (Pepe) Herrero. He passed away at the age of 95, on 15 February 2020. A month after he left us, the world began to change forever. The tragedy of a new pandemic, the Russian invasion of Ukraine, the new redistribution of power in the international order and the threat of an economic recession were coupled to the subjective pain of loss and grief. It seemed that the world would never go back to the way it was, that it had already passed a point of no return. Indeed, the death of my father marked a clear 'tearing of time'. This epochal tearing has strengthened many convictions I owe only to him; present as they are in these pages, so is his memory. Let this book be, then, a trace and testimony of his beautiful life.

Introduction: The Theological Turn in Political Philosophy

Any discourse can only claim to be an untimely intervention in the context of a discursive framework. This book, which aims to elucidate on the theological–political figures present in the constitution of the political, is therefore written against a backdrop. This backdrop is made up of many interwoven threads that are the result of numerous discussions bearing on the question of the political and the sacred. If the characteristics of this backdrop were not made at least minimally explicit, it would not be possible to understand the course of action that is intended to be followed and developed in the rest of the book. This is what this brief introduction intends to do.

The Backdrop

The first clarification to be made is that we speak of the theological instead of the religious, because the concept of "the religious' is much more blurred. When we use the expression 'the theological' we are not referring to positive confessions, that is to say, to a set of dogmatic beliefs held by any one church, which is one of the meanings of 'religion', as in, for example, the Christian religion. As Trevor Stack argues, the proper meaning of *religion* is defined as a counterweight to the modern state.[1] In fact, the category of *religion* appeared and started to be used in opposition to the modern state, meaning those kind of confessions excluded by the state. Nevertheless, religion can be retraced to ancient times, even if, as Talal Asad has suggested, the Reformation was crucial in order to construct the category 'religion'.[2]

We speak of the theological in a similar way that Hent de Vries speaks of 'religion, beyond a concept' to signify a 'set of phenomena whose simultaneous density ("thickness") and elusiveness (or "thinness") belong to the "heart" of this "matter" and constitute its references in their very "essence", that is to say, their logic and grammar'.[3] To move beyond the concept as defined by de Vries means entering into a constellation of particulars, such as words, gestures, texts and practices that have the character of thickness and elusiveness at the same time; that is, that they conceal while they reveal. The absence–presence dialectic is at the core of these phenomena: historical origins, scriptural sources or ritual practices.

Taking this terminological aspect into consideration, the background against which the discourse in this book is built has three derivations: the post-secular context; the theological turn in philosophy; and the consolidation of political theology as a theoretical and practical area.

The post-Secular

Our evolution to a post-secular society is largely seen as inevitable. In fact, there has been a revival of the sacred in contemporary societies that seems to show the failure of the Weberian diagnostic of the progressive disenchantment of the world, which went hand in hand with the historical narrative of its progressive secularisation. Both ideas suppose that the presence of the divine is progressively declining not only in public spaces and in private practice, but also in academic discourse.

In fact, Max Weber's well-known diagnosis has long served as an interpretative framework for explaining the historical fact that religious meanings and practices have been substituted by procedural mechanisms and rationalisation. This is well-documented in his *Essays on Sociology of Religion*, in particular, in *The Protestant Ethic and the Spirit of Capitalism*.[4] Starting in the nineteenth century, his diagnosis even became 'normative' for political action and has tended to confine religion to a violent and uncivilised past.

The philosophy of history has also spread the idea of the progressive secularisation of the world. Karl Löwith's *Weltgeschichte und Heilsgeschehen* has been one of the principal milestones in the popularisation of the so-called 'secularisation thesis'.[5] In Löwith this thesis appears as the progressive replacement of the interpretation of history as being guided by Providence, for the different accounts of history since Voltaire in which history is guided by reason.

Many twentieth-century intellectuals have adopted this thesis almost uncritically. Hans Blumenberg, however, was one of its first critics.[6] The dogma of secularisation – interpreted as an 'expropriation' and involving the idea of 'historical injustice' – is an unjustified construction deriving from the philosophy of history. According to Blumenberg, this characterisation is ideological and it misinterprets the very concept of history. Modernity should be defined independently, and not in relation to an origin that it betrays. The Modern Age justifies reality by the sole fact of its very existence, and not because of a transcendental or precedent order, or any other external reference that might justify its present order. Immanence is the modern category par excellence and modernity affirms its autonomy and authenticity through science and technology. Modernity claims, in the voice of Blumenberg, its own legitimacy through a discontinuity with the Middle Ages. This discontinuity also means a discontinuity with a world in which religion provides legitimation.

Kathleen Davis denounces Blumenberg's position by showing that the mere idea of periodisation is structurally and historically inextricable from that of sovereignty and concludes that Blumenberg's thesis is in itself an application of the principle he wants to deny.[7] Blumenberg is caught in the very trap that he criticises by establishing immanentism as the category of modernity par excellence. Moreover, Davis critically engages this important narrative of modernity (both in Löwith and Blumenberg's view), which implies in this case that the development of history inexorably leads to a progressive vanishing of religion from every place in society – beginning in the public sphere – and from theoretical and practical disciplines.

In fact, does history really testify to such a linear process? Is it true that religion as such is a source of violence or intolerance? Can philosophical reason be completely autonomous and separate from religious experience? The idea that we have evolved into a post-secular society has become commonplace and poses an important challenge to the alleged 'modern thesis'. Enlightened categories related to the presence or absence of religions in the public space, such as John Locke's texts on toleration,[8] have proven themselves so insufficient that Jürgen Habermas was able to declare that we have entered a post-secular age heralding a new discussion in academia.[9]

It seems that enlightened reason has exhausted itself in theory and in practice. Indeed, religions continue to emerge in the public arena, including the media, under the guise of new beliefs and representations, new religious movements and the revival of old religions. We can even speak of a process of re-enchantment or re-mythologisation of the world that involves recovering symbolic and meaningful aspects of culture, against which the past decade has reacted in favour of the structural aspects of linguistic constructions and procedural protocols.

The Theological Turn in Philosophy

Along with the discussion on secularism in the social sciences and in the interpretation of history, different philosophical traditions have also experienced a turn towards 'the theological'.[10] The expression 'theological turn', which avoids the use of the contested term religion, properly comes from Dominique Janicaud, who used it in 1990 to critically designate the phenomenological movement in France from 1975 to 1990. In those years, philosophy took on a decidedly theological agenda, as testified in the works of this movement's most representative French authors, such as Emmanuel Lévinas, Jean-Luc Marion, Michel Henry and Jean Louis Chrétien, among others. In 1999, Hent de Vries followed Janicaud's original diagnostic in his book *Philosophy and the Turn to Religion*, in this case signalling Derrida as one of the protagonists of the theological turn.[11]

Janicaud's opening debate ushered in a variety of publications, including another milestone in the discussion, *God in France: Eight Contemporary French Thinkers on God*, by Peter Jonkers and Rund Welten,[12] which discusses thinkers such as Jacques Derrida, Paul Ricoeur, René Girard, Jean Francois Lyotard and Jean-Yves Lacoste. The volume edited by Hent de Vries and Lawrence E. Sullivan, *Political Theologies: Public Religions in a Post-Secular World*, as the result of different conferences that took place between 2001 and 2004, was, as it were, a report on what was happening at the time in continental philosophy in relation to the theological turn.[13] Another milestones in shaping the 'turn' are Bruce Ellis Benson and Norman Wirzba's book, *Words of Life*, and Aaron Simmons, *God and the Other*.[14] After examining these publications, we can say that one of the most important motivations of this turn is to highlight the idea that overcoming onto-theology is not the same as overcoming God.

The radical theology movement stands as a clear precedent of the theological turn as reported by Janicaud. In this case, it was theology that turned to philosophy assuming a radical interpretation of the Nietzschean trope of the death of God. In fact, in the 1960s, Thomas J. J. Altizer led the theological movement of the death of God.[15] For him, Nietzsche inaugurates with this sentence a new historical–theological phase of the absence of God. We have to suppose, he will say, that the death of God is an event that happened in 'our time, our history and our existence'.[16] This new theological time announces the negation of every form of Christian theology, but it remains Christian insofar as it proclaims Jesus as a model for praxis.

Radical theology has followed its own path and had new representatives in the 1980s, as in the case of Mark C. Taylor, Charles E. Winquist and Carl A. Raschke.[17] An epigone of this kind of theology is Katherine Keller, although she can be better considered as a representative of the 'theology of the process'.[18] The reading of the Christianism practiced by these authors could be considered as a form of post-modern theology following Taylor's assertion that: 'deconstruction is the hermeneutic of the death of God'.[19]

In continental philosophy we can recognise some authors who follow the theological turn in a *sui generis* way. This is the case of Jacques Derrida, Jean-Luc Nancy, Giorgio Agamben, Gianni Vattimo, John D. Caputo, Richard Kearney and Merold Westphal.[20] Some of these theoretical approaches could also be considered as theological philosophies of the death of God.[21]

In addition, the political theology of St Paul has given rise to a slew of academic literature, of which Jacob Taubes was a pioneer. Alain Badiou, Giorgio Agamben, Slavoj Žižek and Eric Santner have all contributed to a Pauline political theology. Through its exegesis, Paul's discourse seems to be a target for deconstruction or an interesting alibi for the creation of subversive bibles. The work of many of these authors remains indebted to a new materialism. They are oriented to the unknowable or the absolute understood as the unprecedented, the encounter, the call, the extraordinary or just the new.[22]

Contemporary with this theological turn is the renewal of apophatic theology in the work of William Franke.[23] Franke tries to recover the traces of the divine in its impossibility to self-express. The way to approach divinity in his view is the reactivation of imagination of the divine. Such is, he claims, the role that literature plays in revelation. In his view, the revelatory claim of literature is transformed by modern approaches to poetry where divine revelation is reconfigured and transfigured by the medium of self-conscious poetic art and invention.

The semiotics of religion, in the way that, for example, Robert Yelle develops it, is also a way of turning to religion nowadays in a post-structuralist direction.[24] To look at the signs of the sacred and their meanings in history helps to discover the consistency of the divine.

Political Theology

Many of the philosophers that participate in the abovementioned theological turn incorporate distinctive elements of what has been called 'political theology'. In fact, political theology, by definition, involves the idea of theology 'intertwining' with philosophy and politics.

The expression can be traced back to the *theologia civilis* which appears in Augustine of Hippo's *City of God* and passes through its modern imprint in Spinoza's *Theological-Political Treatise*, but it must be admitted that it was taken up as common currency by Carl Schmitt in his *Political Theology* of 1922. Thus, configured and disseminated in academic literature by Carl Schmitt, to account for a 'sociology of juristic concepts', consisting of 'radical conceptualization, a consistent thinking that is pushed into metaphysics and theology',[25] this concept has been widely used by scholars as a basis for studying the transferences between the meanings, symbols and practices of the secular and the spiritual realms throughout history.[26]

What Schmitt wanted to point out in his *Political Theology I and II*,[27] is that it is impossible to avoid the transference of meanings between different fields of knowledge and action, particularly between theology and politics, when attempting to understand a given political or juridical phenomenon. Beyond this general description, two different assumptions attributed to political theology can be found in Schmitt's general hypothesis: one related to the secularisation thesis – all significant concepts within modern theory of the state are secularised theological concepts; and the other related to the possibility of establishing a structural analogy between both realms – the political and the theological.[28]

The first part of the hypothesis has been discussed by Ernst Katorowicz and Jan Assmann, who have shown that theopolitical transferences of ideas and concepts may be encountered not only in modernity, but in the Middle Ages as much as in Antiquity. In fact,

Ernst Kantorowicz's *The King's Two Bodies: A Study in Medieval Political Theology*,[29] defends the transference of the ecclesiological idea of the *corpus mysticum* to the juridical sphere in the form of 'two bodies of the King'. Through this concrete example, he demonstrates how the political theological thesis worked in the Middle Ages in both directions from the political and juridical to the theological and vice versa.[30] For his part, Jan Assmann affirms that, in Antiquity, this transference of meanings went against the medieval and early modern broader current, since the central concepts of theology are 'theologised political concepts'.[31] In fact, Jan Assmann, also inspired by Schmitt, has explored how such a thesis operated in the ancient world, particularly in Egypt and Israel; what he has found is 'theologification' (*Theologisierung*) instead of secularisation, suggesting that the transference of meanings at that time and place could be characterised as an appropriation by the religious sphere of the meanings that were alive in the political discourse.[32]

Schmitt's idea has widely influenced research in humanities. His synthetic thesis can be enlarged and has already been enlarged. Graham Hamill and Julia Reinhard Lupton, for example, consider political theology as a critical discourse in the humanities aimed at organising a research field. In fact, for example, within 'political theology' they tend 'to identify the exchanges, pacts and contexts that obtain between religious and political life, especially the use of sacred narratives, motifs and liturgical forms to establish, legitimate, and reflect upon the sovereignty of monarchs, corporations, and parliaments'.[33]

Claude Lefort proposes an alternative way of considering political theology in democracy. Lefort readily admits that society cannot function without some type of representation of unity, which often originates in religion. However, the democratic form of representation is an empty place, and more specifically the absence of a body. Nevertheless, this empty place makes possible a plurality of symbolisations. Lefort's argument on the permanence of the theological–political reveals some ambiguity and tension. In any case, his effort can be understood as affirming that the political is inseparable from theological–political tension.[34]

Giorgio Agamben for his part has developed the 'economical–political' paradigm derived from the trinitarian analogy, affirming also the idea of the 'empty throne'.[35] Certainly, at the core of his thesis is the characterisation of the Christian Trinity as an *oikonomia*. This means that in contrast to the theological–political paradigm of sovereignty, which emphasises the unity of power, the economic paradigm refers primarily to governmentality derived from other *dispositifs* like the assemblage, the network, the complex system. This economical paradigm is analogous to the Trinitarian *oikonomia* as a figure of plural, interdependent and heterogeneous elements that nonetheless form a non-transcendent unity. As Dean attests, '. . . the Holy Trinity marked one of the first, and perhaps most influential, applications of the logic of the dispositive in the Occident'.[36]

These enlargements of the theological–political paradigm imply that the secularisation thesis operates in some examples of early modernity, but cannot be read as an uninterrupted process. I agree with Hans Blumenberg when he argues that to defend theopolitical analogies it is not necessary to accept the secularisation thesis. But the fact that analogies can be established and that they are still comprehensible implies that secularisation, if it had existed, would have been an infinite process that would never be completed. In any case, what is valuable about political theology is not the study of historical causes or historical explanations, but rather its focus on structural and semantical parallels and transferences of meanings between two different spheres that aspire to be absolute and that share the same contexts of meaning in a given age. It should not assume causal derivations or theological–political intentions in the political actors. In this sense, what Schmitt wants to demonstrate through the proposition of the 'structural analogy' is that the relationship between politics and spiritual power or theology will always remain open, and that each historical moment has had to find an answer in a specific manner to the relationship between both. The way in which each historical moment finds such answers may generate new means to interpret history and philosophy.

But, indeed, in recent decades we have seen the emergence of academic discourses that look for political derivations from dogma, of a kind that could be achieved in an 'affirmative political theology', as was the case with Johann Baptist Metz or Jürgen Moltmann in the 1960s. Recent examples of an affirmative political theology in the context of Christianity can be found in the analogies that William T. Cavanaugh proposes in his *Theopolitical Imagination*.[37] He advocates making use of theological concepts in the political context to reverse the theological–political secular movement that originated in modernity. The sacred realm, he proposes, could provide us with concepts that serve as political ideas in the praxis, although this is possible only if we awaken our theological imagination. John Milbank and Catherine Pickstock followed a similar path under the label of 'Radical Orthodoxy'.[38]

On the other hand, the radical theology movement, which we have already considered, advocates an affirmative 'radical political theology'. Among its exponents are Jeffrey W. Robbins,[39] Clayton Crockett[40] and Creston Davis.[41] Even if they are different in their theoretical approaches, they coincide in having a common political agenda. The novelty of radical political theology is the transference of political meanings to the event provoked by the name of God, particularly that of democracy. The image that these theologians would like to deconstruct is not, as in Nietzsche's perspective, that of the Crucified, but that of the 'all powerful God'. As Crockett underlines, the death of God in the political domain means that today it is impossible to believe in a rational, benevolent and sovereign God.[42] Faced with this fact, radical political theology concludes that it not only becomes impossible to refer to God in an intelligible discourse, but that it is also impossible to think of God as an object of faith, and, consequently, it is not possible to restore religion. The only possible path open to a consequent theology in the historical period of the death of God is the substitution of the name of God by other names in a complex game of meanings and metaphors taken from political language.[43] In fact, one of the central questions posed by radical political theology is about the meaning of divinity using democracy as a discursive framework, since democracy is not the name of a constituted regime, but a permanent future, a promise.[44] Democracy, conceived as a utopia, is the sole political form that allows its own deconstruction, since it guarantees its own revision and its own repeatability, and for that reason it assures its impotence in the face of every omnipotence.[45] This happens in multifarious ways and harbours a plurality of differences.[46] This political project functions as an authentic faith.[47]

This complex discussion concerning the post-secular, the theological turn in philosophy and political theology is the backdrop that has inspired the question I would like to reformulate in this book: to what extent is the centrality of the theological discourse in originating meanings, symbols and realities relevant for shaping instituted practices in the political realm.

Figures

At the beginning of his book *Secular Scriptures*, William Franke asserts that 'secularization is intrinsic to theological revelation'.[48]

In fact, the idea of revelation presupposes an inaccessible 'X', which remains beyond any form of knowledge, and which, however, is somehow made noticeable by revelation itself. The divine 'kneels over' the world. The idea of the incarnation of God that is at the centre of the Christian faith expresses an extreme meaning of secularisation. Seen from this perspective, secularisation means the radical inscription of God in the world; so radical that it can be conceived as cutting off all reference to the beyond.[49]

It is in the context of this inscription of God in immanence where some 'theological tropes' begin to matter again in the way human beings think and experience the world. Giorgio Agamben expresses this idea using the term 'signature', an expression already used by Michel de Certeau and Derrida.[50] Agamben maintains that 'secularization operates in the conceptual system of modernity as a *signature* that refers it back to theology'.[51] Didier Franck points out that already in *Einführung in die phänomenologische Forschung*,[52] Martin Heidegger, attributed to the '*clara et distincta* perception' the character of a secularised product of the Christian idea of grace. He spoke of a detheologised understanding under this rubric of the translation or transference of the originary propositions of the Christian faith's domain to the sphere of philosophical knowledge. Following Heidegger's path, Franck remarks, that when a concept comes from the Christian dogmatic, it retains the mark of its original domain, that is, ultimately, the mark of God himself.[53] If a concept marked as Christian is exported from its native domain, some of its theological traces may be erased, but at the same time a surreptitious and radical theologisation of philosophy is being carried out, since a trace of God is introduced into it. The same could be said about other practices as is, for example, the case of the political. In fact, as Derrida has recognised, Christianity over-determines the language of law and politics: 'No alleged disenchantment, no secularization comes to interrupt it. On the contrary.'[54] Certainly, detheologisation cannot avoid carrying the weight of its theological origin. This mark of origin could not be erased as if it were any type of mark, because its origin exceeds all others. For this reason, it can be seen as an infinite task, since it can never be achieved.

The aim of the following pages is to discover the divine marks, the theological signatures, embedded in some institutionalised political practices. These marks speak of God and in a way reveal Him, by saying something about Him or by representing Him. This purpose could be considered a kind of 'theological turn' in political philosophy, interpreted as a way of reinscribing contemporary political concepts and experiences in the 'theological locus', from which they supposedly come.

The name adopted here for designating these signatures is that of figure. Theopolitical figures are signatures of God that we find as roots of political instituted practices. In this second part of the Introduction, I would like to explore how these theological signatures speak of God or name God in a way that is negative, symbolic and definitively figural.

The Names of God

A very lengthy theological and philosophical tradition of negative theology, beginning with Dionysius and passing through Eckhart and Cusa, has come down to us as being representative of the contemporary theological turn in philosophy. In fact, the contemporary theological turn can be characterised as an 'apophatic turn', in a similar way to the Christian tradition of negative theology.[55] Indeed, some of the most representative participants in the 'philosophical turn' in philosophy made, in de Vries words: 'a movement toward God, toward the name of God; and no less a dramatic farewell to almost the canonical, dogmatic or ontotheological interpretations of this very same God'.[56]

In fact, negative theology is based on a critique of all positive and dogmatic formulations regarding divinity, since our senses and our words cannot express accurately what the divine is. Avoiding idolatry is the main task of negative theology. We can only know and say what God is not. Muteness should be the only consequent way to act before God. In fact, the tradition of negative theology tends to be a mysticism.[57] In monotheist revelations, one of the main features of God is His concealment, along with His revelation. The encounter with God always implies a sort of exodus in order to find that concealed luminosity. He is the hidden within this world. To find Him we have some marks or some imprints that at the same time as revealing Him speak of what He is not. Derrida gives the example of the 'seal' as a figure of the unfigurable.[58]

In a negative theological perspective, what cannot be said is actually the basis for all that is said. We could broaden this sentence in an historical–existential perspective by saying that the basis for the events that happen in God's name is the impossibility of what cannot happen in this world at its plenitude – God himself. There is a beyond language and there is a beyond existence. In the same way that the apophatic entails a claim to a yet more powerful comprehensiveness, the unpresentable character of the divine in history entails a claim to a richer existence, which no one can attain.[59]

Contemporary philosophy has recovered the possibilities of this negative access to the divine by substituting God with other names in a metaphorical interplay of meanings and significations. Confronted with a similar problem to that of the old negative theology (an impossible God for human discourse and an unpresentable God for human experience), contemporary philosophy looks for other ways of evoking Him: events, bodies or secular scriptures. These are then reinterpreted in a way that they 'pass under the name' of God, in John Caputo's phrasing: 'God is the event that takes place in the name of God'.[60] He promotes a negative theology of the event. We cannot understand God as a supreme being, nor as the cause or foundation of beings, nor even as a being. It makes no sense either to say that God has a proper name, authentic representatives or orthodoxies. To give God the name of a *res* would be idolatrous. The kingdom of God can act only as a disruption.[61] Every existing order is always the prevailing kingdom for which deconstruction is designed to instigate trouble in the name of the kingdom of God.[62] This is the *via negativa* of Caputo's political theology.

Another way of pursuing this *via negativa* is that of substituting names for bodies, as Jean-Luc Nancy tries to do. His a-theology claims to be the definitive inscription of the infinite in the finite. In fact, for Nancy, every art-image is an incarnation.[63] In this exegesis, the Eucharist is the presence of the absent, of one who is continually withdrawing. When we call on God, we encounter the presence of His death.[64] Religion is a frustrating relationship involving the constant absence of a potential presence. Consequently, for Nancy, art is an expression of the name of God in a *via negativa*.[65] It is a kind of substitute for the divine presence. Every image in its dynamic is in itself divine: 'Image and text are the two holy species of a single withdrawn presence.'[66] There is a desire for the image to speak, a desire to become the body of the word. Both have a common cause: a real presence. Both contribute to fixing the presence, as in the Eucharist, where there is a material image but also the presence of words that make the transubstantiation possible. Briefly, according to Nancy, art reveals the proper sense of the Eucharist: *kenosis*. God empties Himself to the point that what subsists is just a piece of bread.[67] It is the complete alienation of God. In the Eucharist, God is present *qua absent*.[68] Christianity was crucial for the opening of the world to an inaccessible alterity and therefore activated a disclosure that comes down to our times and that will be with us forever. Christianity is not just the object, but also the subject of deconstruction. It is self-deconstruction. What then remains of the divine? The corporeal 'there' of art, that is, of bodies. Art tries to inscribe the 'beyond' in the 'there'.

Nancy's ontology implies a conscious castration of the spirit in its incarnation in worldly phenomena. Yet this castration of the spirit cannot be properly expressed without recurring to a metaphorical use of non-castrated spiritual phenomena, as is the case of Christ's Incarnation and his 'real presence' in the Eucharist. Finite thinking must have recourse to infinite thinking, and if not to a metaphysical language, then at least to its 'images' and 'rituals', such as incarnation, adoration and Eucharist, among others. In fact, in *Adoration*, Nancy seems to acknowledge the dependence of the finite on the infinite: this is, the attitude of adoration. Negation of every determination opens to infinitude, just like the orifices of the body connect it to what is beyond. God is simply excess: an excess that manifests itself in the contingency of the world and in 'fortuity'. Finite thinking is not sufficiently finite, and therefore it always has to be constructed as a result of deconstruction, just as with the case of atheism in relation to Christianity.[69]

William Franke represents another attempt 'to (un)define and (de)situate the theological'.[70] There are many scriptures; and all of them are equally revelatory.[71] Franke has developed a 'critique of apophatic reason', meaning a rational examination of first principles transforming them into a literary hermeneutics or poetics and into religious reflection. Literary hermeneutics means an elucidation of certain rhetorical conditions that make meaningful discourse possible. These conditions of possibility of meaning and therewith also of being are marks of the unsayable. The unsayable is not an object at all, because, if it were, it could be said in some language.[72] For this reason, Franke says that it is better to call it 'Nothing'. Apophatic discourse is the negative for which no positive can be presented. From this point of view, Franke interprets revelation as a 'strong statement in support of total disclosure in the Word'.[73] This revelation, however, leaves the mystery of the divine life intact, since this presence was destroyed by death and the resurrection is a new mystery that remains unrevealed at the very movement of revelation. Christ is an *unmediated presence*, but 'as broken and disseminated, the Word becomes salvific in the eucharistic community in which love silently discourses through charitable *action*'.[74]

This position understands transcendence as the openness of thought towards an infinity that can be reached only by negating every definition and every determination. Consciousness can give content to the divine only through human action, emotion and devotion, but not through definite concepts.

In all these attempts, God cannot be expressed in finite terms, in any one discourse more than another, in any one figuration more than another, and for that reason we have to deduce that it is a Nothing that converts into an Everything. If we can still speak of a 'revelation', that is, of a notice of the divine, the question remains: how to interpret the relationship between God and the plurality of the world in terms other than Nothing, the Indefinite, the pure Other or the Beyond. Could we consider the limit between God and the world, or negativity in some other way?

Jacques Derrida is critical of this *via theologica negativa*. He notes in *How to Avoid Speaking* that negative theology still presupposes a trajectory that is propositional, that is, that privileges the unity of the world and the authority of the name; it reserves beyond all positive predication some hyper-essentiality; and it assumes the promise of a mystical vision.[75] For some negative theological attempts, says Derrida, 'God's name would suit everything that may not be broached, approached or designated, except in an indirect and negative manner.'[76] Almost as if negation would produce divinity, he criticises. Moreover, the apophatic movement cannot contain within itself the principle of its interruption. It always defers the encounter with its own limit. In any event, it seems that the advice to remain silent regarding what one cannot speak about, contradicts the injunction of saying something: 'it is necessary that there *has been* a trace, a sentence that one must simultaneously turn toward a past and toward a future that are as yet unpresentable'.[77] To avoid speaking is to delay the moment when one will have to say something. In fact, Derrida thinks that something has to be said, even if it is inadequate, and preserves the deferring or the '*differance*', which is crucial to avoid idolatry. God appears in the reverse of the finitude as the impossible, beyond any conditions. God is not a condition of possibility, but the impossible that makes any condition possible. He is beyond the limit and because of that He is not. In spite of all this, Derrida enunciates the impossible, in what he calls 'figures of the unconditional': the promise, the gift, hospitality, forgiveness; that is, he concludes, 'what we call God'.[78]

I retain Derrida's motto: something has to be said even if it is inadequate. In fact, as Jean-Louis Chrétien points out, there is an apophatic tradition that considers silence superior to the word, and superior precisely because it withdraws it, negates it and surpasses it. However, there is another tradition of negative theology, such as that of Proclus, for example, in which radical negativity would not prevent knowledge by connaturality. What characterises the negative thinking of the principle in the Platonic tradition is not simply the setting of negations as superior to affirmations; nor is it the showing that of the principle one cannot say what it is, but only what it is not; but what mainly characterises that tradition is the surpassing of the negations themselves. As Proclus himself points out, there can be only negation if there is a previous proposition. The apophasis must be overcome: silence must be overcome. There has to be a beyond to silence and a beyond to the word that is the basis of both, states Chrétien.[79] For his part, John Damascene, whom Chrétien calls the 'greatest deconstructor' in the history of philosophy, tries to eschew even thought. To put the absolute in any relation to us would be to define it, to determine it. In the end, silence is to be silent about ourselves. To this thesis of Damascene, Chrétien adds: isn't this 'representation' of the absolute as someone who cannot even be approached too human? Does it not transform the emptiness of our own spirit into an idol?[80] It was precisely the historical task of Dionysius the Areopagite to wrest negative theology from the impulse that led it to the idolatry of nothingness, in order to introduce the incarnate Word. Excessive silence, illuminating the word, manifests rather than conceals. It is not the silence of Platonism, although Dionysius owes much to it. Chrétien refers to the expression of Maximus the Confessor about Jesus as silence mysteriously hidden behind numerous voices: a polyphonic silence, one that gives voice in a generous way. The praise of silence finds its limit in the revelation of God and in the incarnation of the Word.[81]

At the core of early modernity, we find another tradition of negative theology, that of Nicholas of Cusa. Again, he is looking for an appropriate name for God, noting the impossibility of this task. In different works, he explores different names: *maximum* that coincides with its opposite *minimum* (*De docta ignorantia*); *idem absolutum* or *ipsum idem*; *possest* (*De possest*); *posse ipsum* (*Compendium* and *De apice theoria*); *non aliud* (*Directio speculantis seu de li non aliud*). These names remain possible hypotheses for naming God. The Toledo manuscript of his *Directio speculantis seu de li non aliud* has a subtitle that specifies the enigmatic divine name he explores in the book: *Of the definition that defines everything*. We could also say: of the *determination that determines everything*. The definition of God in these terms is not another, but 'not-other'. God is beyond the distinction between other and not-other. Not-other precedes all definition by virtue of the fact that it defines everything; and everything is other since not-other precedes them.[82] It is this definition that defines everything and itself, and not the undefinable.[83] The definition that defines everything is not-other than what is defined. The 'not-other than' structure is that of definition in itself. At the same time, without the not-other each entity would then cease to be identical to itself and could no longer be different from the others. Difference presupposes unity: there is no otherness without not-otherness. While the other cannot exist without the not-other, the not-other can exist without the other, since nothing precedes it. Definition and being are equalised in Cusa's reflection. Every signification that is other than Not-other terminates in something other than in the Beginning, and this is what we call opposition. Not-other, however, is beyond opposition and indicates that in a world that stands as real, oppositions stand. God is the force of the limitation that creates those oppositions by virtue of defining and of being beyond these definitions as definition itself – the Not-Other – and not as the undefined. This not-other consists of the co-implication of those oppositions and partial definitions: this is Cusa's idea of *coincidentia oppositorum*. Not-Other is for him simpler than the One, since the One takes from Not-Other the fact that it is 'not other than one', whereas the converse is not true. Parmenides and Dionysius placed the one as beyond any contradiction; but for Cusa the Not-Other is a much clearer expression of a divine name than the One. He notes that Not-Other is even before Nothing.[84]

Every aspect of God's reality can be named in as much as it is made manifest by this logic. Reinscribing realities in God means showing the Not-other in other,[85] because He who is Not-other is not *other*; nor is He *other than other*; nor is He *other in another*.[86] When we see something *other*, at the same time we are seeing something *not-other*; and in this way the *other* and *not-other* are distinguished. Since it is before numbers, the *not-other* is not multipliable.[87] A name is what it is as long as it participates in the *not-other*.[88]

Cusa tries to show the concordance of his doctrine with that of Dionysius the Aeropagite. Dionysius asserted for the first time with clarity, as Cusa would later do, that an opposition that pre-exists its opposites does not oppose anything.[89] Just as Dionysius did before him, Cusanus never abandoned his initial insight of the unopposed opposition of the opposites. He even proposes metaphors or symbols to speak about the relationship between God and creatures. Thinking through symbols and neologisms allows us some movement of mind and heart towards the divine mystery with whom we are ever connected.

In the case of Cusa, the unsayable must be said. There is an obligation to say 'before every injunction of remaining silent', using Derrida's expression.[90] The question then is how this beyond is present first through words, but, secondly, in actions, gestures or rituals. Dionysius the Aeropagite at the beginning of his main work *On the Celestial Hierarchy* justifies the necessity of symbolic speech in order to express realities that cannot be perceived by the senses. Derrida himself notes that the largest volume of Dionysius is *Symbolic Theology* and not *Mystical Theology*. Dionysius generates an 'economy' of signs, symbols, metaphors and figures, based on the same language that God Himself uses.[91] The inexpressible must be symbolised; the unpresentable must be figured.

The Symbolic

How to say what is unsayable? 'What cannot be said can only be said,'[92] announces de Certeau. If we can achieve no more than Nicholas of Cusa did in respect of defining Him, at least we can read the speech of the unsayable. In fact, we have His speech and His actions. God has spoken and acted in history.

Gerhard E. Caspary stresses that until the middle of the twelfth century, speech about God was deeply rooted in the symbolic grammar of the Bible.[93] As Robert Markus asserts, the symbolic was 'the Augustinian discovery'.[94] His originality consists in understanding the sign as operating a mimetic mediation in relation to a double alterity: the sign creates meaning by showing itself at the same time to the senses and to the spirit.[95] Moreover, the sign always addresses another. Augustine was completely aware of the importance of the context of communication in the understanding of the sign; and this awareness is grounded in Christian experience. In fact, the emphasis was made on the arbitrariness of signs and symbols that speak of God, in which some refer to others in a way that is immanent in God's speech itself and from which any other extra-discursive reality is interpreted, and not vice versa, as in the referential model of adequacy. Any person who receives God's discourse, the very subject of His revelation, lacks any external reference to access its content other than revelation itself.

We can intuit something of this in Saussure's linguistics, since his idea of a system of signs is also self-referential. The basis of any system of signs and of any symbolisation consists of invoking the concrete presence of an absence. In the case of Saussure's logic, this absence is that of the rest of the signs of the system. In any case, as Benveniste asserts, language is a very specific semiotic system, since it is the mediation of every other kind of significant system of signs, which need not operate as a system.[96]

Gadamer has been an important voice in the rehabilitation of the symbolic. He devotes some paragraphs of *Truth and Method* to elucidate on the specificity of the character of symbols and its differentiation from that of allegories.[97] He states that Winckelmann understood both concepts as synonymous. Both refer to something the meaning of which is beyond its mere manifestation. Symbols have a communitarian character that requires that they be 'instituted' in some way. By 'instituting', Gadamer means the fixation of the being of something as a sign or as a symbolic function. What a sign indicates depends primarily on its institution.[98] The other face of institutionalisation is indeterminacy. The inadequacy between form and meaning is essential to the symbol. Symbols function as substitutes, but they say nothing about what they symbolise: their relationship with what they stand for is a 'negative' one. That is the reason why symbols can be interpreted *ad infinitum*. If one is to understand to what they refer, one must be familiar with the context of the community to which they belong. Visible contemplation and invisible meaning are complicated in the symbolic. When it belongs to the sacred, what is symbolised is undoubtedly in need of representation, inasmuch as it is itself non-sensible, infinite and unpresentable.[99] In this case, the referent for symbolisation can be none other than God's own 'instituted' speech.

Another kind of representation is that of the 'image'. An image as such is not a symbol: symbols do not need to be shaped in images, and images do not supply an increment of meaning that goes beyond what they represent. Images are immediate, visible appearances. They shape the models to which they refer. Thanks to their immediacy, the institution of images is not necessary in determining their ontological valence. As Erich Przywara has pointed out, between a 'pure philosophy in concepts' and a 'pure philosophy in images' there is a gradated progression or regression in the use of analogies, which range from images to 'parables, symbols, myths mysteries and logos'.[100]

Figures

When we speak of 'figures', does this notion add something to the idea of symbolic speech? Or does a figure represent another rhetorical category? Speaking of figures implies going one step beyond symbols, since figures refer to embodied meanings and not simply to meanings in general. Figures refer to symbolic meanings that happen as historical events.[101]

Erich Auerbach is one of the few authors who have devoted some attention to figures.[102] The idea of the figure originally pertains to the field of rhetoric. But, thanks to a transference operated by Tertullian, who introduced pagan terms into Christian contexts, figures begin to be an historical–theological concept: a kerygmatic concordance between the Old and New Testaments, which allowed for a meaningful interpretation of sacred history as a whole and attempted to resolve the conflict between the particular events and the meaning in history. The category of figure becomes the nucleus of Christian hermeneutics. As Auerbach attests, for Tertullian, the figure of the prophet is a concrete historical fact that is substantiated by other concrete historical facts.[103] After him, Origen of Alexandria steered biblical interpretation more towards an allegoric and moral sense. For his part, Augustine tried to reformulate both currents by opposing the purely allegorical interpretation of Origen.[104] Origen's ideal sublimation is substituted in his interpretation by a historical recurrence. *Figura* evokes the possibility of an intermingled coexistence of temporality and timelessness, since in God there is no *differentia temporis*. Augustine's typological or figural vision converts historical events (*facta*) into symbolic forms (*verba*).[105] The divine happens in history in multiples *figurationes*. The beyond is always present, in any time, in its figures. The *figura* is a visible shadow, which, however, reveals.

How can a historical event be interpreted in the light of a subsequent event and at the same time preserving the uniqueness and revelatory character of each one? Not in a causal manner.[106] Figure evokes the idea of an event that is capable of shaping another event that is historically and temporally separate from the former. This shaping occurs by way of mimesis.[107] In fact, '*figura* is something real and historical which announces something else that is also real and historical. The relation between the two events is revealed by an accord of similarity.'[108] Every event is complete in itself and full in its meaning at the moment of its happening, but at the same time, when two or more events are assembled, they become revelatory of a transcendent meaning that is embedded in them. Hence, paradoxically, figures have a trans-historical temporal nature thanks to a certain 'insistence' in historical terms. 'Figural temporality' corresponds to events that 'insist, subsist and resist over time'.[109] The instant of every event is the 'temporal aspect' of figural occurrence.

The relationship between events in figural logic is completely different from the progressive view in which modernity interprets history. In the modern view, a provisional event is conceived as a step in an unbroken horizontal process at the outcome of which that particular event is only a part; however, in figural logic, events are considered not in their unbroken relation to one another, but individually, each one in relation to some meaning that each of them fully represents; and which, while being revealed by them, is nonetheless promised and not yet historically present. Figures have a symbolic texture insofar as they participate in the dialectic between presence and absence typical of symbolic realities.

Auerbach applies this theological idea to his exegesis of European literature. However, when we speak here of theopolitical figures, we apply the figural character to particular institutionalised political practices in which the divine somehow happens historically. Revelatory theopolitical figures must insist, resist and subsist if the community is to stand. Here, figures are considered as practices, and not merely as ideas or symbols, even if ideas and symbols accompany every figure.[110] These practices are interpreted in the light of that of which they are perceived to be signs. This is the idea of the 'figure'.

An idea closely related to this of theopolitical figures is Derrida's 'topolitology'. Interpreting Dionysius Aeropagite, he speaks of topolitology to refer to a 'secret divine place' at the core of the social link.[111] These places are 'sacred allegories which one has had the audacity to use to represent God, projecting outward and multiplying the visible appearances of the mystery . . .'[112] And Derrida makes an important addition to this text: 'Without the divine promise which is also an injunction, the power of these *synthemata* would be merely conventional rhetoric, poetry, fine arts, perhaps literature.'[113] Derrida even asks himself: 'What would be its institutional or political figure?'[114] This is the issue that this book addresses.

Theopolitical Figures

Which then are these 'figurations' of the divine in the political? What would their institutional or political figure be? Here, theopolitical figures are designated as scripture, prophecy, oath, charisma and hospitality. Some central features of contemporary societies are discernible in the symbolic meaning of these figures: the endurance of the law and the unconditional character of justice; the unfeasibility of historical expectation; the stability or instability of the given word; the way political power is legitimised; and the political–ethical imperative of welcoming strangers.

By naming these figures, this book investigates the divine meanings that persist in some of the institutionalised practices that our society considers indispensable. Since they are 'signatures' of the divine, it is not possible to erase them. Put in another way, here theopolitical figures are understood as political practices and institutions in which the divine is embedded.[115] Indeed, a certain number of words, things, gestures and powers might be seen as 'instances' of the 'divine' in political life. We recognise that they are 'theo-', that is, related to the divine, precisely because it is not possible to completely appropriate their presence and their meaning, as happens in the case of God himself. When we perceive the inappropriable character of some realities, we have to suspect that something of the divine is acting upon them. In them, God is 'taking place' without Him being His own place, as Derrida would say.[116]

Through the description of these figures, we address at the same time the implicit question of whether or not society has always to be thought of as being at the same time both sacred and civil. This includes the question of whether or not the 'permanence of the theologico-political', to use Lefort's expression, is inevitable for the subsistence of contemporary societies.

When dealing in the following chapters with these figures, we will, first, offer the meaning they symbolise; secondly, explain why they are figures of the divine; and, thirdly, show their historical 'insistence'-repeatability by offering a historical case as an example of each one.

Notes

1. Trevor Stack, 'Introduction', in *Religion as a Category of Governance and Sovereignty*, Trevor Stack, Naomi R. Goldenberg and Timothy Fitzgerald (eds) (Leiden: Brill, 2015), 1–21.
2. See Talal Asad, *Formations of the Secular: Christianity, Islam, Modernity* (Stanford, CA: Stanford University Press, 2003). Naomi Goldenberg suggests that its roots lie in ancient Greek ways of classifying cults. Naomi R. Goldenberg, 'The Category of Religion in

the Technology of Governance: An Argument for Understanding Religions as Vestigial States', in *Religion as a Category of Governance and Sovereignty*, Trevor Stack, Naomi R. Goldenberg and Timothy Fitzgerald (eds) (Leiden: Brill, 2015), 280–93. In the same vein, Daniel Boyarin, *Border Lines: The Partition of Judaeo Christianity* (Philadelphia: University of Pennsylvania Press, 2004).
3. Hent de Vries, 'Introduction. Why still "Religion"?', in *Religion: Beyond a Concept. The Future of the Religious Past* (New York: Fordham University Press, 2008), 5.
4. In particular, see Max Weber, 'Zwischenbetrachtung. Theorie der Stufen und Richtungen religiöser Weltablehnung', in *Die Wirtschaftsethik der Wertreligionen. Konfuzianismus und Taoismus* (Tübingen: JCB Mohr, 1989). For a discussion of this question, of interest is Marcel Gauchet, *Le désenchantement du monde. Une histoire politique de la religion* (Paris: Gallimard, 1985).
5. Karl Löwith, *Weltgeschichte und Heilsgeschehen. Die theologischen Voraussetzungen der Geschichtsphilosophie* (Munich: Metzler, 2004).
6. Hans Blumenberg, *Die Legitimität der Neuzeit* (Frankfurt: Suhrkamp, 1966).
7. Kathleen Davis, *Periodization and Sovereignty: How Ideas of Feudalism and Sovereignty Govern the Politics of Time* (Philadelphia: Pennsylvania University Press, 2008).
8. See Montserrat Herrero, *La política revolucionaria de John Locke* (Madrid: Tecnos, 2015), 29–120, pages devoted to the question of toleration. And its new re-editions as such of Cecile Laborde, *Liberalism's Religion* (Cambridge, MA: Harvard University Press, 2017). In her approach, political government has the last word in authorising as 'religious' the practices and institutions that it is unable to control. The political sphere defines then the meaning of the religious by recognising it as such and accepting it as lawful and permissible or as unlawful and inadmissible, that is to say, 'tolerating' it. Only the supremacy of political sovereignty makes the expression 'religious freedom' meaningful.
9. Jürgen Habermas, *Glauben und Wissen* (Frankfurt: Suhrkamp, 2001); Jürgen Habermas, *Zwischen Naturalismus und Religion* (Frankfurt: Suhrkamp, 2005). That discussion is enriched by contributions by, among others, Asad, *Formations of the Secular*; Peter Berger (ed.), *The Desecularization of the World: A Global Overview* (Grand Rapids, MI: Eerdmans, 2005); Charles Taylor, *A Secular Age* (Cambridge, MA: Belknap Press of Harvard University Press, 2007); Walter Schweidler (ed.), *Postsäkulare Gesellschaft. Perspektiven interdisziplinärer Forschung* (Munich: Alber, 2007); Hent de Vries (ed.), *Religion: Beyond a Concept. The Future of the Religious Past* (New York: Fordham University Press, 2008);

Josef Bengtson, *Explorations in Post-Secular Metaphysics* (New York: Palgrave Macmillan, 2015).
10. Mary Bryden, *Deleuze and Religion* (London: Routledge, 2000); Jeremy R. Carrette, *Foucault and Religion: Spiritual Corporality and Political Spirituality* (London: Routledge, 2000); Jeffrey Kosky, *Levinas and the Philosophy of Religion* (Bloomington: Indiana University Press, 2001); Laurence Paul Hemming, *Heidegger's Atheism: The Refusal of a Theological Voice* (Notre Dame, IN: Notre Dame University Press, 2002); Michael Purcell, 'Beyond the Limit and Limiting the Beyond', *International Journal for Philosophy of Religion* 68 (2010): 121–38; Roberto Farneti, 'A Political Theology of the Empty Tomb: Christianity and the Return of the Sacred', *Theoria: A Journal of Social and Political Theory* 116 (2008): 22–44; James K. A. Smith, 'Liberating Religion from Theology: Marion and Heidegger on the Possibility of a Phenomenology of Religion', *International Journal for Philosophy of Religion* 46 (1999): 17–33.
11. Hent de Vries, *Philosophy and the Turn to Religion* (Baltimore, MD: Johns Hopkins University Press, 1999). On Derrida's turn to religion, see Arthur Bradley, 'Derrida's God: A Genealogy of the Theological Turn', *Paragraph* 29 (2006): 21–42.
12. Peter Jonkers and Rund Welten, *God in France: Eight Contemporary French Thinkers on God* (Leuven: Peeters, 2005).
13. Hent de Vries and Lawrence E. Sullivan, *Political Theologies: Public Religions in a Post-Secular World* (New York: Fordham University Press, 2006).
14. Bruce Ellis Benson and Norman Wirzba, *Words of Life: New Theological Turns in French Phenomenology* (New York: Fordham University Press, 2010); J. Aaron Simmons, *God and the Other: Ethics and Politics after the Theological Turn* (Bloomington: Indiana University Press, 2011).
15. Thomas J. J. Altizer, 'Theology and the Death of God', *Centennial Review* 8 (1964): 129–46; Thomas J. J. Altizer and William Hamilton, *Radical Theology and the Death of God* (New York: Bobbs-Merrill, 1966); John D. Caputo, Gianni Vattimo and Jeffrey W. Robbins, *After the Death of God* (New York: Columbia University Press, 2007), 68–69: 'My lingering worry is that the death of God theologies are themselves thinly disguised *grand récits*. They are theologies of history that tell the big story of how we go from the religion of the Father of Judaism, to the religion of the Son in the New Testament, to the religion of the Spirit in modernity (Altizer) or in post-modernity (Taylor), which is the final story.' Caputo also alludes to the analogy of this periodisation with that of Joaquin de Fiori in *After the Death of God*, 76. Besides Altizer, John W. Lewis,

Jürgen Moltmann, Ronald G. Smith, Dorothee Solle, Herbert Brown, David Miller, Richard Underwood and Gabriel Vahanian. See Gabriel Vahanian, *The Death of God: The Culture of Our Post-Christian Era* (New York: George Braziller, 1961). Together with these authors, it is important to underline the reformist tentative of John A. T. Robinson, *Honest to God* (Philadelphia, PA: Westminster Press, 1972); Harvey Cox, *The Secular City: Secularization and Urbanization in Theological Perspective* (New York: Macmillan, 1966). The forerunners of these ideas were Dietrich Bonhoeffer and Soren Kierkegaard.

16. Altizer, 'Theology and the Death of God', 129; Altizer and Hamilton, *Radical Theology*, 34–6. According to Altizer, being Christian in the historical context of God's death means expecting the unexpectable, while throwing oneself into the profane to appropriate all its sacramental power; whereas for van Buren, the Christian in this last period of history is the perfect image of Christ, completely free, subject to nothing or nobody and therefore the owner of him/herself. Van Buren proclaims a theology of maturity and represents a non-religious theology that follows the path of Bultmann and affirms the impossibility of finding a language to speak about God. The Christian mission is only an ethical one. William Hamilton proposes a third variant within this theological tradition. He evidences, on the one hand, the experience of the abandonment of God, and, on the other hand, the necessity of making the transition from the cloister to the world through the only possible Christian praxis in our time: remaining close to our neighbour.

17. Mark C. Taylor, *Erring: A Postmodern A/theology* (Chicago: University of Chicago Press, 1984); Charles E. Winquist, *Epiphanies of Darkness* (Minneapolis, MN: Fortress Press, 1986); Carl A. Raschke, *The End of Theology* (Aurora, CO: Davies, 2000).

18. Katherine Keller, *Face of the Deep: A Theology of Becoming* (Abingdon: Routledge, 2003).

19. Taylor, *Erring*, 6.

20. Gianni Vattimo, *Dopo la cristianità. Per un cristianesimo non religioso* (Milan: Garzanti Libri, 2002); John D. Caputo, *The Weakness of God: A Theology of the Event* (Bloomington: Indiana University Press, 2006); Jean-Luc Nancy, *L'Adoration. Déconstruction du christianisme II* (Paris: Galilée, 2010); Richard Kearney, *The God Who May Be: A Hermeneutics of Religion* (Bloomington: Indiana University Press, 2001); Merold Westphal, *Overcoming Onto-theology: Toward a Postmodern Christian Faith* (New York: Fordham University Press, 2001).

21. At least that seems to be suggested in the book edited by Jeffrey Robbins, *After the Death of God*, already quoted. The book consists of an interview with Vattimo and Caputo with an epilogue

by Gabriel Vahanian. For all of them, after the death of God, the question is now about the 'deconstruction of the death of God' in order to achieve another form of post-modern faith in a post-secular context. Caputo in particular develops the theological turn of post-modernism, taking advantage of the Derridian heritage, but also of Deleuze's ideas. Caputo notes: 'On my accounting, things take a theological turn in post-modernism when what we mean by the event shifts to God. Or, alternatively, things take a post-modern turn in theology when the meditation upon *theos* or *theios*, God or the divine, is shifted to events, when the location of God or what is divine about God is shifted from what happens, from constituted words and things, to the plane of events.' 49. On Caputo's theological turn and his consequent political theology, see Montserrat Herrero, 'Sacred Anarchy Instead of Divine Democracy', *Political Theology* 23(3) (2022): 243–51.

22. Jacob Taubes, *The Political Theology of Paul* (Stanford, CA: Stanford University Press, 2003); Alain Badiou, *Saint Paul: The Foundation of Universalism* (Stanford, CA: Stanford University Press, 2003); Slavoj Zizek, *The Fragile Absolute: Or, Why is the Christian Legacy Worth Fighting For?* (New York: Verso, 2009); Eric Santner, *The Psycotheology of Everyday Life: Reflections on Freud and Rosenzweig* (Chicago: University of Chicago Press, 2001). Critical approaches to this way of proceeding can be found, for example, in Dominik Finkelde, *Politische Eschatologie nach Paulus. Badiou, Agamben, Zizek, Santner* (Vienna: Turia, 2007). He thinks that Badiou, Agamben, Zizek and Santner develop Paul's theology as a purely immanent theology. Peter Frick also criticises the way in which continental philosophy deals with Paul. They create a 'Paulus politicus' by inscribing Paul in their own philosophical views. See Peter Frick (ed.), *Paul in the Grip of the Philosophers: The Apostle and Contemporary Continental Philosophy* (Minneapolis, MN: Fortress Press, 2013), 1–13. He considers Nietzschean criticism the archetype of Pauline deconstruction in *Daybreak: Thoughts on the Prejudices of Morality* (Cambridge: Cambridge University Press, 1997), 68. Simon Critchley also openly and critically addresses continental discourse on Paul in its aim to build a political revolutionary. Simon Critchley, *The Faith of the Faithless* (New York: Verso, 2012), 15: 'I argue that the Paulinism of Agamben and Badiou is actually a crypto-Marcionism that risks a radical antinomianism in its attempt to break the connection between law and faith.'

23. William Franke, *A Philosophy of the Unsayable* (Notre Dame, IN: Notre Dame University Press, 2014). Also see William Franke, *Secular Scriptures: Modern Theological Poetics in the Wake of Dante* (Columbus: Ohio University Press, 2016), 5–6: 'The nature of poetic and religious knowledge metamorphoses radically along

this historical trajectory. It becomes decisively grounded in the secular world and in human faculties of imagination, as well as in language, with its inherently self-reflective structure and dynamics, particularly its self-critical capacity of negation. Despite this, the poetic word retains and reformulates its claim to a religiously revelatory power or function – and sometimes even to extending and re-actualizing Holy Scripture. Just as religious revelation is subjected to myriad forms of secularization in the modern world, with its newly discovered, humanly manipulated media and technologies, so the secular world is, in manifold ways, subject to sacralization, to becoming itself a sign or a resource in unprecedented new forms of revelation that are ambiguously poetic and religious in that they extend – and even tend to surpass – human mastery.'

24. Robert Yelle, *Semiotics of Religion: Signs of the Sacred in History* (New York: Bloomsbury, 2013).
25. Carl Schmitt, *Political Theology: Four Chapters on the Concept of Sovereignty* (Chicago: University of Chicago Press, 2005), 42.
26. A general approach to Carl Schmitt's political theology as a method can be found in Montserrat Herrero, *The Political Discourse of Carl Schmitt* (Lanham, MD: Rowman & Littlefield, 2015), chs 7 and 8; Montserrat Herrero, 'Carl Schmitt's Political Theology: The Magic of a Phrase', in *Political Theology in Medieval and Early Modern Europe: Discourses, Rites and Representations*, Montserrat Herrero, Jaume Aurell and Angela Miceli (eds) (Turnhout: Brepols, 2017), 23–43. See also de Vries and Sullivan, *Political Theologies*; W. T. Cavanaugh and P. Scott, *The Blackwell Companion to Political Theology* (Oxford: Blackwell, 2004); William T. Cavanaugh, *Theopolitical Imagination: Discovering the Liturgy as a Political Act in an Age of Global Consumerism* (London: T & T Clark, 2002); Carl A. Raschke, *Force of God: Political Theology and the Crisis of Liberal Democracy* (New York: Columbia University Press, 2015); Graham Hamill and Julia R. Lupton, *Political Theology and Early Modernity* (Chicago: Chicago University Press, 2012); Victoria Kahn, *The Future of Illusion: Political Theology and Early Modern Texts* (Chicago: University of Chicago Press, 2014); Heinrich Meier, *The Lesson of Carl Schmitt: Four Chapters on the Distinction between Political Theology and Political Philosophy* (Chicago: University of Chicago Press, 1998). An accurate new interpretation of Schmitt's political theology to understand the political theology of liberalism, underlining the aspect of political theology as sociology of the juridical concepts is that of Paul W. Kahn, *Political Theology: Four New Chapters on the Concept of Sovereignty* (New York: Columbia University Press, 2011). It is the intrinsic shared world of meanings that allows the transfer of concepts and roles between the theological and political.

27. Schmitt, *Political Theology*; Carl Schmitt, *Political Theology II: The Myth of the Closure of Any Political Theology* (Cambridge: Polity, 2008).
28. As I have argued in Herrero, *The Political Discourse of Carl Schmitt*, following these two assumptions Schmitt developed several political theologies: a 'political theology of the sovereign', a 'political theology of representation', a 'political theology of the *katechon*', a 'romantic political theology' and a 'political theology of revolution'. Each of them, based on a different analogy. The first of these is based on the analogy between God and the modern sovereign, while the second focuses on the analogy between representation in the Church and in the modern state, the third on the analogy between the *katechon* and the political power, the fourth in the occasionalist God of Malebranche and the opportunistic politics of the romantics. Finally, the last is based on the analogy between the Trinitarian relationship and the criteria of the political, the friend–enemy relationship.
29. Ernst H. Kantorowicz, *The King's Two Bodies: A Study in Medieval Political Theology* (Princeton, NJ: Princeton University Press, 1997), 193. What he understands by political theology can be summarised in this text of *The King's Two Bodies*: 'Infinite cross-relations between Church and State, active in every century of the Middle Ages, produced *hybrids* in either camp. Mutual *borrowings and exchanges* of insignia, political symbols, prerogatives, and rights of honour had been carried on perpetually between the spiritual and secular leaders of Christian society . . . These borrowings affected, in the earlier Middle Ages, chiefly the ruling individuals, both spiritual and secular, until finally the *sacerdotium* had an imperial appearance and the *regnum* a clerical touch.' He had already used the phrase in his 1952 publication of *Deus per naturam, Deus per gratiam: Note on the Political Theology of the Middle Ages*, in which there is no further indication of what political theology means. Instead, he again works with a political–theological analogy; in addition, *Mysteries of State* (1953) and *Pro Patria Mori* (1951) include political–theological analogies.
30. For Kantorowicz's use of the concept of 'political theology', see Montserrat Herrero, 'On Political Theology: The Hidden Dialogue between C. Schmitt and Ernst H. Kantorowicz in The King's Two Bodies', *History of European Ideas* 41(8) (2015): 1164–77.
31. Jan Assmann, *Politische Theologie zwischen Ägypten und Israel* (Munich: Carl Friedrich von Siemens, 2006).
32. Jan Assmann, *Herrschaft und Heil* (Munich: Carl Hauser, 2000).
33. Hamill and Lupton, *Political Theology and Early Modernity*, 1.
34. Claude Lefort, 'The Permanence of the Theologico-Political?' in Claude Lefort, *Democracy and Political Theory* (Cambridge: Polity, 1988), 213–55.

35. Giorgio Agamben, *The Kingdom and the Glory: For a Theological Genealogy of Economy and Government* (Stanford, CA: Stanford University Press, 2011).
36. Mitchell Dean, 'What is Economic Theology? A New Governmental–Political Paradigm?' *Theory, Culture and Society* 36(3) (2019): 3–26, 21. When he claims the impossibility of economic theology, Mitchell Dean points out that there have been two previous uses of the term economic theology, that of Robert H. Nelson in 2004, meaning a historical and conceptual critique of economics and, in particular, the American economics profession; and that of Alexander von Rüstow in 1942, meaning an analogy between the 'invisible harmony' posited by laissez-faire economics and the *ordre naturel* of the physiocrats and Adam Smith's 'invisible hand', which came from pre-Socratics, through Stoicism and early Christianity. He further compares economic liberalism to Spinoza's *deus sive natura* (God as nature), and to Taoism. Rüstow then offers a critique of early liberalism as a pantheistic theology and calls this pantheistic liberalism an 'economic theology', a *Wirtschaftstheologie*.
37. Cavanaugh, *Theopolitical Imagination*; William T. Cavanaugh, *Migrations of the Holy* (Grand Rapids, MI: Eerdmans, 2011).
38. John Milbank, Catherine Pickstock and Graham Ward (eds), *Radical Orthodoxy: A New Theology* (London: Routledge, 1999); John Milbank and Catherine Pickstock, *Truth in Aquinas* (London: Routledge, 2000); Stephen Long, *Divine Economy: Theology and the Market* (London: Routledge, 2000); Graham Ward, *Cities of God* (London: Routledge, 2000); Daniel M. Bell, Jr, *Liberation Theology After the End of History: The Refusal to Cease Suffering* (London: Routledge, 2001); Conor Cunningham, *Genealogy of Nihilism: Philosophies of Nothing and the Difference of Theology* (London: Routledge, 2002); James K. A. Smith, *Speech and Theology: Language and the Logic of Incarnation* (London: Routledge, 2002); John Milbank, *Being Reconciled: Ontology and Pardon* (London: Routledge, 2003); John Milbank and Simon Oliver (eds), *The Radical Orthodoxy Reader* (London: Routledge, 2009).
39. Jeffrey Robbins, *Radical Democracy and Political Theology* (New York: Columbia University Press, 2011).
40. Clayton Crockett, *Radical Political Theology: Religion and Politics after Liberalism* (New York: Columbia University Press, 2011).
41. See Ward Blanton, Noelle Vahanian, Jeffrey W. Robbins and Clayton Crockett, *An Insurrectionist Manifesto: Four New Gospels for a Radical Politics* (New York: Columbia University Press, 2016).
42. Crockett, *Radical Political Theology*, 15–16.
43. Crockett, *Radical Political Theology*, 161: 'Now according to the temporalization or periodization of modernity, secular concepts

succeed and replace theological concepts, which is the more conventional reading of modernity.'
44. Crockett, *Radical Political Theology*, 55.
45. This idea of deconstructive democracy is more related with reformation than with revolution as in the case of Zizek or Badiou; closer to the pragmatist project of Rorty.
46. As Caputo says in *After the Death of God*, 122, following Derrida: 'The dream of democracy – let's say it's prayer – is the dream of a world in which we would endlessly be able to reinvent ourselves, in which there would be a profusion of difference rather than fusion or playing in harmony.'
47 Crockett, *Radical Political Theology*, 164: 'Our challenge is to think the possibility of a radically democratic politics and practice, which would be necessarily a religious or quasi-religious politics and practice insofar as religion is inescapable.' Here there is not as such a 'theological turn' as a renewed 'political turn' very similar to that which was inaugurated in early modern politics by means of other exegetical instruments. See Montserrat Herrero, 'The Early Modern "Philosophical Bible" and the Supposedly Secular Modern State', *European Legacy* 22(1) (2017): 31–49.
48. Franke, *Secular Scriptures*, 1.
49. Well described by Giogio Agamben, *Profanations* (New York: Zone Books, 2007), 79: 'Nevertheless, in Christianity, with the entrance of God as the victim of sacrifice and with the strong presence of messianic tendencies that put the distinction between sacred and profane into crisis, the religious machine seems to reach a limit point or zone of undecidability, where the divine sphere is always in the process of collapsing into the human sphere and man always already passes over into the divine.'
50. Michel de Certeau, 'The Gaze of Nicholas of Cusa', *Diacritics* 17(3) (1987): 2–38, 8. He refers of Nicholas of Cusa's idea, according to which 'intellectual intuition has transformed all things into possible mirrors'. And he characterises that intuition as 'a signature, like a received name, the indecipherable of the proper'. Derrida uses it in his discussion with Searle on John Austin's theory of speech acts in *Limited Inc* (Evanston, IL: Northwestern University Press, 1988). There it appears in the context of the source of the utterance. Austin himself pointed out that this source is connoted in written utterances or inscriptions, by the appending of a signature. This must be so, because written utterances are not tethered to their origin in the way spoken ones are. This is Derrida's starting point on the signature as an impossibility of being that source. Precisely because its presence is at the same time its absence: 'By definition, a written signature implies the actual or empirical nonpresence of the signer. But, it will

be claimed, the signature also marks and retains his having-been present in a past now or present [*maintenant*] which will remain a future now or present [*maintenant*], thus in a general *maintenant*, in the transcendental form of presentness [*maintenance*]. That general maintenance is in some way inscribed, pinpointed in the always evident and singular present punctuality of the form of the signature. Such is the enigmatic originality of every paraph. In order for the tethering to the source to occur, what must be retained is the absolute singularity of a signature-event and a signature-form: the pure reproducibility of a pure event.' Derrida, *Limited Inc*, 20. Ten years later, Derrida refers to Augustine's signature at the end of *The City of God* in *Le parjure et le pardon II* (Paris: Seuil, 2020), 159–60. Augustine's signature hides itself because it is conceived as the liberation of a commission from God himself to him, which has been carried out far below what would have been worthy. A signature that asks for forgiveness, while at the same time giving thanks for the gift granted for its writing. God commands it and grants it. Asking for forgiveness while giving thanks: 'this is the double gesture of this signature', which brings to the end a book about the end of history, which is without end, Derrida points out. This signature 'persigns itself with the sign of the Cross', Derrida, *Le parjure et le pardon II*, 160. The editor of the published version of Derrida's lesson adds that, at the end of the lesson, Derrida himself remarked: 'and it may be that (it is the gesture) of every signature. If one analyses what is hidden in the signature, perhaps Augustine would tell us that every signature is this: a performative that asks for forgiveness, thanking.' Derrida, *Le parjure et le pardon II*, 159.

51. The complete text is: 'Secularization operates in the conceptual system of modernity as a *signature* that refers it back to theology . . . The way in which the reference operated by the theological signature is understood is decisive at every turn. Thus, secularization can also be understood (as is the case with Gogarten) as a specific performance of Christian faith that, for the first time, opens the world to man in its worldliness and historicity. The theological signature operates here as a sort of trompe l'oeil in which the very secularization of the world becomes the mark that identifies it as belonging to a divine *oikonomia*.' Agamben, *The Kingdom and the Glory*, 4.
52. Martin Heidegger, *Einführung in die phänomenologische Forschung*, Gesamtausgabe Abt. 2 Vorlesungen Bd. 17 (Frankfurt am Main: Vittorio Klosterman, 2006), 159, 311.
53. Didier Franck, *Nietzsche et l'ombre de Dieu* (Paris: PUF, 2014), 32–3.
54. The complete text is: 'It would be necessary to interrogate from this point of view what is called globalization, and which I elsewhere (Foi et savoir in Derrida and Vattimo, *La Religion*) call globalatinisation

to take into account the effect of Roman Christianity which today over-determines all language of law, of politics and even the interpretation of what is called the "return to the religious". No alleged disenchantment, no secularization comes to interrupt it. On the contrary.' Jacques Derrida, *On Cosmopolitanism and Forgiveness* (London: Routledge, 2001), 32.

55. William Franke has recovered the apophatic tradition in *On What Cannot Be Said: Apophatic Discourses in Philosophy, Religion, Literature, and the Arts*, 2 vols (Notre Dame, IN: Notre Dame University Press, 2014). In *The Universality of What is Not: The Apophatic Turn in Critical Thinking* (Notre Dame, IN: Notre Dame University Press, 2020), Franke explores what he calls the new apophatic universalism of the contemporary atheist. I will not go into more detail as the whole tradition is well expounded by Franke.

56. de Vries, *Philosophy and the Turn to Religion*, 24. In the case of Franke, *A Philosophy of the Unsayable*, 55: 'We need not reject the traditions of onto-theology; rather we need to think them through more deeply -and, above all, in a more timely fashion.'

57. See Franke, *A Philosophy of the Unsayable*, 2–3: 'Ineffability was once a leading theme of the Neoplatonists (particularly Plotinus, Porphyry, Proclus, Iamblichus and Damascius) and of their heirs in the monotheistic traditions of Christian mysticism (Dionysius the Areopagite, John Scotus Eriugena), of the Kabbalah, of Sufism, and again of certain post-Scholastics (Meister Eckhart, Nicholas Cusanus). Baroque mystics such as John of the Cross, Jakob Böhme, and Silesius Angelus share this same obsession with Romantic thinkers like Kierkegaard and the late Schelling, as well as with imaginative writers such as Hölderlin, Emily Dickinson, Rilke and Kafka . . . the apophatical reflections of Wittgenstein, Heidegger and Franz Rosenzweig . . .'

58. Jacques Derrida, 'How to Avoid Speaking: Denials', in *Languages of the Unsayable: The Play of Negativity in Literature and Literary Theory*, Sanford Budick and Wolfgang Iser (eds) (Stanford, CA: Stanford University Press, 1996), 3–70, 50: 'Among all these figures for the unfigurable, there stands the figure of the seal . . . the figure of the seal, which also seals a promise, is valid for the entire text of the creation.'

59. The Catholic faith is the only monotheistic faith that supplements this definitive historical unpresentability of the divinity with the historical and sacramental presence of God in Christ.

60. Caputo, *The Weakness of God*, 10, also 177: 'The name of God harbors an event of interpretation.' For Caputo, the relationship between name and event has a Derridean origin. Hence, the theology of the event consists of a deconstruction of the name of God. This means a deconstruction of the conditioned name in order to release the unconditional event that is found in that name.

This unconditional event is what Derrida called the undeconstructible and is a function of *difference*. Caputo, *The Weakness of God*, 27. See also Caputo et al., *After the Death of God*, 47–85.
61. Caputo, *The Weakness of God*, 163, see also 13: 'My idea is to stop thinking about God as a massive ontological power line that provides power to the world, instead thinking of something that short-circuits such power and provides a provocation of the world that is otherwise than power.'
62. Caputo, *The Weakness of God*, 31.
63. Nancy primarily studies the theme of incarnation in Jean-Luc Nancy, *Corpus* (New York: Fordham University Press, 2008).
64. Jean-Luc Nancy, *The Ground of the Image* (New York: Fordham University Press, 2005), 11: 'if we recall the Christian use of this expression: the "real presence" is precisely not the ordinary presence of the real referred to here: it is not the god present in the world as finding himself there. This presence is a sacred intimacy that a fragment of matter gives to be taken in and absorbed. It is a real presence because it is a contagious presence, participating and participated, communicating and communicated in the distinction of its intimacy. That is in fact why the Christian God, and particularly the Catholic God, will have been the god of the death of God, the god who withdraws from all religion (from every bond with a divine presence) and who departs into his own absence, since he is no longer anything but the passion of the intimate and the intimacy of suffering [*du pâtir*] or of feeling and sensation: what everything gives to be sensed insofar as it is what it is, the thing itself distinguished in its sameness. So, it is as well, according to another exemplarity, with what is called the "poetic image". This is not a decoration provided by a play of analogy, comparison, allegory, metaphor, or symbol. Or else, in each of these possibilities, it is something other than the pleasant game of an encoded displacement.' See also Nancy, *Corpus*, 3–5, and Nancy, *The Ground of the Image*, 5: 'for this intimate force is not "represented" by the image, but the image is it, the image activates it, draws it and withdraws it, extracts it by withholding it, and it is with this force that the image touches us'.
65. Nancy, *The Ground of the Image*, 123: 'an indefinite exchange is played out between representation and non-representation, between visible and non-visible, between art and refusal of art'. In Nancy's view the Christian God – religiously speaking – presents himself as hidden; the Jewish God as an interpellation issuing from the unpronounceable and the invisible; and the Muslim God, incommensurate with any presence. What is common to the three monotheisms is a specific form of alliance, one that is essentially unequal. These signs are also at the core of painting.

66. Nancy, *The Ground of the Image*, 73: 'here is the image, it means . . .; here is the text, it represents . . . But who, then, is the one that is absent? Who is the one that is neither text nor image? Who is the one that would be located precisely at the intersection of this double reference, at the place where the meaning of the image encounters the meaning of the text without either one ever being the meaning of the other?'
67. Or of flesh in the case of Christ. See Jean-Luc Nancy, *Dis-enclosure: The Deconstruction of Christianity* (New York: Fordham University Press, 2007), 81–2. Esposito supposedly alludes 'to the semantics of incarnation as the place, the form, and the symbol of the union between the human and the non-human' and states that 'technology is the non-Christian, post-Christian even, figure of the Incarnation'. Nothing in this statement would contradict Nancy's point of view. See Roberto Esposito, 'Chair et corps dans la déconstruction du christianisme', in *Sens en tous sens. Autour de travaux de Jean-Luc Nancy*, F. Guibal and J-C. Martin (eds) (Paris: Galilée, 2004), 153–64, 162, 158, respectively.
68. Nancy, *Dis-enclosure*, 111.
69. Jean-Luc Nancy, 'In the Midst of the World; or, Why Deconstruct Christianity?' in *Re-treating Religion: Deconstructing Christianity with Jean-Luc Nancy*, Alena Alexandrova (ed.) (New York: Fordham University Press, 2012), 1: 'I'd like to speak of it (Christianity) as little as possible. I'd like to move toward an effacement of this name and of the whole corpus of references that follows it . . . But I do think it is important to follow the movement that this name has named: that of the exit from religion and of the expansion of the atheist world.' This is because in his view Christianity is culpable of the 'immense fracture' between the 'upper' and the 'lower' world. Through this distinction, Christianity has created the possibility of the mundane and atheist world. For the meaning of deconstruction according to Nancy, see Jean-Luc Nancy, *Sense of the World* (Minneapolis: University of Minnesota Press, 1997); Nancy, *Dis-enclosure*, 32. Derrida discusses the topic of the infinite in reference to Nancy saying: 'such a difficult, paradoxical, almost impossible task, always exposed to being nothing more than Christian hyperbole'. Jacques Derrida, *On Touching – Jean Luc Nancy* (Stanford, CA: Stanford University Press, 2005), 220. For a commentary on this Derrida–Nancy discussion, see Ian James, 'Incarnation and Infinity', in *Re-treating Religion: Deconstructing Christianity with Jean-Luc Nancy*, Alena Alexandrova (ed.) (New York: Fordham University Press, 2012), 246–60. Incidentally, making the same point, Franke interprets Nancy in a 'favorable manner' for his own thesis: 'This negation of the "indefinite" is a quintessentially Hegelian gesture, but it should not be converted into a unilateral affirmation of the definite: it is rather apophatic in negating the figure of the indefinite, which like

any figure whatever must be negated in deference to what escapes all figuring. The apophatic cannot be finally qualified as indefinite either: it is made manifest always only in definite, concrete forms – and their surpassing.' Franke, *A Philosophy of the Unsayable*, 170. And also: 'Nancy exemplifies one of the most significant paradoxes of contemporary philosophy of religion. He evolves from a rigorous proponent of the thought of finitude to a proponent of an unrestricted opening to the infinite. Of course, the infinite, cannot simply be opposed to finitude.' Franke, *A Philosophy of the Unsayable*, 196.
70. Franke, *A Philosophy of the Unsayable*, 4.
71. Franke, *Secular Scriptures*.
72. Franke, *A Philosophy of the Unsayable*, 60.
73. Franke, *A Philosophy of the Unsayable*, 68.
74. Franke, *A Philosophy of the Unsayable*, 69.
75. Derrida, 'How to Avoid Speaking', 7–8.
76. Derrida, 'How to Avoid Speaking', 6.
77. Derrida, 'How to Avoid Speaking', 11.
78. Derrida, *Le parjure et le pardon II*, 195, also 146.
79. Jean-Louis Chrétien, *L'arche de la parole* (Paris: PUF, 1998), 91–3.
80. Chrétien, *L'arche de la parole*, 96.
81. Chrétien, *L'arche de la parole*, 99.
82. Nicolas de Cusa, *Nicholas of Cusa on God as Not-Other: A Translation and Appraisal of De Li Non Aliud*, trans. Jasper Hopkins (Minneapolis, MN: Arthur J. Baning Press, 2001), 6, 1110: 'Since all call the First Beginning God, you seem to intend for Him to be signified by the words "Not-other". For we must maintain that *the First is that which defines both itself and all [others]*. For since there is not anything prior to the First and since the First is independent of everything posterior, assuredly it is defined only through itself. But since what is originated has nothing from itself but has from the Beginning whatever it is, assuredly the *Beginning is the ground of being, or the definition*, of what is originated.' My italics.
83. See the interpretation of this text of Cusa's by William Franke, who stresses, contrary to my interpretation, the undefinable character of God, even while lucidly preventing indefinability from becoming itself the definition of divinity. Franke, *The Universality of What is Not*, 93–9.
84. Cusa, *On God as Not-Other*, 24.
85. Cusa, *On God as Not-Other*, 6, 1118.
86. Cusa, *On God as Not-Other*, 6, 1118: 'But because Not-other is not *other* than *any* thing, it does not lack any thing, nor can anything exist outside of it. Hence without Non-other no thing can be spoken of or thought of, because it would not be spoken of or thought of through that without which, since it precedes all things, no thing can exist or be known.'

87. Cusa, *On God as Not-Other*, 31, 38.
88. Cusa, *On God as Not-Other*, 36.
89. Cusa, *On God as Not-Other*, 89.
90. Derrida, 'How to Avoid Speaking', 16.
91. Derrida, 'How to Avoid Speaking', 10.
92. de Certeau, 'The Gaze of Nicholas of Cusa', 2–38. See also Michel de Certeau, *L'absent de l'histoire* (Liège: Mame, 1973). William Franke has commented extensively this expression of de Certeau, taking also the trope as the title of his volumes on the apophatic.
93. Gerard E. Caspary, *Politics and Exegesis: Origen and the Two Swords* (Berkeley: University of California Press, 1979), 190–1: 'Symbols could be interpreted in different ways, but multifaceted surfaces are part of the nature of symbols and are fully expected by those who engage in symbolic discourse . . . With the growth of scholastic and legal modes of thinking, on the other hand, there is a tendency for questions to be reduced to a clear and simple either/or . . . But when the network that sustained the older symbolism collapses, when the unity of exegesis and politics is dissolved, the symbols that remain in use cease in effect to function as genuine symbols. They no longer resonate, they are no longer translucid, the facets that are not in the light have become darkened. From multifaceted and transparent symbols, they have become one-dimensional and opaque emblems; they are turning into slogans, into rather dreary political clichés. They had illuminated; now they merely obscure.'
94. The relevance of Augustine for the symbolic theory of language is shown in Robert A. Markus, 'St. Augustine on Signs', *Phronesis* 2(1) (1957): 60–83, 64. See also Robert A. Markus, *Signs and Meanings: World and Text in Ancient Christianity* (Liverpool: Liverpool University Press, 1996); Daniel Bourgeois, *Être et signifier* (Paris: Vrin, 2016), 207–379.
95 Augustine of Hypo, *De dilectica* V (PL 32, 1410): 'Signum est quod seipsum sensui, et praeter se aliquid animo ostendit. Loqui est articulata voce signum dare.' Augustine of Hypo, *De doctrina christiana* II, I, 1: 'Signum est enim res praeter speciem quam ingerit sensibus, alius aliquid ex se faciens in cogitationem venire.' See Markus, 'St. Augustine on Signs', 72.
96. Émile Benveniste, *Problèmes de linguistique générale II* (Paris: Gallimard, 1974), 50–4.
97. Hans Georg Gadamer, *Truth and Method* (New York: Continuum, 2006), 61.
98. Gadamer, *Truth and Method*, 148.
99. Gadamer, *Truth and Method*, 147: 'It is especially true of religious symbols that they not only function as distinguishing marks, but that the meaning of these symbols is understood by everyone, unites everyone, and can therefore assume a sign function. Hence, what is

symbolized is undoubtedly in need of representation, inasmuch as it is itself non-sensible, infinite, and unrepresentable, but also capable of it. It is only because what is symbolized is present itself that it can be present in the symbol. A symbol not only points to something; it represents it by taking its place. But to take the place of something means to make something present that is not present. Thus, in representing, the symbol takes the place of something: that is, it makes something immediately present. Only because it thus presents the presence of what it represents is the symbol itself treated with the reverence due to the symbolized. Such symbols as a crucifix, a flag, a uniform have so fully taken the place of what is revered that the latter is present in them.' In my view, the case of Goethe that Gadamer refers to by quoting Goethe's letter to Schiller of 17 August 1797, is particularly interesting. Goethe 'describes the sentimental mood brought about by his impressions of Frankfurt, and says of the objects that induce it "that they are properly symbolic – i.e., as I hardly need to say, they are eminent examples which stand in a characteristic multiplicity, as representatives of many others, and embrace a certain totality . . ." He attaches importance to this experience because it is intended to help him escape the "million-headed hydra of empiricism". Schiller supports him in this and finds this sentimental mode of feeling wholly in accord with "what we have agreed on in this sphere". But with Goethe it is, as we know, not so much an aesthetic experience as an experience of reality, and to describe it he apparently draws the concept of the symbolic from early Protestant usage.' Gadamer, *Truth and Method*, 66.

100. Erich Przywara, *Lessons sur Dieu* (Paris: Cerf, 2011), 129–60. David Ratmoko, in his book *On Spectrality: Fantasies of Redemption in the Western Canon* (New York: Peter Lang, 2006), 3, tracks down the 'spectral archive' of revelatory traces – images and words – that haunt the history of the West: 'No innocent or disinterested method is at hand when it comes to interrogating ghosts; significantly, it is here that deconstruction professes allegiance with Marxism, particularly with the "weak messianic force" that Benjamin pinned his hopes on. The "spectral analysis" I have in mind "reads what was never written", to use the phrase of Hofmannsthal, in the sense of unlocking a "spectral archive" of "memory-traces".'

101. An explanation of this set of combinations is that of Ernst von Dobschütz, 'Zeit und Raum im Denken des Urchristentums', *Journal of Biblical Literature* (1922): 212–23, 223: 'Schließlich findet die ganze Geschichte der Exegese mit ihrem großen Gegensatz von Typologie und Allegorie ihre Erklärung von diesen zwei Denkschemata der Menschheit aus. Die Griechen mochten die ganze Geschichte in eine zeitlose Ideenwelt sublimieren. Die Gnostiker sind die radikalsten Allegoristen; sie deuten alle Züge des Evangeliums

auf sich immer wiederholende Erlösungsvorgange der Überwelt. Je kirchlicher ein Theologe, das heißt, je mehr er sich an die geschichtliche Gottesoffenbarung in Jesus halt, desto schwieriger wird ihm das Allegorisieren; die Allegorie hat nur neben der wörtlichen, geschichtlichen Deutung ihren Platz, und ihr tritt bei den syrischen Theologen die Typologie gegenüber, welche das Geschichtliche in dem Bericht festhaltend nur einen zweiten geschichtlichen Sinn hineinlegt, eine Art prästabilierte Harmonie von Weissagung und Erfüllung.' Instead of speaking of types or allegories, I use the terms figures and symbols here.

102. Eric Auerbach, *Mimesis: The Representation of Reality in Western Literature* (Princeton, NJ: Princeton University Press, 1953); see also Eric Auerbach, 'Figura', in *Scenes from the Drama of European Literature*, Eric Auerbach (ed.) (Minneapolis: University of Minnesota Press, 1984).

103. Auerbach, 'Figura', 30.

104. Auerbach, 'Figura', 39.

105. José Mª Cuesta, 'Erich Auerbach. Una poética de la historia', in *Figura*, Erich Auerbach (ed.) (Madrid: Trotta, 1998), 32.

106. Hayden White has noted the significance of Auerbach's 'figurality', but he misunderstands the core of this idea by introducing causality. Hayden White, "Auerbach's Literary History: Figural Causation and Modernist Historicism', in *Figural Realism: Studies in the Mimesis Effect* (Baltimore, MD: Johns Hopkins University Press, 1999), 87–100, 88: 'progress toward a goal that is never ultimately realizable nor even fully specifiable. It gives him a concept of a peculiarly historical mode of causation, different from ancient teleological notions, on the one side, and modern scientific, mechanistic notions, on the other. This distinctively historical mode of causation I propose to call figural causation.'

107. Hans Urs von Balthasar interprets this mimesis as hermeneutical faith. The relationship between the Old and the New dispensations turns into a relationship between image and reality. Although Jesus took Isaiah, 53 as his own life programme, his ultimate achievement can be affirmed only through faith. But, in fact, as Auerbach perceives, both are equally real and equally historical. Hans Urs von Balthasar, *The Glory of the Lord: A Theological Aesthetics*, vol. 1 (San Francisco, CA: Ignatius Press, 1989).

108. Auerbach, 'Figura', 11–76, 29, also 53: 'Figural interpretation establishes a connection between two events or persons, the first of which signifies not only itself but also the second, while the second encompasses or fulfils the first. The two poles of the figure are separate in time, but both, being real events of figures, are within time, within the stream of historical life.'

109. Cuesta, 'Erich Auerbach', 30.

110. We use the term figuration instead of instantiation as it has been common in the abovementioned turn of philosophy to religion. In the words of Hent de Vries: 'Resuscitating, reactivating, remobilizing the archive – what Bergson and Deleuze call the pure or absolute past, the virtual – would mean bringing it into his own, letting it emerge for the first time, giving minimal differences their maximal impact, or, again letting it condense in the singularity of words, things, gestures and powers. There would be no pre-, para-, or post-figuration of a single – eternal/historical, spiritual/material, subjective/collective – Truth, but rather the emergence of an infinite, yet incomplete, set of instantiations of truth.' de Vries, 'Introduction. Why still "Religion"?', 80.
111. Derrida, 'How to Avoid Speaking', 23. There is a 'secret divine place' that nobody can reach, but: 'between the secret place and the topography of the social link which must protect the non-divulgence, there must be a certain homology. This must govern some (secret) relation between the topology of what stands beyond Being, without being-without Being, and the topology, the initiatory politopology which at once organises the mystical community and makes possible the address to the other, this quasi-pedagogical and mystagogical speech, which Dionysius singularly directs to Timothy.' Derrida, 'How to Avoid Speaking', 21.
112. Derrida defines this 'topolitology' with the same words as Dionysius in Letter 9 (1105 b): 'sacred allegories which one has had the audacity to use to represent God, projecting outward and multiplying the visible appearances of the mystery, dividing the unique and indivisible, figuring in multiple forms what has neither form nor figure, so that one who could see the beauty hidden in the interior (of this allegories) would find them entirely mystical consistent with God and full of a great theological light'. Derrida, 'How to Avoid Speaking', 21.
113. Derrida, 'How to Avoid Speaking', 23.
114. Derrida, 'How to Avoid Speaking', 24.
115. Theopolitical figures represent examples of what de Vries with reference to Derrida calls 'reverse implication', that is, the motion of folding the transcendental back into the empirical and the historical. Hent de Vries, *Religion and Violence: Philosophical Perspectives from Kant to Derrida* (Baltimore, MD: Johns Hopkins University Press, 2001), 299. Other ways of naming them are 'placeholders of the infinite', 'instantiations of the extraordinary' (Derrida); 'divine places' (Nancy); 'marked concepts', 'signatures' (Agamben); or 'religious or theological tropes' (de Vries).
116. Derrida, 'How to Avoid Speaking', 26.

Chapter 1

Scripture or the Unconditional Character of Justice

> The most negative discourse, even beyond all nihilisms and negative dialectics, preserves a trace of the other. A trace of an event older than it or of a 'taking-place' to come, both of them: here there is neither an alternative nor a contradiction. Translated into the Christian apophatic of Dionysius (although other translations of the same necessity are possible), this signifies that the power of speaking and of speaking well of God already proceeds from God.[1]

The 'speaking well of God [that] already proceeds from God' has a name: Scripture. Scripture is the already-there of a phrase 'of which the singularity would have to remain irreducible and its reference indispensable in a given idiom'.[2] With these thoughts, Derrida evokes the question that will be addressed in this chapter: why every historical–political epoch has confronted the particular texts we call Scriptures as a figure of the divine.

Sacred Scriptures are not only the most read and studied scriptures, but also the most translated, and the most transformed into different practices. Literature, art, philosophy, morality and politics have all been significantly 'steeped' in biblical imaginaries.[3] God is the unsayable, nobody can reach Him discursively; except Himself. Scripture is not a book about God, but God's speech that has been written down. In the beginning was the Word, and the Word was with God, and the Word was God says John at the beginning of his Gospel. We encounter that Word written down in the form of sacred Scriptures. The Scriptures are unique because they speak of God and at the same time claim that it is God who speaks. Other 'scriptures', which we find in every political community, such as contracts, covenants, constitutions, core literary texts of every civilisation can be interpreted, in a theological–political transposition, as figures of that trace. In fact, as Derrida asserts, 'the very idea of institution – hence of the arbitrariness of the sign – is unthinkable before the possibility of writing and outside of its horizon'.[4]

The Scriptural Turn: Translation, Interpretation, Deconstruction

At the beginning of the twentieth century, language began to be at the centre of philosophical interest. If the ideal of scientific knowledge had been inspired by the Galilean model of the mathematical conception of nature, natural language began to be the specific object of philosophy and eventually constituted the field of human sciences. Semiotics, linguistics and logic and, in general, theories of language of any kind, flourished as a means to explain the alleged 'effective' dimension of reality. The way we experience the world is called linguicity. Or to use Benjamin's even more radical expression, 'language communicates the linguistic being of things'.[5] Dilthey, Humboldt, Heidegger, Gadamer and Rorty among many others were the central figures in bringing about this linguistic turn. As Derrida has formulated it: 'a historic-metaphysical epoch must finally determine as language the totality of its problematic horizon'.[6]

Accelerating the closure of this last step in the history of the metaphysics of presence, Derrida tries to be radical in his position regarding the priority of writing.[7] As he notes in *Writing and Difference*: 'The question of writing could be opened only if the book was closed. The joyous wandering of the *graphein* then became wandering without return. The opening into the text was adventure, expenditure without reserve.'[8]

He tries to hasten that closure and the new adventure of the 'scriptural turn' by proclaiming, more rigorously than Saussure did, the arbitrariness of the sign. Derrida is completely aware of the as yet theological character of the Saussurian turn and says: 'The sign and divinity have the same place and time of birth. The age of the sign is essentially theological. Perhaps it will never end. Its historical closure is, however, outlined.'[9] Saussure, however, disregards any belief in a God behind the sign; but for Derrida, the sign still retains a theological residue, in what he calls a 'transcendental meaning' – an ultimate presence – that generates all meaning: the presence of the God of the history of metaphysics is simply replaced by the presence of the sign.[10] This affirmation goes beyond Saussure's distinction between signifier and signified; a distinction that in Derrida's views remains within the heritage of the logocentrism he seeks to criticise.[11] He deconstructs Saussure by radicalising his own affirmation of the 'arbitrariness of the sign': this position cannot be held at the same time as the differentiation between an ideographic and a phonetic writing as Saussure does.[12]

Derrida tries to be more radical. Language is derived from writing and not vice versa: 'there is no linguistic sign before writing. Without that exteriority, the very idea of the sign falls into decay'.[13] The written signifier has no constitutive meaning. Indeed, Derrida's movement places the question of writing at the centre of any possibility of the constitution of meaning. Bearing in mind that writing is a particular case of the trace, he proposes to think the entity, any presence, from pure mediation.[14] In fact, the idea of trace implies the deep, real structure of mediation. Every sign is inhabited by the trace insofar it as it is related to every other. This is the first consequence of the supposed principle of Derrida's scenario: deferral or *différance*.[15] *Différance* is then at the source of linguistic value: 'The trace is in fact the absolute origin of sense in general. Which amounts to saying once again that there is no absolute origin of sense in general. The trace is the *différance* which opens appearance and signification.'[16]

In this context, the theological appears hidden as a moment of the total movement of the trace.[17] This is what Derrida thought when he wrote *Grammatology* in 1967. In 1996, as we have seen in the opening of this chapter, he declares that the trace is of an 'event older than it', or of a 'taking place to come'. It is the trace of a 'past injunction'. To the abstract structure of semiotic mediation, he adds a temporalisation, which is open to the absence of a certain event. We have, however, only the here and now, the trace, the writing, the inscription, which, on the one hand, is inaugural and, on the other hand, is always secondary and supplementary.

Writing is inaugural insofar as it opens up the possibility of language and meaning: 'the meaning that it constitutes and that is, primarily, its future'.[18] This idea can be particularly evidenced in inscriptions, since we receive them emancipated from an authorised meaning. Every possible meaning we ascribe to them refers to the disposition of a contingent situation.

The priority of writing implies two other features beyond inauguration: secondarity and supplementarity. In fact, the origin is the process of emptying from which every reference takes its secondarity:

'the origin is always already eluded on the basis of an organized field of speech in which the speaking subject vainly seeks a place that is always missing'.[19] Writing is then a 'crossed out origin'[20]: 'That speech and writing are always unavowably taken from a reading is the form of the original theft, the most archaic elusion, which simultaneously hides me and purloins my powers of inauguration.'[21]

Everything begins with reproduction. All the traces or writings we can find are made out of references: a lattice without a centre, without presence. Words and concepts receive meaning only in sequences of differences; there is not full meaning. One can choose the terms of one's own discourse only within a topic and with a historical strategy. The justification of that choice can never be absolute and definitive; moreover, it shows a condition of forces and a historical calculation.[22]

The logic of supplement – far from the idea of writing as 'a supplement to the spoken word' – comes in Derrida from a reading of some parts of Rousseau's *Emile* and *Confessions* where he designates masturbation as 'that dangerous supplement'. Supplement designates then auto-affection: experience of immediate restitution, not deferred pleasure; but what is no longer deferred is by the same token, absolutely deferred: 'The presence that is thus delivered to us in the present is a chimera. Auto-affection is a pure speculation. The sign, the image, the representation, which come to supplement the absent presence are the illusions that sidetrack us.'[23] In this sense, the supplement is 'maddening because it is neither presence nor absence and because it consequently breaches both our pleasure and our virginity'.[24] The supplement then does not add to what was once a pure or complete presence, but rather compensates for a presence that never actually existed in the first place. The desire for the origin or the pure presence, necessary in order to achieve an idea of the supplement, should be crossed out after being desired: 'There is a point in the system where the signifier can no longer be replaced by its signified, so that in consequence no signifier can be so replaced, purely and simply.'[25] An origin ought to have been and however it has never been: 'its history is that of the supplement of (from) origin: of the originary substitute and the substitute of the origin'.[26] Originary *différance* is neither absence nor presence, neither negative nor positive. It is supplementarity as structure. And here structure means irreducible complexity. This kind of 'structural supplementarity' is opposed to the idea that there is a natural writing that is immediately united to the voice and to breath, whose nature is pneumatological instead of grammatological.[27]

Derrida's *via negativa* to account for the origin, whose first principle is writing, gives a relevant account of the founding nature of sacred Scriptures as the inscription of an absence. This absence, nevertheless, must be understood not only as a past injunction, but also as a trace in relation to which the significant multiplicity of all other discourses is generated. Sacred Scriptures seem to be the proper name of writing. Here, it is worth repeating the quotation at the beginning of this chapter: Scripture is the already-there of a phrase 'of which the singularity would have to remain irreducible and its reference indispensable in a given idiom.'[28] But Derrida also says that it is a trace of an event older than itself.[29] But this event always remains behind the trace – it is never present. And at the same time 'all graphemes are of a testamentary essence'.[30]

Insofar as all writing, as an iterable mark, is repeated independently of the moment of its enunciation and of the intention of its issuer, it makes the historical treatment of the event problematical, to the point where the event becomes unpredictable and impossible to apprehend.[31] The writing of the event prevents what has happened or what is happening from being fully present; it does not refer to a full origin, nor does it show it as it is in its uniqueness: the event is a fractured structure. It is an impossible possibility for saying. This impossible possibility of writing the event has to be understood as accepting the fracture of the event that cancels it as such.[32] The written form derealises the event itself by the very condition of its iterability. The written sign is left to drift, which allows it to be taken out of its context and grafted onto another in order to have an intelligibility that is not anchored to its origin. This is why the original context of a text is not absolutely determinable for it to have a meaning, nor can it be stabilised as what the author wished to say. Every sign, every writing, as a material mark, implies that meaning is always postponed, deferred and open to semantic drift. And, as Derrida himself recognised, this has a political implication.[33] Scripture of an event older than itself is an impossible that becomes the very experience of the possible.[34]

Benjamin expresses this idea by saying that sacred texts are the only access to pure language: 'The sanctity of what is written is inextricably bound up with the idea of its strict codification. For sacred script always takes the form of certain complexes of words which ultimately constitute, or aspire to become, one single and inalterable complex.'[35] Beyond God's word, there is only translation, Benjamin goes on to say.[36] Since in conditions of finitude pure language, except the biblical narrative, cannot exist, one language has to supplement the others.[37] The afterlife of a text depends on the kind of translatability it is able to receive.[38] Scriptures cannot be read as a definitive system of meaning: they are open to the past and to the future, and can still be interpreted and reinterpreted by human languages, which are finite and not pure. Scriptures are therefore being indefinitely interpreted up to the end of time. Moreover, it is the only word that passes judgement in what it says: 'This judging word expels the first human beings from Paradise; they themselves have aroused it in accordance with the immutable law by which this judging word punishes – and expects – its own awakening as the sole and deepest guilt.'[39] In exchange for the loss of the immediacy of name that was damaged by original sin, a new immediacy arises: the magic of judgement, which no longer rests blissfully on itself, but on a political power. Every prosecution is a figure of that judging, by means of a positive law that is written not in a pure language, but in a human language, the symbol of decay.

Gadamer epitomises the opposite of Derrida and Benjamin's position.[40] He also prioritises writing, but what characterises written texts is that instead of derealising events, they give an account of them. Texts appear as a register of something that happened in the past, but that is always looking to the future: looking for a reader. As in Derrida's description, events become fractured in writing; but in this case not because they can only be described within the text, but because they are torn between the intentions of the author and the addressee.[41] A text embodies always a complexity of writers, readers and contexts, achieving meanings that will never be complete, full or satisfactory. Texts not only have meaning, but also produce meaning; but, in the case of the Gadamerian approach, they produce self-understanding.[42]

In Gadamer's theory of writing we find the metaphysics of presence that Derrida was trying to exorcise with his assumption of archi-writing,[43] since the interpretation of a text is always motivated by an actual interest. This is what Gadamer calls the problem of application.[44] Motivated actual interest and the practical dimension combine to produce understanding that is never a purely theoretical act. Writing is no mere accident or mere supplement that qualitatively changes things which are part of the course of oral tradition. Certainly, there can be a will to permanence or durability without writing, but only a written tradition can detach itself from the mere continuance of the vestiges of past life. Only by writing is continuity made possible through discontinuity. The understanding of something written is never a repetition of something past but the sharing of a present meaning, Gadamer would say.[45]

The priority of the aspect of reading and applying every text leads Gadamer away from the Derridian perspective, even if there are some common points in both, such as the primacy of writing and the impossibility of achieving a definitive meaning of any text. In fact, for Gadamer, texts originate in language and return to language,[46] whereas for Derrida, as we have seen, language originates in texts and remains in texts. Gadamer considers that reading has the form of a conversation, something impossible in the Derridian perspective of the complete autonomy of the text.

As Gadamer asserts in *Text and Interpretation*, the essay in which he tried to enter into a dialogue with Derrida during their encounter in 1981, even if the unfinished character of every experience of meaning is a fact, the desire to achieve full meaning provokes our understanding. The mediation made by the linguicity can be understood as a bridge or as a barrier. In the movement of this dialectic between full understanding and derealisation appears the dialectic between the community of meaning in which the reader is immersed, that is tradition, and the opacity of the other in the text. Does this mean, Gadamer asks himself, that if we cannot achieve a true meaning or a full meaning, we cannot 'find' meaning at all? Is the only alternative to 'construct' it in a 'position of meaning', as Derrida postulates? Gadamer would answer no, because the horizon of his method is that of truth.

Gadamer has reflected profoundly on the theological weight of the scriptural turn when he characterises philological and biblical hermeneutics as the prehistory of philosophical hermeneutics.[47] In his view, theological hermeneutics lead the way to the philosophical question of hermeneutics. In this case, the general condition of application is apparent in preaching.[48] Preaching cannot be considered as a creative supplement to the text it is interpreting. Hence, the gospel acquires no new content in being preached. But, certainly preaching is concerned with interpreting a valid truth. The validity of the interpretation is in the power of the word itself, which can call men to repentance even though the sermon is a bad one. The proclamation cannot be detached from its fulfilment. In Gadamer's view, Scripture is the word of God and hence it has absolute priority over the doctrine of those who interpret it. The priority of the written is independent of every interpreter and according to Gadamer cannot be manipulated.

The philosophical import of the scriptural turn, which has been described here in the dialogue between Derrida, Gadamer and Benjamin, reveals the crossroads at which sacred Scripture finds itself. Indeed, the question of writing is a theological one; and, at the same time, the question of writing is from the beginning, as we have seen, a question related to historicity. Sacred Scriptures, God's proper speech, are plural in their immediate production: they have many historical authors, from different sources and from different time layers, but what makes these Scriptures so singular is that they give an account of the event of God, who appears for their immediate author. Beyond this remote authorship, which is not historically verifiable, the possible unity of these written words of God comes from their reception, that is, from their reading. It is over the course of time that they become, through the idea of the canon, a kind of authorised book. The canon is in itself already a kind of reading. It is the context of reading, which makes the plurality of Scriptures something like a book, the Bible.[49] In fact, the Catholic Church understands itself as being 'the primary setting for biblical hermeneutics',[50] because it is a community of faith through a continued tradition. It claims that Scripture itself was written in the bosom of that community of faith and meaning, and for that reason the Catholic Church takes itself to be the rightful interpreter.

In any case, a certain autonomy of the written cannot prevent interpretations which proceed from very different angles. We cannot merge the normative aspect evoked by the churches with the multiple possibilities consummated in history. Actually, already the complex process of translation increases the flow of meanings of the original text. In fact, first the Greek translation and later the Latin translation of the Bible, the Vulgate, carried out by Jerome, were decisive steps in shaping meanings. Tertullian was a key person for the West in appropriating terms and meanings to express the spiritual experience contained in the Scriptures. The Hebrew context, the Jewish way of thinking, acting and writing were completely different from the Greek of the third and second centuries BC; and no less so from Tertullian's background and from the fourth century of Jerome's Rome. In fact, it seems that the translation into Latin was irremediably a Romanisation of the Bible. A new appropriation of the meaning of Scriptures influenced by the cultural context and background occurred with every translation.

Texts and Events

Sacred Scriptures are a paradigmatic example of both Gadamer's hermeneutical circle and Derrida's inaugural character of writing. Both speak of the possibility of texts that produce not only interpretations but also events. This idea opens up the possibility of speaking of a circularity between texts and historical events. Indeed, for Christian hermeneutics, Scriptures are about a unique event: 'in the beginning was the Word' (John 1:1) and 'the Word became flesh and dwelt among us' (John 1:14). This is the event folded into the very text that requires interpretation. In fact, there is a conversion between writing and historical eventuality in Scriptures. The written word becomes event, particularly the event of Christ. But before this event, the prophetical word has also been converted into historical existence: writing as such happens and has happened.

Sacred Scripture is a singular writing because it transpires in history, otherwise it would be one among others. It is the specific relationship that this writing has with history that makes it completely unique. Scriptures are fulfilled, not in a progressive, but in a figurative sense. The very idea of figure is transformed through Scriptures from a literary artefact into a historical event. In recounting the event, texts become history: that is, they not only produce events, but events entrenched in that particular narrative.

Certainly, the idea of the fulfilment of the Scriptures is a complex one, since it has three dimensions: a basic aspect of continuity between the Old and the New Testament revelation; an aspect of discontinuity, since the New Testament is completely new; and an aspect of transcendence. The mystery of Christ is the fulfilment of the figure of sacrificial worship of the old dispensation, but it came to happen in a very different way from the expected. The paschal mystery of Christ is in complete conformity with prophecy, albeit in a way that could not have been anticipated and that presents clear aspects of discontinuity with regard to the institutions of the community of the Jewish faith.

This performativity of Scriptures shown in Christ has several complex dimensions in the course of the after-history. Holiness is the most common way in which Scripture still acts in history.[51] Indeed, in the case of the saints, Scripture acts upon the life of the subjects who read it, mediating the spirit that lives within it. But also, the performative character of Scriptures implies that the written words continue to await events. Sacred Scriptures are not a narrative of past events, but a narrative of a coming future that cannot be performed as such by the interpreters.[52] The whole Scripture has the character of a prophetic word. It has a 'figural' character insofar as new figures will take place in history shaped by this particular prophetic writing. In fact, the structure of the figural character is already contained in Scripture. Its performativity, however, is not just based on the decision of the historical actors, but transcends them since it is grounded in its prophetical character according to which God does what he says: 'For the word of God is living, and active.'[53]

This idea of Paul inspires the exegetical approach of Thomas Aquinas. Sacred Scripture is the *testimonium* of revelation.[54] God speaks not only with his words, but also through the events which happen in history and are rendered scripturally.[55] Something has 'taken-place', is 'taking-place' and will 'take-place'.[56] The text is entrenched in history: to the past event in the literal sense, and to the future event in the anagogical sense, rejoicing in the excess of meaning. This is the main feature of the theology of revelation.[57] The text comes from the spirit and returns to the spirit.[58] This is a third alternative way of conceiving this particular priority of writing, beyond Derrida's language coming from texts and returning to texts; and Gadamer's texts coming from language and returning to language. In any of the three ways of approaching text, the impossibility of the definitive presence of total and complete meaning is recognised. The text is neither meaningfully nor temporally closed. Scripture is still always revealing. Its trace refers to many other texts and many other texts refer to its trace. In a paradigmatic way, sacred writing shows the very character of writing. In fact, sacred Scripture displays a complex arrangement of intertextuality and interpretive processes that make it a hermeneutical artefact or a text ready to be deconstructed.[59] In fact, sacred Scripture is an enigmatic text that can be put at the core of the poststructuralist philosophical debate.

The many historical and political vicissitudes that the scriptural texts have undergone, show their character as theopolitical figure. The destiny of every core text of a community is associated with that of Scripture. In particular, the text of the law. In fact, legal dogmatic in itself is a figure of Scripture, when Scripture itself loses its dogmatic place in the political arena.[60]

Theopolitical Figurations of Scripture: The Case of the Political Interpretation of the Bible

The use of the interpretation of sacred Scriptures in the legitimisation of power throughout history speaks of their founding character for the political community. Indeed, the struggle to appropriate the meaning of Scriptures has governed the legitimacy of power since Antiquity. As Philippe Buc asserts, the metaphors and categories of

Scripture constitute imaginaries that influence political praxis and its intelligibility.[61] The mediation of the interpreters and of the very theory and methodology of interpretation itself is crucial for political legitimation. In fact, interpretation of sacred Scriptures can be understood throughout history as an exercise to achieve political power.

Examples of direct or indirect application of biblical interpretation in government can be found in every age, however, the Bible does not contain a unique way of speaking about power, politics or government. In fact, it is not only in the Middle Ages that there many examples of this kind of practice. The two last parts of Hobbes' *Leviathan* are devoted to biblical exegesis. Locke has his own interpretation of the Gospel, *The Reasonableness of Christianity* and *A Paraphrase and Notes on the Epistles of St. Paul*. And Spinoza's *Theological–Political Treatise* is a paradigmatic case for the connection between biblical interpretation and politics in early modernity. But even in the eighteenth and nineteenth centuries, biblical interpretation continued to be present and to transform philosophy into hermeneutics, not without political consequences: first, for legal theory, but also for the meaning of authority.[62] Even the twentieth century proclaims a political theology of the death of God, which sacralises democracy as the new name of God, again through biblical interpretation. The following pages will attest to the capacity of Scripture to shape historical–political constellations. Indeed, I will try to unravel the shift from the 'theological Bible' to the 'philosophical Bible'. A passage that also represents a shift from the political theology of the lordship to that of the sovereign.

In fact, Percy E. Schramm and Walter Ullmann have insisted on the relevance of biblical commentaries in shaping medieval political thought.[63] We can say that the Bible provided the Middle Ages with the vocabulary to speak about power and authority. However, there is not a fixed set of ideas which can be considered as the Bible's medieval political theology. Biblical vocabulary is embedded in narratives that cannot be interpreted univocally. Scriptures were from the beginning an area of confrontation. Both an anti-monarchical Bible and the political constitution of monarchies in the West could be justified through the words of interpreters.[64]

Luke's text on the 'two swords' (22:38) was one of the first theological–political fragments that forced exegesis to define itself. Indeed, since the Christian owes obedience to God, what place does temporal power have in this obedience? In Origen, we find the first exegesis of this passage, which for centuries dominated Western thinking regarding the separation between Church and State.[65] The hermeneutical methodology used by Origen combines allegorical with logical elements in a discretionary equilibrium. Origen's exegetical scheme demands that some moments be interpreted on a purely spiritual level, while others be interpreted on a purely literal level; it requires, paradoxically, that each moment should equally express the underlying tension between letter and spirit. In the case of the sword, his exegesis depends on the tension between the spiritual or allegorical sword, which the disciples are first enjoined to buy, and the corporeal or literal sword, for the use of which they are later rebuked. In particular, transfiguration of the corporeal sword into the sword of the spirit becomes the symbol of the conversion from the Old into the New Testament. The tension between letter and spirit must be conserved in every interpreted passage.[66]

However, the spiritual warfare of the Christian not only has an inner, moral or tropological aspect but also a historical, Christological and eschatological dimension. The inner struggle takes place as part of the cosmic struggle between Christ and the devil. For the Christian, cosmic forces of evil will remain at work as long as this world persists. This evil must be resisted, but not in the same manner by Christians and non-Christians. Non-Christians continue to fight with the carnal weapons of the old dispensation. Christians, however, because they are participating in the eschatological struggle, fight with weapons of another kind. Therefore, despite the mildness of the New Testament, the coming of Christ has not abolished the warlike qualities of the God of hosts. For that reason, Origen considers that when the Christian first encounters the name of Jesus, it should be under the figure of Joshua the Warrior. Paradoxically, the New Testament rejects, but at the same time re-edits the wars of the Old Testament in terms of the metaphor of the sword.

Origen's pacifism is visible not only in his comments on Luke 22:38 and also on Matthew 26:52, but mainly in his *Contra Celsum*. He refutes Celso's idea that Christians drew their origin from a revolt against the Jews in the same manner as the Jews did against the Egyptians. Christians are radical pacifists. They do not fight for the empire, even if pressed to do so.[67] For him, the Roman Empire was not the fourth empire referred to in Daniel 2:40; nor the power that 'holdeth' Antichrist in 2 Thessalonians 2:7, as it was for Tertullian. His contemporary Hippolytus thought that the empire was under the apocalyptic sign of the beast. This was also the case made by Irenaeus. Even for Hippolytus, the empire was an anti-church, and even though he was Christian, he was obliged to obey its civil laws as far as possible. For him, however, the only providential role of the empire is linked to the birth of the Church as a non-political structure, and therefore with the secret unfolding of the Christ-event. Origen considered the blurring of national differences that the Roman Empire implied as a providential coincidence favouring the expansion of Christianity, but in no case as a means to achieve that end. In his view, if the totality of the empire were to convert, the Romans could defeat their enemies just by prayer. The idea of a pacified unity of the world was for him very tempting. In a sense, he had a proto-Eusebian vision of the Christian empire that fulfils an eschatological role. However, every Christian ought to resist the imperial power if it issued orders that contradicted Christian precepts.

Origen's political theology remained in the exegetical tradition, but not without changes. In fact, in the fourth and fifth centuries, the main idea was that the sword that Christians were forbidden to use was not necessarily the physical sword. However, condemnation was not of war, but of anger. Ambrose, for example, celebrates the power of self-defence, which neither the Lord nor his disciples had lost: in rebuking Peter, the Lord forbids his disciples to use a power that they nevertheless possessed. Be that as it may, Ambrose gives an allegorical interpretation of Luke 22:38: the two swords represent the Old and the New Testament, respectively; together they suffice to defend Christian doctrine.

The patristic commentaries mediated through Beda successively suggest other alternatives, such as the two swords represent the power of self-defence and the obligation not to make use of that power; body and soul, or works and faith; the sword of excommunication and the sword of life. Through all these commentaries, a theology of two separate jurisdictional powers was achieved, which received its classical formulation in the fifth century by Pope Gelasius I.

Consultation of patristic sources has, little by little, been substituted by the gloss. The gloss was an eclectic commentary on the Scriptures. Instead of being systematised, the different glosses were independent of each other. They were rewritten and corrected. The gloss contributed to shape the ideas of the clerical estate. Around 1179, the pope prohibited the reading of Scripture without gloss. It is at this time that the gloss begins to have an official status.[68] And it was at this time that the central idea of the 'authorised interpretation', in this case the gloss, began to take hold. But in an almost contradictory way that authoritative character of the gloss was tempered by the great openness allowed by its a-systematic character. In fact, the most precious exegetical principle was that of the *concordantia oppositorum*, according to which different meanings have to be arranged until a possible interpretation is arrived at, which does not allow one of the opinions in contention be considered be false. The reading of Scripture was not linear; it was moreover a *catena* – that is, a linkage of different sentences of the Bible to the exclusion of others – that could be interpreted as containing different aspects of the truth. The interpretation always had to be referred to a chain of sentences. Therefore, the understanding of the opinions of one commentator depends on three elements: first, on the chain to which he has alluded; secondly, to the meaning he has attributed to the elements of the chain; and, thirdly to the nuances and shifts with which he contributes to tradition. This exegetical logic can be easily transferred into other practices, as long as equilibrium is maintained. In any event, concord can easily become discord or conflict.

One of the most incredible results that accompanied this new kind of exegesis is the variety of political opinions that result from it.[69] In fact, in the eleventh century, three different theological–political argumentations ran parallel with regard to the pericope of the two swords. For the defenders of the monarchy, the two swords pericope legitimises a defensive dualism; there are two powers that must remain distinct and without interference. For the curialists, in a misinterpretation of St. Bernard that seems to go back to John of Salisbury's 'Policraticus', Peter had both swords, and the fact that he may not use the material sword only demonstrates that the kings and emperors are his delegates. Finally, for the neutralists it is clear that there are two distinct powers, but the form of their relationship is always an open question. In fact, for Gregory VII, kingship could be so worldly that it could be considered as a weapon of the devil, and yet, at the same time, capable of functioning as an ecclesiastical office.[70]

In addition to the pericope of the two swords, another semantic pair became prominent in the battlefield of scriptural interpretation, the dialectic between *iustitia* and *misericordia*. Through this semantic pair, the conflict between *sacerdotium* and *regnum*, hierarchy and equality, was settled.[71] Buc's study on the Gloss of Nord France and Paris between the twelfth and fourteenth centuries concludes that the force of the egalitarian trend was prominent until 1215 in France, and it seems also to be the case in other parts of

Europe.[72] Ullmann, for his part, states that the hierarchical trend began to be mainstream around 1330.[73]

In fact, the idea of 'sacred kingship', perhaps the most original feature of medieval political imaginary, is not, however, that of an 'absolute monarch', an early modern concept, but that of lordship. The Middle Ages lacked the idea of absolutism, except for that used by medieval canonists and ecclesiologists, who designated as absolute the jurisdictional power of the papacy (*plenitudo potestatis papalis*). Innocent III (pope from 1198 to 1216) was the first to make regular use of the term, in opposition to, in hierarchical logic, the *pars sollicitudinis*, the 'share of solicitude' held by the bishops. But for an interpretation of the two swords pericope, the ideas of Giles of Rome were decisive. In fact, Giles of Rome, who based his thinking on Pseudo-Dionysius the Areopagite, explains reality as operating a reduction from the inferior to the superior through intermediaries. Spiritual power constitutes the essence of power; temporal power is a kind of intermediary. Thus, in the *casus imminens*, the original power should include all the different powers. Giles of Rome uses the distinction between *potestas absoluta* and *ordinate*, applying to the pontiff the *potestas absoluta* and to the king the *potestas regulata*, comparing the miraculous acts of God with the exceptional power of the pope in temporal matters. This idea was accepted in the Church, albeit for a short time. In fact, Boniface VIII, after defending the *plenitudo potestatis* of the pope against the power of political monarchs, such as Felipe IV, wrote the *Unam Sanctam* bull in 1302, substituting the expression *plenitudo potestatis* for *potestas Petri*.[74]

As Ullmann writes, the Middle Ages lack not only the idea of absolutism, but also that of political sovereignty, since the idea of the state is missing.[75] However, it is indeed true that the theocratic-descendant forms of government typical of the Middle Ages have biblical origins and influenced the modern shaping of the idea of sovereignty. The introduction of the term *superioritas* in the Vulgate of Jerome was not without political consequences.[76] The medieval *superioritas* always operated with its counterpart, that is, the *subditus* or *subjectus*. Otto Brunner sees this separation between the king and his people, particularly the estates, as the most revolutionary political feature of the Low Middle Ages, because it channels the idea of the monarch into the idea of the modern sovereign. In his view, this separation was a confrontation in the cases of exception to the law, since the question of deciding on those occasions gave voice to the royal power. Also, the disappearance of the *Fehde* – the private defence – was crucial in his view for the consolidation of sovereignty in the face of the empire and the papacy.[77] Ironically, this superiority makes the king an ecclesiastical servant in a way. In fact, first, making the king superior meant separating him from his people and ascending him to the estate of the clerical, which was contrary to the use of traditional medieval societies, where the king always governed with the estates. The people were not a mass of subjects deprived of their will, but a plural community that had political rights and acted with the king in judicial and military matters. All kinds of assembly took place at that time.[78] Secondly, making him superior presupposes that he receives from God the government of his people – 'rex Dei gratia' – in competition with church officers, that is, with the bishops. In particular, it was the political theology of the Carolingians, starting in the nineth century, which shaped the king's aura in the image of the Old Testament kings. This idea was embedded in the ceremonies of the Crown, through which all these meanings were shaped. In fact, the unction of the king was intentionally similar to that of the bishops, even if it never had an indelible character as in the case of holy orders; the coronation, however, was a secular matter.[79] In sum, Ullmann asserts that this theocratic kingship was a product of exegesis, theology and the liturgy, and not a 'natural' course of Roman history.[80]

We can imagine how important scriptural comments were in this period, particularly in the interpretation of authority and hierarchy. We can also imagine how arguments flow from one sphere to the other, from ecclesiastical to political and vice versa: democrats, monarchists and theocrats disputed the semantic field.[81]

Sacred Scripture continues to be insidious for philosophy, and particularly for political action, in early modernity. Indeed, between 1650 and 1690, an intense scriptural movement took place.[82] Hobbes, Spinoza and Locke, the founders of Modern State theory, were immersed in that scriptural movement.[83] They recognised the potential of the interpretation of Scripture in shaping political legitimation; and for the sake of peace after the religious wars, they tried to diminish its 'force of truth' through their epistemological considerations. For sure, the three thinkers influenced each other to a certain extent. Spinoza incorporated the doctrine of the third part of Hobbes' *Leviathan* into his *Theological Political Treatise*.[84] Locke, for his part, was definitely influenced by Spinoza, as is shown by the notes about the *Tractatus theologico politicus* contained in Locke's Bentley Bible;[85] furthermore, he was familiar with, and sometimes criticised, Hobbes' *Leviathan*. Moreover, the three philosophers shared a common fate: censorship by the ecclesiastical authority.[86]

In their view, God speaks to people's minds in a different way from the way the empirical world does: through the narrative called sacred Scriptures. But sacred Scriptures are confusing to such an extent that they provoke all kind of controversies in the political arena. Hence, these enlightened philosophers try to liberate men from the authority of the sacred Scriptures through interpretation.

In fact, among their epistemologies, different as they are, there is a certain common nucleus of philosophical ideas about language that transformed the status of the sacred Scriptures. This is mainly through the idea that in the discourse called 'sacred Scriptures', in which we find the prophetic word of God, nothing can be demonstrated, and nothing refuted, because we do not have information from the senses about the things related therein. Words and language are enemies of the truth. They represent things as they are in the imagination, not as they are in the intellect. Because of that fact, the meaning of words varies from one person to another. Words became stable in their meanings through their usage. Ordinary language, as expressed in natural languages, is constantly changing. As a result, the interpretation of the Bible was a disputed question.[87] Locke will say that this is why there are millions of commentators on and interpreters of the Old and New Testaments; it is also why we have to be charitable with one another in our interpretations or misunderstandings of those ancient writings.[88]

In this interpretative context, it was Hobbes who first raised the political question related to the Scriptures: who is the authorised interpreter? By what authority are those Scriptures made law?[89] He is not now thinking of any possible true knowledge that Scripture can provide, but of its political efficacy. Common sense says that God's words have efficacy only for those to whom God has directly communicated their meaning. Outside that group, these words are effective, as for any other law, only through the action of the sovereign power. In Hobbes' view, the Christian monarch enters into sacred history as an interpreter of the divine word. Therefore, not only must the sovereign be regarded as the definitive interpreter of the doctrine 'Jesus is the Christ', he must also have the power to speak truthfully about the second sign of true prophecy: the working of miracles. Hobbes rejected the notion that the Church might have a public prerogative in the representation of divine power.[90] Indeed, the Church is primarily an association within the commonwealth, and thus cannot make or enforce any law. The purpose of Hobbes' argument throughout chapter 42 of *Leviathan* was to provide conclusive proof of the ecclesiastical supremacy of civil sovereigns over their subjects, supplanting the alleged power of the pope. This line of argument also prompted Hobbes to write of the need to establish national churches under a theocratic monarchy.[91] Sovereignty is the most revolutionary creation of the early modern political world and this creation would not have been possible without a certain interpretation of the Scriptures.

Spinoza, for his part, concludes his *Political-Theological Treatise* with a justification of a kind of theocratic democracy he calls for as the 'new Christian religion'. Not surprisingly, criticism of the 'old Christian religion' abounds in the *Theological-Political Treatise*. The first of these criticisms accuses the old Christian religion of only maintaining its external forms, since such great importance is given to ecclesiastical ministries. The second criticism asserts that the ability to discern between truth and falsity, between good and evil, is delegated to those same ministries, particularly to the pope's infallibility, thus alienating the free judgement of men and turning them into brutes.[92] He insists on the idea that once the Hebrew state had been destroyed, revealed religion only had any immediate force in civil law through supreme authority. He then concludes by saying that jurisdiction over all the sacred lies with the supreme authorities.[93] But if this is so, then every political power immediately becomes a theocracy, even if it is a democratic one.[94]

According to Locke, the use of reason makes men free; in contrast, believing in principles and authorities in order to obtain justification turns men into slaves.[95] The liberation of reason from the yoke of dogmatism, authority and tradition leads to political liberation as well.[96] For Locke, this kind of liberation is impeded by two primary obstacles: infallibility, which gives rise to the power of the Church; and tradition, which supports patriarchal government in both the Church and the civil state. Free interpretation diminishes the weight of both, giving rise to autonomous reason and, hence, to individual liberty. From the institutional point of view, the two enemies of Locke's political freedom were the Church and the monarchy, but he did not consider religion and politics to be enemies as such.[97] However, it is the elimination of the significance of the Church that clears the path to 'true religion'. Through his interpretation of Scripture, Locke was able to achieve a deinstitutionalisation of religion that preserves and guarantees the autonomous jurisdiction of political power. If conflict arises, political jurisdiction should decide in religious affairs. The great separation between religious and political jurisdictions was the aim of his writings on toleration.

Although Locke's republicanism and Spinoza's radical democracy stand in complete contrast to Hobbes' conservative monarchism, all three philosophers sacralised political reason by defending the supremacy of the sovereign's decisions over religious doctrine in response to the constant danger of political unrest. They accomplished a theological–political transposition: the place of the churches was taken over by the state, and the sovereign's *'raison d'état'* was not to be limited by the 'reason' of any other institution. For all three, scriptural interpretation was the political–theological instrument to achieve political changes in a world in which religious matters held weight.

The main task that enlightened 'tradition' begins with is to constitute a 'theological–political Bible', instead of simply denying the legitimacy of the Bible. Perhaps the reason is because of the indestructible character of 'the written' as such. Only an infinite critical movement can achieve something like the negation of what remains irremediably written.

Notes

1. Derrida, 'How to Avoid Speaking', 28.
2. Derrida, 'How to Avoid Speaking', 29.
3. We could also say with Brian Britt that those manifestations frequently have a 'scriptural function' to indicate the idea of 'a text that participates significantly in a religious or sacred tradition'. Brian Britt, *Walter Benjamin and the Bible* (New York: Continuum, 1996), 19. My option has been, however, to speak of 'scriptural figure', since 'figure' has a historical character that 'function' lacks.
4. Jacques Derrida, *Of Grammatology* (Baltimore, MD: Johns Hopkins University Press, 1997), 44.
5. Walter Benjamin, *On Language as Such and on the Language of Man*, in Walter Benjamin, *Selected Writings, vol. 1: 1913–1926*, ed. Marcus Bullock and Michael W. Jennings (Cambridge, MA: Harvard University Press, 2002), 62–74, 63.
6. Derrida, *Of Grammatology*, 6.
7. Derrida, *Of Grammatology*, 6: 'By a slow movement whose necessity is hardly perceptible, everything that for at least some twenty centuries tended toward and finally succeeded in being gathered under the name of language is beginning to let itself be transferred to, or at least summarized under, the name of writing.' For an account of the

philosophical contribution of Derrida's *Grammatology* to philosophy, see Arthur Bradley, *Derrida's Of Grammatology: An Edinburgh Philosophical Guide* (Edinburgh: Edinburgh University Press, 2008).

8. Jacques Derrida, *Writing and Difference* (Chicago: University of Chicago Press, 1978), 295. Also, Derrida, *Of Grammatology*, 18: 'The idea of the book, which always refers to a natural totality, is profoundly alien to the sense of writing. It is the encyclopaedic protection of theology and of logocentrism against the disruption of writing, against its aphoristic energy, and, as I shall specify later, against difference in general. If I distinguish the text from the book, I shall say that the destruction of the book, as it is now under way in all domains, denudes the surface of the text. That necessary violence responds to a violence that was no less necessary.' By writing we must understand not only the physical gestures of literal pictographic or ideographic inscriptions, but also all that makes them possible, whether or not it is literal and even if what it produces is not imparted by the voice: pictorial, musical, sculptural, cinematographical, choreographical, cybernetical, etc. See Derrida, *Of Grammatology*, 8–9.
9. Derrida, *Of Grammatology*, 13–14.
10. So, Bradley, *Derrida's Of Grammatology*, 46.
11. Derrida, *Of Grammatology*, 11. Logocentrism presupposes the absolute proximity of voice and being, of voice and the meaning of being, of voice and the ideality of meaning.
12. Derrida, *Of Grammatology*, 44: 'The thesis of the arbitrariness of the sign (so grossly misnamed, and not only for the reasons Saussure himself recognizes) must forbid a radical distinction between the linguistic and the graphic sign. Now from the moment that one considers the totality of determined signs, spoken, and *a fortiori* written, as unmotivated institutions, one must exclude any relationship of natural subordination, any natural hierarchy among signifiers or orders of signifiers. If "writing" signifies inscription and especially the durable institution of a sign (and that is the only irreducible kernel of the concept of writing), writing in general covers the entire field of linguistic signs. In that field a certain sort of instituted signifiers may then appear, "graphic" in the narrow and derivative sense of the word, ordered by a certain relationship with other instituted –hence "written", even if they are "phonic" – signifiers. The very idea of institution – hence of the arbitrariness of the sign – is unthinkable before the possibility of writing and outside of its horizon. Quite simply, that is, outside of the horizon itself, outside the world as space of inscription, as the opening to the emission and to the spatial distribution of signs, to the regulated play of their differences, even if they are "phonic".'
13. Derrida, *Of Grammatology*, 14–15.

14. Derrida, *Of Grammatology*, 47: 'The trace, where the relationship with the other is marked, articulates its possibility in the entire field of the entity [*etant*], which metaphysics has defined as the being-present starting from the occulted movement of the trace. The trace must be thought before the entity.' And Derrida, *Of Grammatology*, 167: 'Writing is one of the representatives of the trace in general, it is not the trace itself. The trace itself does not exist. (To exist is to be, to be an entity, a being-present, *to on*). In a way, this displacement leaves the place of the decision hidden, but it also indicates it unmistakably.' To designate this notion, Derrida uses the idea of *archi-writing*. Bradley, *Derrida's Of Grammatology*, 9, 146: archi-writing 'describes the mediated nature of perception, consciousness and our experience of "reality" in general: we think, act and live through signs'.
15. Derrida, *Writing and Difference*, 20: 'To say that *différance* is originary is simultaneously to erase the myth of a present origin. Which is why "originary" must be understood as having been crossed out, without which differance would be derived from an original plenitude. It is a non-origin which is originary.'
16. Derrida, *Of Grammatology*, 65. Derrida, *Writing and Difference*, 178–9, where with reference to Poe's 'The Purloined Letter', Derrida explains: 'The letter, inscribed or propounded speech, is always stolen. Always stolen because it is always open. It never belongs to its author or to its addressee, and by nature, it never follows the trajectory that leads from subject to subject. Which amounts to acknowledging the autonomy of the signifier as the letter's historicity; before me, the signifier on its own says more than I believe that I mean to say, and in relation to it, my meaning-to-say is submissive rather than active. My meaning-to-say finds itself lacking something in relation to the signifier, and is inscribed passively, we might say, even if the reflection of this lack determines the urgency of expression as excess: the autonomy of the signifier as the stratification and historical potentialization of meaning, as a historical system, that is, a system that is open at some point.'
17. The complete text is Derrida, *Of Grammatology*, 47: 'The "theological" is a determined moment in the total movement of the trace. The field of the entity, before being determined as the field of presence, is structured according to the diverse possibilities – genetic and structural – of the trace. The presentation of the other as such, that is to say the dissimulation of its "as such", has always already begun and no structure of the entity escapes it.'
18. Derrida, *Writing and Difference*, 11: 'It is because writing is inaugural, in the fresh sense of the word, that it is dangerous and anguishing. It does not know where it is going, no knowledge can keep it from the essential precipitation toward the meaning that it constitutes and that is, primarily, its future. However, it is capricious only through

cowardice. There is thus no insurance against the risk of writing. Writing is an initial and graceless recourse for the writer, even if he is not an atheist but, rather, a writer. Did Saint John Chrysostom speak of the writer? "It were indeed meet for us not at all to require the aid of the written Word, but to exhibit a life so pure, that the grace of the spirit should be instead of books to our souls, and that as these are inscribed with ink, even so should our hearts be with the Spirit. But, since we have utterly put away from us this grace, come let us at any rate embrace the second-best course." But, all faith or theological assurance aside, is not the experience of secondarity tied to the strange redoubling by means of which constituted-written-meaning presents itself as prerequisitely and simultaneously read: and does not meaning present itself as such at the point at which the other is found, the other who maintains both the vigil and the back-and-forth motion, the work, that comes between writing and reading, making this work irreducible? Meaning is neither before nor after the act.'

19. Derrida, *Writing and Difference*, 178.
20. Derrida, *Of Grammatology*, 61: 'What I call the erasure of concepts ought to mark the places of that future meditation. For example, the value of the transcendental *arche* [archie] must make its necessity felt before letting itself be erased. The concept of arche-trace must comply with both that necessity and that erasure. It is in fact contradictory and not acceptable within the logic of identity. The trace is not only the disappearance of origin – within the discourse that we sustain and according to the path that we follow it means that the origin did not even disappear, that it was never constituted except reciprocally by a non-origin, the trace, which thus becomes the origin of the origin. From then on, to wrench the concept of the trace from the classical scheme, which would derive it from a presence or from an originary nontrace and which would make of it an empirical mark, one must indeed speak of an originary trace or arche-trace. Yet we know that that concept destroys its name and that, if all begins with the trace, there is above all no originary trace.'
21. Derrida, *Writing and Difference*, 178, see also, 11: 'Is not that which is called God, that which imprints every human course and recourse with its secondarity, the passageway of deferred reciprocity between reading and writing? or the absolute witness to the dialogue in which what one sets out to write has already been read, and what one sets out to say is already a response, the third party as the transparency of meaning? Simultaneously part of creation and the Father of Logos. The circularity and traditionality of Logos. The strange labor of conversion and adventure in which grace can only be that which is missing.'
22. Derrida, *Of Grammatology*, 70. The idea of bricolage evoked by Levi-Strauss is used by Derrida to explain this idea about the constitution or deconstitution of texts, Derrida, *Writing and Difference*,

285: 'If one calls bricolage the necessity of borrowing one's concepts from the text of a heritage which is more or less coherent or ruined, it must be said that every discourse is bricoleur. The engineer, whom Levi-Strauss opposes to the bricoleur, should be the one to construct the totality of his language, syntax, and lexicon. In this sense the engineer is a myth. A subject who supposedly would be the absolute origin of his own discourse and supposedly would construct it "out of nothing", "out of whole cloth", would be the creator of the verb, the verb itself.'

23. Derrida, *Of Grammatology*, 154.
24. Derrida, *Of Grammatology*, 154.
25. Derrida, *Of Grammatology*, 266: 'there is a point in the system where the signifier can no longer be replaced by its signified, so that in consequence no signifier can be so replaced, purely and simply. For the point of non-replacement is also the point of orientation for the entire system of signification, the point where the fundamental signified is promised as the terminal-point of all references and conceals itself as that which would destroy at one blow the entire system of signs. It is at once spoken and forbidden by all signs. Language is neither prohibition nor transgression, it couples the two endlessly. That point does not exist, it is always elusive or, what comes to the same thing, always already inscribed in what it ought to escape or ought to have escaped, according to our indestructible and mortal desire.'
26. Derrida, *Of Grammatology*, 244.
27. Derrida, *Of Grammatology*, 17.
28. Derrida, 'How to Avoid Speaking', 29.
29. Derrida, *Of Grammatology*, 66: 'This impossibility of reanimating absolutely the manifest evidence of an originary presence refers us therefore to an absolute past. That is what authorized us to call trace that which does not let itself be summed up in the simplicity of a present. It could in fact have been objected that, in the indecomposable synthesis of temporalization, protention is as indispensable as retention. And their two dimensions are not added up but the one implies the other in a strange fashion. To be sure, what is anticipated in protention does not sever the present any less from its self-identity than does that which is retained in the trace. But if anticipation were privileged, the irreducibility of the always-already-there and the fundamental passivity that is called time would risk effacement. On the other hand, if the trace refers to an absolute past, it is because it obliges us to think a past that can no longer be understood in the form of a modified presence, as a present-past. Since past has always signified present-past, the absolute past that is retained in the trace no longer rigorously merits the name of past.'
30. Derrida, *Of Grammatology*, 69, see also 27: 'That historicity itself is tied to the possibility of writing; to the possibility of writing in

general, beyond those particular forms of writing in the name of which we have long spoken of peoples without writing and without history. Before being the object of a history – of an historical science – writing opens the field of history – of historical-becoming. And the former (*Historie* in German) presupposes the latter (*Geschichte*).'

31. When Derrida speaks here of 'event' it is something that happens in historical time, to which we can attribute the nature of the unconditional: what comes once, in a singular, exceptional, irreplaceable, unpredictable and incalculable way. See Jacques Derrida, *Voyous: deux essays sur la raison* (Paris: Galilée, 2003), 189.
32. Jacques Derrida, 'A Certain Impossible Possibility of Saying the Event', *Critical Inquiry* 33(2) (2007): 441–61, 452: 'the saying of the event presupposed some sort of inevitable neutralization of the event by its iterability, that saying always harbors the possibility of resaying'.
33. Derrida, 'A Certain Impossible Possibility', 447.
34. Derrida, 'A Certain Impossible Possibility', 454.
35. Walter Benjamin, *The Origin of German Tragic Drama* (London: Verso, 1998), 175; Walter Benjamin, *Gesammelte Schriften* (Frankfurt am Main: Suhrkamp, 1991), I, 351.
36. In fact, God is above all a creative word, creative omnipotence of language. In his creative word, God called everything into being, calling them by their proper names. In the language of men, however, they are overnamed. Benjamin, *On Language as Such*, 74: 'The language of an entity is the medium in which its mental being is communicated. The uninterrupted flow of this communication runs through the whole of nature, from the lowest forms of existence to man and from man to God. Man communicates himself to God through name, which he gives to nature and (in proper names) to his own kind; and to nature he gives names according to the communication that he receives from her, for the whole of nature, too, is imbued with a nameless, unspoken language, the residue of the creative word of God, which is preserved in man as the cognizing name and above man as the judgment suspended over him. The language of nature is comparable to a secret password that each sentry passes to the next in his own language, but the meaning of the password is the sentry's language itself. All higher language is a translation of lower ones, until in ultimate clarity the word of God unfolds, which is the unity of this movement made up of language.' See also Benjamin, *Gesammelte Schriften*, 4, 9. There are three main consequences of original sin in respect of language: first, men lose the purer language of name, making language a means, or a mere sign (which amounts to the same) of what he calls the 'bourgeois conception of language'; and this fact later results in the plurality of languages. Secondly, in exchange for the immediacy of name, a new immediacy arises: the

magic of judgement. The third consequence is the origin of abstraction, as a faculty of the spirit of language. It is through abstraction that philosophy seeks to restore pure language. These three aspects incline human language to presume that the word should communicate something other than itself.

37. Walter Benjamin, *The Task of the Translator*, in Walter Benjamin, *Selected Writings, vol. 1: 1913–1926*, ed. Marcus Bullock and Michael W. Jennings (Cambridge, MA: Harvard University Press, 2002), 253–63, 257.
38. For Benjamin, translation means more than an effect of idiomatic pluralism. Benjamin, *The Task of the Translator*, 254: 'Just as the manifestations of life are intimately connected with the phenomenon of life without being of importance to it, a translation issues from the original – not so much from its life as from its afterlife. For a translation comes later than the original, and since the important works of world literature never find their chosen translators at the time of their origin, their translation marks their stage of continued life. The idea of life and afterlife in works of art should be regarded with an entirely unmetaphorical objectivity.'
39. Benjamin, *On the Language as Such*, 71. See also Britt, *Walter Benjamin and the Bible*, 11. Sacred texts are the only access to pure language, even if they do not provide a magical power to recover that pure language as such. Again, the cross-out of origin.
40. P. Fofget (ed.), *Text und Interpretation. Eine deutsch-franzosische Debatte* mit Beiträgen von Jacques Derrida, Philippe Forget, Manfred Frank, Hans-Georg Gadamer, Jean Greisch and François Laruelle (Munich: Wilhelm Fink, 1984).
41. Gadamer, *Truth and Method*, 2nd rev. edn; translation revd. Joel Weinsheimer and Donald G. Marshall (London: Continuum, 2006), 297: 'Thus the reference to the original reader, like that to the meaning of the author, seems to offer only a very crude historic-hermeneutical criterion that cannot really limit the horizon of a text's meaning. What is fixed in writing has detached itself from the contingency of its origin and its author and made itself free for new relationships. Normative concepts such as the author's meaning or the original reader's understanding in fact represent only an empty space that is filled from time to time in understanding.'
42. Gadamer, *Truth and Method*, 251: 'It still remains true that all such understanding is ultimately self-understanding (*Sichverstehen*: knowing one's way around).'
43. Derrida, *Writing and Difference*, 211: 'There is no present text in general, and there is not even a past present text, a text which is past as having been present. The text is not conceivable in an originary or modified form of presence'; see also 14: 'This history of the work is not only its past, the eve or the sleep in which it precedes itself in

an author's intentions, but is also the impossibility of its ever being present, of its ever being summarized by some absolute simultaneity or instantaneousness. This is why, as we will verify, there is no space of the work, if by space we mean presence and synopsis.'

44. Gadamer, *Truth and Method*, 307–8: 'The fact that philological, legal, and theological hermeneutics originally belonged closely together depended on recognizing application as an integral element of all understanding. In both legal and theological hermeneutics there is an essential tension between the fixed text – the law or the gospel – on the one hand, and, on the other, the sense arrived at by applying it at the concrete moment of interpretation, either in judgment or in preaching. A law does not exist in order to be understood historically, but to be concretized in its legal validity by being interpreted. Similarly, the gospel does not exist in order to be understood as a merely historical document, but to be taken in such a way that it exercises its saving effect. This implies that the text, whether law or gospel, if it is to be understood properly – i.e., according to the claim it makes – must be understood every moment, in every concrete situation, in a new and different way. Understanding here is always application.'

45. Gadamer, *Truth and Method*, 394: 'Certainly, in relation to language, writing seems a secondary phenomenon. The sign language of writing refers to the actual language of speech. But that language is capable of being written is by no means incidental to its nature. Rather, this capacity for being written down is based on the fact that speech itself shares in the pure ideality of the meaning that communicates itself in it. In writing, the meaning of what is spoken exists purely for itself, completely detached from all emotional elements of expression and communication. A text is not to be understood as an expression of life but with respect to what it says. Writing is the abstract ideality of language. Hence the meaning of something written is fundamentally identifiable and repeatable. What is identical in the repetition is only what was actually deposited in the written record. This indicates that "repetition" cannot be meant here in its strict sense. It does not mean referring back to the original source where something is said or written. The understanding of something written is not a repetition of something past but the sharing of a present meaning.'

46. Gadamer, *Truth and Method*, 392: 'Thus, written texts present the real hermeneutical task. Writing is self-alienation. Overcoming it, reading the text, is thus the highest task of understanding. Even the pure signs of an inscription can be seen properly and articulated correctly only if the text can be transformed back into language.' And also: 'all writing is a kind of alienated speech, and its signs need to be transformed back into speech and meaning'. Gadamer, *Truth and Method*, 394.

47. Gadamer, *Truth and Method*, 175–6: 'The art or technique of understanding and interpretation developed from analogous impulses along two paths – theological and philological. Theological hermeneutics, as Dilthey showed, developed from the reformers' defense of their own understanding of Scripture against the attack of the Tridentine theologians and their appeal to the indispensability of tradition; philological hermeneutics developed as instrumental to the humanist claim to revive classical literature. Both involve a rediscovery: a rediscovery of something that was not absolutely unknown, but whose meaning had become alien and inaccessible. Classical literature, though constantly present as material for humanistic education, had been completely absorbed within the Christian world. Similarly, the Bible was the church's sacred book and as such was constantly read, but the understanding of it was determined, and – as the reformers insisted – obscured, by the dogmatic tradition of the church. Both traditions are dealing with a foreign language and not with the scholar's universal language of the Latin Middle Ages, so studying the tradition in the original made it necessary to learn Greek and Hebrew as well as to purify Latin. By applying specialized techniques, hermeneutics claimed to reveal the original meaning of the texts in both traditions – humanistic literature and the Bible. It is of decisive importance that through Luther and Melanchthon the humanistic tradition was united with the reform. Insofar as scriptural hermeneutics is regarded as the prehistory of the hermeneutics of the modern human sciences, it is based on the scriptural principle of the Reformation.'
48. Gadamer, *Truth and Method*, 326.
49. Josef Ratzinger, 'Discurso en la Investidura de Doctor Honoris Causa del Cardenal Joseph Ratzinger en la Universidad de Navarra', *Scripta Theologica* 30 (1998): 390–2. On the canon in contemporary continental philosophy, see Colby Dickinson, *Between the Canon and the Messiah: The Structure of Faith in Contemporary Continental Thought* (London: Bloomsbury, 2013).
50. Benedict XVI, *Post-synodal Apostolic Exhortation Verbum Domini* (Vatican: Libreria Editrice Vaticana, 2010), 29: 'Here we can point to a fundamental criterion of biblical hermeneutics: the primary setting for scriptural interpretation is the life of the Church. This is not to uphold the ecclesial context as an extrinsic rule to which exegetes must submit, but rather is something demanded by the very nature of the Scriptures and the way they gradually came into being . . . The Holy Spirit, who gives life to the Church, enables us to interpret the Scriptures authoritatively. The Bible is the Church's book, and its essential place in the Church's life gives rise to its genuine interpretation.' See also Paul Ricoeur, 'The Sacred Text and the Community',

in *The Critical Study of Sacred Texts*, Wendy D. O'Flaherty (ed.) (Berkeley, CA: Berkeley Religious Studies Series, 1979), 271–6.
51. Benedict XVI, *Verbum Domini*, 49: 'holiness in the Church constitutes an interpretation of Scripture which cannot be overlooked'.
52. Benedict XVI, *Jesus of Nazareth* (London: Bloomsbury, 2007).
53. St Paul, Hebrews 4:12.
54. Beyond the dialectic between writing and events and concerning the discussion that we have had previously between writing and meaning, Piotr Roszak underlines, that in Aquinas' metaphysics of writing, writing appears as a 'lesser evil' in revelation and quotes: 'on account of the excellence of Christ's doctrine, which cannot be expressed in writing; according to John 21:25: "There are also many other things which Jesus did: which, if they were written everyone, the world itself, I think, would not be able to contain the books that should be written." Which Augustine explains by saying: "We are not to believe that in respect of space the world could not contain them . . . but that by the capacity of the readers they could not be comprehended." And if Christ had committed His doctrine to writing, men would have had no deeper thought of His doctrine than that which appears on the surface of the writing [S. Th. III, 42, 4c].' See Piotr Roszak, 'Language, Metaphysics and the Bible: The Philosophical Background of Aquinas's Exegesis of Sacred Scripture', *European Journal of Science and Theology* 14 (2018): 123–35, 130. For that reason, Aquinas considers that meaning and message come after writing.
55. Roszak, 'Language, Metaphysics and the Bible', 129.
56. Fáinche Ryan, *Formation in Holiness: Thomas Aquinas on Sacra doctrina* (Leuven: Peeters, 2007), 118. He calls this a post-modern sacramental ontology.
57. Olivier-Thomas Venard, 'Is There a Thomist Hermeneutic?' in *Redeeming Truth: Considering Faith and Reason*, S. S. Parsons and L-P. Hemming (eds) (London: SCM Press, 2007), 125–53.
58. Benedict XVI, *Verbum Domini*, 38.
59. Michael Fishbane, *Biblical Interpretation in Ancient Israel* (New York: Oxford University Press, 1985), 4: 'What needs to be noted here is that this development cannot simply be explained as a consequence of rival systems of exegesis, but must be seen, just as surely, as a natural theological consequence of the notion that the contents of interpretation are part of the written divine revelation (implicitly or explicitly).'
60. Gadamer, *Truth and Method*, 321: 'legal hermeneutics is no special case but is, on the contrary, capable of restoring the hermeneutical problem to its full breadth and so re-establishing the former unity of hermeneutics, in which jurist and theologian meet the philologist'.

61. Philippe Buc, *L'ambigüité du Livre. Prince, pouvoir et peuple dans les commentaires de la Bible au Moyen Age* (Paris: Beauchesnes, 1994), 26. Scriptures enter into the flow of history and act politically depending on interpretation. Interpretation was and is about authority and power, says Philippe Buc, in this case in 'Ritual and Interpretation: The Early Medieval Case', *Early Medieval Europe* 9(2) (2000): 183–210. The idea of Scriptures as a theological–political figure shares this fundamental conviction that Buc deduces from the study of the medieval exegetical sources of Scripture. Before him, Caspary, *Politics and Exegesis*, had asked himself rhetorically in the introduction of his book, 'what has politics in common with biblical exegesis?' And he responds by focusing on the contested reading of Scripture implicit in the battle of the investitures, or what might be called the mystery of ever-unified and ever-divided power.
62. See, e.g., Montserrat Herrero, 'Variaciones hegelianas de la crítica bíblica ilustrada. El espíritu frente a la letra', *Scripta Theologica* 50 (2018): 275–302.
63. Walter Ullmann, 'The Bible and the Principles of Government in the Middle Ages', in *La Bibbia nell'alto medioevo* (Spoleto: Settimane di Studio del Centro italiano di studi sull'alto medioevo 10, 1963), 181–227; Percy E. Schramm, *Herrschaftszeichen und Staatssymbolik. Beiträge zu Ihrer Geschichte vom Dritten bis zum Sechzehnten Jahrhundert*, Monumenta Germaniae historica, Schriften, XIII/1 (Stuttgart: Hiersemann, 1954).
64. See Markus, *Signs and Meanings*, 45–70.
65. Caspary, *Politics and Exegesis*, 9.
66. Origen, *De Principiis*, 4. 2. 9, 321 f. Robert McQueen Grant, *The Earliest Lives of Jesus* (London: SPCK, 1961), emphasised the debt of Origen's exegesis to Hellenistic rhetoric. For the exegesis of the sword, see Caspary, *Politics and Exegesis*, 40–103. See also Jean Danielou, *Origen* (New York: Sheed & Ward, 1955); Henri de Lubac, *Medieval Exegesis: The Four Senses of Scripture* (Grand Rapids, MI: Eerdmans, 1998).
67. Origen, *Contra Celsum* (Leiden: Brill, 2001), 8.73, 4, 346.
68. Guy Lobrichon, 'Une nouveauté, les gloses de la Bible', in *Le Moyen Age et la Bible*, Pierre Riche and Guy Lobrichon (eds) (Paris: Beauchesne, 1984), 111. The glosses circulated as manuscripts until the birth of the press, and were printed along with the Church Fathers' comments in the Counter Reformation.
69. Buc, *L'ambiguité*, 38.
70. Caspary, *Politics and Exegesis*, 189.
71. Buc, *L'ambiguité*, 51–4.
72. Buc, *L'ambiguité*, 399.
73. Ullmann, 'The Bible', 195.

74. See Hans-Joachim Schmidt, 'The Papal and Imperial Concept of *plenitudo potestatis*: The influence of Pope Innocent III on Emperor Frederick II', in *Pope Innocent III and his World*, J. C. Moore (ed.) (Aldershot: Ashgate, 1999), 305–14. See also Francis Oakley, 'The Absolute and Ordained Power of God and King in the Sixteenth and Seventeenth', *Journal of the History of Ideas* 59 (1998): 669–90, 683: 'Bodin spoke of the prince as being able by his "absolute power" to "derogate from the ordinary right" (i.e., "the laws of his country"), though not from the laws of God or of nature.' See also Mika Ojakangas, 'Potentia absoluta et potentia ordinata Dei: On the Theological Origins of Carl Schmitt's Theory of Constitution', *Continental Philosophy Review* 45 (2012): 505–17, 514, signals that it is 'the juristic notion of *potentia absoluta* applied first to describe papal power that became a theological notion, not vice versa: God can act outside of the order of nature and grace he has already established, like the pope can act outside his own laws.' See also María L. Lukac de Stier, 'Potentia Dei. De Tomás de Aquino a Hobbes', *Intus-Legere Filosofía* 7 (2013): 43–57.
75. Walter Ullmann, 'Der Souveränitätsgedanke in der mittelalterlichen Krönungsordines', in *Festschrift für Percy Ernst Schramm*, P. Classen and P. Scheibert (eds) (Wiesbaden: Franz Steiner, 1964), 72–89. In fact, there are some meaningful elements of the early modern idea of sovereignty that were present not only in the Middle Ages, but even in Rome. It is the case of the idea of *majestas*, applied by Cicero first to the people and later to the Caesar. Two Roman maxims evoke this kind of superior power: *majestas legibus solute est* and *quod principit placet, habet legis vigorem*. The idea of the prince as a specific force of law was already in Roman political thinking, but what was lacking was the idea of superiority as such.
76. Ullmann, 'Der Souveränitätsgedanke', 74.
77. Otto Brunner, *Sozialgeschichte Europas in Mittelalter* (Göttingen: Vandenhoeck & Ruprecht, 1978), 91.
78. Brunner, *Sozialgeschichte Europas*, 19.
79. The book discussing the heterogeneous character of these coronations and self-coronations ceremonies is that of Jaume Aurell, *Medieval Self-Coronations: The History and Symbolism of a Ritual* (Cambridge: Cambridge University Press, 2020).
80. Ullmann, 'Der Souveränitätsgedanke', 86.
81. Buc, *L'ambiguité*, 339–400. Buc affirms that we have to imagine an academic milieu divided by many controversies: never a unique ideology within the church or the laity. The disputes on the myth of origins, the end of time, the egalitarian ways of accession to power of princes, reflections on popular resistance, were aimed at putting pressure on princes and their agents.

82. For information on this discussion, see Herschel C. Baker, *The Wars of Truth: Studies in the Decay of Christian Humanism in the Earlier Seventeenth Century* (Cambridge, MA: Harvard University Press, 1952); Gerard Reedy, *The Bible and Reason: Anglicans and Scripture in Late Seventeenth-Century England* (Philadelphia: University of Pennsylvania Press, 1985). In addition, Jeffrey L. Morrow explains the transformation of the sacred Scriptures into a commonplace book. See Jeffrey L. Morrow, 'The Bible in Captivity: Hobbes, Spinoza, and the Politics of Defining Religion', *Pro Ecclesia* 19 (2010): 285–99.
83. See Herrero, 'The Early Modern "Philosophical Bible"', 31–49. See also Luisa Simonutti, *Locke and Biblical Hermeneutics: Conscience and Scripture* (Cham: Springer, 2019); S. W. Hahn and B. Wiker, *Politicizing the Bible: The Roots of Historical Criticism and the Secularization of Scripture 1300–1700* (New York: Crossroads Publishing, 2013); Henning Graf Reventlow, *The Authority of the Bible and the Rise of the Modern World* (London: SCM Press, 1984). Reventlow recognises that: '[t]he whole of Locke's scriptural exegesis is a further example of the way in which at this period exegesis is not done for its own sake but because of the normative validity of scripture for quite specific questions of political life or in the associated search for the foundations of social ethics which would serve as a criterion in current controversies over the form of state and society in England'. Reventlow, *The Authority of the Bible*, 285.
84. This is the judgement of Noel Malcolm, 'Hobbes and Spinoza', in *Aspects of Hobbes* (Oxford: Oxford University Press, 2004), 47. It is also the thesis of Steven Nadler, *A Book Forged in Hell* (Princeton, NJ: Princeton University Press, 2011), 30–1. In any case, the article by Mogens Laerke shows us that this is a controversial issue. See Mogens Laerke, 'Jus Circa Sacra. Elements of Theological Politics in 17th Century Rationalism: From Hobbes and Spinoza to Leibniz', *Distinktion: Scandinavian Journal of Social Theory* 6(1) (2005): 41–64.
85. Wim Klever sees 'Spinoza as the real philosophical master of John Locke'. Wim Klever, 'Locke's Disguised Spinozism', *Conatus* 11 (2012): 61–82.
86. Indeed, around 1674 the Dutch Government prohibited the printing or sale of four books: Hobbes' *Leviathan*, first published in 1651, but with a Latin edition that appeared in 1668; the *Biblioteca Fratrum Polonorum*, published between 1665 and 1692 by Frans Kuyper and including Socinian works; Spinoza's *Political Philosophical Treatise* (1669); and Meyer's *Philosophy, the Interpreter of Sacred Scripture* (1666). Some years later, Locke's *Reasonableness of Christianity as Delivered in the Scriptures*, written in 1695 and influenced by Spinoza and the Socinians, would also be stigmatised as heretical.

See Victor Nuovo, *Christianity, Antiquity, and Enlightenment* (Dordrecht: Springer, 2011). Reventlow hesitates to characterise Locke as a Socinian or Unitarian; he is, in any case, a Latitudinarian in *The Authority of the Bible*, 244.

87. Hobbes' nominalism conceives of language as providing an uncertain path to knowledge. In *De Homine*, optics is held to be the most important science for the interpretation of human knowledge. Thomas Hobbes, *De Homine* (Paris: Albert Blanchard, 1974), III, 70–80. In English there is only a short version beginning in chapter X: *Man and Citizen* (De Homine and De Cive) (Indianapolis, IN: Hackett, 1991). In this text he claims that an idea could be very clear and at the same time completely false. Also see Thomas Hobbes, *Leviathan* (Oxford: Oxford University Press, 1998), 1. Also in Thomas Hobbes, *The Elements of Law Natural and Politic* (Oxford: Oxford University Press, 1994). In the part devoted to human nature (III, 8, 30), he says that a man cannot know if he is dreaming or not from the point of view of the knowledge he has. Therefore, to perceive does not mean perceiving something [external to the mind], but rather perceiving on the occasion of a sensation in the body. Hobbes, *Leviathan*, 10. See also Thomas Hobbes, *On the Body: The English Works of Thomas Hobbes of Malmesbury* (Aalen: Scientia, 1966) I, XXV, 7. 396. The composition of images is a 'spiritual fiction' – called 'mental discourse' – that shapes language. On Hobbes' theory of language, see Martin A. Bertman, 'Hobbes on Language and Reality', *Revue Internationale de Philosophie* 32(126/4) (1978): 536–50. A summary of some of the studies on Hobbes and language is found in the book by Philippe Pettit, *Made with Words: Hobbes on Language, Mind, and Politics* (Princeton, NJ: Princeton University Press, 2008). An approach to the topic of language and fiction can be found in Montserrat Herrero, *Ficciones políticas. El eco de Thomas Hobbes en el ocaso de la modernidad* (Buenos Aires: Katz, 2012), 11–30. The status and use of language, is also one of the most intricate problems in Spinoza's philosophy. In academic literature there are three possible ways of considering Spinoza's conception of language, arguing from within Spinoza's philosophy: first, language is a means that is intrinsically incapable of expressing philosophical truth. An example of this opinion is David Savan, 'Spinoza and Language', *Philosophical Review* 67 (1958): 212–25. Secondly, Spinoza suggests the development of a specifically philosophical language purified of the uncertainties of ordinary language. An example of this position is François Zourabichvili, *Spinoza. Une physique de la pensée* (Paris: PUF, 2002). And, thirdly, the midway position, that is, while ordinary language is confusing, it is possible to develop a philosophical adaptation of it. An example of it is Edwin Curley, *Behind the Geometrical Method* (Princeton, NJ: Princeton University Press, 1988);

Edwin Curley (ed. and trans.), 'Introduction to the *Ethics*', *The Collected Works of Spinoza* (Princeton, NJ: Princeton University Press, 1985). In addition, the interpretation of Pierre-François Moreau, *Spinoza. L'experience de l'eternité* (Paris: PUF, 1994), could be considered as taking this position. Nevertheless, in the case of Scripture, it is clear that it is built on ordinary language and not on a specialised philosophical language. For this case, we can adopt the pessimistic view of the first possibility of interpretation. Something similar occurs with John Locke. A good example is Walter R. Ott, *Locke's Philosophy of Language* (Cambridge: Cambridge University Press, 2003). However, it is infrequent to see attempts to relate his philosophy of language to his scriptural interpretation and his political philosophy. An exception is Hannah Dawson, 'Locke on Language and (Civil) Society', *History of Political Thought* 26(3) (2005): 397–425; Hannah Dawson, *Locke, Language and Early-Modern Philosophy* (Cambridge: Cambridge University Press, 2007).
88. John Locke, *An Essay concerning Human Understanding* (Stansted: Wordsworth Editions, 1998), III, 9, § 23; Locke, *An Essay*, III, 2, § 1.
89. Hobbes, *Leviathan*, 32, 259.
90. Hobbes, *Leviathan*, 36, 290.
91. Hobbes, *Leviathan*, 42, 397.
92. Baruch Spinoza, *Theological-Political Treatise*, ed. Jonathan Israel (Cambridge: Cambridge University Press, 2007), 116. VII [116].
93. Spinoza, *Theological-Political*, 245. XIX [235]: 'We cannot doubt, therefore, that in our day sacred matters remain under the sole jurisdiction of sovereigns . . .' And also, Spinoza, *Theological-Political*, 207. XVI [199–200]: '[T]he supreme right of deciding about religion belongs to the sovereign power, whatever judgment he may make, since it falls to him alone to preserve the rights of the state and to protect them both by divine and by natural law.' This very same thesis is repeated several times, for example, in Spinoza, *Theological-Political*, 238. XIX [228]. In these texts Spinoza's 'theocratic democracy', based on a supposed 'philosophical' interpretation of the Scriptures, is well demonstrated. It is difficult to deduce, as Laerke does, that 'in opposition to Hobbes, Spinoza refuses to identify the State-controlled theology of the Church with true or "universal" religion'. See Laerke, 'Jus Circa Sacra', 51. Hobbes had already made the distinction between exterior interior worship that remains free.
94. In this same vein, see Norman O. Brown, 'Philosophy and Prophecy: Spinoza's Hermeneutics', *Political Theory* 14(2) (1986): 195–213, 209: 'Democracy is the most perfect form of theocracy, the only true theocracy'. See also Andy Alexis-Baker, 'Spinoza's Political Theology: Theocracy, Democracy and Monism', *Journal of Church and State* 54(3) (2012): 426–44. He argues that Spinoza was convinced that democracy requires the unity of politics and religion. The idea of a

civil religion in Spinoza has been studied by André Tosel, 'Démocratie du commun et religion civile', in *L'actualité du Tractatus de Spinoza et la question théologico-politique*, Q. Landenne and T. Storme (eds) (Bruxelles: Edition de l'Université de Bruxelles, 2014), 165–89, 169. Fraenkel points out that even Spinoza, who has the most critical account of religion of the three, did not resolve the tension between his philosophical reinterpretation of Christianity and his critique of religion. Carlos Fraenkel, *Philosophical Religions from Plato to Spinoza* (Cambridge: Cambridge University Press, 2012).

95. Locke, *An Essay*, I, 4, § 25.
96. The political intentions of Locke's *Reasonableness* are shown in Richard Sherlock, 'The Theology of Toleration: A Reading of Locke's The Reasonableness of Christianity', *Jewish Political Studies Review* 9 (1997): 19–49. Sherlock argues that the purpose of *Reasonableness* was not to offer a rational basis for religion, but to reinterpret it in such a way as to make it safe for liberal regimes.
97. Nuovo, *Christianity, Antiquity, and Enlightenment*, 98: 'Locke's place in the Enlightenment must be represented in the light of his Christian commitments.' For J. Israel, the main difference between Locke and Spinoza's approaches is that Locke's toleration revolves primarily around freedom of worship and theological discussion, while Spinoza's toleration is essentially philosophical, republican and explicitly anti-theological. As a result, he does not consider Locke a 'radical'. Jonathan Israel, *Radical Enlightenment: Philosophy and the Making of Modernity 1650–1750* (Oxford: Oxford University Press, 2002), 265. See also John Dunn, *The Political Thought of John Locke* (Cambridge: Cambridge University Press, 1969), 99. See also Montserrat Herrero, 'The Quest for Locke's Political Theology', *Ethics & Politics* 18 (2016): 83–109.

Chapter 2

Prophecy or the Deconstruction of Historical Expectation

> The past always speaks as an oracle.[1]

The previous chapter focused on the Scriptures as a figure that speaks of the instituted practice of writing as a constitutive element of any political community. What makes sacred Scriptures an exceptional type of writing is their prophetic character. This means that Scriptures unfolds figuratively in historical time, but also contains an idea of historical time. It is to this aspect that this chapter is devoted.

Every historical narrative is written in a present time – a now – which is not only pervaded by the past, but also looks towards something in the future. In fact, the act of writing historical narratives – the usual way of interpreting history, that is, of building history as such – is at the same time a way of shaping destiny. In this sense, historians seem to be like prophets. But can the historian achieve the future he or she imagines? The future cannot be master-built from the present. Nietzsche himself once said that 'the past always speaks as an oracle'.[2] In fact, past, present and future are intermingled in every twist of history in an enigmatic way that is structurally analogical to the representation of time in prophecy.

Prophetic Time: Historical Time from the Future

Prophetic literature is central to divine revelations. We find it not only in Israel, but in every ancient civilisation.[3] The prophet is not a soothsayer, who interprets exterior signs; he is not a theologian, who interprets a given revelation. The prophet is the voice of

God moved by his divine spirit to interpret the 'signs of the times'. Certainly, prophets coexisted with the soothsayers and the augurs in ancient civilisations; but unlike them they did not try to initiate a course of action or to legitimise a situation. The role of prophets was rather to make a historical interpretation.

Prophetic history and human history are uncoupled from the point of view of their factuality and of their possible interpretations.[4] However, from the point of view of meaning, they cannot be completely separated: first, because prophetical narratives imply a definite judgement of the events of history; and, secondly, because profane history can only expect a future to come, but not assure the future as prophetic history does. Both of these claims are important in order to achieve meaning in history, and historical narratives of other kinds cannot realise them.

Prophetism as an institution in Israel emerged around the tenth century BC, along with monarchy. Samuel is considered the oldest prophet of Israel, even though Moses was in fact a prophet. Taking him as an example, we can speak of a regulated function in Israel that sought to incarnate God's voice for the sake of the people, or for a particular person, chosen by God for a particular task. In Israel and in the vicinity of the temple, we also find groups of prophets who act together (1 Samuel 10:5–13), although not all the prophets were associated with the temple. There were charismatic prophets whose interventions were important for Israel, as in the case of Elias and Elisha, who were prophets in the nineteenth century BC and had important political influence. There were also 'oppositional prophets', who challenged the predictions of contemporary 'official prophets' during, for example, Acab's reign (875–853 BC).

A prophetic message always appeared in the context of certain historical circumstances, as if they were part of the message. In any event, the prophets did not limit themselves to testifying to historical events, but rather went deeper into their meaning; they judged persons and situations, intervening in them and revealing their aim.[5] They provided an interpretation of historical events based on three principal ideas: monotheism, Israel as God's elect and the universality of salvation. In fact, the prophecies manifest a messianic hope. Contemporary exegesis speaks of an evolution in prophetic practice in the direction of a more spiritualised and generalised interpretation. Before the Babylonian exile, the prophets spoke about a royal messianism; during the deportation, the prophets did not mention that kind of messianism, but rather the idea that God himself would be the saviour; in the post-exile period, prophets spiritualise messianism, noting that, in any case, salvation will be effected through the people of Israel. Thirdly, prophecies speak of the necessity of preserving morality and worship. Whatever the case may be, prophetism always adapts to the social and political context while being critical of the functioning of its institutions; and it always presages a revolution to come based on the power of the great beyond.

New Testament prophecies are of another kind: they are centred on the end of time and the second coming of Christ. Indeed, the book of Daniel divides history into successive periods which are characterised as being *the end of a time*. All of these periods will terminate in the end of history, characterised as *the end of time*; after this end of history, the definitive instauration of the kingdom of God will happen (Daniel 7:17–23, 11:8–40, 12:3). This book, as well as John's Revelation, do not provide a linear description of the last times, but rather they present several cycles of visions that warn about coming tribulations before the second coming of Christ, which they refer to as the coming of the Antichrist. The adversaries of God's people are depicted as a beast and a harlot, who are finally destroyed. At the end of each cycle, readers return to the heavenly throne room (Revelation 7:9–17, 11:15–19, 15:2–4, 19:1–8). The final chapters culminate in the New Jerusalem, the city of God (Revelation 21:1–22:5). Through its warnings and promises, the book of Revelation seeks to bring readers to renewed faith in God and the Lamb, who are the Alpha and the Omega of history, a beginning and an end that cannot be understood as chronological temporal concepts (Revelation 1:8, 22:13).

Revelation of a concrete future is not the essential function of prophets. This idea is a distortion produced by an audience who desired to know the future in order to achieve political success or to avoid fear and seek security. Rather, the prophecies reveal the existence of an absolute future that intersects with every present. They thus 'translocate' the order of the categories of past, present and future as they are commonly understood.

How can we interpret the temporal translocation inaugurated by these prophetical narratives and their historical periodisation? How have they changed Greek and Hebrew assumptions about historical temporality? Is there any conception of time in these prophetical narratives? Is then Christian revelation responsible for our linear image of historical time?

Concerning the question of the possibility or not of finding a specific idea of historical time in the Bible, the first thing to note is that Hebrew and Greek historiography are completely distinguishable between them and also from the abstractions of Greek philosophy about time. In Momigliano's opinion, the connection between truth and history in Hebrew tradition reflected to the connections between prophets and historians. The historian subordinates himself to the prophet and derives his values from him. The Hebrew relation between the historian and the prophet is the counterpart of the Greek relation between the historian and the philosopher at least since Plato.[6]

It was a classic *topos* in biblical studies, particularly since the 1930s, to oppose Hebrew to Greek thought. James Barr has criticised this naive approach, particularly when it concerns the idea of time.[7] He argues that the topic 'time' is not a biblical one, but a philosophical one; in addition, it is not so easy to contrast a circular vision of time by the Greeks and a linear vision by the Hebrews.[8] Moreover, what the Greeks called cyclical did not refer to historical time, but rather to the movement of the heavenly bodies by which time was commonly measured as is the case in the *Timaeus*.[9] Incidentally, we can also find cyclical representations of time in the Bible, as is the case in *Qohelet*, the only book that contains an explicit discussion regarding time. Barr struggles with the firm position of Cullmann, who had strongly supported the particularly Christian linear conception of history, and who began a great theological discussion on the topic. In fact, Cullmann, in disputing the extreme eschatological interpretation of the New Testament of Karl Barth, on the one hand, and the *Entmythologisierung* (demythologisation) of the Gospel by Albert Schweitzer and Rudolph Bultmann, respectively, on the other, wanted to reinstate the historical character of Christian revelation and he does so by researching etymologically the scriptural concept of time. Cullmann stresses the idea of linearity in contrast to the emphasis on eternity attributed to God by some systematic or dogmatic theologians, as is the case of Barth in his distinction between before time, above time and after time; even if he tries to temporalise the very idea of eternity.[10] Confronting Barth, Cullmann insists that the idea of eternity is not present in the New Testament as it was in Greek thought. But, again, Barr is highly critical of this idea.[11] A close examination of the contexts in which *aeon* appears shows, according to Barr, that in almost every case, it means 'the totality of time', 'something other than time' or everything that should 'last forever'.[12] He explains that in biblical Hebrew three words are distinguishable in speaking about time: *'et,* meaning time in cases such as 'several times', 'occasion' or 'the time of'; *moʻed*, a word meaning appointment, which comes to be used of sacred seasons fixed in the calendar; and *ʻolam*, which refers to the remotest time, meaning perpetuity, and appears in contexts such as eternal destruction, eternal fire, for all the ages of eternity. After the appearance of post-biblical documents, such as the Qumran literature and Mishnaic sources, we find the word *qe s* for divine periodisation, sometimes meaning a moment, sometimes an extended period.

In the Septuagint, the first translation of the Hebrew Bible, *ʻet* is translated by *kairos* more frequently than by *chronos*, but they are frequently interchangeable. *Chronos* is used for more quantitative accounts and *kairos* for meaning opportunity. The strong eschatological expectation and the sense of fulfilment of past eschatological promises produce frequent contexts like 'the time is coming', in which *kairos* is usual.[13] But it can also have the sense of season, natural and sacred. *Ora* is also used for translating *ʻet* in phrases such as 'at this time tomorrow', 'all the time', 'at the right time', 'in the time of'. *ʻOlam* is rendered as *Aeon* and frequently has a meaning of 'for ever'; in particular, the everlasting covenant, eternal sign, eternal joy and permanent slave.[14] Certainly, the sense of eternity in a free syntactical context is uncommon. Cullmann argues that even the well-known passage in Revelation 10:6, where it is said that there will be no more *chronos*, is not to be understood as an era of timelessness; rather, in the analogy of Habakkuk 2:3 and Hebrews 10:37, we should translate as: 'There will be no more delay'.[15] With the translation into Latin the different nuances of the experience of time were lost: in the Latin Vulgate, all cases of *chronos* and *kairos* were translated as *tempus*; and *aeon* as *saeculum* or *aeternum*.

Cullmann advances yet another term: if *chronos*, *kairos* and *eon* are biblical words used to qualify time, *prophecy* is the word that indicates the historical narrative of the Bible.[16] In fact, Christian revelation affects the idea of history insofar as it happens through history. It is a dispensation (*oikonomia*) in the form of a history of salvation.[17] The absolute Christian norm is itself also history – an incision in historical time – and is not, as is the philosophical norm, just a transcendent datum that lies beyond all history. In Cullmann's expression, it is 'redemptive history' that measures every historical event and not an abstract norm.[18] However, the kind of narrative that the Bible presents is always an interpreted history that escapes from all historical evidence.[19] Indeed, prophecy represents a 'paradigmatic' structure of historical time. In fact, it is always an interpretation of events made in a 'present' time that does not just simply recover the past, but also embraces a promise that opens an expectation. Future is not an imaginable destiny, foreseeable or calculable, but rather one which is given in the form of a divine promise throughout the course of history speaking of an absolute future. Where Christ acts, the future is already accomplished. Nevertheless, prophecy is not history. We cannot equate the history of salvation with other histories or even with what has been labelled universal history. Historical events are the 'backdrop' of the redemptive event. This can be demonstrated in many examples, such as the mentions of Tiberius or Augustus in the Gospel of Luke. The very mention of Pontius Pilate in the apostles' symbol of faith shows how the course of the so-called 'secular events' stand in relation to redemptive history. While historical events are common, historical narratives, whether secular or sacred, might differ.

Apart from this interwoven relationship between redemptive history and other stories, between historians and prophets, what is specifically remarkable in the prophetical narratives is the temporal structure inaugurated by the last prophecy, the book of Revelation. If in the exploration of the biblical language of temporality we have found an anarchic variety, when it comes to historical temporality we find a new logic that goes beyond the prophetic logic of the Old Testament, which could be summed up in the linearity of a fulfilment directed towards the future.

In fact, the representation of time that the last prophecy contains is not a merely linear one; or, we might say, the linear conception of historical time it evokes cannot be interpreted as a simple succession of present, past and future. In fact, by distinguishing between the Christian and Jewish periodisation of historical time, Cullmann emphasises the particular moment of the incarnation as a *caesura* in the middle of Christian history: after Easter, the future to come no longer lies only in the *parousia*, but penetrates history through the incarnation of Christ, which becomes the 'centrality of time'.[20] In his view the centre of history has already been reached, even if the end is still to come, in the same way that the decisive battle can have happened already even though the war has not yet ended. Thus, we stand in a section of time in which we are already redeemed through Christ, but also in which the sin that is characteristic of the entire period before the *parousia* is still present. The expectation thus continues to exist as in Judaism, but the experience of time is different. As Cullman himself clarifies in the introduction to the third edition of his book *Christ and Time*: 'Besides, linear time is weakened by this tension and by the orientation from the middle, but both presuppose it as the framework of biblical thinking about time.'[21] In fact, the new prophetic logic for understanding historical time is the logic of the 'already and not yet'. This is the particular temporal tension inaugurated by the incarnation and redemption: events which happened in the past are still waiting for a future. This is the main translocation of historical time that happens in the fulfilment of the last prophecy.

Erik Peterson has called this temporal logic 'der eschatologische Vorbehalt',[22] the 'eschatological reservation'. Instead of prophetic time, he speaks of eschatological time. He used this phrase for the first time in a course on mysticism in the ancient church suggesting that the paschal events brought about a new kind of reality; thanks to them, the Church is now 'in Christ' and this new way of being is already eschatological. This means that it is a present reality which nevertheless refers to the future: we have died and been buried with Christ and will rise with Him. This present being of the Church refers immediately to a past and to a future. In Peterson's interpretation, which differs from Cullmann's 'already, but not yet' logic, the specific 'place' where the categories of historical time come together is the reality of the sacraments, which ultimately happens cyclically as the repetition of the same instant.

In the prophetic representation of time, the kingdom of God is not a beyond, but an 'absolute future'. It is a future that happens simultaneously with the past of the incarnation and with this 'now' and every possible 'now'. In particular, Werner G. Kümmel has shown that the temporal tension between present and future exists for Jesus insofar as the future is already fulfilled in his person, and yet is still awaited. Even for Jesus, the preaching that the kingdom of God is present stands with all emphasis alongside the preaching that the kingdom of God is still to come. Jesus' historical presence is the fulfilment of eschatology. In fact, we are living *now* in the *last days*, because now the consummation of salvation cannot be long delayed. In the same vein, alongside the words of John saying that the judgement has already occurred (John 3:18), there stands the other assertion that it will take place only in the future, 'at the last day' (John 12:48, 5:28 f.). It seems that Jesus' message about the imminent coming of the kingdom of God is intended to confront men with the end of history in the now.[23]

This idea of an 'absolute future' has been interpreted by Koselleck as an absolute limit to experience: 'the legibility of the future, despite possible prognoses confronts an absolute limit, for it cannot be experienced'.[24] This 'absolute limit' is what we should be thinking about, instead of simply trying to transpose it to an always-deferred temporal line. Gadamer calls it the 'absolute epoch'.[25] From his point of view, the end of time is an epochal experience of the discontinuity of time which entered ancient historical consciousness with Christian history and which added new meanings: in particular, that there is a destiny that is not rationally cognizable and yet it is in this destiny that the reality of history is given to us and not in the cognitive actualisation of the past, nor in the domain of happening. It is precisely this nuance, which Gadamer brings out, that appears in the idea of prophecy.

In fact, an absolute limit to experience cannot be an extension of the present time forward. An absolute limit implies a hiatus for the experience that can be thought of only as an *aporia*. Every interpretation of the future has to confront this aspect, which makes history into something 'undisposable'.[26] The historical future cannot be derived from the past or from the present. The future does not depend on the past; rather, it is always an absolute limit for experience.[27] Something different from what is expected will always happen.

How to reconcile this absolute limit with the 'already'? Peterson points to sacramental reality, the ontological dimension of which is irreplaceable. But is there any other kind of anticipation of this absolute future? Koselleck evokes the 'prophetic logic' in some paragraphs of his analysis of the concept of crisis.[28] Following the argument of Kittel in *Theologisches Wörterbuch des Neuen Testaments*, he points out how the forensic meaning of the term 'crisis' has been transferred to the theological vocabulary in the Septuagint. The only relevant crisis is the final judgement, in which true justice will be done. However, that criterion of justice has been partly revealed here and now, even though in historical terms it has not yet become completely effective. This final event is a theologically qualified horizon of expectation, thanks to which the crisis always remains open as a cosmic event, even though it is being realised in the judgement of each conscience. The Last Judgement remains historically temporalised in the moral judgement of consciences; and through them, it acts in the present of history.

In the eighteenth century a new appropriation of the Last Judgement changed the meaning of the relationship between history and eschatology. Schiller was the first to capitalise on this sense: 'Die Weltgeschichte ist das Weltgericht.'[29] According to this maxim, every event carries its own judgement without any kind of postponement. At the end of the idealist narrative, the crisis loses its apocalyptic or transitional meaning and simply becomes a structural element of history as future: 'eschatology is, so to speak, historically monopolised', says Koselleck.[30]

The temporal structure implicit in the idea of prophecy brings about a radical union and temporal tension between experience and expectation which illuminate the understanding of historical time and of any interpretation of history. The idea of prophecy tells us that expectation can be founded only on a promise, that is, in an absolute future and is not constructed from past experiences; hence, we lack any representation of it that is not 'a revelation'. And, despite the absence of its representation, we cannot completely dispense with it when interpreting history, even if it only appears as a question of meaning.

We have referred with Koselleck to the idea of an 'absolute limit' of experience; and with Gadamer to the expression 'absolute epoch'. Both cases refer to that expectation that cannot be indefinitely displaced, and which gives notice, in the sense of a negative theology, of a beyond time. Before both, Nietzsche had already characterised 'real time' as 'absolute time':[31] but in this case, time is inaugurated by the experience of 'eternal recurrence'.[32] It is simply an idea of temporality that attempts to replace Christianity's temporal centre of gravity of a futurisable past. Nietzschean temporal perspectivism came into being by negating the old structure of prophetical time and instituting a new prophetical time announced by Zarathustra. This new time castrates the past and future by enhancing the now in connection with eternity: 'eternal recurrence'.[33] Wanting to live in this instance by 'affirming' (saying yes to life) is a fundamental decision, in both individual and political terms.[34] Jesus' good news is a vital praxis guided by the instance at present and not an institutional configuration. Zarathustra then announces a new way of interpreting time that annuls past as negative memory and future as expectation and rolls back both dimensions into the present action.

The temporal structure of prophecy joins in a radical way the temporal tension between experience and expectative – understood as an absolute limit to experience – which enlightens the comprehension of historical temporality without castrating any dimension of time. In this sense, Christian temporality gives no priority to past, present or future. A three-dimensional schema of time is organised by the prophets in order to achieve an interpretation of history. Its distinctive feature is found in the idea that an 'absolute future' penetrates every present and has been effective in every past.

This possibility – which is consistent with the ways of experiencing time that appear in the sacred narrative and which only makes sense within it – annuls the simple linear interpretation of history. In fact, characteristic of the prophetic timeline is that the 'decisive incision' in historical time occurs not at the beginning, and not completely at the end, but in the middle of the times. Then there is a double *parousia*: one that happens with the incarnation, sacrifice and resurrection, and the other with the second coming of Christ, which will be complete enlightenment in respect of justice and judgement. If the eschatological future has to be expected, it is because of the past resurrection of Christ, and this has effects in every present time. It is in this sense that we must interpret the 'already and not yet': the centre of history is *already* in the past, but this past has *not* completely passed *yet*; it is a word and a flesh acting every time, a promise that accomplishes the end of history.

Katechon: A Theological–Political Category

Only in the context of a prophetic time can a theopolitical category such as the Pauline *katechon* make sense. The relevance of Paul's idea of *katechon*, already alluded to by Tertullian's *Apology* and which was central in Augustine's *City of God*, was recovered in the twentieth century by Carl Schmitt. In fact, for Schmitt, eschatological power is the real governing power in history.[35] The central facts of the Christian era – Christ's birth, crucifixion and resurrection – remain alive throughout history with an 'unaltered presence'.[36]

The concept of *katechon* refers to St. Paul's passage in 2 Thessalonians 3–9. There, St. Paul related how, before the coming end of the world, an adversary would appear and try to remove God from his throne: '*Et nunc quid detineat scitis, ut revelatur in suo tempore. Nam mysterium iam operatur iniquitatis: tantum ut qui tenet nunc, tenent, donec de medio fiet.*' History will end with the coming of the Antichrist before the establishment of the kingdom of God with the second coming of Christ. A kingdom of righteousness and peace that will overcome the mystery of iniquity. The mystery of iniquity is already at work and is being halted by he who is holding the Antichrist back. When St. Paul says, 'you all know', he assumes something that has not been revealed to us yet and that held back the Antichrist until now, and prevented his coming until 'it is time'. There is a time for the anarchy and a time for justice and peace. In any case, is this intervention of anarchy and this final establishment to be understood in a linear way, as a progressive conception of history would have it? We have already referred to the book of Daniel and John's Revelation which do not provide a linear description of the last times, but rather they present several cycles of visions that warn about coming tribulations before the second coming of Christ. Thus, we can think that neither the Antichrist nor the end of time are unrepeatable figures, although, on the one hand, in all cases they have an exceptional character; on the other hand, there will be an *end of a time*, which will be the *end of time*. As Augustine points out in *The City of God*, good and evil, wheat and tares in the language of the Gospel, the forces of creation and destruction, are intermingled until the end of time.[37] Indeed, Augustine already conveyed the relationship between the eschatological vision and political history through the idea of *katechon*: it is a real historical force that, before the end of time, represents the eschatological saving event by repressing the spirit of evil – the Antichrist – and *momentarily* halts the end of time.[38]

This force, therefore, seems to be a political–theological figure that connects historical and political events with the great beyond. That is, it makes absolute future relevant for the course of history. One of the most well-known quotes of Schmitt on *katechon* is the following from *Glossarium*:

> On the *katechon*: It is the only way for me to understand history as Christian and encounter its full meaning . . . I would like to hear from you: who today is the *katechon*? It cannot be considered Churchill or John Foster Dulles . . . Its place has never been empty, otherwise we would not be here anymore.[39]

Schmitt argues with historical examples: 'The medieval kingdom of German lords historically understands itself as *katechon*. Even Luther understood this, thus Calvin took a decisive turn by making the *katechon* no longer the Empire, but the preaching of the word of God.'[40] In *Land and Sea* he refers to the Byzantine Empire as *katechon*, which prevented the Muslims from conquering Italy, thus making the extermination of ancient and Christian culture impossible.[41] In the same book, he designates as *katechon* the German King Rudolph II, who, rather than being an active hero, simply delayed and contained the Thirty Years' War.[42] Another example, in this case from *Ex captivitate salus*, refers to the *katechon* in discussing the religious idea contained in European civilisation.[43] In other places Schmitt refers the *katechon* to the Christian empire.[44]

In his view, the conceptions of empire that do not correspond to the *Respublica Christiana* immediately foster Caesarism instead of being *katechon*. When the idea of *katechon* faded out, the Antichrist appeared in the form of secularisation, identified with secularism or secular humanism.[45] Schmitt refers to Hegel and Savigny as two examples of those who have occupied the place of the *katechon* without being political figures as such: 'These two were genuine *katechon* halters (*Aufhalter*) in the true sense of the word, both were halters against the voluntary and involuntary accelerators on the way to complete functionalization.'[46] Therefore, the *katechon* need not be a political force, but in any case, a political institution or person can be a figure of Christ in his function of *katechon*.

Paradoxically, as Bradley points out in his acute interpretation of Schmittian *katechon*, which takes central account of the first text in which the term appears – *Beschleuniger wider Wille* – retention in the face of functionalisation can introduce elements of anarchy. This becomes clear, for example, in a paragraph of the letter to Álvaro d'Ors: 'My lecture on the unity of the earth corresponded perfectly to your conception of the *unum ovile* and the *una sancta*, and this because any other than this Christian unity of the earth is the work of the Antichrist. For me, therefore, the dualism of the world today is not necessarily a transition to unity. Rather, I am convinced that today's dualistic tension must lead to pluralism and thus to balance.'[47]

Functionalisation for Schmitt was undoubtedly a figure of the Antichrist. But, as Koselleck has pointed out, even this functionalisation was the product of an interpretation of the figure of the *katechon*. Indeed, the Reformation with its particular interpretation of the *parousia* emphasised a new temporal category, namely, that of the "shortening of time'. According to Luther, the end of the world was fast approaching, so that the last prophecy would be fulfilled immediately. The 'shortening of time' was for Luther a blessing and, at the same time, a call to be vigilant, because the time remaining was getting shorter and shorter.[48] The ancient theological idea of a linear time that is shortened by the representation of an imminent horizon of expectation is given a functional substitute in a progressively secularised world: the 'acceleration of time'. The new experience that opens the context of secular intelligibility to this temporal reference is the progressive dominance of technology. Indeed, primary experience is no longer constituted by the experience of salvation with religious overtones, but by that of technical success, which integrates the human communicative network and raises productivity in shorter and shorter temporal intervals.[49]

Even the apocalypse is a real possibility for history today, more than ever before.[50] In fact, Günther Anders speaks of the 'technically possible apocalypse'.[51] The course of history seems to lead directly to the apocalypse that already began on 6 August 1945 with the bombing of Hiroshima. In fact, Anders compares the Christian with the nuclear apocalypse. In his view, both share the conscience of living in a 'term', that is, in a waiting for the end. But they are different; first, because the nuclear apocalypse is an apocalypse without a final kingdom; and, secondly, because the nuclear version is made possible by a human decision and the theological apocalypse will be an 'incision' in history from outside, a *kairos*. Anders very expressively declares that the Christian apocalypse states that the future has already begun; the nuclear apocalypse, however, can only warn us that the lack of future has already begun. History and prophecy, just as the future and the end of time, cannot be completely decoupled.

Certainly, in Koselleck's texts, as also in those of Löwith, Christianity's understanding of time appears as the inauguration of an image of linear time.[52] But, the transposition of eschatology would not necessarily result in a merely linear conception of time, as did the Reformation, as I am arguing.

In sum, the force that halts the counter-figure of Christ, which can even take the same form as the kingdom of God in worldly imagination, can be seen as the real ruler of history in a prophetic perspective; and, for that reason, Schmitt can say that salvation is the decisive meaning of history.[53] However, historical, political and moral judgements are not necessarily linked in the course of history and, hence, the theological–political meaning of historical events in time is always an open question; and even if the events have been judged morally once and for all, we do not know that judgement with certainty either. If we accept that this interpretation is contained in the concept of *katechon*, it can be recognised as the theological–political category *par excellence* related to the figure of prophetical time.[54]

The Messianic and the Recovering of Absolute Time in History

Another theological–political category alternative to 'prophetic time' is that of 'messianic time'. The messianic view of interpreting historical time also combines the three temporal axes of time in a perspectivistic way. In fact, messianism is another way to escape historicism.[55]

Walter Benjamin was one of the interpreters of historical time who has contributed most to the elaboration of an alternative temporal structure to linear progressivism. Theology is crucial for Benjamin in the creation of a 'grammar of time', which will articulate the figure of the 'Messianic cessation' (*messianische Stillstellung*); a temporal form discovered early on by Benjamin but which crystallise in his last five theses on the philosophy of history. Benjamin distinguishes two forms of time: the tragic and the messianic. Tragic time is restricted to the experience of the individual plan of the hero, who could not achieve fulfilment at the historical level. Messianic time, however, is specifically historical time. The two temporal forms seem to be asymptotic.[56] According to Benjamin, history is not based on the linear flow of 'homogeneous, empty time', but on an idea of time as something that can be interrupted. Messianic time should be thought of as a *Jetztzeit*, which is an anti-teleological temporal 'constellation' of past, present and future. History is not a chronological order but a constellation that, by means of a messianic static charge, can rearrange itself in an instant. This anarchical principle of construction of history in constellations eclipses the notion of causality in history. Every 'now' is not a transition but a real 'state of emergency'.[57] Each day is lived as the day of judgement when the Messiah will come not only to redeem, but also to subdue the Antichrist.[58] The historian is the person who is conscious of that. Messianic time is specifically a historical time that connects that exceptional present with a past that has to be redeemed. In fact, Benjamin writes of a 'weak Messianic power, a power to which the past has a claim'.[59] His messianism never produces images of future salvation, but rather images of a past that demands to be saved.[60] Messianic time is more than anything a 'past present', but of a peculiar kind: it is 'remembrance' (*Eingedenken*), made up of involuntary memory, dream contents and the moment of its recognisability (*Augenblick seiner Erkennbarkeit*) that combines with reflective work. Remembrance, hence, telescopes the past through the present, so that it almost results in a 'translation' of the past into the present. Through this figure of *Eingedenken*, Benjamin introduces the idea of the past, as something persistent in the present in a dialectic relationship: 'For while the relation of the present to the past is purely temporal, the relation of what has been to the now is dialectical: not temporal in nature but figural (*bildlich*). Only dialectical images are genuinely historical.'[61] The past intermingles with the present through an anarchical and discontinued connection of images.

Benjamin understands this vision as the prophetic element inherent in the political intuition of the present.[62] The past bears in itself a demand (*Anspruch*) which we can extract from the present to change its meaning retrospectively inasmuch as we have been endowed with the 'weak Messianic power' of the oppressed. This is the messianic theological–political action *par excellence*.[63]

Messianic time has also been examined, albeit in another way, by Jacques Derrida.[64] In the footsteps of Levinas, who interprets the messianic as an infinite demand of justice for the other, Derrida coined the term messianicity to denote a universal structure of experience that affirms otherness and justice.[65] To make justice happen now is to live in a messianic time. In any event, it is a messianicity without a messiah, that is, it is non-identifiable with any form of explicitly religious messianism, be it Jewish or Christian: 'The figures of messianism would have to be . . . deconstructed as "religious", ideological, or fetishist formations, whereas messianicity without messianism remains, for its part, undeconstructible, like justice. It remains undeconstructible because the movement of any deconstruction presupposes it.'[66]

Messianicity is then a quasi-transcendental structure of experience, which is a dislocated time.[67] Disjointed time is the temporal site of justice. In fact, justice is not presentable. In remaining eternally indescribable, justice enjoys the form of a haunting spectre. Ultimate justice is the name of the messianic spectre, which haunts the living. The messianic means to go where you cannot go.[68] This is one of the topics Derrida returns to when he speaks of the *aporia* of origin.[69] Messianic time is expressly not just a 'horizon of possibility' or a 'horizon of expectation' for the future and, therefore, a kind of anticipatory encircling of what is to come. The condition of the 'to come' is the experience of coming.[70] The spectre simply works against being and its ontological tendency to represent not only everything that exists but also everything that is possible. Messianicity only manifests itself properly as a trace, which cannot find a home in the conditions of immanence. Messianic time is the impossible.

Even if faith, in Derrida's view, is always anti-foundational, insofar as it cannot become absolute knowledge without losing its character of faith, the messianic is the foundation of a faith-based approach to the philosophy of history and its historical representations: faith in what is to come (or whatever the particular historian wants to come), faith in the wholly other (*tout autre*). The great challenge for him is to not convert eschatology into teleology.

Only in this way is history thinkable as historicity beyond the privilege of the present and linear progress. The messianic future must pass through the empirical without being reducible to it. The historical *kairos* permits the very possibility of invention, which, in turn, enables the future to open up. There is a never-to-be realised longing in the accounts that historians produce.[71]

The temporal structure of this Derridian messianic promise is 'always not-yet', and 'anything but already'; which is almost the opposite of the prophetic temporality of the 'already and not yet'. The question that we can put to Derrida is how is it possible that this 'not-yet' manages to transform into 'never'. This *aporia* is at the heart of his idea of messianicity. As Bradley diagnoses: 'Derrida's attempt to think the political through the vehicle of messianic rather than historical time risks foreclosing history as the site in which political invention must take place.'[72] In fact, Derrida argues that in every politico-religious ideology '[t]he effectivity or actuality of the democratic promise, like that of the communist promise, will always keep within it . . . this absolutely undetermined messianic hope at its heart, this eschatological relation to the to-come of an event, and of a singularity, of an alterity that cannot be anticipated'.[73]

Giorgio Agamben has also tried to consider the temporal structure of history through the messianic.[74] He introduces a remainder into historical time, the 'time that is now', which re-divides the division between the old age and the world to come. The Messiah has already come; the messianic event has already been fulfilled, but His presence contains within itself another time that lasts until the *parousia*, not to defer it but to make it apprehensible: 'The messiah always makes his time, that is, he makes time his own and at the same time fulfils it.'[75] Messianic time, after the incision of incarnation, is 'the time that time takes to make an end'.[76] It is an operational time, a supplement. It is the time in which time and eternity transform each other in the *caesura* of chronos. This experience of time inaugurates the messianic ethic of the *hos me* – the Pauline 'as if not'. It is therefore a time of judgement. In fact, Paul yearns to 'make the most of the time (*kairos*)' (Galatians 6:10; Ephesians 5:16; Colossians 4:5) – seizing it not as a proprietary possession, but as a loving 'bringing to fulfilment' (the 'fullness = *pleroma* of time', Ephesians 1:9–10), in keeping with the messianic agency of the *hos me*. For Paul, profane time is messianically configured – in a parabolic, not a noetic configuration. Paul insists: 'Those who think they know something do not yet know as they ought to know. But whoever loves God is known by God' (1 Corinthians 8:2, 3). To be known by God is to participate in the messianic motion of kenotic love, a 'fullness of time' that unites – literally, 'recapitulates' – all things in heaven and on earth (Ephesians 1:10). Such a process is not a hermeneutical one that seeks to 'replace' one meaning with another in a supersessionist dualism, or a movement from a particular to a universal possession of meaning; it is a state of exception, which interrupts the normal meaning of the laws.[77]

What differentiates the prophetic from the strictly messianic approaches concerning the historical structure of time is the content, or absence of content, of the promise, of the given word. In the scriptural prophecies, faith in a future expectation is not without dogma, as Derrida likes to say.[78] Since, as Murchadha argues, dogmas are inseparable from the event 'as it is retold, retained, and instituted through time . . . Dogmas are illuminated accounts of nocturnal events.'[79] Instead of speaking of dogmas, we could speak of prophetic announcements, which define a monotheistic faith, its rituals of worship and its moral prescriptions.[80] These announcements will persist in every future time as a persistent word – final justice – and have achieved a historical concretisation in Christ's incarnation. The meaning of this 'word become flesh' constitutes the character of figural events in the course of history; therefore, it has the character of a judgement and hence of justice.

Theopolitical Figurations of Prophetical Time: The Lisbon Earthquake of 1755

In order to ensure the success of its enterprises, every civilisation has felt the need to inquire into the course of the future. In fact, as Norman Cohn attests, ancient civilisations such as that of the Egyptians, the Sumerians, the Babylonians and the Indo-Iranians, as well as their Iranian and Indian descendants, envisaged a destiny related to a conception of the world with a divine origin.[81] Their image of the world was an ordered and immutable cosmos that was sometimes threatened by destructive forces of different kinds, that is, political, natural or supernatural. The interpretation of history in this cosmovision, which was the realm of theologians and priests, follows the pattern of a struggle between cosmos and chaos. Between 1500 and 1200 BC, Zoroastro changed this static representation of divine history through a reinterpretation of the

Iranian myth: the world is moving through incessant conflict to a final stage, imagined as a final battle in which God and his allies will defeat chaos. As Cohn asserts, Qumram testified to the influence of this belief among the Hebrews even before Zoroastro. In addition, Minois notes how ancient civilisations not only tried to interpret the history of the world as a whole by looking for divine traces, but also practised divination and prediction to ensure the success of concrete actions. Astrology was also a common practice in order to inquire into the future.[82]

Greco-Roman culture did not ignore the voice of the highest in order to ensure a political future. The oracles in Greece and the augurs in Rome were always at the origin of every kind of political action. Political actors tried to attract the favourable will of the divinities in pursuing political goals. Cicero in *De divinatione* can be cited here as one of the first critics of those practices. With the establishment of the empire, divination by astrologers, augurs and haruspices was forbidden; and the emperor reserved any consultation with the divinities for himself. Knowledge of the future became a matter reserved to the state and any other attempts to foretell the future were considered treason.[83]

The presence of particular messengers of divinity called prophets has been testified in Mesopotamia and Egypt long before Israel. In Assyria around 1800 BC, prophets were a state institution similar to a counsel of consultants.[84] In addition, a new sovereign benefactor who was to restore the cosmic and national order was announced prophetically in Egypt. Catastrophe, grace and salvation are found in Nefer-Rohu's prophecy written in 1991–1786 BC, almost a thousand years before Nathan's prophecy to David.

We can see through these examples how, in early civilisations, the politics of time connected with pre-existing theological representations, which aimed to appropriate knowledge of the future in order to control the present. This practice persists to the present day in different forms. We can think of a whole series of messianisms, millenarianisms and apocalypticisms.[85] Enlightenment's philosophy had a particular effect in transfiguring 'prophetic time' into a 'horizon for political action'. The idea of the 'to come' is converted into progressive action. The future begins to be a human task to reach a foreseen type of state. But even at this historical moment, prophetic thought was not absent from historical interpretations of unexpected historical events.

Such is the case of the Lisbon earthquake of 1755. On 1 November 1755, some twenty thousand people died when the city of Lisbon was hit by an earthquake which probably measured 9 on the Richter scale. Floods and fires followed the shocks:

> the singularly disastrous character of the catastrophe cannot be 'equalled' by anything in the annals of the world. It cannot be domesticated within a common taxonomy of known, memorisable, historical events. It becomes an event of biblical proportions, a 'disaster' in the most radical sense of the Old Testament.[86]

Indeed, different texts of the time introduce biblical references for the sake of comparison, such us Sodom and Gomorrah in the story of Lot.[87] A great earthquake affecting one of the main capitals of Europe built upon the successes of the Portuguese maritime empire, posed a challenge to the enlightened intellectuals of the age. Their belief in the power of the intellect, in the triumph of the mind projected in science and technology was shattered by a historical event which made them aware that history cannot be completely mastered. The substantial impression made on the spirits of that time remains as a figure to this day: the Lisbon earthquake comes to represent an exceptional position within a narrative that describes the eighteenth and nineteenth centuries as developing a more secular outlook, particularly in response to natural phenomena. In fact, almost every time a similar catastrophe occurs, reflection on the Lisbon earthquake returns; this is demonstrated by the prolific bibliography on the subject produced in subsequent years and up to the present century. The disruptive event always recalls the prophetic force of the apocalypse. That is to say, it re-opens the difficult question of the irruption of an absolute time or of the divine in history.[88] In fact, in November of that year, Voltaire wrote the poem on the Lisbon disaster in which he expressed his sentiment that rationalist optimism had been demolished along with the city of Lisbon. He incisively underscores the idea that nature reveals itself as the empire of destruction, a chaos of suffering and horrors. He examined the claim in Alexander Pope's *An Essay on Man* (1733–4) that: 'Whatever is, is right.' Pope's point seems to be that the harmony of the world requires the admission of some discordant notes. A few years before, in 1752, Voltaire had published a poem on natural law in which he was more optimistic about the existence, on the one hand, of an invisible God whose law is morality and, on the other hand, of the idea of justice imprinted on one's conscience, in all times and places. He also denounced the excesses of fanaticism and superstition. The poem ended with a prayer to the God who is unknown, to that God who announces everything.

A year after the earthquake, Voltaire wrote the first philosophy of history liberated from theology, the *Essai sur le moeurs et l'esprit des nations*. His intention was to discredit the biblical interpretation of history. In fact, in his view and after a detailed review of historical events, it can be said that providence does not act in history. But it is in *Candide, ou l'Optimisme* (1759) where he unravels a satirical critique of the Christian doctrine of providence and Leibniz's theodicy; this is represented by the figure of Mr Pangloss, who tries to prove that everything in this world has a certain end and ultimately the best of all ends. These theses were revised in the light of the experience of the earthquake. In fact, as Fergusson has explained, the placid deist's providentialism of early modernity was questioned on many fronts, not only by Voltaire, following reflection on the Lisbon earthquake.[89]

Rousseau reacted critically to Voltaire's poem in a letter dated 18 August 1756. The central points of disagreement were the feelings provoked by the reading of Voltaire's poem, which, by making the picture of miseries more extreme, instead of offering consolation, embittered. He recognises that the dimensions of the problem of evil and suffering force him to alter his view of some of God's perfections. But he prefers to opt for God's goodness.[90]

In 1756, Kant wrote *Geschichte und Naturbeschreibung der merkwürdigsten Vorfälle des Erdbebens* ('History and Physiography of the Most Remarkable Cases of the Earthquake which towards the End of the year 1755 Shook a Great Part of the Earth'), where he tried to find the natural causes of the disaster. Thanks to his book, this line of argument gained strongly in credibility compared with the moral, theological and philosophical formulations. The disaster becomes a peculiarity, which triggers fear, because it cannot be classified and explained. Kant announces a change of paradigm in the apprehension of natural catastrophes. Concerning the possibility of an earthquake in Prussia, he answers with irony all the clergymen who defend the idea of retribution, like his colleague Gottsched, for example, who presents the earthquake as the result of the sins of the Prussians. Kant asserts that these violent events of nature can inform us about the particular order of the laws of nature; and about the need for men to learn to live in harmony with them. In 1784, he wrote *Idee zu einer allgemeinen Geschichte in weltbürgerlicher Absicht*, where he assigned to nature a role that was not without plan or purpose, despite the historical intervention of human freedom. In fact, he supposes that the human race will finally achieve the condition in which all the seeds planted in it by nature can fully develop and in which the destiny of the race can be fulfilled on earth. He does not doubt to equate nature to providence on the only occasion he uses the term. The order of the natural causes and no other explanation is what has to be looked for in order to give an account of the earthquake.

Much of enlightened literature was directed against theodicy, whether Leibnizian or catholic, which assumed that the world as such is good and that what happens is for the best; and that both assertions are a justification of God's existence. But along with these kind of arguments, there was also prophetic literature that easily became theological–political. This was the case of Gabriele Malagrida (1689–1761).[91] After the earthquake, he wrote an opuscule on the causes of the catastrophe, which served as a pretext for the Marquis of Pombal to banish him. While in prison, he was tried by the Inquisition as a heretic and, at the instigation of the minister, he was burnt in a public square and his ashes thrown into the Tagus on 21 September 1761.

The Jesuit Malagrida attributed the earthquake to divine punishment for undue leniency towards heretics in the sermon which he published titled *Judgement of the True Cause of the Earthquake that Struck the Court of Lisbon on the first of November 1755*.[92] As if he were a prophetic voice, he called on the people of Lisbon to banish sin and to understand the language of God, who spoke through the natural causes of the earthquake. The immediate cause is not God, of course. The prophetic voice is not attributing the cause of the catastrophe to God. Rather, the prophetic voice is making an interpretation of a historical event, of which the meaning is independent of its natural causes. The interpretation then made of Malagrida's book was political: an attack on Pombal and his allies. It was nothing less than a first class theological–political action. But Malagrida's discourse was like that of the old prophets: he does not accuse, but appeals for a reform of customs as a means of recovery for the city and the people in general. These instruments of possible re-edification hardly touch on the future.

Certainly, Malagrida's interpretation could be confused with the prophecies of Bandarra, in which the return of King Don Sebastian was guaranteed after his disappearance at the Battle of Alcazarquivir in August 1578, and which had political consequences in the Sebastianism movement in the context of Portuguese messianism.[93]

From England, too, came apocalyptic voices like that of the Methodist preacher John Wesley: he was disturbed by the news from Lisbon, because he thought that God might have been punishing the Portuguese, in his view, for their support of the Inquisition.[94] The action of God directly overwhelms us in the earthquake, not through the ordinary powers of nature. Earthquakes do not have a sufficient natural explanation. As such, these are peculiar events wrought by God without intermediate secondary causes. In short, Wesley understands the earthquake in judicial terms: this was God's judgement on Lisbon. The question for him was whether or not the object of God's anger was a particular religion, in this case Catholicism, or whether it was due to human sinfulness.[95]

Prophetism does not cease to be present in the history of Portugal. In 1815, a new edition of Bandarra's prophecies was published under the title *Trovas Inéditas do Bandarra*. Between 1822 and 1823 another edition with the title *Verdade e Complemento das Profecías* was added to the collection. Bandarra's troves influenced the *sebastianismo* (the idea that King Sebastian would one day return to rule the Portuguese nation) of the Jesuit António Vieira and the poet Fernando Pessoa. The Jesuit António Vieira discovered in Bandarra's verses evidence for his idea of a universal empire in which Christians and Jews would be united in a new church, an idea to which he gave the name of the Fifth Empire.

Years after 1852, the book *The Fulfilment of Prophecy, Or, A Prophetic History of the World, Including a Few Suggestions on the Probable Termini of the Chronological Periods*, written by Francis H. Berick and John Couch, edited by Lowell, included the Lisbon earthquake under the 'Events connected with the Sixth Seal'. In fact, the Book of Revelation says: 'And I beheld when he had opened the sixth seal, and there was a great earthquake.' Berick and Couch do not hesitate in writing: '1st ITEM . – "A great earthquake". This occurred A.D., 1755, at which time the city of Lisbon was sunk, and not less than 60,000 persons lost their lives. The effects of this earthquake were felt throughout the world.'[96]

As Neves suggests, Portuguese Jesuit prophetism in the seventeenth and eighteenth centuries, is not irrational. Prophetic writings do not imply a repudiation of history. Rather, their prophetism is a reflection on history, an interpretation of history. And this interpretation is an alternative to other possible interpretations, which had been expressed in different terms: as a 'natural cause', which the Enlightenment attempted to do, or as a 'social cause', which Rousseau seems to have been inclined to do, or as a 'third cause' or 'neutral cause'. This is Neves' understanding of events from the viewpoint of the biblical proclamation.[97]

In the opening book of his autobiography, *Dichtung und Wahrheit* (1811–32), Goethe records the Lisbon earthquake as one of his most important childhood experiences.[98] The line of argument of this third chapter presents the Lisbon earthquake as an event whose metaphorical force provides a conceptual springboard for a reading of some central texts on the sublime. As Regier shows, for the post-Enlightenment romantic generation, the Lisbon earthquake still represented a figure of the extraordinary, which Goethe called the sublime.[99] He insists in particular in the structural and logical interdependence between fragmentation and the sublime, while he at the same time argues that the fragmenting moment exceeds the possible taxonomies of a discourse of aesthetics, including the sublime. In any case, we can also recover biblical categories here: the catastrophe is associated with the epiphany of the divine.

Notes

1. Friedrich Nietzsche, *On the Use and Abuse of History for Life* (Indianapolis, IN: Hackett, 1980), 38.
2. The complete text is Nietzsche, *On the Use and Abuse of History for Life*, 38: 'history is written by the experienced and superior man. If you have not had some higher and greater experiences than all others you will not know how to interpret anything great and high in the past. The past always speaks as an oracle: only as master builders of the future who know the present will you understand it.' See also Friedrich Nietzsche, *Nachgelassene Fragmente*, Winter 1883, 22(3), *Kritische Gesamtausgabe*, Giorgio Colli and Mazzino Montinari (eds) (Berlin: de Gruyter, 1977), 624: 'Alles Vergangene ist eine Schrift mit hundert Sinnen und Deutungen und wharlich! Ein Weg zu vielen Zukünften! Wer aber der Zukunft Einen Sinn giebt, der bestimmt auch die Eine Deutung des Vergangenen.' The other illustrious testimony is that of Johann Georg Hamann: 'Can one know the past if one does not even understand the present? And who will take the right concepts from the present, without knowing the future?' Johann Georg Hamann, *Kleeblatt Hellenistischer Briefe* (1792).
3. Georges Minois, *Histoire de l'avenir. Des prophètes à la prospective* (Paris: Fayard, 2014), 24.
4. This is also the position of Taubes, as Agata Bielik-Robson confirms in *Jewish Cryptotheologies of Late Modernity: Philosophical Marranos* (London: Routledge, 2014), 166–212, 171: 'In Taubes' unstable apocalyptic narrative two worlds clash all the time: the Kierkegaardian–Barthian universe of the antithesis so strong that it can only be called a diathesis, a static alternative of either/or between the worldly and the divine, and the Hegelian universe of dialectics

which turns the antithetical separation of revelation and reality into a stage of the holy–historical process, ultimately "aiming at union with God".' She sees, however, an incongruence in Taubes' position that she calls antinomianism. I consider it to be a *complexio oppositorum*, often found in the way of reasoning of a negative theology.

5. See Menachem Lorberbaum, in *The Jewish Political Tradition, vol. 1: Authority*, Michael Walzer, Menachem Lorberbaum, Noam J. Zohar and Yair Lorberbaum (eds) (New Haven, CT: Yale University Press, 2000), ch. 5, 202, where prophecy is more closely connected to the task of criticising its own times than with a political function. Prophets seem to look for wisdom and not for power.

6. Arnaldo Momigliano, 'Time in Ancient Historiography', *History and Theory*, Supplement 6: *History and the Concept of Time* 6 (1966): 1–23. Momigliano suggests that the first task is to disentangle Greek historians from Greek philosophy. Greek historians were not as quick to make generalisations as the philosophers were and consequently they did not interpret time in cycles, as we usually suppose. In this sense, Biblical authors are closer to the Greek historians than to the Greek philosophers. But in any case, Momigliano asserts that there are at least important differences between Hebrew and Greek historians: (1) the idea of a historical continuum from the creation prevails in Biblical history. (2) Hebrew historians did not use reliability of source as a criterion for selecting and graduating events even within this continuum. In any event, they based their account of history on written records while other aspects of history were entrusted to collective memory. Incidentally, Hebrew historians did not emphasise the distinction between a mythical age and a historical age. (3) The Biblical historian gave an authoritative version of what everybody was supposed to know, whereas the Greek historian recorded what was in danger of being forgotten. (4) The Hebrew historian never claimed to be a prophet, but the pages of the historical books of the Bible are full of prophets who interpret the events because they know what was, is and will be. To summarise, Momigliano is saying that even in the Greeks there are no philosophical assumptions about historiography, and it comes as no surprise that those kinds of generalisation do not appear in Hebrew historiography. Incidentally, the possible Christian notion of time, if we can speak of it as such, offended all the classical notions concerning Antiquity, memory and evidence in Momigliano's view: 'the modern notion of historical periods selected according to the intrinsic importance of the facts and according to the reliability of the evidence is quite clearly part of our pagan inheritance. Experience seems to show that it can somehow be reconciled with the Jewish idea of a history from the creation of the world. The reconciliation with the Christian notion of a history divided into two by Incarnation is a more difficult problem' (Momigliano, *Time in*

Ancient Historiography, 22). Felix Ó Murchadha, *A Phenomenology of Christian Life: Glory and Night* (Bloomington: Indiana University Press, 2013), 178–98, repeats the thesis that the scriptural approach to time is far removed from the philosophical – or at that time 'scientific' – approaches to time that we can read in Heraclitus, Plato's *Timaeus* or Aristotle's *Physics*.

7. James Barr, *Biblical Words for Time* (London: SCM Press, 1962), 158: 'The fact that the Greek philosophers had theories about time does not mean that the Bible will necessarily have a view of time which contrasts strongly with theirs, or indeed have a view of time at all.' He criticises not only Oscar Cullmann, *Christ and Time: The Primitive Christian Conception of Time and History* (London: SCM Press, 1962), but also John Marsh, *The Fullness of Time* (London: Nisbet, 1952); John A. T. Robinson, *In the End, God: A Study of the Christian Doctrine of the Last Things* (London: James Clarke, 1950).
8. Barr, *Biblical Words for Time*, 137. Barr also refers to Boman to justify the assertion that it is not necessary to conclude that the Greek conception of time was cyclical. Moreover, Boman maintains that the popular time conception of the Greeks was linear. Thorleif Boman, *Das hebräische Denken im Vergleich mit dem griechischen* (Göttingen: Vandenhoeck & Ruprecht, 1965).
9. For a theological discussion about the theological interpretations of the cyclical or linear conception of time in the Bible in Greek and Hebrew thought, see the synthesis in Barr, *Biblical Words for Time*, 143–4.
10. Karl Barth, *Kirchliche Dogmatik*, II, Part 1 (Zürich: Theologische, 1940), 698.
11. Barr, *Biblical Words for Time*, 146.
12. Barr, *Biblical Words for Time*, 147.
13. Murchadha speaks of a 'time of revelation' as a 'time beyond adequation', as a *kairos* in a similar manner as Cullmann. *Kairos* is the figure of time inaugurated by the event of Incarnation. It is a time that concentrates the occurrence of eternity breaking into chronological time. The idea of the event or of the 'sudden' as Murchadha denominates it happens in another kind of temporality that is not comprehended either as an 'space of experience', or as an 'horizon of expectation' in Koselleck's terms (Ó Murchadha, *A Phenomenology*, 188). The 'sudden' has to be, however, recognised as such and this presupposes some knowledge. That knowledge is given by the content of a promise. And for this reason, I personally prefer to speak of prophetic time more than just of *kairos*.
14. Cullmann says that *aion* assumes different meanings: first, time in its entire unending extension, which is unlimited in both directions, past and future; in other words, something similar to what the Greeks understand as eternity. Secondly, the limited time that lies between

creation and the eschatological drama, and thus is identical with the 'present' age or 'this' age. A third meaning is that of a period of time that is limited in one direction but unlimited in the other, and specifically: the time that lies before the creation, and the time that extends beyond the end of the present age and before the 'coming age'. See Cullmann, *Christ and Time*, 48.
15. Cullmann, *Christ and Time*, 50. Otherwise, this argument is in line with Dobschütz in distinguishing that Greek thought was more spatial and Hebrew thought more dominated by temporal categories. See Dobschütz, 'Zeit und Raum im Denken des Urchristentums', 212–23.
16. Cullmann asserts that the history of redemption as a whole is 'prophecy'. Cullmann, *Christ and Time*, 97. He argues about prophecy in relationship to the dichotomy between history and myth. He rejects this dichotomy while speaking about prophecy and distinguishes between a prophecy that has been developed through symbolic language and another developed through historical facts. He calls the first 'just prophecy' and the second 'history and prophecy'. Hence, the first should be at the same time mythical and prophetical.
17. Ephesians. 1:10, 3:2, 3:9; Colossians 1:25.
18. In any event, he discusses the work of Johann Christian K. von Hofmann, *Weissagung und Erfüllung im alten und im neuen Testamente* (Nördlingen: C. H. Beck, 1841–4). For him all history is prophecy and at the same time every prediction becomes history. Christ's incarnation is the figure of all history. Thus, it is not the end that here gives meaning to the whole; it is rather the incarnate Christ. Cullman, *Christ and Time*, 184: 'a brilliant representative of the so-called "theology of redemptive history" (referring Hofmann) in the nineteenth century, seeks an explanation of the relation between the redemptive movement and the general process of history that would preserve the particular character of the New Testament redemptive history. He bases his explanation upon the concept of prediction. Everything that occurs is a prediction of an occurrence to come. Thus, he so connects the secular history that it forms one line with the Biblical course of events, but nevertheless he does not thereby do justice to the specific claim of the Biblical revelation.'
19. Cullman, *Christ and Time*, 98: 'the main fact, that Israel is chosen by God, no historian can test. The same thing holds true of the Gospels, which relate the history of Jesus the Son of God. Here, too, much can be tested by the historian. But the main thing, that this Jesus is the Son of God, remains concealed from the historian as such.' However, it is difficult to distinguish between prophets and historians in the Bible. For Jacob Taubes, the prophets were simply the historians of the ancient world. See Jacob Taubes, *From Cult to Culture: Fragments toward a Critique of Historical Reason* (Stanford, CA:

Stanford University Press, 2009); Jacob Taubes, *Occidental Eschatology* (Stanford, CA: Stanford University Press, 2009). See also Momigliano, 'Time in Ancient Historiography', 20, who asserted: 'I do not know of any satisfactory study of the relations between prophets and historians in the Bible.' For an illuminating paper on the prophet's predicament, see E-J. Bickerman, 'Les deux erreurs du prophète Jonas', *Revue d'histoire et de philosophie religieuses* 45 (1965): 232–64. See also Artur Weiser, *Glaube und Geschichte im Alten Testament* (Stuttgart: W. Kothlhammer, 1931; reprinted Göttingen, 1961); Sigmund Mowinckel, 'Israelite Historiography', *Annals of the Swedish Theological Institute* 2 (1963): 4–26; Georg Fohrer, 'Prophetie und Geschichte', *Theologische Literaturzeitung* 89 (1964): 481–500; Johannes Hempel, *Geschichten und Geschichte im Alten Testament* (Giltersloh: Gerd Mohn, 1964); Hans Walter Wolff, 'Das Geschichtsverstindnis der alt-testamentlichen Prophetie', *Gesammelte Studien zum Alten Testament* (Munich: Kaiser, 1964), 289–307.

20. Cullmann, *Christ and Time*, 81. This experience is an interpretation of time, not a new conception of time: this is the central thesis of Cullmann in *Christ and Time*, 49: 'that only this simple rectilinear conception of unending time can be considered as the framework for the New Testament history of redemption. Along this consistently rectilinear line of the ages lie the *kairoi* determined by God.' In the same vein, Rudolf Otto, *The Kingdom of God and the Son of Man: A Study in the History of Religion* (Eugene, OR: Wipf & Stock, 2009). He notes that the idea that was entirely unique and peculiar to Jesus was that the Kingdom – supramundane, future and belonging to a new era – penetrates from the future into the present and is operatively redemptive as a divine power.

21. Cullmann in *Christ and Time*, XXV. Walter Kreck, *Die Zukunft des Gekommenens* (Berlin: Evangelische Verlagsanstalt, 1968) was critical of Cullmann's approach, since he thinks that linear time is not necessarily a Christian interpretation of time. In his defence, Cullmann accepts that the most specific time derived from Christian revelation is not linear time: 'It is characteristic that in that work my view is mentioned only in connection with "linear" time (which Kreck rejects), and with the "ascending line". No reference to my views appears in his discussion of the "already and not yet" tension, which is the most essential matter of my book' (Cullmann, *Christ and Time*, XXVI). Also, Josef Ratzinger points to the idea that the subdivision of history into a 'before and after Christ' – or, in different words, into an unredeemed time and a redeemed time – was a response to Joaquin de Fiore's thirteenth-century account of the three ages. If the Church condemned this doctrine of de Fiore, at least the idea of the incarnation of Christ as an intra-historical, time-periodisation

event remained. But in his opinion, this is not the only possible view. See Josef Ratzinger, *The Theology of History in St. Bonaventure* (Chicago: Franciscan Herald Press, 1971).

22. Erik Peterson, 4 *Vorlesung Altchristiche Mystik*, unedited text of 1924. See Gabino Uríbarri, 'La reserva escatológica: un concepto originario de Erik Peterson (1890–1960)', *Estudios Eclesiásticos* 78 (2003); and also Gabino Uríbarri, *La vivencia cristiana del tiempo* (Madrid: BAC, 2020). Both are an accurate study on this concept in Peterson. Philippe Büttgen and Alain Rauwel, *Théologie politique et sciences sociales. Autour d'Erik Peterson* (Paris: EHESS, 2019), 43, attest that the first to trace this idea back to Peterson was Ernst Käsermann, *An die Römer* (Tübingen: Mohr, 1980).

23. Werner Georg Kümmel, *Promise and Fulfilment* (London: SCM Press, 1957), 142: 'Jesus connects the present, being by its very nature an eschatologically fulfilled present, with the expected future, because the encounter with the man Jesus in the present demands a decision which will be determining factor for the eschatological verdict of Jesus when he comes as the son of man.' And 151: 'Jesus' message concerning the future was not intended to be an apocalyptic revelation, but a prophetic message concerning the imminent Kingdom of God, so that the apocalyptic interest in the date and the premonitory signs is necessary lacking in Jesus.'

24. Reinhart Koselleck, *Futures Past* (New York: Columbia University Press, 2004), 261, also 13: 'The unknown *eschaton* must be understood as one of the Church's integrating factors, enabling its self-constitution as world and as institution. The Church is itself eschatological. But the moment the figures of the apocalypse are applied to concrete events or instances, the eschatology has disintegrative effects. The end of the world is only an integrating factor so long as its politico-historical meaning remains indeterminate. The Church integrates the future as the possible end of the world within its organization of time; it is not placed at the end point of time in a strictly linear fashion. The end of time can be experienced only because it is always already sublimated in the Church. The history of the Church remains the history of salvation so long as this condition held.'

25. Hans-Georg Gadamer, 'The Continuity of History and the Existential Moment', *Philosophy Today* 16(3) (1972): 230–40.

26. Koselleck, *Futures Past*, 192–205. See also the development of his thesis carried out by Christophe Bouton, *Faire l'histoire* (Paris: Cerf, 2013). In this book, Bouton makes a genealogy of the 'feasibility of history' and analyses the objections to that same feasibility drawn from the theory of history.

27. This was clear for some early modern philosophers like Hobbes (*Leviathan*, ch. 30) and Spinoza, (*The Theological-Political Treatise*,

ch. 1), who devote many pages to making the sovereign the unique interpreter of prophecies. They were convinced that power depends on the idea of the future. Also, Koselleck underlines that: 'The genesis of the absolutist state is accompanied by a sporadic struggle against all manner of religious and political predictions. The state enforced a monopoly on the control of the future by suppressing apocalyptic and astrological readings of the future. In doing so, it assumed a function of the old Church for anti-Church objectives. Henry VIII, Edward VI, and Elizabeth I all proscribed in strong terms any prediction of this nature. Disobedient prophets could expect lifelong imprisonment.' Koselleck, *Futures Past*, 16.

28. Reinhart Koselleck, 'Krise', in *Geschichtliche Grundbegriffe. Historisches Lexikon zur politisch-sozialen Sprache in Deutschland*, O. Brunner, W. Conze and R. Koselleck (eds), 8 vols (Stuttgart: Klett-Cotta, 1972–97, vol. III, 1982), 617–50. See also Reinhart Koselleck, *The Practice of Conceptual History: Timing History. Spacing Concepts* (Stanford: Stanford University Press, 2002), 237: 'In theology, specifically since the New Testament, *krisis* and *judicium* both gain a new and, to a certain extent, unsurpassable meaning taken up from legal language: the judgment before God. This might be that crisis meant the Last Judgment at the end of time, or the judgment that appeared with Christ's Second Coming through the light that he brought to this world, something that would already be present to all believers during their lifetimes.' And 240: 'The associative power of both God's judgment and the Apocalypse constantly contributed to the use of the word such that no doubt can be raised as to the theological origin of the new form of the concept. Not least of all, this is proven by the fact that historico-philosophical diagnoses of crises often operate within rigid compulsory alternatives which preclude a differentiated diagnosis but which appear to be all the more effective and plausible because of their prophetic associations.'

29. Friedrich Schiller, *Resignation. Eine Phantasie* (1781/1784). Commenting on this aphorism, Koselleck, *The Practice of Conceptual History*, 241 says: 'Formally, this concerns the temporalization of the Last Judgment which is always and constantly enforced. It has a pronounced anti-Christian thrust because all guilt mercilessly enters into the personal life of the individual, into the history of political communities, into world history in its entirety. This model is compatible with fate, which in Herodotus appears behind all individual histories and which can be read again and again as the consummation of a world-immanent justice. However, Schiller's dictum raises a greater claim. An inherent justice, one which acquires almost a magical air, is not only required of individual histories but of all world history *in toto*. Logically, every injustice, every incommensurability, every unatoned crime, every senselessness and uselessness is apodictically

excluded. Thus, the burden of proof for the meaning of this history increases enormously. It is no longer historians who, because of their better knowledge, believe themselves to be able to morally judge the past ex post facto, but rather it is assumed that history, as an acting subject, enforces justice. Hegel took it upon himself to settle the moral discrepancies and shortcomings resulting from this dictum. His world history remains the judgment of the world because the world spirit or the thoughts of God are realized in it in order to achieve their identity. Seen theologically, it is a question of the last imaginable heresy which wants to fully reckon with a Christian interpretation of history.'

30. Koselleck, *The Practice of Conceptual History*, 242.
31. In *Posthumous Fragments* 1884 25[406] he says: 'Unsere Ableitung des Zeitgefühls usw. setzt immer noch die Zeit als absolut voraus' ('Our way of experiencing time, etc., presupposes time as absolute').
32. It is 'Der mächtigste Gedänke', as Nietzsche would say. *Nachgelassene Fragmente* 1881 11[220] KSA 9. 526–7: 'Der mächtigste Gedanke verbraucht viele Kraft, die früher anderen Zielen zu Gebote stand, so wirkt er umbildend, er schafft neue Bewegungsgesetze der Kraft, aber keine neue Kraft. 'It is difficult not to understand cosmologically the idea of the eternal recurrence, as Valadier notes. He interprets it as an 'amen to the eternity' (Paul Valadier, *Nietzsche et la critique du christianisme* (Paris: Ed. du Cerf, 1974), 542. In the last phase of its development, this doctrine does not signify a dull permanence of conjunctures. A pronounced 'yes' to life will return once and again, but between them, radical alteration occurs. Every 'yes' is a new beginning. The will is always open to that which is 'to come'.
33. See María Guibert, 'La memoire et l'oubli chez Nietzsche. Une approche à partir de la Généalogie du moral', PhD dissertation, Université Sorbonne/Universidad de Navarra, 2021. See also Franck, *Nietzsche et l'ombre de Dieu*. One of Franck's central theses is that the Nietzschean–Christianism controversy originates with the Pauline doctrine of justification that Nietzsche interpreted through Luther. He tries to overcome the justice of God with the justice of the will to power and the death and resurrection of Christ with a new source of resurrection by eternal recurrence. Nietzsche considers himself the apostle of a Gospel to come, whose prophet is Zarathustra and whose main prophecy is eternal recurrence. See also Manfred Riedel, *Vorspiele zur Ewigen Wiederkunft. Nietzsches Grundlehre* (Vienna: Böhlau, 2012), 82–102. Manfred Riedel, who interprets eternal recurrence as a theory of time, has pointed out that it can be thought of according to the image of Janus – the union of two opposed heads that represent the two vectors of time in an instant. It symbolises the unity of the instance that immediately dissolves into duality, an instance that is barely observable. This instance, in the infinite

weakness of its passing from one dimension of time to the other, represents the redemptory and transformative counterpoint of an unstable body. This figure of time also has its appropriate sacramental character: Zarathustra celebrates his own Eucharist as being the true one, since it is the Church that did not understand what Eucharist means, as Nietzsche would say. Z-IV-Abendmahl KSA 4. 353: 'Das Abendmahl. An dieser Stelle nämlich unterbrach der Wahrsager die Begrüssung Zarathustra's und seiner Gäste: er drängte sich vor, wie Einer, der keine Zeit zu verlieren hat, fasste die Hand Zarathustra's und rief: "Aber Zarathustra! Diess aber war der Anfang von jener langen Mahlzeit, welche 'das Abendmahl' in den Historien-Büchern genannt wird. Bei derselben aber wurde von nichts anderem geredet als vom höheren Menschen".' Nachgelassene Fragmente 1884, 31 (63) KSA 11. 391: 'Das Abendmahl. Das Lied des Lachenden. Die Begrüssung. Das Abendmahl. Die Improvisation. Die Rosenrede.' NF-1884,32[16] KSA 11. 415–16: 'Die Begrüßung. Das Abendmahl. Vom höheren Menschen. Das Lied des Zauberers. Von der Wissenschaft. Der Nachtisch-Psalm. Der Auferstandene.' See also Montserrat Herrero, 'Political Theologies Surrounding the Nietzschean "Death of God's Trope"', *Nietzsche-Studien. Internationales Jahrbuch fur die Nietzsche-Forschung* 49 (2020): 125–49.

34. To live the way you desire to live is the only possible action that deserves resurrection. Nachgelassene Fragmente 1881 11[161]: 'Nicht nach fernen unbekannten Seligkeiten und Segnungen und Begnadigungen ausschauen, sondern so leben, daß wir nochmals leben wollen in Ewigkeit so leben wollen! – Unsere Aufgabe tritt in jedem Augenblick an uns heran.'

35. Numerous works have dealt with this subject in the work of Carl Schmitt. Among others: Massimo Maraviglia, *La penultima guerra. Il 'katéchon' nella dottrina dell'ordine politico di Carl Schmitt* (Milan: LED, 2006); Alfons Motschenbacher, *Katechon oder Grossinquisitor? Eine Studie zu Inhalt und Struktur der Politischen Theologie Carl Schmit* (Marburg: Tectum, 2000); Bernd A. Laska, *'Katechon' und 'Anarch'. Carl Schmitts und Ernst Jüngers Reaktionen auf Max Stirner* (Nürnberg : LSR, 1997); Felix Grossheutschi, *Carl Schmitt und die Lehre vom Katechon* (Berlin: Duncker & Humblot, 1996); Günter Meuter, *Der Katechon. Zu Carl Schmitts fundamentalistischer Kritik der Zeit* (Berlin: Duncker & Humblot, 1994). Beyond these works, many articles have been published on the topic: Julia Hell, 'Katechon: Carl Schmitt's Imperial Theology and the Ruins of the Future', *Germanic Review: Literature, Culture, Theory* 84(4) (2009): 283–326; Michael Dillon, 'Specters of Biopolitics: Finitude, Eschaton, and Katechon', *South Atlantic Quarterly* 1 (2011): 780–92; Sergei Prozorov, 'The Katechon in the Age of Biopolitical Nihilism', *Continental Philosophy Review* 45 (2012): 483–503; Arthur Bradley,

'Unleashed: "Schmitt and the Katechon"', in Arthur Bradley, *Unbearable Life* (New York: Columbia University Press, 2019), 141–62. On the difficult interpretation of *Katechon* in Paul, see Paul Metzger, *Katechon: II Thess 2,1-12 im Horizont apokalyptischen Denkens* (Berlin: De Gruyter, 2005); Otto Betz, 'Der Katechon', *New Testament Studies* 9(3) (1963): 276–91.

36. Carl Schmitt, 'Tres posibilidades de una visión cristiana de la historia', *Arbor* 62 (1951): 239. I quote here the Spanish version where it does not coincide with the German version.
37. Hence, Bradley's hypothesis of the restrainer as a complex figure that brings together a dialectic of order and chaos, rather than simply being a conservative figure of a status quo, is entirely plausible. It is also very illuminating that he has interpreted Schmitt's position in this sense, which he understands as genuinely Pauline. See Bradley, *Unbearable Life*, 152–3.
38. Augustine of Hippo, *City of God*, XX, 19. As he discusses in XX, 13, it is not clear how that happens in history. Whether the saints will reign with Christ at the same time as the devil is unleashed or not.
39. Carl Schmitt, *Glossarium. Aufzeichnungen der Jahre 1947–1951* (Berlin: Duncker & Humblot, 1991), 63.
40. Carl Schmitt, 'Drei Stufen historischer Sinngebung', *Universitas. Zeitschrift für Wissenschaft, Kunst und Literatur* 5(8) (1950): 929–30.
41. Carl Schmitt, *Land and Sea* (Washington, DC: Plutarch, 1997), 8.
42. Schmitt, *Land and Sea*, 43.
43. Carl Schmitt, *Ex Captivitate Salus. Experiencias de los años 1945–1947*, trans. A. Schmitt (Santiago de Compostela: Porto y Cia., 1960), 35, 36.
44. Carl Schmitt, *La Unidad del Mundo* (Madrid: Ateneo, 1951), 34, 35; Schmitt, *Political Theology II*, 92. In addition Schmitt, 'Drei Stufen historischer Sinngebung', 929, or in the Spanish translation, 'Tres posibilidades de una visión cristiana de la historia', 239.
45. This idea appears for the first time in Carl Schmitt, *Theodor Däublers 'Nordlicht'. Drei Studien über die Elemente, den Geist und die Aktualität des Werkes* (Munich: Georg Müller, 1916), 65. It also appears many times in Schmitt, *Glossarium*, 12, 30, 63. Also Carl Schmitt, *Die Lage der europäischen Rechtswissenschaft*, in *Verfassungsrechtliche Aufsätze*, C. Schmitt (ed.) (Berlin: Duncker & Humblot, 1958), 386–430, 429.
46. Schmitt, *Die Lage der europäischen Rechtswissenschaft*, 429. There is no English translation of this note.
47. Montserrat Herrero (ed.), *Carl Schmitt und Álvaro d'Ors Briefwechsel* (Berlin: Duncker & Humblot, 2004), 120. Brief 13.9.1951.
48. Koselleck, *The Practice of Conceptual History*, 245: 'In Christian preaching, before the end of the world arrives, God is said to make time pass by more quickly. Behind this teaching stands the cosmological idea that God, as master of times, could bring about the planned

end of the world earlier than scheduled and, in fact, would do so for the sake of the elect whose suffering would be alleviated (Mark 13:20, Matthew 24:22). Of course, one might psychologize or ideologize this mythological language of apocalyptic expectation. Within this belief in the imminent foreshortening of time, it is not difficult to see the wish of the suffering and the oppressed to exchange misery as fast as possible for paradise. However, if one observes the *topos* of the eschatological foreshortening of time in terms of its historical interpretations, one arrives at the astonishing finding that from the initially suprahistorical foreshortening of time came a gradual acceleration of history itself. Luther, for example, strongly believed that God would foreshorten time before the unknown end of the world. But he no longer believed years would turn into months, months into weeks, and weeks into days before the eternal light would negate the difference between day and night; instead, he already interpreted the foreshortening of time historically: events themselves, with the disintegration of the church rapidly rushing onward, were for him a harbinger of the coming end of the world. The burden of proof for the engulfing Last Judgment was no longer summed up in the mythological imagination that time itself is able to be foreshortened, but rather it was expected from empirically observable historical events as such.' See also Philippe Büttgen, 'Eschatologie et temps présent chez Martin Luther', in Éric Alliez, Gerhart Schröder, Barbara Cassin, Gisela Febel and Michel Narcy (eds), *Metamorphosen der Zeit* (Munich: Wilhelm Fink, 1999), 343–61.

49. Reinhart Koselleck, *Zeitschichten. Studien zur Historik* (Frankfurt: Suhrkamp, 2000), 194 (there is not an English translation of this chapter of the book titled *Zeitverkürzung und Beschleunigung. Eine Studie zur Säkularisation.* The English *Sediments of Time* omitted this chapter): 'Primar Erfahrung war nicht mehr die religiös eingefärbte Heilserwartung, sondern sie des technischen Erfolges, die in immer kürzeren Zeitabständen des menschliche Kommunikationsnetz zusammenführte und die Produktivität erhöhte.' Koselleck, *Zeitschichten*, 196–97: 'Während sich inhaltlich der Geschichte nur wiederholen könne, liege das eigentlich innovative dieser französischen Revolutionserfahrung darin, dass alles schneller als bisher gelaufen sei. Damit wurde das Beschleunigungsaxiom um sein apokalyptisches Erbe gebracht und aus der progressiven, fortschrittlichen Erwartung herausgedreht, um gleichwohl al sein geschichtlicher Erfahrungssatz für Neuzeit bestehen.' And he quotes Barthold Georg Niebhur who expresses this idea in *Geschichte des Zeitalters der Revolution* (Hamburg, 1845) I, 54.

50. Koselleck, *The Practice of Conceptual History*, 247: 'the question can be raised as to whether our semantic model of crisis as final decision has gained more chances of realization than it has ever had before.

If this is the case, everything would depend upon directing all our powers toward deterring destruction. The *katechon* is also a theological answer to crisis.'

51. Günther Anders, *Die Antiquiertheit des Menschen. 1, Über die Seele im Zeitalter der zweiten industriellen Revolution* (Munich: Beck, 1961). See also Günther Anders, *Endzeit und Zeitsende. Gedanke über die atomare Situation* (Munich: Beck, 1972), 217–21. See also Bernard Stiegler, *La technique et le temps*, 3 vols (Paris: Galilée, 1994), 2001, 2003.

52. Karl Löwith, *Weltgeschichte und Heilsgeschehen* (Stuttgart: Kohlhammer, 1953). He supposes that the conscious anticipation of an imagined future that will never be achieved is an inversion of the eschatological or messianic hope.

53. Schmitt, *Land and Sea*, 45. This is what is present when Schmitt argues that any political decision between friend and enemy is historically resolved as a theological–political decision, in the sense that it represents an approach taken (or not) to the coming of the Antichrist, that is, the end of time. Every political decision is already critically judged and will indeed be judged at the end of time from a theological–political perspective. In other words, the political perspective is not identified with the theological perspective, but rather the two intersect. See Carl Schmitt, 'Coloquio sobre el poder y el acceso al poderoso', *Revista de Estudios Políticos* 52(78) (1954): 3–20, 14. Álvaro d'Ors, *De la Guerra y de la Paz* (Madrid: Rialp, 1954), 195–9, interprets that eschatological power, that is, the final judgement regarding every man's salvation or damnation, governs history in two ways; the first being historical (Providence as the effective force of events), and a second, no less fundamental, giving meaning to history, i.e., making a moral judgement.

54. Schmitt, *Glossarium*, 63. For an account of the meaning of this category, see the correspondence between Carl Schmitt and Álvaro d'Ors and Montserrat Herrero (eds), *Carl Schmitt und Álvaro d'Ors Briefwechsel* (Berlin: Duncker & Humblot, 2004), particularly letters 13.9.1951, 17.12.51, 29.2.1952. The correspondence with Hans Blumenberg, in Alexander Schmitz and Martin Lepper (eds), is also interesting in this respect. *Hans Blumenberg. Carl Schmitt. Briefwechsel* (Frankfurt: Suhrkamp, 2007). The critical account of Heinrich Meier in the last edition of *The Lesson of Carl Schmitt* is also relevant insofar as he comments on the relationship between Blumenberg and Schmitt and focuses on the *katechon* theory.

55. See Vassilios Paipais, '"Already/Not Yet": St Paul's Eschatology and the Modern Critique of Historicism', *Philosophy and Social Criticism* 44(9) (2018): 1015–38: 'The central concern of this renewed interest in Paul's messianic imaginary seems to be the critique of Marxist historicism, that is, a rigid interpretation of Marxist thought that views

history as moving toward a predetermined telos and society operating according to iron-clad socio-economic laws destined to turn the very instruments of capitalist exploitation into the midwives of a society free from want and oppression.' See also John D. Caputo, 'Philosophy and Prophetic Postmodernism: Toward a Catholic Postmodernism', *American Catholic Philosophical Quarterly* LXXIV (2000): 549–67; Travis Kroeker, 'Messianic Ethics? Paul as Political Theorist', *Journal of the Society of Christian Ethics* 25(2) (2005): 37–58. Agata Bielik-Robson speaks of a messianic vocation of contemporary apocalyptic Jewish thinkers starting with Lukács and Landauer, and continuing with Bloch, Scholem, Benjamin and Taubes. For her, the last was also the fiercest campaigner for the Jewish messianic vocation. In her view, he was closer to ancient Hebraism than to Judaism and the common denominator between Hebraism and early Christianity is *apocalyptic messianism*. She denominates this group of Jewish thinkers 'new Marcionites'. Bielik-Robson, *Jewish Cryptotheologies of Late Modernity*, 185: 'With Marcion's intransigent Gnostic dualism in the background, the issue of "unbridgeability" between history and redemption acquires an uncompromising poignancy which found its best expression in the text chosen by Taubes as the paradigmatic text of neo-Marcionism: Walter Benjamin's *Theologico-Political Fragment*. Later in his career, Taubes will move closer to Benjamin, whom he will stubbornly interpret along the Marcionite dualistic lines (*pace* Scholem seeing no essential difference between his early "Fragment" and his late "Theses on the Concept of History"), and away from Ernst Bloch, whose "philosophy of Exodus", conducted under the Hegelian auspices, emphasizes the historical, dialectical potency of the exodic act, issuing in an earthly messianic practice (deemed by Taubes as ultimately "wishy-washy", against Benjamin's highly praised "hard theocracy").'

56. Benjamin, *Gesammelte Schriften*, I, 2, 701–4. See Francisco Naishtat, 'Benjamin's Profane Uses of Theology: The Invisible Organon', *Religions* 10(93) (2019): 1–16, 5; Britt, *Walter Benjamin and the Bible*, 101–4.
57. Walter Benjamin, 'Theses on the Philosophy of History', in *Illuminations* (New York: Schocken, 1969), 259, theses XVII and XVIII: 'The here-and-now, which as the model of messianic time summarizes the entire history of humanity into a monstrous abbreviation, coincides to a hair with the figure, which the history of humanity makes in the universe.' And in addendum B: 'It is well-known that the Jews were forbidden to look into the future. The Torah and the prayers instructed them, by contrast, in remembrance. This disenchanted those who fell prey to the future, who sought advice from the soothsayers. For that reason, the future did not, however, turn into a homogeneous and empty time for the Jews. For in it every

second was the narrow gate through which the Messiah could enter.' See also Walter Benjamin, *Selected Writings* (Cambridge, MA: Harvard University Press, 2002) 1, 55–6; Benjamin, *Gesammelte Schriften* II, 1, 134: 'And without specifying what goes beyond this, what else determines historical time – in short, without defining how it differs from mechanical time – we may assert that the determining force (*bestimmende Kraft*) of historical time (*historischen Zeitform*) cannot be fully grasped by, or wholly concentrated in, any empirical process (*von keinem empirischen Geschehen völlig erfaßt*). Rather, a process that is perfect in historical terms is quite indeterminate empirically; it is in fact an idea. This idea of fulfilled time (*erfüllten Zeit*) is the dominant historical idea of the Bible: it is the idea of messianic time.' My translation.

58. James Martel compared Nietzsche's political theology with Walter Benjamin's messianism. In his opinion, both present a 'negative messianism' insofar as Benjamin's messiah and Nietzsche's prophet 'do' nothing except preserve us from false hopes that could lead to phantasmagoria. Thus, humans should bear the weight of all responsibility. Given this, Martel affirms that their political theologies are similar. James Martel, *Divine Violence: Walter Benjamin and the Eschatology of Sovereignty* (New York: Routledge, 2012), 132–3.

59. Benjamin, *Gesammelte Schriften*, I, 2, 693–94; Benjamin, *Selected Writings*, 4, 389.

60. Walter Benjamin, 'Theologico-Political Fragment', in *Reflections: Essays, Aphorisms, Autobiographical Writings*, trans. E. Jephcott (New York: Schocken, 1978), 312; which is a translation from 'Theologisch-politisches Fragment', in *Illuminationen: Ausgewahlte Schriften* (Frankfurt am Main: Suhrkamp, 1977), 262. Benjamin, *Selected Writings*, 3, 305; Benjamin, *Gesammelte Schriften*, II, 1, 203–4: 'Only the Messiah himself consummates [*vollendet*] all history [*historisches Geschehen*], in the sense that he alone redeems, completes, creates its relation to the Messianic. For this reason, nothing historical can relate itself on its own account [*von sich aus sich*] to anything Messianic. Therefore, the Kingdom of God is not the *telos* of the historical dynamic; it cannot be set as a goal [*Ziel*]. From the standpoint of history, it is not the goal but the end. Therefore, the order of the profane cannot be built up on the idea of the Divine Kingdom [*Gedanken des Gottesreiches*].' Benjamin never published the 'Theologico-Political Fragment', whose title was added by Theodor W. Adorno (on the basis of the author's indications) and whose date of writing is unknown. Adorno thought the text was written in 1937. Gershom Scholem and Rolf Tiedemann, date it *c.* 1920–1. In his fragment on *The Meaning of Time in the Moral World*, *Gesammelte Schriften* (Frankfurt am Main: Suhrkamp, 2017), VI, 98, he writes: 'The last judgement is valued as the date

on which all postponements will have ended and all punishment (*Vergeltung*) will be realised. This idea, however, which simulates every delay as a vain postponement, fails to grasp the immeasurable significance of the final judgement, of that constantly postponed day which so determinately escapes into the future after the commission of every crime. This meaning is not revealed in the world of the law, where punishment has rules, but only in the moral universe, where forgiveness comes to meet it . . . The storm is not only the voice in which the evil cry of terror is drowned; it is also the hand that erases the traces of its crimes, even if it has to devastate the world in the process. Like the purifying hurricane speeds ahead of the thunder and lightning, God's fury roars through history in the storm of forgiveness, in order to sweep away all that can be consumed forever in the flashes of divine wrath . . . Time not only extinguishes the traces of all crimes but also – by virtue of its duration, beyond all remembrance or forgetting – helps, in ways that are utterly mysterious, to complete the process of forgiveness, though never of reconciliation [*Versöhnung*].' My translation.

61. The complete text is in Walter Benjamin, *The Arcades Project* (Cambridge, MA: Belknap Press of Harvard University, 1999), 462–3; Walter Benjamin, *Das Passagen-Werk* (Frankfurt am Main: Suhrkamp, 1982), N3, 1: 'each now is the now of a particular recognizability . . . It is not that what is past casts its light on what is present, or what is present its light on what is past; rather, image is that wherein what has been comes together in a flash with the now to form a constellation. In other words: image is dialectic at standstill. For while the relation of the present to the past is purely temporal, the relation of what has been to the now is dialectical: not temporal in nature but figural (*bildlich*). Only dialectical images are genuinely historical – that is, not archaic – images. The image that is read – which is to say, the image in the now of its recognizability – bears to the highest degree the imprint of the perilous critical moment on which all reading is founded.' I owe this quote to Francisco Naishtat. See Naishtat, 'Benjamin's Profane Uses of Theology', 11–12.

62. See Stéphane Moses, 'The Theological–Political Model of History in the Thought of Walter Benjamin', *History and Memory* 1 (1989): 5–33, 9: 'Benjamin could have echoed the formula of the *Confessions* in his own regard: "The past's present is memory; the present's present is vision; the future's present is expectation." (St. Augustine, *Confessions*, XI, 20, 26).' However, we must realise that all these notions for Benjamin represent historical categories. Memory is what evokes the recollection of previous generations; expectation is the collective salvation of humanity. Benjamin understands vision to be the prophetic element inherent in the political intuition of the present. *Gesammelte Schriften*, I, 3, 1237: 'It is no accident that Turgot defines

the notion of a present, the intentional object of a prophecy, as a fundamentally political reality: "Even before we could have found out about a certain state of things," says Turgot, "this state had already changed numerous times. Thus, we always apprehend too late what has happened. One could thus say that politics is destined, as it were, to anticipate the present." The actuality of an authentic writing of history is founded on just such a conception of the present.' Also, regarding remembrance, see Moses, 'The Theological–Political Model of History', 26: 'remembrance is the tool of the retroactive effect of the present on the past; thanks to it, historical time ceases to seem irreversible. That the law of historical time be opposed to that of physical time – this, says Benjamin, is theology. Thus, one may understand that for Benjamin, the term "theology" signifies the very specificity of historical time as the "time of the today", that is, as time in which human activity can intervene in order to change its meaning retrospectively.' For an interesting interpretation of this pervasion of the past into the present and viceversa see Bradley, *Unbearable Life*, 164: 'In Benjamin's famous claim that we still possess a "weak Messianic power [messianische Kraft]" to redeem the past, I propose that we encounter a weak, profane, and immanent rewriting of Damiani's own idea of the past as a theater for the exercise of divine power.'

63. As Brian Britt notes, 'there is very little in Benjamin's work to show what kind of power that might be, apart from a critical awareness of the tragic circumstances of modernity'. Brian Britt, 'The Schmittian Messiah in Agamben's The Time That Remains', *Critical Inquiry* 36 (2010): 262–87, 284. Or as Paipais asserts, the messianic has to be interpreted politically as 'an "interruption" of the dynamics of secular capitalist progressivism'. Paipais, '"Already/Not Yet": St Paul's Eschatology and the Modern Critique of Historicism', 121.

64. For a neat distinction between 'Benjamin's past-gazing messianism and Derrida's disjointed messianism, a messianic affirming both the past and the future', see Owen Ware, 'Dialectic of the Past/Disjuncture of the Future: Derrida and Benjamin on the Concept of Messianism', *Journal for Cultural and Religious Theory* 5(2) (2004): 99–114.

65. Jacques Derrida, 'Marx & Sons', in *Ghostly Demarcations: A Symposium on Jacques Derrida's 'Specters of Marx'*, Michael Sprinker (ed.) (London: Verso, 2008), 213–69, 248–9: 'Messianicity (which I regard as a universal structure of experience, and which cannot be reduced to religious messianism of any stripe) is anything but utopian: it refers, in every here-now, to the coming of an eminently real, concrete event, that is, to the most irreducible heterogenous otherness. Nothing is more "realistic" or "immediate" than this messianic apprehension, straining forward toward the event of him who/that which is coming. I say "apprehension", because this experience, strained forward toward the event, is at the same time a waiting

without expectation, an active preparation, anticipation against the backdrop of a horizon, but also exposure without horizon, and therefore an irreducible amalgam of desire and anguish, affirmation and fear, promise and threat . . . Anything but utopian, messianicity mandates that we interrupt the ordinary course of things, time and history here-now; it is inseparable from an affirmation of otherness and justice.' See also Agata Bielik-Robson, 'The Messiah and the Great Architect: On the Difference Between the Messianic and the Utopian', *Utopian Studies* 29(2) (2018): 133–58, see 136–40, where she attempts another interpretation of Bloch's typical utopianism in terms of a messianic hope. In my view the difference between both kinds of project lies in the question of the feasibility of history. Followers of utopianism think that the future is our task, even if the imagined future can never be achieved, as if it were the case of Bloch's utopianism, which puts the force of imagination in favour of the emancipatory revolutionary task.

66. Derrida, 'Marx & Sons', 253. And also, Jacques Derrida, *Specters of Marx: The State of the Debt, the Work of Mourning and the New International* (New York: Routledge, 1993), 74: 'Well, what remains irreducible to any deconstruction, what remains as undeconstructible as the possibility itself of deconstruction is, perhaps, a certain experience of the emancipatory promise; it is perhaps even the formality of a structural messianism, a messianism without religion, even a messianic without messianism, an idea of justice – which distinguish from law or right and even from human rights – and an idea of democracy – which we distinguish from its current concept and from its determined predicates today [permit me to refer here to "Force of Law" and The Other Heading].' Derrida insists that his use of the word messianism is free from religious connotations, yet it remains in the Abrahamic tradition. See Jacques Derrida, 'Force of Law: "The Mystical Foundation of Authority"', in *Deconstruction and the Possibility of Justice*, Drucilla Cornell and Michael Rosenfeld (eds) (New York: Routledge, 1992).

67. Derrida, *Specters of Marx*, 20: 'Not a time whose joinings are negated, broken, mistreated, dysfunctional, disadjusted, according to a dys – of negative opposition and dialectical disjunction, but a time without certain joining or determinable conjunction. What is said here about time is also valid, consequently and by the same token, for history, even if the latter can consist in repairing, with effects of conjuncture (and that is the world), the temporal disjoining. "The time is out of joint": time is disarticulated, dislocated, dislodged, time is run down, on the run and run down [*traqué et détraqué*], deranged, both out of order and mad. Time is off its hinges, time is off course, beside itself, disadjusted.'

68. Jacques Derrida and Bernard Stiegler, *Echographies of Television* (New York: Polity, 2002), 13: 'The most difficult thing is to justify, at

least provisionally, pedagogically, this attribute "messianic": at issue is an *a priori* messianic experience, but *a priori* exposed, in its very awaiting, to what will only be determined *a posteriori* by the event. Desert in the desert (one gesturing toward the other [faisant signe vers l'autre]), desert of a messianic without messianism, where, without doctrine and without religious dogma, this arid waiting devoid of any horizon retains from the grand messianisms of the book only the relation [le rapport] to the one who arrives [or the arrival, l'arrivant], who [or that] can arrive – or never arrive – but about whom [which] I ought, by definition, not to know anything in advance.' For Hent de Vries, this passage recapitulates the central question of the relationship between and co-implication of ideality and empiricity. De Vries, *Religion and Violence*, 393. In *Deconstruction in a Nutshell*, (New York: Fordham University Press, 1997), 3–28, 24, Derrida confesses that he oscillates between the two possibilities, that is, the messianic and the determined messianisms; and he thinks that it might be possible to think of both together.

69. So, Arthur Bradley meant in 'Derrida's God', 21–42. In his view, Derrida's theological turn can be seen as a 'transcendentalizing' of the *aporia* of origin in expressions such as immemorial promise, originary hospitality and messianic time.

70. Derrida and Stiegler, *Echographies*, 12: 'There is not even a horizon of expectation for this messianicity before messianism. If there were a horizon of expectation, if there were anticipation or programming, there would be neither event nor history. (A hypothesis which, paradoxically, and for the same reasons, can never be rationally excluded: it is practically impossible to think the absence of a horizon of expectation.) In order for there to be event and history, there must be a "come" that opens and addresses itself to someone, to someone else that cannot and must not determine in advance, not as subject, self, consciousness, nor even as animal, god, or person, man or woman, living or nonliving thing.' See also John D. Caputo, *The Prayers and Tears of Jacques Derrida: Religion without Religion* (Bloomington: Indiana University Press, 1997), 157.

71. See Mark Mason, 'Exploring the Impossible: Jacques Derrida, John Caputo and the Philosophy of History', *Rethinking History* 10(4) (2016): 501–22.

72. Bradley, 'Derrida's God', 36. In fact, he argues that this idea makes him avoid political committment. For her part, Bielik-Robson, 'The Messiah and the Great Architect', 135, interprets contemporary messianism as intrinsically modern and as an alternative to both: utopian thinking and a passive waiting for the Messiah or expecting providential care from God.

73. Derrida, *Specters of Marx*, 35.

74. Giorgio Agamben, *The Time that Remains: A Commentary on the Letter to the Romans* (Stanford, CA: Stanford University Press, 2005).
75. Agamben, *The Time that Remains*, 65.
76. Agamben, *The Time that Remains*, 112.
77. For a highly critical approach of this reading of Paul, see Britt, 'The Schmittian Messiah', 272: 'Though *The Time that Remains* is really about Paul and Schmitt. Agamben uses Benjamin as a methodological link between Paul and Schmitt, even while Agamben reads Benjamin through Schmitt.'
78. Jacques Derrida, 'Faith and Knowledge', in *Acts of Religion* (London: Routledge, 2002), 40–101.
79. Murchadha, *A Phenomenology*, 194.
80. I prefer not to talk about dogmas, because the word dogma has a particular meaning in the context of the churches, since Peterson wrote that there is not dogma outside the Church's pronouncements. Erik Peterson, 'The Church', in *Theological Tractates* (Stanford: Stanford University Press, 2011), 30–40. In fact, as Murchadha has recognised in *A Phenomenology*, 195: 'the genius of Christianity is to embody justice in a time and place, as the materialization of time in a figure who in claiming to speak on the authority of a non-worldly mission, by incarnating that mission, contaminates all things with an unworldly destiny and in so doing doubles experience: as reason and faith . . . Justice in this context is only the movement beyond the world, which is always also a movement toward the world.'
81. Norman Cohn, *Cosmos, Chaos and the World to Come* (New Haven, CT: Yale University Press, 1993).
82. Minois, *Histoire de l'avenir*, 17–23. See Wolfgang Hübner, 'The Culture of Astrology from Ancient to Renaissance', in *A Companion to Astrology in the Renaissance*, B. Dooley (ed.) (Leuven: Brill, 2014), 17–58; Franz Boll and Carl Bezold, *Le Stelle. Credenza e interpretazione* (Turin: Bollati Boringhieri, 2011); Steven van den Broecke, 'Astrology and Politics', in *A Companion to Astrology in the Renaissance*, B. Dooley (ed.) (Leuven: Brill, 2014), 193–232; Franz Cumont, *Astrology and Religion among the Greeks and Romans* (New York: Dover, 1960).
83. On Roman divination, see Minois, *Histoire de l'avenir*, 89–127. See also Álvaro d'Ors, 'Inauguratio', in *Ensayos de teoría política* (Pamplona: Eunsa, 1979), 79–94.
84. Georges Contenau, *La Divination chez les Assyriens et les Babyloniens* (Paris: Payot, 1940).
85. Taubes, *Occidental Eschatology*, reflects on the apocalypticisms, the chiliastic movements at the end of medieval period (Joachim da Fiore), and finally the development of modern historicism (from Hegel to Marx). In fact, Taubes attributes the awakening of the

messianic-historical spirit in some sectors of Christianity to the *rehebraisation* and, accordingly, *dehellenisation* of the Gospel; these movements reclaimed the messianic elements of Jewish revelation, which were operative in the Gospels themselves but were subsequently repressed by the catholisation of Christianism with its purified pneumatic-spiritual orientation, at least from Origen onwards. The most salient feature of this awakening is the dialectical sublation of the difference between the sacred and the profane, the spiritual and the secular, which completely transfigures the traditional discourse of the religious.

86. Alexander Regier, *Fracture and Fragmentation in British Romanticism* (Cambridge: Cambridge University Press, 2010), 79.
87. Judite Noze (ed.), *The Lisbon Earthquake of 1755: British Accounts* (Lisbon: British Historical Society of Portugal and Lisóptima, 1990), 36, 54; John Biddulph, *A Poem on the Earthquake of Lisbon* (London: W. Owen, 1755).
88. Theodore E. D. Braun and John B. Radner (eds), *The Lisbon Earthquake of 1755: Representations and Reactions* (Oxford: Voltaire Foundation, 2005); Horst Günther, *Das Erdbeben von Lissabon und die Erschütterung des aufgeklärten Europa* (Frankfurt am Main: Fischer, 2005); Grégory Quenet, *Les tremblements de terre aux XVIIe et XVIIIe siècles. La naissanced'un risqué* (Seyssel: Champ Vallon, 2005); Jean Mondot (ed.), *Lisbonne 1755. Un tremblement de terre et de ciel* (Bordeaux: Presses Universitaires de Bordeaux, 2005); Jan T. Kozák, Victor S. Moreira and David R. Oldroyd, *Iconography of the 1755 Lisbon Earthquake* (Prague: Geophysical Institute of the Academy of Sciences of the Czech Republic, 2005); Susan Neiman, *Evil in Modern Thought: An Alternative History of Philosophy* (Princeton: Princeton University Press, 2002); Theodor W. Adorno, *Negative Dialectics* (London: Routledge,1990), 361; Richard Hamblyn, 'Notes from the Underground: Lisbon after the Earthquake', *Romanticism* 14(2) (2008): 108–18; Wolfgang Breidert (ed.), *Die Erschütterung der vollkommenen Welt. Die Wirkung des Erdbebens von Lissabon im Spiegel europäischer Zeitgenossen* (Darmstadt: Wissenschaftliche Buchgesellschaft, 1994); Olaf Briese, *Die Macht der Metaphern. Blitz, Erdbeben, Kometen im Gefüge der Aufklärung* (Stuttgart: Metzler, 1998); Horst Günther, *Das Erdbeben von Lissabon erschüttert die Meinungen und setzt das Denken in Bewegung* (Berlin: Wagenbach, 1994); Andreas Schmidt, 'Wolken krachen, Berge zittern, und die ganze Erde weint'. *Zur kulturellen Vermittlung von Naturkatastrophen in Deutschland 1755 bis 1855* (Münster: Waxmann,1999); Harald Weinrich, 'Literaturgeschichte eines Weltereignisses. Das Erdbeben von Lissabon', *Literatur für Leser. Essays und Aufsätze zur Literaturwissenschaft* (Stuttgart: Kohlhammer, 1971), 64–76.

89. David Fergusson, *The Providence of God: A Polyphonic Approach* (Cambridge: Cambridge University Press, 2018), 110–66. In his view, the different positions on providence that the discussion about the earthquake generated at that time have to do with the relationship between God as ultimate cause and second causes. In his view, 'Lisbon proved a hinge event in uncoupling moral and natural evil. Catastrophes could no longer be viewed as divine acts expressing a moral intention such as retribution.' 130.
90. Russell Dynes, 'The Dialogue between Voltaire and Rousseau on the Lisbon Earthquake: The Emergence of a Social Science View', *International Journal of Mass Emergencies and Disasters* 18(1) (2000): 97–115. See also the discussion in Jonathan Israel, *The Democratic Enlightenment: Philosophy, Revolution and Human Rights 1750–1790* (Oxford: Oxford University Press, 2011), 41–55.
91. See Luiz Felipe Baêta Neves, 'Profetismo e Iluminismo no Terremoto de Lisboa de 1755', *Revista Convergência Lusiada* 24 (2007): 145–56.
92. For an account of this position in Spain, see Agustín Udías, 'Earthquakes as God's Punishment in 17th- and 18th-century Spain', in M. Kölbl-Ebert (ed.), *Geology and Religion: A History of Harmony and Hostility* (London: Geological Society, 2009), 41–8.
93. João de Castro, *Paráfrase e Concordância de Algumas Profecías de Bandarra*, João Carlos Gonçalves Serafim (ed.) (Porto: University of Porto Press, 2018). In this Paraphrase, for the first time, an edition is made of the pieces attributed to the notorious cobbler from Beira, António Gonçalves Annes Bandarra. The inquisitorial process in which the silence of the poet and the censorship of his verses was ordered had already taken place sixty-two years before (1541) the first publication of this text. See also Renato Samuel Lima, *Revolta e esperança. A Guerra do Contestado e o messianismo portugués* (Lisbon: Gramma, 2018).
94. John Wesley, *Serious Thoughts Occasioned by the Late Earthquake at Lisbon, 1755*, in *The Works of John Wesley, vol. II: Thoughts, Addresses, Prayers, Letters* (Grand Rapids, MI: Baker Books, 1996). See on Wesley also Fergusson, *The Providence of God*, 126–8.
95. His tradition was that of a radical Protestant with an anti-Catholic bias. For a discussion of Wesley's position, see Susan Bassnett, 'Seismic Aftershocks: Responses to the Great Lisbon Earthquake of 1755', in *Sites of Exchange: European Crossroads and Faultlines*, Maurizio Ascari and Adriana Corrado (eds) (Amsterdam: Rodopi, 2006), 177–87. She quotes two books that were important in England for knowledge of the event: Thomas Dawning Kendrick, *The Lisbon Earthquake* (London: Methuen, 1956) and Rose Macaulay, *They Went to Portugal* (London: Cape, 1946).
96. Francis H. Berick and John Couch, *The Fulfilment of Prophecy, Or, A Prophetic History of the World, Including a Few Suggestions on the*

Probable Termini of the Chronological Periods written (Lowell: S. J. Varney, 1852), 95.
97. Neves, 'Profetismo e Iluminismo', 151.
98. Johann Wolfgang von Goethe, *From My Life: Poetry and Truth*, trans. Eithne Wilkins and Ernst Kaiser (Princeton: Princeton University Press, 1994), 34; Hans Blumenberg, *Begriffe in Geschichten* (Frankfurt am Main: Suhrkamp, 1998), 230–5. Blumenberg writes about Goethe's changing reception and conceptualisation of the disaster. For the significance of the catastrophe in German literature as a whole, see Karl-Heinz Bohrer, *Nach der Natur. Über Politik und Ästhetik* (Munich: Hanser, 1988), 133–61.
99. For a reflection on the sublime apropos of the Lisbon earthquake, see Regier, *Fracture and Fragmentation in British Romanticism*. Before him, Gene Ray, 'Reading the Lisbon Earthquake: Adorno, Lyotard, and the Contemporary Sublime', *Yale Journal of Criticism* 17(1) (2004): 1–18. See also Walter Benjamin, 'The Lisbon Earthquake', in *Selected Writings*, vol. 2, Michael W. Jennings, Howard Eiland and Gary Smith (eds) (Cambridge, MA: Harvard University Press, 1999), 536–40.

Chapter 3

Oath or the Given Word

> Et nous ne pouvons rien donner de plus, ni de plus haut, que notre parole, car elle est ce en quoi nous nous donnons nous-mêmes.[1]

It is because of their potency in generating obligations that oaths are at the heart of the constitution of political communities. The oath is one of those concepts that have undergone numerous theological–political transfers, to which Carl Schmitt referred when talking about political theology. Schmitt himself thought that the oath will always remain a necessary institution, no matter how much it might seem to have disappeared from public life: whatever the formula, it ensures internal disposition, so that the institutions of the modern state are not abused and their very foundations destroyed.[2] In fact, when written constitutions emerge, legislatures seek to institute and sanction their identity through solemn declarations, for example, by appealing to God or some other moral or ideological formula. Paolo Prodi, following Schmitt's theological–political hypothesis, declares that the oath is the basis of the political covenant in Western societies.[3] Prodi's main theological–political argument is that the modern state has taken the place of God as the absolute witness of every oath as a result of the secularisation process. Hence, the oath has become a prerogative of sovereignty.[4]

The oath, as a mutual promise between two or more persons to trust each other's word under the sight of the 'immortal God', can be understood as a meta-political guarantor of the political bond. Consequently, it is possible to think as Prodi does, that the decline of the oath to the status of a solely secular commitment, which can be broken at any time, carries with it the crisis of the very idea of political community.⁵ In contrast to this catastrophist thesis, Aroney still perceives that oaths of office and oaths of allegiance have marked the path of the authority of the modern state and continue to do so until today. In fact, he argues, that we can still find the theological–political paradox at the core of the state's institutional proceedings and arrangements. On the one hand, oaths seek to guarantee the performance of official duties; on the other hand, they subject the content of those duties to another *potestas* external to that of the state, that of God. The resolution of this contradiction has been developed by smoothing over the ritual of the gesture of oath-taking: acceptance of affirmations instead of oaths, of statutory declarations instead of sworn affidavits, of different kinds of qualified witnesses depending on the personal credo of the person who swears the oath. But still we keep a gesture that comes from an act of religion.⁶ In Dean's formulation, the oath presents a 'political-theological case'.⁷

The Sacred–Civil Character of Oaths

This dual valence of the sacred and the profane, attested not only by constitutionalists, but also by historians, was already present in Ancient Greece and Rome.⁸ In ancient political communities, legal and community bonds were at the same time religious and civil acts; for example, pronouncements on laws were ritual actions.⁹ In Rome, the force of the *iuramentum* was essential for the community and for the *ius*. *Iurare* – if we accept the explanation of Benveniste, who based his opinion on Plautus' and Pliny's use of the word – consisted of repeating a given formula, while touching a sacred object. This sacred object was supposed to have the power to ensure fulfilment of what was being promised, thus preventing perjury. In this rite, the commitment itself was called *sacramentum* – a kind of consecration to the gods through words – and *iurare* was simply the act of repeating the formula.¹⁰ An oath was not taken using words of any kind – such as might be used in a simple statement – but words that pointed to an act of force carried out by a person and recognised by society as appropriate. Part of this force derived from Iovis-Iupiter, the god who punished perjury. The oath that ensured the efficacy of the word – or the connection of a pronounced word with an invoked power, as Benveniste explains¹¹ – had a close relationship with religion. The force of oaths had nothing to do with magic; it derived from faith in Jupiter (*fides deorum*).¹²

The Middle Ages inherited this tradition and were full of different kinds of private and public oaths, often in conflict with one another.[13] It is not valid to oppose the theocratical–monarchical vision of the Middle Ages – which arose from sacral kingship – to early modern constitutionalism – which evolved from the feudal system of oaths – since both paths were already active at the same time in the Middle Ages.[14] In fact, different kinds of civil associations emerge from oaths: for example, the collective oath of the *coniuratio*, the electoral bodies and the universities, which in the Middle Ages were sworn societies. At that time, the prevailing opinion was that the stability of promises and oaths made economic growth and the security of the city possible. Not in vain, as history moved forward, did the sovereign power try to take control over the validity of oaths in order to safeguard the possession of power. However, the sovereign power achieved this only with difficulty, once the Church had declared the oath sacramental character; this can be verified from the second century onwards.[15] Indeed, in the Middle Ages the Church also fought for control over the form and validity of the oaths that bound the will of men.

In early modernity, the extent of the use and type of oaths was almost as wide as that of the Middle Ages: oaths of coronation, oaths of allegiance, vows, oaths of passage, oaths of office, oaths of succession, oaths of supremacy, oaths of association and so on. From the Reformation, trust was severely compromised by the perceived need to impose uniformities of religious practice owing to the possible insincerity of those forced to comply. It was the case, for example, in the Church of England with the practice of the Oath of Allegiance of 1606.[16] In early modernity, the covenant also produced sovereignty and the system of law, as we can see in the writings of Hobbes and Locke. Both dedicate a number of pages to elucidate the role of oaths in the generation of the commonwealth. In the case of Hobbes, the oath need only be implicit.[17] In fact, since Hobbes was determined to make the state an absolute power and, in the process, eliminate ecclesiastical jurisdiction by merging it with civil jurisdiction, he argued that an oath adds nothing to obligations that already exist and have been generated by his second law of nature. However, John Locke thought that an explicit oath was required in order to found a commonwealth.[18] Arguing in favour of the separation of jurisdictions, Locke saw in atheism a threat to the civil state: since atheists lack the faith necessary to swear oaths, they cannot participate in the constitution of the civil state. Thus, in his view, to eliminate God even in one's own thoughts undermines everything.[19]

Rousseau again merges both spheres and declares a civil religion, to whose jurisdiction oaths belong.[20] Also Schmitt, speaking about the conventional nature of any constitution, quotes Ferdinand Lassalle and states with him: 'A constitution is a pact, affirmed by oath, between king and people that establishes the fundamental principles of law-making and government in a country.'[21]

The presence of oaths in the historical development of the West expresses the conviction that the structure of society implies loyalty to the given word, the supreme example of which is that of God's promise. The oath is taken before men, as it seeks to confirm before them the truth of what is asserted or to give the assertion greater force as a guarantee of the fulfilment of a promise.

Oaths can take very different forms, as can be seen in the great variety of concrete formulas designed to give one's word throughout history. However, oaths are usually performed and accompanied by a number of gestures and in the presence of a divinity. Thanks to this special witness, who guarantees one's truthfulness, whoever commits perjury is execrated. In fact, the *execratio* that is produced by perjury and other crimes exposes the offender to divine revenge (*sacer esto*) to the extent of being precluded from human protection and being directly punished by the gods. The punishment of a god who sees everything, the past, the present and even the darkest thoughts, is the guarantee of truthfulness.

The Divine Witness

In monotheistic theological traditions, God's word alone is seen to be stable and effective, making Him an indispensable witness to the most important commitments. God is the ultimate force behind every oath, since He is the only one whose word is always effective (Isaiah 45:23). Other oaths, those that men can pronounce, can fail. Only God has the exclusivity of the absolute efficacy of His word not only in the present, but also in the future.[22] It is no coincidence that oath in Hebrew means a promise. The oath reinforced God's promises to his people (Exodus 33:1; Deuteronomy 6:18, 7:8; Psalm 132:11), established boundaries for human speech and set guidelines for human conduct (Numbers 30:1; Deuteronomy 23:21). In the New Testament, God is also often represented as taking an oath (Hebrews 6:13–18), as did Christ (Matthew 26:64) and Paul (Romans 9:1; Galatians 1:20; Philippians 1:8).

In fact, for the Jews of the Old Testament, the oath was the most solemn commitment that anyone could make. It was even an act of worship, a monotheist profession of the faith to such an extent that to take an oath by a strange divinity was considered idolatry.[23] Israel's covenant with God includes the provision that all oaths must be pronounced in the name of God, since they are protected by Him through His alliance with Israel. Israel ratified its treaties by oaths (Joshua 9:15, 9:18, 9:20), and the writer of Ecclesiastes reminded his readers that it is better not to make a vow than to make a vow and not keep it (Ecclesiastes 5:4–5).[24]

One of these important commitments for the Jews was the Covenant of Sinai, through which the nation gained its identity and its history, both its past as a people redeemed from slavery and its future, which is given by the promise of becoming ministers of the Lord (Exodus 19:6). The covenant is enacted over and over again through the ethical, ritual and political ceremonials of the community.[25] The various acts and rituals performed in the making of a covenant usually included an oath to underscore its binding character. In fact, the parties made oaths to enforce awareness that a violator of the covenant would suffer the same fate as the sacrificed animal. Using God's name in an oath appeals directly to His involvement regarding testimony and establishes Him as the supreme enforcer and judge.

God's given word – whether in the form of sacred language, speech and writing or in an incarnate form through Christ – is the condition of possibility of every faithfully given word. However, and this is a disruptive gesture in the New Testament, we find the assertion of Christ commanding us not to swear. Jesus' injunction, 'swear not at all',[26] seems to indicate that the proper state of Christians requires no oaths: when evil is expelled from among them, every yes and no will be as decisive as an oath and every promise as binding as an oath.[27] Language itself suffices as an oath.

This completely new approach to oaths is inaugurated by Christianity. Is it really a secularisation as Prodi has judged it? Or, is it rather a question of not entrusting the performance of our oaths to an exceptional or divine witness, but to the truthfulness and faithfulness implicit in our own saying? No one has seen this evolution of the oath with the arrival of Christ as well as Michel Foucault. Foucault argues that while discouraging oaths, Christianity accelerated a subjectivation process that required truth to be manifested in subjectivity and the verification of the self in order to be saved and free.[28]

In fact, he identified that the production of the truth of and by the subject began to be a central question for society in early

Christianity. Indeed, the effective possibility of separating the inner and outer spheres of the self in oaths, such as baptism, made false conversion possible. As Foucault asserts, constructing identities was not a philosophical problem in the third century; instead, the problem lay in uncertain conversion. How then is the unity of both spheres of human action ensured? How could truthful identity be promoted?[29] New rituals of veridiction beyond oaths succeeded in internalising the divine witness.

The Testimonial and Promissory Aspects of Oaths

Oaths are temporally marked. In fact, oaths lend verification to the given word, be it about the past or about the future. If the oath is about the past, its content is usually a testimony. If it is about the future, the oath takes the form of a reinforced promise articulated as a vow, an alliance or a covenant. Because of this double temporal reference, Thomas Aquinas already distinguished between *juramentum assertorium* and *juramentum promissorium*.[30]

In fact, oaths are usually taken in circumstances in which testimonies must be given. To act as a witness in a trial is the typical case. In these cases, the validity of the judgement rests on the truth of certain statements. And this truth must be told by individuals who take part in the proceedings only as bearers of truth. The truth about something has to be uttered by someone. Apparently, the subject who swears seems not to be of significance. Not only that, but it is even important that the swearer is not related to the case in which he is a witness. In fact, in trials, testimony must come from subjects who are not parties in the case itself, but who were its mere spectators. What is required of them is simply their 'objective' knowledge about something that they have seen or heard: a basic knowledge that does not require reflection; a knowledge, however, that would otherwise not be known. For that reason, the witness cannot be anyone, but only this particular person who was present in that particular circumstance. What constitutes someone as a witness is their particular position as having a particular knowledge. The constitution of a witness is therefore in some way circumstantial and at the same time mandatory. However, to be compelled to 'tell the truth', or what the witness considers to be the truth, is a complete interior disposition of the subject who has to give their testimony. Since oaths are used to reinforce the internal disposition to tell the truth, they are usually taken at the beginning of these processes. Oaths are, in this context, a judicial procedure that underscores the importance of telling the truth 'as it is' in a given case, that is, of telling the truth when justice has to be done. Given their importance, in these cases, the trial witness is placed explicitly in the sight of the absolute witness – God or a divine object. If a person swears an oath falsely, he risks falling foul of the wrath of the gods. In the case of oaths, there is no reversion without malediction.[31] However, this is neither certain nor automatic; and if there is punishment, its time and form remain shrouded until the last moment. In fact, the *execratio* produced by perjury exposes the wrongdoer to divine vengeance (*sacer esto*) and also deprives him or her of civil protection.[32] So, as Foucault asserts, the risks involved in making a false oath are incommensurable.[33]

If oaths are an important part of judicial procedure, they are no less important as a guarantee of promises. As Agamben points out, Cicero realised that the faithfulness established in promissory oaths does not only depend on religiosity, but mainly on the institution of *fides*.[34] Whoever violates the oath, violates trust and this violence is the strongest attack on society.[35] Faithfulness operates as a temporal dimension, which looks into the future and creates rights and duties. For that reason, apart from the testimonial aspect of some oaths, we have the promissory aspect of others. In fact, every alliance or covenant binds its subjects to some future obligations. However, it is never possible to ensure the performance of a promissory oath. Promises exclude what is automatically or naturally given, for their object can only be something that will not occur without some positive form of commitment. The promise has its own conditions of possibility, the most important of which is that what it aims to obtain is made possible by the sole act of promising. Which is at the same time almost its condition of impossibility.

As Chrétien says: 'the promise carries in its heart a noetic darkness that is essential to it. Only prophecy carries clarity.'[36] In fact, prophecy ensures a future that is in a way independent of the prophet or that transcends his action. A prophecy offers a secured future, but a promise does not. The unexpected can make us unable to fulfil our promises, since we cannot appropriate the future. And, nevertheless, our approach to the future can only be in the form of a promise. In this sense, we can say that to make a promise or to swear a promissory oath is a 'possibility within the impossible', in Chrétien's words.[37] For that reason, Derrida can say that perjury is the other face of oath. In a finite world nobody can give their word as such regarding the future, because such a word cannot be completely owned.[38] However, there is an immemorial promise woven from the threads of language. Language opposes resistance to the person who uses it. We are tied to the language we have inherited, insofar as we want to use it meaningfully; in fact, that inheritance protects the language against manipulation. For Derrida, language has the character of an absolute past: 'Having come from the past, language before language, a past that was never present and yet remains unforgettable.'[39] Misunderstandings are possible, but provoking them involves a kind of perjury in a language that 'having come from the past' has the structure of the promise. Attack on language is the first type of perjury, says Derrida. And vice versa, loyalty to the meanings embodied in language is what makes swearing possible. Hence, even if God were not invoked, He is already present in the very possibilities offered by language.

In his reading of Shylock's oath in the *Merchant of Venice*, Derrida raises this question: is it possible to countersign one's own act of faith by swearing on what one has already sworn? 'When I swear, I swear in a language that no human language has the power to make me abjure, to disrupt, that is to say, to make me perjure myself. The oath passes through language, but it passes beyond human language.'[40] God is ceaselessly invoked in every human oath through the structure of language. A strange and complex relationship occurs between this kind of pronouncement, language and the divine, which makes every oath sacred.[41]

Not only language but also the law has the structure of a sworn promise.[42] Every legal system is based on the promise to impose a penalty on whoever commits a crime. Where crime still retains a moral connotation, that is, when a wrong has been committed, a harm has been done. When this is lost sight of, the law is functionalised, becoming a technical means of state power devoid of the two characteristics of the oath: truthfulness and faithfulness. Schmitt was obsessed with the famous exclamation, 'Be silent, theologians! *Silete theologi!*,' which was launched at the beginning of the modern state era by an international lawyer against theologians of Catholic and Protestant confessions.[43] Schmitt describes the path of legal science over the last two centuries as the development of this cry.[44] The substitution of divine compromises, such as the respect for the given word, by the utilitarian decision of the state resulted in legal positivism: the law as a command of the sovereign. In the twentieth century, another step was taken, which Schmitt called the 'motorization of the law', through which the legislation process and its reform became easy and fast: the word given through the law could rapidly change if driven by political interests of any kind.

The last step emerged with liberal economism, under which the law became an elastic instrument that can be formed or deformed depending on all kinds of economic interest. A moralised natural law, as well as general propositions within a theory of values, were also attempts to overcome the motorisation of the law that legal positivism entails. Ultimately, the consequence of the loss of theological legitimation or, we can say, the impossibility of swearing or making an oath endure, is that the law has ceased to be a promise and has become a means to revolution.[45]

Certainly, after swearing an oath or making a promise, our most important political commitment is to commit it to memory. Registering, archiving, retaining, tracing are crucial actions which ensure the memory of a political community. They constitute a referential resistance as much to forgetfulness as to discursive re-appropriation.[46] In fact, if promises have to endure over generations, they have to be somehow inscribed or scripted and accompanied by oaths or solemn declarations that imply some kind of ritual.

Oaths as Rituals of Veridiction

Oaths are a kind of rite.[47] They cannot be produced as the result of a set of practices. Moreover, they must be represented or depicted by means of symbols, analogies or metonymies. Buc defines a ritual act, inasmuch as it can be deduced from the European medieval matrix, as the manifestation of a superior reality, a kind of divinity, which functions as an archetype for a historical action, whether represented by God's kingdom, the state or the law.[48]

The fact that oaths are normally oral is their central characteristic, even if the verbal expression is also usually accompanied by other gestures and by a narrative.[49] Their recording in writing always has a secondary role, mainly that of confirming the public consequences the oath may have, since the given word is not just a word, but a word addressed to someone. Characteristic of the ritual action is a formal over-determination. This means that its formal register is not a method aimed at achieving a result following technical rules. On the contrary, this over-determined formal aspect aims to symbolise the meaning of the action and it is not a particular means to achieve a specific result. There is no displaced end outside the self-referred operation of the ritual. The end of the ritual is its performance, which embodies the full meaning of the actions that will follow after the new context has been established. The efficacy of the ritual falls on to the subject that carries it out.

It transforms the subject, establishing a new context. For this reason, we say that oaths have a foundational character opposed to the functionality of the ordinary actions.

The specifically ritual character of oaths shows the impossibility for the unconditional to be operationalised. The unconditional – in this case, the word that has to be kept – cannot become an end that must be achieved, but is the meaning implicit in the word that will be given thereafter. Ritual forms have specific sense when technical forms cannot be applied to achieve a particular goal. They are the paradigm of the performative action, in which intention and meaning coincide insofar as language and gestures create the reality they depict.[50] The symbolic representation announces that something has changed in an irreversible way. Indeed, the veracity of those kinds of action lies in their transference to reality. In addition, oaths have a moral content.[51] The ritual character of the action does not annul the logos and this is an important difference with respect to magic.

The consideration of the oath as a sacred ritual in the strong sense carries within it the original *rapprochement* between the oath and the sacrament, which will be dealt with in the last section of this chapter. However, there are other types of action with similar characteristics to those of the ritual, but which are completely civil, as is the case of ceremonies or ceremonials. The obsession with replacing ritual by ceremonial actions dates back to the Lutheran Reformation.[52] The principal difference between ritual and ceremonial happens when the latter abandons any mystical element and acquires a merely pragmatic and political dimension. What is at stake, therefore, in the serious case of the oath, is the limit to the functionalisation of action, that is, the political utilitarianism of which lies and falsehood are always a channel.

Truth in the Form of Subjectivity as Substitutive Oath

The consistence of human testimonies and promises cannot be divine; but, paradoxically, if men wish to found a community, the human gesture of giving the word must be as stable as are divine oaths. God alone is absolutely truthful and faithful: without the archetypical example of His promise, that is, without the experience of the absolute stability and effectivity of His word, the very possibility of human testimonies or promises is at stake. In fact, as Derrida points out, the name of God designates the absolute identity and synchrony between the promise made and the promise verified.⁵³ Hence, to take an oath is impossible, as we have heard from Chrétien, but it must, however, be possible, according to Derrida.⁵⁴ Such is the problematical nature of human oaths: they are human, but they are marked by the divine. Oaths are a visible sign of the possible eruption of the divine in the midst of the established social order.⁵⁵

The oath, which traditionally had been necessary to ensure the inner disposition of the one giving the word, gives way, as a consequence of the mandatory doctrine of Christianity of not swearing, to other forms of verification of subjectivity that also seek to ensure that inner disposition. In the absence of the divine witness, the gesture of giving one's word has no other authority than that which we ourselves have, no other guarantee than what we are and what we have proved to be.

As mentioned, it was Foucault who placed most emphasis on the new forms of rituals of veridiction introduced by Christianity.⁵⁶ Indeed, Foucault points out two forms of the theological–political transfer of the truth of the word given in the oath under the divine gaze to more or less socially stipulated procedures of attesting the inhabitation of truth in subjectivity: on the one hand, there is confession, which is a routine device of veridiction; on the other hand, there is parrhesia, the exceptional example of which is martyrdom, that is, an exceptional ritual of veridiction for extreme cases in which one's own life is at stake. The two rituals of veridiction seem to be either alternatives to the oath, or even conditions of possibility for the sincerity of an oath. Both are at the root of the human possibility of not swearing falsely. Both represent a double value of truthfulness. Both are somehow permeated by the theopolitical mixture.

In Foucault's view, these new rituals of veridiction have resulted in a new form of truthful and faithful subjectivity constitutive of the West; among other consequences of the political transference it embodies, this new form of subjectivity made the constitution of the Western criminal legal system possible.

Foucault defines confession in *Mal faire, dire vrai* as 'a verbal act by which the subject, in an affirmation of what he is, binds himself to this truth, places himself in a relationship of dependence with regard to others and at the same time modifies the relationship that he has with himself'.⁵⁷ Confession is a procedure of *alèthurgie*, that is, a ritual which acts upon the subject.⁵⁸ Foucault calls the manifestation of truth by means of these procedures 'veridiction'. This process began to be a requirement for baptism in early Christianity.

For this reason, Foucault speaks of a *'régime de vérité'*.⁵⁹ A truth regime involves that which (*ce que*) obliges the individual to a certain number of acts of truth. And this regime is necessary because, '*il n'est pas vrai que la vérité ne contraigne pas que par le vrai.*'⁶⁰ It is possible to speak falsely once and again.⁶¹ This possibility constitutes veridiction as a duty and allows for the construction of a *dispositif* consisting of the repetition of penance. In fact, at the very moment when Christianity first faced the risk of false conversions, it was realised that the purely external formality of the oath was insufficient to produce truthfulness. Hence, new rituals of veridiction were required that would prepare the subject for that sacrament–oath, which is baptism. Only a truthful subject can 'give his word' in a way that compromises his future in the sight of God.

Foucault claims that the reiterated practice of confession brings with it a process of subjectification constituted by the relationship between the manifestation of the truth about oneself and the suppression of evil. To prove this thesis, Foucault explores early Christian literature, which greatly influenced medieval writers. Over time the ancient *exomologein* – a 'public confession', or public acknowledgement of one's status as a sinner – which took place before baptism, became auricular and private and took the form of *exagoreusis*, bringing penance closer to juridification.⁶²

As time went by, the relationship between the manifestation of individual truth and the remission and reduction of sins was organised in Christianity around three practices: baptism, penance (ecclesiastical or canonical) and the *dispositif* of examination–direction of conscience. All of them include acts of faith and acts of confession, which are not completely independent since practices of truth depend on the assimilation of the truths of the faith and vice versa.⁶³ In Christianity, confession is the procedure thanks to which the subject incorporates faith in his practices, the self becomes conscious of his relationship with that truth, and consequently can be tested by an ongoing community of truth. Confession and spiritual direction produce truthfulness. The truth of the self is the price one has to pay in order to enter into any kind of loyalty.

In Foucault's opinion, two historical facts helped confession to become a recurrent penance, namely, the monastic rule that aimed to typify faults and the system of Germanic law that interpreted the sanction of faults as an absolution from them. And there is an analogy between the two elements to the extent that for Foucault the major theological–political imprint of Christianity is the transference of an economy of salvation – that is, a canonical system with penalties for every fault – to a juridical system of civil penalties.[64] The modern state in fact employs a similar truth regime in order to enable governmentality.

Taking the argument to the extreme, Foucault says that the imperative 'tell me who you are', which originated in Christianity, is the fundamental imperative of Western civilisation;[65] a statement which is analogical to that of Prodi, 'the oath is the basis of the political covenant in Western societies'.[66] Foucault adds that in the nineteenth century a point of diffraction emerges that was to change the whole juridical system: when confessions seemed deficient or insufficient, they were replaced by or reinforced with something else. That other process that replaced the subject's self-veridiction was psychiatric or criminal examination of concrete cases; this process covered the possible gaps, filled in the deficiencies of information and, above all, was objective.[67] A regime of transparency and surveillance appears and replaces confession: a purely positive ideal of truth immanent to the very event that is happening. Indeed, as Foucault himself points out, there is a dispersion of regimes of veridiction in our societies.[68] The truth is 'revealed' by the access to data, by surveillance cameras, without the need for a confession. However, this production of truth does not resolve the problem of the truthfulness of the subject as a condition for commitment.

With these questions in mind, Foucault returns to Ancient Greece to analyse another form of veridiction that does not conclude in a penal system or in a kind of pastoral or sovereign power; for that reason, it seems to function as the exception to the rule: parrhesia. In fact, parrhesia 'does not produce a codified effect; it opens up an unspecified risk'.[69] Undertaking a genealogy of *parrhesia* – raging from the public orator, through the prince's counsellor and the minister of the modern state up to the revolutionary – Foucault tries to bring into play one of the practices of truth-telling that also implies a mode of philosophical subjectivation and veridiction, that is, the constitution of a truthful subject. The practice called parrhesia is 'having the courage to tell the truth without concealing anything and regardless of the dangers this involves'.[70] Parrhesia is also an *aléthurgie*, which reveals truth in the form of subjectivity, in such a way that it is interpreted as an irruption in the context in which it takes place. In this case, the production of the truth about the subject does not happen in privacy, but publicly, contrasting the subject's own truth with the public truth regime; this represents, in Foucault's words, 'the political dramatics of true discourse'.[71]

Parrhesia puts to the test one's own life and that of the other by a word of truth. In fact, not only does the parrhesiast tell the truth, but, what is more, this truth must really be his personal position. The truthful man is he in whom the obligation to tell the truth is at the same time an exercise of freedom and courage; as such, they also demand the interlocutor's courage in agreeing to accept the unpleasant truth that he hears.[72] This description presupposes that the parrhesiast's discourse contrasts to the prevalent regime of discourses at a given historical moment. This is the main difference between this kind of veridiction and that of confession. Indeed, the expressed truth in parrhesia is not regulated by a 'regime of truth'. The mere possibility of the figure of the parrhesiast contradicts the usual Foucaultian parameters of the co-implication between discourses and epistemological regimes.[73] From what historical, epistemological and discursive conditions do the parrhesiast's manifestations of truth come? How is it possible that the parrhesiast remains independent from the compelling character of the truth regime in which he is living? Is this figure an exception in the epistemological regime? Finally, is it possible to pronounce a 'pure truth on the subject', which is not committed to an aspiration to power, as the pronouncement of the parrhesiast seems to be? In the end, is philosophical life the only possibility to escape power? Is the parrhesiast the only subject capable of swearing without any utilitarian motive? All these questions arise when we contemplate the figure of the parrhesiast, the only subject who is personally confronted with truth beyond any kind of *dispositif*. Philosophical life transforms the subject's own life and dangerously aspires to transform and disturb the life of others. The philosophical subject is not let establish any *dispositif*, as occurs in the case of the confessing subject. There is no power attached to the veridiction operated by him, nor an announced truth, but rather a disturbance of the political power, a permanent criticism of the world caused by the transference of sovereignty to the parrhesiastic subject.[74] The parrhesiast points out the subversive nature of truthfulness as much as the oaths taken in secret by a group to carry out an illegal act together.[75] For Foucault, the paradigmatic figure of the parrhesiast is the cynic.[76] Foucault is well aware of the two kinds of cynic who appear in history: one being an 'ostentatious, noisy, and aggressive cynicism which denies the laws, traditions, and rules'; and the other, 'measured, thoughtful, well-bred, discreet, honest, and really austere cynicism'.[77] Christian asceticism is for him a religious descendant of the cynics.[78] In fact, Christianity has produced some parrhesiastic figures such as the monk, the preacher and above all the martyr, who assumes the greatest risk. The martyr is the epitome of the pahrresiast, because he accepts death by giving public testimony about the truth concerning another world in which he will be saved while relativising his own world.[79] The two types of veridiction, confession and parrhesia, come together in the martyr's sacrifice; hence, they become completely trustful. Their actions imply a 'pact of frankness'. In fact, an important difference between martyrs and other kinds of parrhesiasts is the appearance of the transcendent axis.[80] The revolutionary is a similar figure in modern times, but Foucault is reluctant to include him as another example of a parrhesiast.[81]

By describing the two veridiction rituals of confession and parrhesia, Foucault gives us a hint of what Victor Turner calls the 'liminal' practices of society.[82] The possibility of constituting a stable community through the stability of the word given by verifiable subjects implies at the same time the possibility of the deconstitution of the community by those same subjects. Absolutely verifiable subjects can always act in one direction or the other. Martyrs and parrhesiasts are the exception that ensures the rule. The existence of subjects who can give their word makes the community possible, while at the same time puts it at risk.

Theopolitical Figurations of Oath: The Case of the Transferences between Oath and Sacrament

The vocabulary of the Church was formed in the three first centuries after Christ. The fact that in the second century the vocabulary of Christian theology appropriates the meaning of 'sacramentum', meaning mainly 'oath', shows in a paradigmatic historical case the double theological and political valence of the oath, which allows for the transference of meaning from the juridical to the theological realm.[83] In Prodi's opinion, this became possible through the confluence of different traditions: the biblical, the classical and traditional Germanic customs such as *Treue* (fidelity).[84] After that appropriation by the Church, there was a complete 'sacralization of the oath' in the Middle Ages, even though oaths had always been somehow related to the sacral realm in ancient tradition.[85]

Originally, in the Roman juridical context, *sacramentum* means the money deposited by the parties in a suit, either because the sum was deposited by the losing party and used for a religious purpose, or, more likely, because it was deposited in a sacred place.

It was called *sacramentum* because to violate what one had solemnly promised was perfidy, since the money in that context was a *sacro*, as Mommsen confirms.[86] The word later came to mean any civil suit or process, particularly the vindicatory procedure of ownership. It was a part of the two kinds of procedural action (*legis actionis*): *sacramentum in re*, which had the effect of an appropriation of things; and *manus iniectio*, which had the effect of an appropriation for an unpaid debt. Each of these procedures was completely typified.[87]

But there is another Roman meaning of *sacramentum* which particularly influenced Christian vocabulary and theological reflection: in the Roman Empire, *sacramentum* also referred to the preliminary oath taken by newly enlisted troops. This latter was voluntary until after the Second Punic War (218–201 BC), when the military tribune required it. After the Augustan age (27 BC–14 AD), *sacramentum* just means 'any oath, solemn obligation or sacred engagement'.[88] As Foster has noted, the idea of sacredness persists in both meanings – the military use does not supersede the juridical – and the implication throughout is that there is something like a divine sanction or concern with a person's actions.[89] Émile Backer notes that 'sacrament' and 'military oath' were recognised as equivalents in North Africa before Tertullian, and were in common usage by Christians as early as the second century.

Indeed, the concept of sacrament appears in early theological reflection as signifying the *sacramentum militiae* (oath of allegiance), as it was considered in the Roman–Italic context.[90] This kind of oath transforms the legal status of the person who pronounces it. The military oath put the soldier under the power of his commander and tied him to military law. Through this ceremony the soldier's previous ties with other kinds of community were neutralised and he no longer had civil status.[91]

How is it possible that this kind of relationship could exist between military and Christian vocabulary, given that Jesus' preaching – as recorded in the New Testament – on the duty to renounce the practice and actions of violence showed his rejection of any violent resistance to evil? How is it possible that juridical and military meanings would make their way into the Christian theological vocabulary?[92] The military metaphor found no home in the Eastern Church, as we can see from the example of Clement of Alexandria or Origen, but it was widely disseminated in the Latin Church from Tertullian onwards.[93] He affirmed that baptism excluded the commitment acquired through a 'military oath', and in emphasising this exclusion, he confirmed the similarity of the two kinds of commitment. Indeed, Tertullian was responsible for the coinage of 'sacrament' as a specifically religious word, and of the transference of meaning from '*sacramentum*' as 'military oath' to mystery.⁹⁴

What happened in the second century is of significance for the subsequent development of the concept and practice of the oath, which generated two different rituals of veridiction: oaths and sacraments. As Backer asserts, from a total of 134 examples of the use of the word 'sacrament' in Tertullian's work, 84 refer to oath and 50 to mystery.⁹⁵ Neither meaning seems to derive from the other. They simply enter into the Christian vocabulary from different sources; in any case, they constitute a symbolic reality that fuses multiple meanings. As recent writers have asserted, Tertullian does not ordinarily quote from the various Latin versions of the Bible, but translates directly from a Greek text.⁹⁶ Nevertheless, von Soden, who does not believe that Tertullian had access to any Latin version of the New Testament, still virtually admits that at least a standard Latin translation of part of the Gospels was in use in Tertullian's time.⁹⁷ The fact is that in the translations of the Bible prior to Jerome (late fourth century), the word μυστήριον (the only word that appeared in the Septuagint) was already rendered as *sacramentum*.⁹⁸

The two relevant temporal aspects of an oath, the *testimonial* that looks to the past and the present and the *providential* that looks to the future, are also implied in the two source meanings attributed to *sacramentum* in early theological reflection, that is, oath and mystery.⁹⁹ Oath appears frequently in the New Testament, rendered in Greek as ορκους (oath), ομοση (to take an oath). However, the occurrence of the word *sacramentum* in the Latin Vulgate (382) seems to come mostly from the Greek 'mystery' and not from the correspondent 'oath'.¹⁰⁰ The question is why Jerome made that replacement. To give an answer, Foster undertakes a study of the old Latin versions of the New Testament, concluding that Jerome had probably been influenced by one of the New Testament manuscripts available in African Latin. Additionally, this replacement is also present in New Testament quotations by Tertullian, Cyprian and Novatian. In Novatian and Cyprian 'mystery' is not present, only 'sacrament'. Foster ventures that the consolidation of the meaning of 'sacrament' in Jerome's Latin Vulgate – together with the various old ante-Hieronimian versions – was the responsibility of the Church Fathers and especially of Tertullian.

Harnack classifies the meanings of *sacramentum* found in Tertullian's works into two broad senses: the first, is similar to the

Roman idea of procedure, a notion that will also be recovered in Hugh of Saint Victor: it is a sensible sign somehow similar to the sacred thing it represents. The second sense refers directly to a 'military oath'.[101] For the African theologian, Christians have sworn an oath through their baptism; they have made a commitment to Christ to be his warriors. This sense is represented in the new disciple's change of name. Backer adds to Harnack's argument that the sense of oath used by Tertullian is embodied in baptism, which is the *initiation rite* of the *militiam Dei*. The one who has been initiated into the mysteries of Christ becomes a *sacratus*. The oath expressed in the rite is a means of consecration. Nevertheless, Tertullian uses the word *sacramentum* to indicate many other realities, such as: first, a religion, worship or the objects of worship, for example, holy water; secondly, the faith or doctrine itself, the *regula veritatis* which is not visible to the non-initiated; thirdly, every access to the sacred, as well as the various means of blessing; fourthly, the rites perceived by the senses which entail the production of the desired supernatural effects; fifthly, a sacrifice, in connection with the Eucharist; and sixth, *signaculum*: the guarantee that the oath promises, which was also present in military oaths. In addition, in Cyprian's works, baptism remains the *sacramentum*, the oath of allegiance; Christ is the 'emperor' and Christians are his '*milites*'.

Indeed, *sacramentum* appears in Tertullian's texts with this broader meaning; there is a unifying meaning that derives from the meaning of sacrament in the ancient military oath. If baptism is called a sacrament, it is because it involves a commitment to and acceptance of an obligation that transforms the civil position of the person who takes the baptismal oath. The denominations of other rites as sacraments are just an extension of this one. The primitive Roman idea of the *sacrare*, making *sacer*, means separating some things as non-appropriable. All the material things or persons in which God reveals his designs in the Bible are sacraments. These objective or subjective elements that refer to God always imply a mystery. They are symbols that outwardly express grace and at the same time communicate it. This is one of the reasons why the juridical and military meanings of 'sacrament' could be related to the meaning of 'mystery', could thereby become immediately related to faith, and, finally, acquire a strictly religious meaning.

The pagan use of the word 'mystery' came from mystery religions and cults such as the Eleusinian Mysteries and even earlier from the oriental mysteries. In any event, such words as *mysterium*, *mysta*, *mystagogus, mysticus* were quite frequent in Greek, and also acquired a broad spectrum of meanings. Mystery became a synonym for sacred rites. But the sense of *mysterium* present when Tertullian speaks of sacrament is related to the idea of the future in four ways: first, as a type, figure and allegory, to designate the different persons, realities or even fictional stories in the Old Testament that are bearers of the name of Christ; secondly, as the economy of that which is hidden and will one day be revealed. As Foster says, even if there is no immediate connection with 'secret' in the term 'sacrament', that is no obstacle to the assimilation of the two words, in fact quite the reverse. For according to the New Testament, the Christian Mysteries, as distinguished from heathen mysteries, are for the many and for that reason seek publicity not concealment. Thirdly, as mysterious dispositions (*ordo divinae dispositionis*) of the divine will that are in part hidden and in part pre-announced by symbolic figures; and fourthly, as prophecy, to the extent that prophesies always involve something secret and hidden that has efficacy in history. They show the efficacy and the performativity of God's words. All these four possibilities are mutually inclusive. In sum, a kind of relationship with the future is what relates oath as sacrament to mystery, like the idea underlying the promissory oath. In fact, in the time of Charles the Great, the word to designate the rite of oath was *sacramentum mysterium*.[102]

Even as late as the twelfth century, during the High Middle Ages, we can still hear an echo of the strictly juridical influence in Hugh of Saint Victor's theological reflection – even if he also recovers the meaning of military oath – expressed in his monumental work *De Sacramentis Christianae Fidei* (1134). He defines a sacrament as: 'A corporeal or material element set before the senses without, representing by similitude and signifying by institution and containing by sanctification some invisible and spiritual grace.'[103] Three elements are necessary in order to be in the presence of a sacrament: a sensible sign similar to the real thing that it represents – he says 'similitude to the thing itself of which it is the sacrament'; a mediating, verbal act of institution; and the 'applied benediction of word or sign'. Of particular interest is his description of 'the sacrament of faith' (at that time the number of sacraments had not yet been settled by the Church[104]); in his *De Sacramentis* he makes a comparison with the 'military sacraments by which soldiers are obligated by their promise to preserve faith with their general'.[105] In his view any action employed by the faithful and accepted with faith for the purpose of sanctification is a kind of sacrament. 'Faith itself is a sacrament' means: what is seen in an image is a sacrament, what is seen in a thing is the matter of the sacrament and what we now see darkly through the glass (of faith) is the sacrament of what we will see face to face in manifest contemplation.[106] So all sacraments are a promise of something that is not immediately available, and instead of which we use a sign that might be water, images or words. We can recognise then two characteristics which are common to both the Roman juridical meaning and that of Hugh of Saint Victor: the importance of the formula and the relationship with a 'thing'. The vindication of the 'real thing', that is, that which is the cause of the dispute, must be present at the trial, or at least symbolically represented.[107]

In this case study of the shift in meaning between *sacramentum* as a military oath and as mystery, we find a clear example of transference from the civil realm – which in Roman Antiquity was at the same time sacred – to a strictly theological–ecclesiastical one. In fact, the word sacrament appears in early theological reflection as signifying the *sacramentum militiae* in the Roman–Italic context. To that meaning subsequent theological reflection adds the broad meaning of mystery. Neither of these two meanings seem to derive from one another, they simply enter into the Christian vocabulary from different sources; in both cases, they configure a symbolic reality, that of sacrament, which fuses multiple meanings together. These multiple meanings recover the two relevant aspects that would be attributed to the oath: the *testimonial aspect*, that looks to the past and to the present; and the *providential aspect* (promissory oath), that looks to the future.

This common origin for oath/*sacramentum* and ecclesiastical sacrament and their associated multiple analogies and transferences of meaning make us aware of two further general assumptions. First, that in a sense, both communities, the civil and the ecclesiastical in their sacramental character, are founded on the kind of symbolic form that is based on the performativity of the pronounced word. Oaths have a societal or communal character. Even vows – a typical medieval institution – make sense in the context of the community. Secondly, that even if church and state developed different institutional jurisdictions in Christianity, the constitution of society was at the same time both civil and religious. This happened to such an extent that even the non-theological sense of the word 'sacrament' was transferred to a theological context that totally appropriated its original, preponderant civil sense.

Notes

1. Jean-Louis Chrétien, *La voix nue. Phénoménologie de la promesse* (Paris: Les Éditions de Minuit, 1990), 45.
2. Carl Schmitt, *Constitutional Theory* (Durham, NC: Duke University Press, 2008), 69, 81, 118.
3. Paolo Prodi, *Il sacramento del potere. Il giuramento político nella storia constituzionale dell' Occidente* (Bologna: Il Mulino, 1992), 11.
4. Prodi, *Il sacramento del potere*, 231.
5. In addition to Prodi, see the classic works of Ernst Friesenhahn, *Der politische Eid* (Bonn: L. Röhrscheid, 1928); Bernard Guindon, *Le Serment. Son histoire, son caractère sacré* (Ottawa: Éditions de l'Université Ottawa, 1957); Rudolf Hirzel, *Der Eid. Ein Beitrag zu seiner Geschichte* (Aalen: Sciencia, 1966), who had previously written a history of the oath in the twentieth century. See also Émile Benveniste, *Vocabulaire des institutions indo-européennes* 2 (Paris: Les Editions de Minuit, 1969), who has reflected on the oath in its Greek and Roman uses from an etymological point of view. Gorgio Agamben, *The Sacrament of Language* (Sandford, CA: Standford University Press, 2011), used the results of most of this historical material for a contemporary reflection, even though his archaeological studies are related mainly to the ancient world.
6. See Nicholas Aroney, 'Faith in Public Office: The Meaning, Persistence and Importance of Oaths', paper in Conference Faith in Public Office, Centre for the Study of Science, Religion and Society, Emmanuel College, University of Queensland, 3 September, 2015. Published on ABC *Religion and Ethics* website. Along with Aroney's narrative, there are other narratives like that of Spurr which undermine the significance of oaths and accordingly the irrelevance of their disappearance in political community-building. John Spurr, 'A Profane History of Early Modern Oaths', *Transactions of the Royal Historical Society* 11 (2001): 37–63, 41.
7. See Mitchell Dean, 'Oath and Office', *Telos* 185 (2018): 67–91, 67, 90: 'The oath acts as something like a signature: something that marks and brackets statements, and facilitates their movement from the profane to the sacred, the immanent to the transcendent, and is indeed very close to the "signature of power".'
8. Guindon was one of the first historians to point out the sacral character of oaths. He asserts in his history of the oath that in every epoch taking an oath has been considered both a civil and a religious act. Guindon, *Le Serment*, 27–8. From the point of view of linguistic research, Benveniste shows that oaths are as much rites as juridical instruments. Benveniste, *Vocabulaire*, 367–75, 406–15. Giorgio Agamben also corroborates this mixed character of the notion of oath in his *The Sacrament of Language*, defending again that the oath is neither merely juridical nor merely religious.

9. Numa Denis Fustel de Coulanges, *The Ancient City: A Study on the Religion, Laws, and Institutions of Greece and Rome* (Kitchener: Batoche, 2001).
10. Benveniste, *Vocabulaire*, 118. From *iurare* comes *ius iurandum*: the formula that fixes the norm. *Sacramentum*, on the other hand, was the act of making a commitment with the gods.
11. See Benveniste, *Vocabulaire*, 112: 'Le dictionnaire d'Ernout-Meillet allègue une expression *ius iurare* qui signifierait "prononcer la formule sacré qui engage", malheureusement sans donner de référence. A notre connaissance une telle locution ne se rencontré pas. Nous n'en avons que la forme résiduelle *ius iurandum*, qui laisse subsister l'écart entre *ius* et *iuro*,' 113.
12. As Álvaro d'Ors points out, etymologically *ius* has the same root as *iurare* and even more so, it can be related to Iovis or Iupiter, the God who punishes perjury. Álvaro d'Ors, *Derecho privado romano* (Pamplona: Eunsa, 1997), §12.
13. The book, edited by Martin Aurell, Jaume Aurell and Montserrat Herrero, *Le Sacré et la Parole. Le Serment au Moyen Age* (Paris: Classiques Garnier, 2018), demonstrates this assertion by means of several study cases.
14. A differentiation between the political oath and the private oath was already alive at that time, but the two coexisted without too much trouble. In Prodi's words, the '*consensum fidelium*' was already displaced from the Church to civil society in the tenth century. Prodi, *Il sacramento del potere*, 88.
15. For the transference from the juridical–political arena to the Church, see Montserrat Herrero, 'Sacrament and Oath: A Theological–Political Displacement', *Political Theology* 19(1) (2018): 35–49.
16. See Conal Condren, *Argument and Authority in Early Modern England: The Presupposition of Oaths and Offices* (Cambridge: Cambridge University Press, 2006), 285: 'The oath of allegiance insisted with laborious repetition that it must be sworn sincerely, without equivocation or mental reservation, as the words were normally understood. These formulas echoed down the rest of the century but were never empty. They attested to the fear not just of insincerity, but the English Jesuit doctrine of equivocation. At risk were the integrity of all oath-taking, human trust and the destruction of social office, because ultimately the very function of language was perverted by it.'
17. Hobbes, *Leviathan*, ch. XIV.
18. John Locke, *The Second Treatise of Civil Government* (Indianapolis, IN: Hackett, 1980), 8.121. See the discussion on engagement with a free state in Condren, *Argument and Authority in Early Modern England*, 290–313.
19. John Locke, *A Letter on Toleration* (Oxford: Oxford University Press, 1968).

20. Jean Jacques Rousseau, *The Social Contract and Other Political Essays* (Cambridge: Cambridge University Press, 1997), IV 8. There, Rousseau praises Hobbes for daring to reunify the two 'eagle heads'.
21. Schmitt, *Constitutional Theory*, 69.
22. See Ernst Jenni and Claus Westermann, *Theological Lexicon of the Old Testament* (Peabody, MA: Hendrickson, 1994), vol. 2. The words of Deuteronomy (7:6–10) reveal this: '. . . because the Lord loved you and kept the oath he swore to your ancestors that he brought you out with a mighty hand and redeemed you from the land of slavery, from the power of Pharaoh king of Egypt. Know therefore that the Lord your God is God; he is the faithful God, keeping his covenant of love to a thousand generations of those who love him and keep his commandments.' Chapter 6 of the Letter of Paul to the Hebrews is clear about, on the one hand, the relationship between oaths and covenant, and, on the other, about the relevance and the irrelevance of God's promise, Hebrews 6:13–19: 'For when God made a promise to Abraham, since he had no one greater by whom to swear, he swore by himself, saying: "Surely I will bless you and multiply you." And thus Abraham, having patiently endured, obtained the promise. Men indeed swear by a greater than themselves, and in all their disputes an oath is final for confirmation. So, when God desired to show more convincingly to the heirs of the promise the unchangeable character of his purpose, he interposed with an oath, so that through two unchangeable things, in which it is impossible that God should prove false, we who had fled for refuge might have strong encouragement to seize the hope set before us.' And in Chapter 7, speaking now about the new priesthood inaugurated by the new alliance, Paul continues, 7:20–28: 'And it was not without an oath. Those who formerly became priests took their office without an oath, but this one was addressed with an oath: "The Lord has sworn and will not change his mind, you are priest forever." This makes Jesus the surety of a better covenant . . . Indeed, the law appoints men in their weakness as high priests, but the word of the oath, which came later than the law, appoints a Son who has been made perfect for ever.'
23. Guindon, *Le Serment*, 27–8.
24. On oaths in the Old Testament, see Friedrich Horst and Hans Walter Wolff, *Gottes Recht. Gesammelte Studien zu dem Recht im Alten Testament* (Munich: Kaiser, 1961). See also Charles W. Draper, Chad Brand and Archie England (eds), *Holman Bible Dictionary* (Nashville, Tennessee: Holman Bible Publishers, 2003). The article mixes oath and vow as identical kinds of action. See Benveniste, *Vocabulaire*, 233–43. See also Ira M. Price, 'The Oath in Court Procedure in Early Babylonia and the Old Testament', *Journal of the American Oriental Society* 49 (1929): 22–9, 26.

25. We can see this in the Bible: the acceptance of the Torah (Exodus 19:7–20:18); the Covenant at Sinai (Exodus 24:1, 12–18; the Covenant at Moab (Deuteronomy 29:1; 30:11–20); the Covenant at Shechem (Joshua 24:1–28); the Forced Covenant (Ezekiel 20:1–6, 10–22, 30–38); the Pledging of a Renewed Covenant (Nehemiah 9:1–8, 24–26, 30–37, 10:1–40). See also Michael Walzer, Menachem Lorberbaum and Noam J. Zohar (eds), *The Jewish Political Tradition, vol. 1: Authority* (New Haven, CT: Yale University Press, 2000), 24.
26. Matthew 5:34–37: '. . . you have heard that it was said to the men of old, "You shall not swear falsely, but shall perform to the Lord what you have sworn." But I say to you, do not swear at all, either by heaven, for it is the throne of God, or by the earth, for it is his footstool, or by Jerusalem, for it is the city of the great King. And do not swear by your head, for you cannot make one hair white or black. Let what you say be simply "yes" or "no"; anything more than this comes from evil.'
27. See Olivier Delouis, 'Eglise et serment à Byzance: norme et pratique', in *Oralité et lien social au Moyen Age*, Marie-France Auzépy et al. (ed.) (Paris: Association des amis du Centre d'histoire et civilisation de Byzance, 2008), 211–46. He points out the contradictions in Byzantium between the norm and the practice of the oath, given the restrictions the Church placed on making oaths. In any case, he holds that: 'l'interdiction du serment par le Christ . . . procède ainsi d'une théologie positive . . . c'est vouloir que l'homme qu'il parle aussi vrai que le Verbe, c'est substituer à l'instabilité visible de la raison humaine la stabilité invisible de la parole divine.' Delouis, 'Eglise et serment', 245.
28. Michel Foucault, *Du gouvernement des vivants* (Paris: Gallimard/Seuil, 2012), 73, 79.
29. These questions were at the centre of Foucault's philosophical preoccupations from the 1980s, but not completely absent before then. Michel Foucault in *Dits et Écrits* IV (Paris: Gallimard, 1994), No. 304, 213 announces the course on *Subjectivité et Verité* (1981) and defines the 'technologies of the self' as procedures required from individuals in order to constitute or fix their own identity or to transform it in conformity with external aims by means of self-dominion or self-knowledge. Only through this reflexive exercise can a subjectivity constitute an identity. In *L'hermenéutique du sujet* (Paris: Gallimard/Seuil, 2001), 343–5, Foucault then consolidates the thesis that the different ways the ancient and modern worlds structured the subject depend on an inverse subordination between care of the self and knowledge of the self. In Foucault's perspective, ever since early Christianity confession has been one of the techniques of taking care of the self, that is, 'techniques by which a subject constructs a definite relationship to self, gives form to his or

her own existence and establishes a well-ordered relationship to the world and to others', in the words of Frédéric Gros (Frédéric Gros, 'Course Context', in Michel Foucault, *The Government of Self and Others*, Lectures at the College of France 1982–1983 (New York: Palgrave Macmillan, 2011), 377–8). The truthful subjectivity provided by confession makes governmentality possible. See Philippe Chevalier, *Michel Foucault et le christianisme* (Lyon: ENS Editions, 2011).

30. Thomas Aquinas *Sth* II–II, Q. 89, a. 1. For a contemporary distinction between the two kinds of oath, following John Austin's theory of speech acts instead of their temporal aspect, see Condren, *Argument and Authority in Early Modern England*, 233–4: 'The assertory oath was in Augustinian terms a constative: it attested to a state of affairs, such as one's identity in a court of law. The promissory, however, was an Augustinian performative; like a wager, it was a creative act, having "constructive power". The assertory, then, could easily be synonymous with declaring and it might only require subscription to its terms. The promissory oath was more problematic and accepted as binding only on tacit conditions.'

31. Henri Levy-Bruhl, 'Reflexions sur le serment', *Études d'histoire du droit privé offertes à Pierre Petot* (Paris: Dalloz, 1959), 392: 'Le serment, nous l'avons vu, contient en lui-même une auto-malédiction pour le cas où le jureur manquerait à la vérité ou à la bonne foi. Cette malédiction s'accomplira tôt ou tard, mais automatiquement, sans qu'une intervention humaine soit nécessaire, suivant le principe que l'on voit encore énoncé par Tacite sous la forme d'un proverbe: *Diis injuria deorum cura*.'

32. Benveniste, *Vocabulaire*, 172: '*Sacramentum* est un dérivé, non de *sacer*, mais du verbe nominative *sacrare*, "déclarer *sacer*", "déclarer anathème" celui qui commettent tel délit. Le *sacramentum* est proprement le fait ou l'objet par lequel on anathématise par avance sa propre personne (*sacramentum* militaire) ou encore le gage déposé (dans le *sacramentum* judiciaire). Dès que la parole est prononcée dans les formes, on est potentiellement dans l'état de *sacer*. C'est état devient effective et appelle la vengeance divine si on transgresse l'engagement pris.' See more in Roberto Fiori, *Homo sacer. La dinámica político-constituzionale di una sanzione giuridico-religiosa* (Naples: Jovene Editori, 1996).

33. Michel Foucault, *Lectures on the Will to Know: Lectures at the Collège de France, 1970–1971* (New York: Palgrave Macmillan, 2013), 27 January 1971, 76–7: 'the oath does not mean entry into the invisible realm of a truth which will shine forth one day; it shifts the combat into a region where the risks are incommensurable with those of the struggle and where the laws governing these risks are absolutely hidden from human sight.' Also, Foucault, *Lectures on*

the Will to Know, 3 February 1971, 85: 'in archaic juridical practices the non-verbal equivalent for the word of truth is the ordeal, the test: being exposed or exposing someone to undefined danger. Taking the oath of truth or exposing oneself to the danger of blows, the thunderbolt, the sea, wild beasts – this has the same form and the same operational property. In archaic judicial practice, the word of truth is not linked to light and looking at things; it is linked to the obscurity of the future and uncertain event.' The study of Foucault in these lectures covers the genealogy of the form of trials in different historical stages. He studies the variations of procedures in oaths, the place reserved to the truth and the systems of sovereignty. In my view, whoever swears an oath decides to place him/herself under the sovereignty of the divine, and this is what matters independently of being at the same time subject to other spheres of sovereignty. Foucault, however, analyses the sequence of changes: in the discourse of truth, discourse of justice and political discourse, at different historical moments.

34. Agamben, *The Sacrament of Language*, 23: 'What is decisive here is the reasoning with which Cicero goes on to establish the vis of the oath. It is not a matter of the anger of the gods, which does not exist (*quae nulla esi*), but of trust (*fides*). Contrary to the opinion very often repeated by modern scholars, the obligatory nature of the oath does not derive from the gods, who are called only as witnesses, but from the fact that it is situated in the sphere of a more far-reaching institution, the *fides*, which regulates relations among men as much as those between peoples and cities.'

35. As Agamben asserts, beyond regulating personal relationships, *fides* also performs an important function in international public law, where common civil law has no jurisdiction. Agamben, *The Sacrament of Language*, 26.

36. Chrétien, *La voix nue*, 149.

37. Chrétien, *La voix nue*, 148.

38. Jacques Derrida, *Le parjure et le pardon I* (Paris: Seuil, 2019), 110: 'c'est que quiconque n'est pas fidèle à l'héritage et se méprend ou introduit une méprise dans l'usage de ces mots (par exemple, pardon et parjure) est lui-même déjà en faute, donc parjure, infidèle a l'injonction inscrite dans la langue, au contrat implicite qu'il a signé en se servant d'un mot de la langue supposé avoir un sens admis et compris par autres.' Also Agamben, *The Sacrament of Language*, 54: 'The name of God names the name that is always and only true, that is, that experience of language that it is not possible to doubt. For man this experience is the oath. In this sense every name is an oath, and in every name a "faith" is in question, because the certainty of the name is not of an empirico-constative or logico-epistemic type

but rather always puts in play the commitment and praxis of men. To speak is, above all, to swear, to believe in the name.'
39. Derrida, 'How to Avoid Speaking', 30. See Bradley, 'A Genealogy of the Theological Turn', 30. 'Language as promise' is another expression used by Derrida in relation to the aporia of origin.
40. Jacques Derrida, 'What Is a "Relevant" Translation?' *Critical Inquiry* 27(2) (2001): 174–200, 185: 'Thus, the oath is, in the human tongue, a promise that human language, however, cannot itself undo, control, obliterate, subject by loosening it. An oath is a bond in human language that the human tongue, as such, insofar as it is human, cannot loosen. In human language is a bond stronger than human language . . . The oath, the sworn faith, the act of swearing is transcendence itself, the experience of passing beyond man, the origin of the divine or, if one prefers, the divine origin of the oath. No sin is more serious than perjury, and Shylock repeats, while swearing, that he cannot perjure himself; he therefore confirms the first oath by a second oath in the time of a repetition. This is called fidelity, which is the very essence and vocation of an oath. When I swear, I swear in a language that no human language has the power to make me abjure, to disrupt, that is to say, to make me perjure myself. The oath passes through language, but it passes beyond human language.'
41. Something similar is expressed by John Spurr when he describes seventeenth-century common-sense knowledge about oaths saying: 'In short, an oath is a provisional self-curse. A profane oath is one sworn in inappropriate circumstances, to support a lie or a frivolous statement. It is a breach of the third commandment's ban on the misuse of God's name.' Spurr, 'A Profane History', 38.
42. This is the thesis of Adolf Reinach, who bases the structure of law on the promise. Adolf Reinach, *Zur Phänomenologie des Rechts. Die apriorischen Grundlagen des bürgerlichen Rechts*, in *Sämtliche Werke. Textkritische Ausgabe in 2 Bänden* (Munich: Philosophia, 1989), 147.
43. Carl Schmitt, *Der Begriff des Politischen. Text von 1932 mit einem Vorwort und drei Corollarien* (Berlin: Duncker & Humblot, 1979), 15; Vorwort. This Foreword has not been included in the English translation. See also Carl Schmitt, 'Die vollendete Reformation. Bemerkungen und Hinweise zu neuen Leviathan Interpretationen', *Der Staat* 4 (1965): 55: 'Hood demonstrates that Hobbes was not anticlerical. It must also be stated that his famous mandate to silence theologians, during the time of the religious civil war, did not come from Hobbes, but from Albericus Gentilis.' Also Carl Schmitt, *Ex Captivitate Salus. Erfahrungen der Zeit 1945–1947* (Cologne: Greven, 1950), 74: 'Thus, the *jus publicum europaeum* was born

from the religious civil wars of the sixteenth and seventeenth centuries. In the beginning there was a slogan pronounced against theologians, a call to silence, which a founder of modern international law directed towards theologians: *Silete theologi, in munere alieno!* Such was the cry of Albericus Gentilis regarding the controversy of just war. Even today, I can hear him shout.' (translation is mine). Also see, Carl Schmitt, *The Nomos of the Earth in the International Law of the Jus Publicum Europaeum* (New York: Telos, 2003), 158–9.

44. Carl Schmitt, 'The Plight of European Jurisprudence', *Telos* 83 (1990): 35–70.
45. Carl Schmitt, 'The Legal World Revolution', *Telos* 72 (1987): 73–89. In this 1987 article, Schmitt describes Hitler's rise to power as a result of a legal revolution. He argues that Hitler shows legalism's last step: legality has not only become the most important means for legitimate political power, a revolutionary instrument. In a modern industrial society, he adds, only legal revolutions have a chance. We know that the solution that Schmitt proposed is not simply to recover the divine or theological character of the law, but mainly a 'substantial' legal idea rooted in *nomos* instead of an 'empty' legality. Certainly, his idea of the *nomos* can also be developed as a political theology of place. See Herrero, *The Political Discourse of Carl Schmitt*. Recent developments of a theology of place in Katherine Keller, *Political Theology of the Earth: Our Planetary Emergency and the Struggle for a New Public* (New York: Columbia University Press, 2018); Jeff Malpas, *The Ethics of Place* (Abingdon: Routledge, 2021); John Inge, *A Christian Theology of Place* (Abingdon: Routledge, 2016).
46. Derrida, *Le parjure et le pardon I*, 330.
47. Benveniste, *Vocabulaire*, 334.
48. Philippe Buc, *The Dangers of Ritual: Between Early Medieval Texts and Social Scientific Theory* (Princeton, NJ: Princeton University Press, 2001). The list of publications that have analysed ritual behaviour in the field of social anthropology is long. Let us cite Clifford Geertz as a pioneer in his *The Iinterpretation of Culture* (New York: Basic Books, 1973). In his view, ritual was said to dramatise, enact, materialise or perform a system of symbols; secondly, ritual was said to integrate the two aspects of symbols, conceptual and dispositional (ethos); and, thirdly, rituals as performances integrate conceptual categories with cultural particularities. A classical work is also, Jonathan Z. Smith, *To Take Place: Toward Theory in Ritual* (Chicago: University of Chicago Press, 1987). For a work on social anthropology that summarises the achievements of ritual, see Catherine Bell, *Ritual Theory, Ritual Practice* (Oxford: Oxford University Press, 1992). She deconstructs the idea of ritual

by functionalising it. She challenges the traditional association of belief and ritual by arguing that 'the projection and embodiment of schemes in ritualization is more effective viewed as a mastering of relationships of power relations within an arena that affords a negotiated appropriation of the dominant values embedded in the symbolic schemes'. 182. See also Catherine Bell, *Ritual: Perspectives and Dimensions* (Oxford: Oxford University Press, 1997). The second and third parts of the book, where she describes different rituals, show the centrality of oaths in very different kinds of rituals. See Robert Spaemann, 'Lo ritual y lo moral', *Anuario Filosófico* 34 (2001): 655–72, 656. From what he argues we can conclude that oaths can be conceived as instantiations of divinity.

49. Marie-France Auzépy, 'Introduction', in Marie-France Auzépy et al. (eds), *Oralité et lien social au Moyen Age (Occident, Byzance, Islam)* (Paris: ACHCByz, 2008), 7–16. She insists that in relation to oaths, it is clear that the written form validates the words, even though the oath is mainly an oral act. Only the given word engages the individual. This sense had been also underlined in Levy-Bruhl, 'Reflexions', 385–96.

50. As Jan Assmann defines it by referring to the biblical narratives, 'performative are texts or speech acts that produce by depicting'. Jan Assmann, *Exodus. Die Revolution der Alten Welt* (Munich: Beck, 2015), 390.

51. On the question of perjury in the *Summa Theologiae*, Thomas Aquinas says that for an oath to be valid as such, its content must be morally acceptable. Thomas Aquinas *Sth* II–II, Q. 89 a. 2: 'Reply to Objection 1. He that swears to do what is unlawful is thereby guilty of perjury through lack of justice: though, if he fails to keep his oath, he is not guilty of perjury in this respect, since that which he swore to do was not a fit matter of an oath. Reply to Objection 2. A person who swears not to enter religion, or not to give alms, or the like, is guilty of perjury through lack of judgement. Hence when he does that which is best it is not an act of perjury, but contrary thereto: for the contrary of that which he is doing could not be a matter of an oath. Reply to Objection 3. When one man swears or promises to do another's will, there is to be understood this requisite condition – that the thing commanded be lawful and virtuous, and not unbearable or immoderate. Reply to Objection 4. An oath is a personal act, and so when a man becomes a citizen of a state, he is not bound, as by oath, to fulfill whatever the state has sworn to do. Yet he is bound by a kind of fidelity, the nature of which obligation is that he should take his share of the state's burdens if he takes a share of its goods. The canon who swears to keep the statutes that have force in some particular "college" is not bound by his oath to keep any that may be made in the future, unless he intends to bind

himself to keep all, past and future. Nevertheless, he is bound to keep them by virtue of the statutes themselves, since they are possessed of coercive force, as stated above.' Cicero expresses the same idea in *De Officiis* III, 29: 'For what was so sworn that the mind of him who took the oath at the time confessed the obligation, ought to be fulfilled; what was not so sworn may be left unfulfilled without perjury. Thus, you would not pay robbers a price that you had agreed to pay for your life; it is no wrong if you fail to do this after having promised with an oath. For a robber is not included in the list of belligerents, but is the common enemy of all. Between him and other men there ought to be neither mutual confidence nor binding oath. For it is not simply swearing what is false that constitutes perjury; but it is perjury not to perform what you have sworn, as it is expressed in our legal form, in the purpose of your own mind.'

52. Peter Burke, 'The Repudiation of Ritual in Early Modern Europe', in *The Historical Anthropology of Early Modern Italy*, Peter Burke (ed.) (Cambridge: Cambridge University Press, 1987), 227–38. See also Buc, *Dangers of the Ritual*, 164–202, in particular 176: 'we owe the fuzziness of our modern concept of ritual in part to the sixteenth century . . . Catholics and Protestants of all stripes polemized about the exact position of the boundaries between sacraments, permissible ceremonies and superstitious ceremonies, as well as about the nature of these subdivisions'. It was the French Revolution that finally broke down these conceptual boundaries by declaring the cult of reason in 1793 and abolishing Catholic public worship. A civil cult with new rites and ceremonies replaced mystical worship. In Buc's view this was a 'routinisation', to use the Weberian term, of the Lutheran position. See Buc, *Dangers of the Ritual*, 203–4.
53. Derrida, *Le parjure et le pardon II*, 181 ff. And he refers to Augustine of Hippo's *The City of God*, where he points out that God's omnipotence consists precisely in not being able to lie. A non-power that is a power.
54. Derrida refers to something similar when he speaks of God's frail presence. Without God, even without an absent God, it is not possible to think of an absolute witness. Given this witness, every other testimony begins to be superfluous. But because it is not, as he asserts in 'Faith and Knowledge', everything begins with the presence of that absence. When God is not positively present, we count mainly on 'secular oaths'. Derrida, 'Faith and Knowledge', 65. Also, in Derrida, *Le parjure et le pardon I*, 81. For Chrétien, *La voix nue*, 148.
55. Delouis, 'Eglise et serment', 246.
56. The discovery of the 'confessing subject' in the 1980s was a turning point in Foucault's project of writing a history of sexuality. Foucault published *La Volonté de savoir* in 1976 as a methodological and preliminary essay for five more volumes on several strategies of the

modern *dispositif* of sexuality. However, in 1984, he shifted his attention to the genealogy of concupiscence, what he called 'the principle of the desiring man', taking advantage of the phenomenology expressed in the practice of confession in Western Christianity. At first, his project was politically oriented and aimed at discovering new power *dispositifs* through a genealogy of political systems based on power over life. At the beginning, sexuality interested Foucault as an indicator of normalisation processes in Western culture. In some ways, Foucault developed his ideas about normalisation produced by power, not in a series of books, but in his Collège de France lectures between 1971 and 1979. Only eight years after the publication of the first volume of his *History of Sexuality*, two more volumes of the *History of Sexuality*, including *l'Usage des plaisirs* and *Souci de soi*, were both published in 1984 after the lectures on *Gouvernement des vivants* (1979–80), *Subjectivité et Vérité* (1980–1), *L'hermeneutique du subject* (1981–2), *Gouvernement de soi et des autres* (1982–3), and *Le Courage de la verité. Gouvernement de soi et des autres* II (1982–4). After these lectures, the framework for his history of sexuality changed completely: the temporal index went from early Western modernity (sixteenth and seventeenth centuries) to Greek–Roman antiquity (second–fifth centuries); it went from a reading of the power *dispositifs* of Western culture to a reading on the practices of the self, a problematisation of the subject and a genealogy of subjectivity. The *Gouvernement des vivants* lecture centred on the idea of '*actes de verité*', which are at the core of the conceptual revolution in Foucault's project. In this new context, *History of Sexuality* must be conceived of as a series of books about the emergence of the subject in the practices of the self.

57. Michel Foucault, *Mal faire, dire vrai. Fonction de l'Aveu en Justice*, Course de Louvain, 1981 (Louvain: Presses universitaires de Louvain/University of Chicago Press Press, 2012), 7: 'l'aveu est un acte verbal par lequel le sujet, dans une affirmation sur ce qu'il est, se lie à cette vérité, se place dans un rapport de dépendance à l'égard d'autrui et modifie en même temps le rapport qu'il a à lui-même' (the translation is mine).

58. Foucault adopted the term *alèthurgie* – taking the expression from the grammarian Heraclides of Pontus (third or fourth century BC) – as a set of verbal and non-verbal procedures conducted to discover something that was hidden, invisible or impossible to know. Foucault, *Du gouvernement des vivants*, 8.

59. Foucault, *Du gouvernement des vivants*, 91 and 99: 'Comment les hommes, en Occident, se sont-ils liés ou ont-ils été amenés à se lier à des manifestations bien particulières de la vérité, manifestations de vérité dans lesquelles précisément, ce sont eux-mêmes qui doivent être manifestés en vérité?'

60. Foucault, *Du gouvernement des vivants*, 94.
61. With the idea of original sin, that is the possibility of failing, Christianity departs from the gnostic idea of perfection. The idea of relapse was completely alien to Greek philosophy and culture. In Antiquity, perfection was an achieved state. For the Gnostics, this perfection was the key to salvation. In Christianity, although salvation does not necessarily imply perfection, it does at least imply a path of conversion that includes the whole of life, from baptism to death. Tertullian, according to Foucault, '"invented"' original sin, which must exist as an obligation of self-veridiction. Evil is found inside ourselves. The subject has no identity, but does have a constitutive rupture, namely, Satan, inside his soul. Who am I, then? The subject must be constituted by the purification of evil, which is impossible without *discrectio* between the good and evil inside the subject. Veridiction corresponds to this kind of discrimination in the process of confessing oneself. This rupture makes 'confessing oneself' problematic and puts one in need of help. The *metanoia* into oneself cannot be done alone; it requires assistance in terms of temptation in the *probatio*, doctrine in the *fides*, and direction in the confession. See Foucault, *Du gouvernement des vivants*, 110, 119, 148, 154, 175; Michel Foucault, *Confessions of the Flesh: The History of Sexuality*, vol. 4 (New York: Penguin, 2021).
62. This genealogy leads to the *dispositif* examination-confession. Foucault, *Du gouvernement des vivants*, 206: 'la mise en public de ce qu'on est comme pécheur ne passera plus que par le filtre verbal et le quadrillage juridique d'un *expositio casus* . . . C'est tout le pivotement de la culture occidentale autour du problème de la pratique du discours et autour des formes de droit, c'est tout cela que qui est engagé dans cet histoire de la pénitence; le droit, la loi, le discours et par conséquent, tous les types de rapport entre vérité et subjectivité.' This evolution is described in great detail in the *Du gouvernement des vivants*, as well as in *Les aveux de la chair*. See chapter 1 of the latter, where he follows different doctrines from Clement of Alexandria, Tertullian, Origen, St. Augustine and Thomas Aquinas, among others. In sum, from the second to the fifth centuries, baptism was the only form of penance. It happened once in a lifetime; the only other opportunity for pardon came by waiting for the jubilee year. As time went by, the second penance – called canonical – emerged; later, the possibility of repeated penance developed, because people were seen to be in need of verifying who they were, up to and including the last moments before death. It is possible that this evolution resulted from the changing conception regarding the moment of the Parousia. The first Christians thought that the Parousia would come immediately; they therefore tried to postpone baptism in order to be purified immediately before the arrival of

death. When it became clear that Christ's second coming would be delayed, repeated penance became a necessity. The practice of repeated penance carries with it the need for examination. There are no Christian texts on examination of conscience before the fourth century. Foucault interprets examination as a practice transferred from philosophical life to Christianity. In fact, Pythagoras was the first to practice examination as a way of achieving perfection. Cicero and Seneca also employed it as a practice reserved to the wise. Foucault also insists that within Christianity this practice was expanded by the Casian institution of the coenobium. Monastic life is impossible without spiritual direction, which implies self-examination to bring out the secret mysteries of the heart – mysteries of which even the subject himself may have been ignorant before articulating them out loud. In fact, this 'articulating' is the *dispositif* of the 'discretio', that is, a discrimination between good and evil in the interior of the soul; as mentioned, the soul is divided by the presence of evil. The penitent does not so much have to 'tell the truth' about what he has done, as 'make the truth' by manifesting what he himself is.

63. This is similar to what Nietzsche called 'digestion'; the truth must be 'embodied' – something that we can do only by acting it out. On this comparison, see Vanessa Lemm, 'The Embodiment of the Truth and the Politics of Community: Foucault and the Cynics', in *The Government of Life: Foucault, Biopolitics, and Neoliberalism*, Vanessa Lemm and Miguel Vatter (eds) (New York: Fordham University Press, 2014), 208–23. This interdependence is what Foucault wanted to stress in his *History of Sexuality* when he writes in volume 4, that 'the flesh' emerged within the *dispositif* of confession. The flesh has to be understood as a unique experience constituted thanks to particular knowledge of the self; that is, by a transformation of the self by himself through a kind of relationship between suppression of evil and manifestation of truth. The novelty of Christianity was not in the sexual code organised around marriage and procreation – which was already present in Ancient cultures – but, rather, in the way the self related to that code.

64. Foucault, *Du gouvernement des vivants*, 190.

65. Foucault, *Du gouvernement des vivants*, 143. Foucault, *Mal faire, dire vrai*, 201: 'la mise en place privilégiée de l'aveu dans les pratiques pénales s'est inscrite, d'une façon générale, dans une sorte de grande juridification de la société et de la culture occidentales au Moyen-Âge, juridification qui est sensible . . . dans les institutions, les pratiques, les représentations propres au christianisme'. See also Morris on the 'individualization' aspect of confession as one of the practices that led towards the discovery of the individual. Colin Morris, *The Discovery of the Individual, 1050–1200* (Toronto: University of Toronto Press, 1987), 70–5. In his seminar

of 25 February 1998, Derrida devotes his lesson to a comparative of confessions in the context of the excuse in Augustine, Rousseau and Paul de Man. Derrida, *Le parjure et le pardon I*, 259–95.
66. Prodi, *Il sacramento del potere*, 11.
67. Foucault, *Mal faire, dire vrai*, 211.
68. Foucault, *Mal faire, dire vrai*, 8–10. Foucault points out that there are many fields that require the subject to confess, not only the field of justice, as is evident, but also the fields of medicine and psychiatry.
69. The complete text is Foucault, *The Government of Self*, 62: 'In a performative utterance, the given elements of the situation are such that, when the utterance is made, the effect which follows is known and ordered in advance, it is codified, and this is precisely what constitutes the performative character of the utterance. In *parrhesia* on the other hand, whatever the usual, familiar, and quasi-institutionalized character of the situation in which it is effectuated, what makes it *parrhesia* is that the introduction, the irruption of the true discourse determines an open situation, or rather opens the situation and makes possible effects which are precisely, not known. *Parrhesia* does not produce a codified effect; it opens up an unspecified risk.' The main difference between Foucault's idea of *parrhesia* and that which is evoked in the 'speech acts', or, as Foucault says, the 'performative utterance' of the analytical tradition, is the subject's commitment and his capacity to introduce new elements in the historical world. Moreover, for the performative character of an utterance, what matters is the enunciation not the status of the subject who enounces, whereas to the parrhesiastic the authenticity of the subject who performs the enunciation is crucial.
70. Michel Foucault, *The Courage of the Truth: The Government of Self and Others II*, Lectures at the Collège de France 1983–1984 (New York: Palgrave Macmillan, 2011), 339.
71. Foucault, *The Courage of the Truth*, 69.
72. Foucault, *The Courage of the Truth*, 66: 'it is a way of telling the truth that lays one open to a risk by the very fact that one tells the truth . . . by binding oneself to the statement of the truth and to the act of stating the truth . . . in the form of a courageous act.' He underlines that this notion was initially a political one, but he carries its meaning beyond this context by identifying Socrates as the first parrhesiastic figure of this new kind. In the case of Socrates, first, there is a transposition of prophetic veridiction to a field of truth, and, secondly, he does not speak of the being of things or the order of the world; he speaks of the test of the soul (Foucault, *The Courage of the Truth*, 88–9). The 'care of the self' that philosophy implies is not a natural attitude but a technique, except in degraded forms of the care of the self, like narcissism or hedonism, and for that reason it has to be introduced by a 'master of existence'. This

figure existed before the institutionalisation of the spiritual director of Christianity. This master could be anyone, but his character should be that of the parrhesiast (Foucault, *The Courage of the Truth*, 6).

73. Cynics play a fundamental role in this topic. First, thanks to the immediate link they experience between their mode of life and truth-telling; and, secondly, because their mode of life reduces all pointless conventions and all superfluous opinions to a sort of general stripping of existence and opinions in order to reveal the truth. The relativisation they make of the truth regime in which they speak, makes 'another world with other rules and convictions' emerge, the advent of which would mean a transformation of the present world; and for that reason, Foucault identifies the 'scandal of the truth' with the cynics. For Foucault, what is manifested in cynicism is also life as the immediate, striking and unrestrained presence of the truth. Art and artists have been historically the bearers of cynicism in the modern world. Foucault, *The Courage of the Truth*, 166.

74. Foucault, *The Courage of the Truth*, 307–8: 'I think that this sovereignty, by which the Cynic life characterized itself, expressed a double derision towards political sovereignty, the sovereignty of kings of the world. First, because Cynic sovereignty asserted itself aggressively, in a critical, polemical mode, as the only real monarchy ... On the other hand – this was the other side of the Cynic derision of monarchies – the Cynic's real monarchy inverted all the signs and distinguishing features of political monarchies. It practiced solitude, whereas sovereigns were surrounded by their court, soldiers, and allies. It practiced destitution, whereas kings of the world gave themselves all the outward signs of wealth and power. It practiced endurance and ascetic exercises, whereas monarchs of the world practiced the enjoyment of pleasures. So, there is a double derision of this real monarchy.'

75. Conspiracy is often equated with treason, even if, *conjuratio, conspiratio* or *conventiculum* do not always have to be illegal or unfair. In fact, conspirators often resorted to negotiation to cause the emperor to reverse a decision or even to abdicate. Their common oath gives weight to their claims in the course of talks with the established authority. At least at first, they do not claim to overturn authority by force, but to compel the emperor to revoke a decision. See Gerd Althoff, '*Conventiculum, conspiratio, coniuratio*: The Political Power of Sworn Associations in 10th and 11th Century Germany', in *Le Sacré et la Parole. Le Serment au Moyen Age*, M. Aurell, J. Aurell and M. Herrero (eds) (Paris: Classiques Garnier, 2018), 57–69. In the same volume, Antonio Bento, 'Machiavelli's Treatment of *congiure* and the Modern Oath', 267–97.

76. Foucault, *The Courage of the Truth*, 339. The difference between the ways the Platonic and the Cynic approach truth is that while Plato gives knowledge of oneself the form of contemplation, Cynics gives knowledge of oneself the privileged form of an exercise: tests and practices of endurance. Foucault, *The Courage of the Truth*, 161: 'in one case we have a mode of giving an account of oneself which leads to the psukhe – and which, in doing this, marks out the site of a possible metaphysical discourse. In the other case, we have a giving an account of oneself, an "accounting for oneself", which is directed towards bios as existence, towards [a] mode of existence which is to be examined and tested throughout its life.' But still the question remains: are the Cynics living the 'true life' or are they simply 'truly' living their own life? In my view, this is the great difference between courage and provocation. Foucault fixed his attention on 'the scandalous banality' with which the Cynics represent for the sake of their own philosophical context the exhibition of their own life as it is, true or not, good or bad. It could also be called shamelessness or impudence. In any event, it is a veridiction, a truthfulness that can incline another to trust or not to trust that scandalous person; but in any case, it is not opacity. Foucault himself poses this question in *The Courage of the Truth*, 218: 'What is a true life? True life is, according to the Greek tradition, unconcealed, unalloyed, straight, stable, incorruptible and happy. But, by pushing these themes to their extreme consequences, Cynics reveal a life which is precisely the very opposite of what was traditionally recognized as the true life.' Foucault puts the focus on one of the precepts of the Cynics, taken first as an example of the alteration of currency and later as an oracle addressed to Diogenes: in order to become famous, 'alter your currency'. What does that mean? For Foucault, it means that 'the forms and habits which usually stamp existence and give it its features must be replaced by the effigy of the principles traditionally accepted by philosophy' (Foucault, *The Courage of the Truth*, 244). True life then is another life. That other provocative life is not one that is beyond the 'currency', but below it: it is shamelessness, poverty, dishonour and natural life or animality. That means a life on the borders of *nomos*. In any event, for Foucault, the mark of the true life is otherness: 'But what I would like to stress in conclusion is this: there is no establishment of the truth without an essential position of otherness; the truth is never the same; there can be truth only in the form of the other world and the other life (*l'autre monde et de la vie autre*)' (Foucault, *The Courage of the Truth*, 340). These were the last words written in the manuscript of the last course by Foucault in the College, on 28 March 1984. Here we recover again the figure of the third: of the absolute witness of the truth 'from outside' a given truth regime.

77. Foucault, *The Courage of the Truth*, 198.
78. Foucault, *The Courage of the Truth*, 29: 'These great preachers played the role of both prophet and parrhesiast in that society. Those who speak of the threatening imminence of the future, of the Kingdom of the Last Day, of the Final Judgement, or of approaching death, at the same time tell men what they are, and tell them frankly, with complete parrhesia, what their faults and crimes are, and in what respects and how they must change their mode of being. Counterposed to this, it seems to me that the same medieval society, the same medieval civilization tended to bring together the other two modes of veridiction: that of wisdom, which tells of the being of things and their nature, and that of teaching. Telling the truth of being and telling the truth of knowledge was the task of an institution which was as specific to the Middle Ages as was preaching: the University. Preaching and the University appear to me to be institutions specific to the Middle Ages, in which we see the functions I have spoken about grouping together, in pairs, and defining a regime of veridiction, a regime of truth-telling, which is very different from the regime we could find in the Hellenistic and Greco-Roman world, where instead was parrhesia and wisdom that were combined.'
79. Foucault signals this point in quoting Gregory of Nazianz, Oration 25 in St. Gregory of Nazianzus, *Select Orations* (Washington, DC: Catholic University of America Press, 2003), who praises Maximus for being 'the best and most perfect philosopher, the martyr, the witness of the truth . . . in Gregory's mouth, it is not a question of just the verbal testimony of someone who speaks the truth. It involves someone who, in his very life, his dog's life, from the moment of embracing asceticism until the present, in his body, his life, his acts, his frugality, his renunciations, and his ascesis, has never ceased being the living witness of the truth. He has suffered, endured, and deprived himself so that the truth takes shape in his own life, as it were, in his own existence, his own body'. Foucault, *The Courage of the Truth*, 173. Instead of simply an act of violence and propaganda, as in the historical plot of Philippe Buc, 'Martyre et ritualité dans l'Antiquité tardive. Horizons de l'écriture médiévale des rituels', *Annales. Histoire, Sciences Sociales* 48(1) (1997): 63–92.
80. Foucault, *The Courage of the Truth*, 332: 'What distinguishes the courage of someone like Socrates, or Diogenes, for example, from the martyr's courage – I think it is Saint Jerome who says this – is precisely that the former is only the courage of man addressing other men, whereas the courage of the Christian martyrs rests on this other aspect, this other dimension of the same parrhesia, which is trust in God; confidence in salvation, in God's goodness, and also in His listening. And here a whole set of texts show that the theme of parrhesia joins up with the theme of faith and trust in God.'

81. Foucault, *The Courage of the Truth*, 30.
82. Victor Turner, *Celebration: Studies in Festivity and Ritual* (Washington, DC: Smithsonian Institution Press; University of Michigan, 1982), who takes the expression from Arnold van Gennep, *Rites of Passage* (London: Routledge, 1960).
83. For an extended argument, see Herrero, 'Sacrament and Oath', 35–49.
84. Prodi, *Il sacramento del potere*, 64. Stefan Esders holds that the custom of pronouncing an oath in front of the political sovereign once seemed to derive from an ancient German tradition, but today it has been established that it comes from the military institutions of the late Roman Empire. Stefan Esders, 'Les origines militaires du serment dans les royaumes barbares (V–VII siècles)', *Oralité et lien social au Moyen Age (Occident, Byzance, Islam)* Marie-France Auzépy et al. (eds) (Paris: ACHCByz, 2008), 19–27.
85. On the Roman–Germanic context, see Cristophe Camby, 'Le serment dans la société franque. Innovation germanique ou continuité romaine?' in *Le Sacré et la Parole. Le Serment au Moyen Age*, M. Aurell, J. Aurell and M. Herrero (eds) (Paris: Classiques Garnier, 2018), 17–33.
86. Theodor Mommsen, *The History of Rome under the Emperors* (London: Routledge, 1999) I. ch. V: 'The victims needed for the public service of the gods were procured by a tax on actions at law; the defeated party in an ordinary process paid down to the state a cattle-fine (*sacramentum*) proportioned to the value of the object in dispute.'
87. d'Ors, *Derecho privado romano*, §72. See also Guindon, *Le Serment*, 64.
88. Theodore B. Foster, '*Mysterium* and *Sacramentum* in the Vulgate and Old Latin Versions', *American Journal of Theology* 19 (1915): 402–15, 412. Also see Benveniste, *Vocabulaire*, 163: 'C'est que le serment n'est ce pas une institution autonome, il n'est pas un acte qui ait sa signification en soi ni se suffise à lui-même. C'est un rite qui garantit et sacralise une affirmation. L'intention du serment est toujours la même dans toutes les civilisations. Mais l'institution peut revêtir des caractères bien différents.' This explains why there is no unique Indo-European term for 'oath', which nevertheless can be found in all languages.
89. Foster, '*Mysterium* and *Sacramentum*', 413.
90. Salvatore Tondo, 'Il "sacramentum militiae" nell' ambiente culturale romano-italico', *Studia et documenta historiae iuris* 29 (1963): 1–123.
91. Esders, 'Les origines', 19, 26.
92. Harnack asked a similar question in Adolf von Harnack, *Militia Christi. Die Christliche Religion und der Soldatenstand in den ersten Drei Jahrhunderten* (Darmstadt: Wissenschaftliche Buchgesellschaft, 1963).

He explains the transference of meaning from the 'military oath' to the Church's sacramental experience by the idea that war is one of life's basic forms and one where every human being can easily achieve virtue. In fact, there are military elements in the theological idea of *sacramentum*. Harnack, *Militia*, 59–60: 'Nun, der göttliche und der menschliche Fahneneid, das Feldzeichen Christi und das Feldzeichen des Teufels, das Lager des Lichts und das Lager der Finsternis sind unverträglich; eine und dieselbe Seele kann nicht Zweien verpflichtet sein, Gott und dem Kaiser.' Also: 'Eben deshalb darf kein Christ Soldat, darf kein Soldat Christ werden. Nicht um den Krieg handelt es sich; nein, auch im Frieden darf kein Christ im Heere stehen.' This question was re-edited centuries later in the dispute between James I of England and Robert Bellarmin about the 'oath of allegiance'. The work of Francisco Suárez, *De iuramento fidelitatis* was also motivated by that controversy: the oath imposed by James implied renouncing a mediation of the Church; the sacred was identified with the political.

93. For the differences between the approach of the Great Eastern Fathers and that of Tertullian regarding the sacramentality of Christian life, see Eliseo Ruffini and Enzo Lodi, *Mysterion e Sacramentum. La sacramentalità negli scritti dei Padri e nei testi liturgici primitive* (Bologna: Centro Editoriale Dehoniano, 1987), 118–19. For the Eastern Fathers 'mystery' always refers to history, that is, to an event to come that will reveal the truth, while for Tertullian it is more a static and immoveable reality. Indeed, the word 'mystery' is also used by those Fathers for all those realities that are effective in the economy of salvation related to the covenant.

94. Tertullian was the person principally responsible for the development of the theological terminology of the Latin West; after him came Cyprian of Carthage and Hilary of Poitiers. This was also the case for the theological coinage of the word 'sacrament'.

95. Émile Backer, 'Tertullien', in *Pour l'histoire du mot 'sacramentum'. Les Anténicéans*, Joseph de Ghellinck (ed.) (Paris: Honoré Champion, 1924). In this book various authors explore the meaning of the word 'sacramentum' in the writings of the Fathers of the Church prior to the Council of Nicaea, that is, before the year 325.

96. See Hoppe for the Old Testament and Zahn for the New Testament: Heinrich Hoppe, *Syntax und Stil des Tertullians* (Leipzig: Teubner, 1903); Theodor Zahn, *Geschichte des neutestamentlichen Kanons* (Hildesheim: Georg Olms, 1975).

97. Hans von Soden, *Das Lateinische Neue Testament in Afrika zur Zeit Cyprians* (Leipzig: J. C. Hinrichs, 1909), 1611.

98. Foster, '*Mysterium* and *Sacramentum*', 413: 'the mystery-sense had by that time become firmly attached to sacramentum'.

99. Benveniste, *Vocabulaire*, 334.

100. Foster, '*Mysterium* and *Sacramentum*'. In fact, the occurrence of the word *sacramentum* in the Latin Vulgate is a disputed question. As Foster notes, it is in eight passages out of a total of twenty-eight occurrences in the Septuagint that the word 'mystery' – and not oath or covenant – is rendered as *sacramentum* in the Latin Vulgate.
101. Harnack, *Militia*, 33. Also Valentine de Gröne, *'Sacramentum' oder Begriff und Bedeutung von Sakrament in der alten Kirche bis zur Scholastik* (Soest: Nasse in Comm, 1853). Also Hans von Soden, 'Μυστήριον und *sacramentum* in den ersten drei Jahrhunderten der Kirche', *Zeitschrift für den neutestamentarische Wissenschaft* 12 (1911): 188–227.
102. Philippe Depreux, 'Les carolingiens et le serment', in *Oralité et lien social au Moyen Age (Occident, Byzance, Islam)* Marie-France Auzépy et al. (eds), (Paris: ACHCByz, 2008), 63–80, 65.
103. Hugh of Saint Victor, *On the Sacraments of the Christian Faith*, ed. Roy J. Deferrari (Cambridge, MA: Mediaeval Academy of America, 1951), I.1.10, 180.
104. It was not until Alexander III (1259) that the structural constitution of the Church began to be divided into sacramental (seven sacraments) and jurisdictional spheres. Oaths were now considered a matter for the jurisdictional sphere, not for the sacramental. After the Church had completely sacralised the oath, through the construction of sacramental doctrine, it returned to the secularisation of the oath in order to differentiate it from the sacrament. In other words, sacramental doctrine delimits the civil–legal sphere from the ecclesiastical–legal sphere. Hence, Thomas Aquinas could say that sacrament has nothing to do with oath and perjury.
105. Hugh of Saint Victor, *On the Sacraments*, I.1.10, 180.
106. Hugh of Saint Victor, *On the Sacraments*, I.1.10, 180.
107. d'Ors, *Derecho*, §148.

Chapter 4

Charisma or the Power as Gift

'Il faut savoir calculer ce qui excède le calcul . . .'[1]

The theopolitical reasons for legitimate power are associated with the figure of charisma. In fact, *charisma* is one of those terms derived from *charis*, which, while being scarcely used in the ancient world, was appropriated by the Christian language, particularly by Paul of Tarsus. It was only much later that it was transferred into the language of politics, chiefly, but not only, by Max Weber. Clifford Geertz describes charisma as a manifestation of 'the inherent sacredness of sovereign power'[2] and makes particular mention of the inherently theopolitical character of political power that is apparent in charisma.

Indeed, the theopolitical character of power has been compromised in the discursive journey of the word charisma. Many different aspects related to the sacredness of power are indicated within the meaning of a word, which is far from ever being fixed. In what follows, I will pursue those meanings and in particular the theopolitical transferences of meanings between the theological and the political discursive registers. In the semantic trajectory of the signifier charisma, if Paul marked a first point of inflection by appropriating it to Christian discourse, Weber marked a second and, so far, almost definitive point of inflection by appropriating it to the field of political theory and sociology. The aim of these pages, after briefly tracing the genealogy of the meaning of charisma, is to reinscribe the political idea of charisma in its theological locus, that is, to discover the political charisma as a figure of the divine.

The Genealogy of Charisma: A Crooked Line of Meaning

The word *charis* was already present in Greek literature and mythology. It can be found in Homer's *Iliad* (18, 382–8), where it is used to describe both a personification of grace and beauty and the wife of Hephaestus. Also in the *Iliad* (Il. 14.269), Pasiphae, who is destined to be the wife of Sleep, is called one of the younger *charites*. The plural *charites* occurs several times in the Homeric poems (Od. 18.194). Hesiod (Hes. Th. 945) for his part, in the *Theogony* names Aglaia as the wife of Hephaestus, and describes her as the youngest of the *charites*. But, according to the *Odyssey*, the wife of Hephaestus is Aphrodite; from this we may infer, if not the identity of Aphrodite and Charis, at least a close connection and resemblance in the notions entertained about the two divinities. *Charites* lend their grace and beauty to everything that delights and elevates gods and men. This notion was probably the reason why Charis was named as being the wife of Hephaestus, the divine artist. The most perfect works of art are thus called the works of the *charites*, and the greatest artists are their favourites.[3] The idea of personified grace and beauty was divided into a plurality of beings at a very early stage, probably to indicate the various ways in which the beautiful is manifested in the world and adorns it. Always understood to be God-given, *charis* was first considered to be a wholly embodied quality. However, the genealogy of the term shows a gradual evaporation of *charis* from the body, although the certain correspondence between the spiritual and the bodily appearance does not dispel. Plato already begins to consider *charis* as a function of the beautiful soul instead of as a quality that radiated through the body, as if it were a force unto itself.[4]

A general meaning of *charis* in the *koine* was gift or present, with connotations such as free, given out of free goodwill and good. The general use of the word was not necessarily a religious one, even though we have seen that in poetics it is. What is certain is that it meant a concrete good or gift.[5] In fact, in first-century Graeco-Roman culture, *charis* could refer to both the ritual of giving and that of receiving. An ethic of the counter-gift was present and constituted a complex system of conventions governing reciprocity. This system could apply to the relationship between a wealthy benefactor and his city or community, within a domestic household, between the caesars and local political associations, and between states.[6]

The convention governing the roles of giver and receiver was so strong that it was described by Seneca as the bond of human society. The type of giving discussed in his *De Beneficiis* is no longer the ceremony of gift-giving but the internal conditions to be acknowledged as a giver. The requirement of purity of intention is proportional to the risk that self-interested considerations might be involved in giving. He denounces the classic symbolic benefits of the practice of gift-giving: prestige, glory and honour. In this context of suspicion, Seneca comes to celebrate unreciprocated giving. The joy of the giver in this case results from doing good for its own sake because giving is beautiful.[7]

These general meanings are what Paul of Tarsus found to be part of the language of his own time when he coined the word *charisma* in the context of Christian revelation.[8] His particular appropriation allows some scholars to speak of 'Paul's invention of charisma'.[9] Paul refers to *charisma* sixteen times. Apart from three individual references – in 1 Timothy 4:14, 2 Timothy 1:6 and 2 Corinthians 1:11 – Paul elaborates his conception of *charisma* and *charismata* primarily in his epistles to the Romans (six references) and 1 Corinthians (seven references). In these references, we find a broad meaning of gifts and a more general one of service; and other more specific meanings such as government, prophecy, preaching, miracle, healing, tongues, revelation, giving, mercy and interpretation among others also appear. In Ephesians 4, 1, Paul designates all of them as gifts or presents;[10] he has no interest in systematising. Baumert affirms that, to the general Greek meaning of *charis*, Paul, by using the term *charisma*, adds two more aspects: the given gift comes from God and it is inscribed in the order of salvation. But also for him, as in the common use of the *koine*, the good was 'objective': in other words, something given to someone, such as the gift of prophecy or the gift of tongues; it was not 'subjective', like a personal state or a virtue, or a power to do something.

From Paul's texts onwards, Christian literature continues to refer to the *charismas*, although the meaning of what they are is progressively modified and increased. Ritter speaks of a polyphony.[11] Many nuances and derivations are added to the original meaning. Tertullian (160–220) retains the Greek word *charismata* instead of translating it, but the Vulgate (382) renders the word as *gratia*. Origin (185–254) and John of Damascus (675–749) understood *charismata* as a present bestowed by the Holy Spirit to an individual; an endowment, or talent or capability given to someone, that is, a 'subjective gift'. It could be both ordinary or extraordinary, a process or a content; and it did not aim only at helping the construction of the Church.[12] The emphasis on this aspect, that the *charismata* are for the salvation of the Christian community and not only for personal salvation, which was otherwise clearly present in Paul, was the work of John Chrysostom, Theodore of Mopsuestia, Theodoret of Cyrus and Cyril of Alexandria. Particularly in Chrysostom, every Christian has a charismatic call to be in the midst of the world in order to unify the body of Christ, in Paul's expression.

Certainly, in the transit from the seventh to the eighth centuries, the meaning of the term varies in almost every writer. But the clear idea of a hierarchy was still not present, nor was the idea of an 'office'. Over time, however, the idea of *charisma* was displaced from the individual to the institution of the Church. It is the Church which becomes charismatic. In fact, the *Treatise of Grace* (STh 1–2 q. 109–112) of Thomas Aquinas begins to speak of *charisma* as a 'service', something already close to 'office'.

This displacement of meaning generated a polemic in the context of the Reformed Church's theology of the nineteenth and twentieth centuries, and was decisive for the transfer of the signifier *charisma* to the political sphere. In fact, the discussion begins with the debate between Julius Friedrich Stahl and Johann Wilhelm Friedrich Höfling about the structural character of the Church; Stahl was a defender of the hierarchical view, while Höfling supported the communitarian view.[13] Rudolph Sohm and Adolf von Harnack revisit these positions to a certain extent. The discussion focuses in this case on the question of to what extent the idea of having a church law is compatible with the essence of the Church. In his *Kirchenrecht*, Sohm took the step of characterising the Church as a 'charismatic organization',[14] arguing that the primitive Church was organised in *charisma*s without having any legal constitution ('*keine rechtliche Verfassung*'). The communitarian character of the assembled Christians is accentuated by Sohm to the detriment of the juridical–constitutional aspect. In his interpretation, the Catholic Church deviates from that origin, and it was Luther who partly restored the original idea.[15] The *charismata* have been continually given to apostles, prophets and preachers until now. For this reason, the leadership of the community has to be borne by those gifted persons and not by election.

However, for Harnack, the idea of the Church as a purely spiritual and religious entity, as the people of God or the body of Christ, without a legal body is a spiritualist error.[16] Harnack understands the Church as a historical institution and, hence, he justifies its structure as one that is historically generated. He elaborates a double principle of organisation of the community: one, *charisma*-based; and the other, administration-based. He speaks of three hierarchical levels: first, the apostles, prophets and teachers, who are gifted with *charisma*; secondly, the seniors, whose capacity for organisation comes from their character; and, thirdly, the bishops and deacons who are merely an administrative organisation. With this structure he wanted to mediate in the discussion, trying to justify both points of view; in his opinion, both *charisma* and office were necessary for the historical constitution of the Church. In any event, both viewpoints disappoint what they consider the Catholic position of a law-based, hierarchically constituted structure of the Church with well-defined offices. In Sohm's view, this idea of the Church is a reification of the *charisma*, since it is the office which confers *charisma*, an idea far removed from the apostolic tradition.

After Sohm, the dispute persisted in twentieth-century theology. In fact, the charismatic movement in the Church originated in the reformed churches in an open *Kulturkampf* with Catholicism. In that dispute, *charismatic* means democratic as opposed to a hierarchical or 'monarchical' idea of the Church.[17] On the one hand, Hans Kung saw the Church as a plural community of *charisma*s, and, on the other hand, Karl Rahner joined the first discussion by distinguishing between 'charisma of office' and 'non-institutional charisma'. But it was Jürgen Moltmann, who recovered the theological charismatic aspect of the Church in its primitive sense.[18] The key aspect of his idea of *charisma* is the ordinary way of its manifestation. These ordinary gifts are called *charisma*s precisely because they are by nature a gift for others. Hence, the word *charisma* already carries in itself the mark of the community. Along with these ordinary *charisma*s, there are also some special *charisma*s, called supernatural, like the gift of tongues, the gift of prophecy and the gift of healing, which are granted to some for the construction of the community of Christ and which bear particular witness to the future kingdom.[19] There is a distribution of powers in the Church, which assures that it will be non-totalitarian. The gift of the Holy Spirit descends in a plural way on to each person with different results. The unity of the community should not degenerate into a compulsion to seek equality, and less still an equalisation of the different gifts. Call and gift, *kleis* and *charisma*, are closely interrelated. Through the different *charisma*s, Christ's lordship is inserted into the world. The dominion and power of Jesus are shown in His capacity to suffer in order to generate these gifts in men. The Holy Spirit makes the existence of men shine through their *charisma*s.

Many generations have represented this force as an aureole, which illuminates existence and expresses a life that is pervaded by God and, therefore, reflects divine radiance and glory (*kabod, doxa*).[20]

Prompted by the dispute between Sohm and Harnack, the term *charisma* has been transferred to Max Weber's sociology in a very different context from that of the development of Paul's theology.[21] In fact, Paul does not use the word charisma to refer to political power. He uses other words in that context: κύριος, δεσπότης, βασιλεύω, ἄρχω, ἐξουσιάζω, δύναμαι, ἐνέργεια, κυβέρνησις.[22] In any event, *charisma* was never associated with power; although, in fact, the poetic primitive term *charis*, referring to divine splendour, was appropriated by ancient emperors and kings to associate their power to the divinities. However, this line of derivation from the poetic pagan *charis* should not be confused with the Pauline *charisma*, which was transferred to the political sphere by Weber. In fact, we can attribute to Max Weber the political popularisation of one of the central terms in the vocabulary of Christianity: *charisma* as a 'gift of grace'.[23] Appropriating Sohm's ideas, Weber understands *charisma* as certain qualities of an individual personality as a result of which he or she is considered extraordinary and supernaturally endowed. Hence, it may be justified that exceptionally his or her action does not conform to established legality.[24] However, there is a great difference between the conception of *charisma* in which the apostle knows that something is being accomplished through him, which was Sohm's viewpoint, and Weber's idea that the charismatic person possesses something that renders him attractive. Moreover, in Sohm's view, *charisma*s come from God, that is, their origin is theological; this is far from clear in Weber's account of *charisma*, since he never discusses where a personal *charisma* comes from. In addition, Weber considers charismatic legitimation one of the three ideal types of legitimation and he opposes it to the other two – the legal and traditional ones; and he implicitly equals legal with democratic legitimacy, displacing *charisma* towards authoritarianism. Thus, in the transfer from the theological to the political sphere, the word *charisma* has changed position; from being the democratic paradigm of the Church, it has become the authoritarian paradigm of the state: an authoritarian turn has been achieved in the conception of charismatic power.[25]

Another response to Sohm's defence of the *charisma* contemporary with that of Weber was Carl Schmitt's *Romischer Katholizismus und politischer Form* (1923). Schmitt supports the idea of office by arguing, in accordance with the medieval Thomistic tradition, that the Church mediates the personality of Christ and that its whole structure is *charismatic* in its offices. He tries to reconcile both aspects, even making the Church a paradigm of political representation that captures the legal *pathos* and the *pathos* of glory at the same time.[26] Not surprisingly, Schmitt was also attentive to Max Weber's concept of charismatic legitimacy in his *Politische Theologie*, where he waxed ironically about Weber's charismatic legitimation as a protestant derivation of ecclesiastical *charisma*.[27] Following this confessional bias, Weber would have interpreted the *charismatic* as irrational, subjective and almost impossible to 'routinise' in any institutional aspect. On the contrary, for Schmitt, the charismatic character of the Church is due to the fact that it embodies a superior 'idea' that is expressed in a juridical form; in other words, it is due to hyper-rationality.

Post-Weberian anthropologists such as Edward Shils or Clifford Geertz were influenced by the idea of the relationship between *charisma* and 'office'. Shils argued that the charismatic propensity is a function of the need for order.[28] *Charisma* appears automatically in connection with the entities and institutions from which emanate the necessary order. This paradigm was explicitly followed by Clifford Geertz. He renders a disenchanted account of *charisma* in which sacred is named directly as a 'centre of meanings'. He follows Shils in his intention to restore the 'connection between the symbolic value individuals possess and their relation to the active centers of the social order'.[29] Such charismatic centres are 'essentially concentrated loci of serious acts': stories, ceremonies, insignia, liturgies embody serious values, mark the centre as such and give it its aura.[30] Geertz says that rulers and gods, insofar as they both exercise power, share common properties, and so he also speaks of political theology.

The 'cultural turn' of *charisma* made by Geertz has made it possible to reinterpret charisma in the modern world and abandon the Weberian idea that charismatic legitimacy was present only in ancient or archaic societies. In fact, as Geertz asserts, a wholly demystified world is a world wholly depoliticised, even if we have to accept that modernity has anthropomorphised power: 'the extraordinary has not gone out of modern politics, however much the banal may have entered; power not only still intoxicates, it still exalts'.[31] This is the conviction of many contemporary scholars. Indeed, recent texts have pointed out that the political arena is unthinkable without the idea of legitimation based on an event exhibiting charismatic aspects. In the religious studies of the twentieth century, we can again see the double paradigm of power, authoritarian versus democratic, which is present in the discussion of *charisma* to this day.[32] Furthermore, sociologists and historians still appropriate the theological voice of *charisma*.[33]

Focusing on the ambivalence of sacred and sovereign power, Robert Yelle has pointed out that what we usually call 'religion' includes not only institutions that reinforce the social order, but also acts of transgression. In his view, *charisma* could be found on both sides.[34] The examples he explores are the biblical *herem*, the *jubilee* or the *sabbatical year*, which can be associated with the classic divine gestures of sacrifice and pardon. But are they as such 'authoritarian gestures'?; or, are they in addition, as Yelle argues, 'exit signs', that is, functions of transcendence within a total social order? In a way the charismatic aspect of power speaks of the character of those 'exit signs' of an immanent political order.

In many of these texts, *charisma* is a long way from Paul's idea; they mainly consider *charisma* as a matter of representation and production of effects on or of the audience in the leader in a constructive path not only of persons, but also and even mainly of objects. As we have shown, however, the theological tradition following Paul of Tarsus tends to interpret the *charismatic* in a non-authoritarian way; that is, it stresses the ordinary aspect of *charisma* as a gift to every member of a community.

The aim of this chapter, however, is not to develop a history of the meaning of *charisma*; nor is it to investigate the topic from different points of view, such as management, culture or film theory, as recent bibliography tends to do.[35] Rather, it is to reinscribe the figure of charismatic power in its theological locus. This movement implies a recovery of aspects of Paul's meaning of *charisma* going beyond the dialectic between democracy and autocracy. Charismatic power, then, means an interpretation of power as gift and consequently as sacrifice, pardon and glory. Indeed, from the charismatic root of power, understood as gift, an alternative paradigm of legitimation of power can be advanced, which does not coincide with the criteria expressed by Weber. In the following pages, therefore, an attempt will be made to give an account of the features of another paradigm of legitimisation of power defined by *charisma*.

Power, Gift and Sacrifice

The idea of gift is at the centre of the theological meaning of *charisma*. Reflection on the communal gift in the social sciences originates in the school of Emile Durkheim, in particular, from the work of Marcel Mauss, although other anthropological researchers such as Boas, Swanton, Thurnwald, Best and Malinowski have also worked on case studies. The work of Mauss was crucial, not only in universalising the phenomenon of the gift but also by provoking a reappropriation of the topic by philosophy.

In fact, Mauss presents the first systematic study of the custom of exchanging gifts.[36] He produced a comparative analysis identifying the universal character of the phenomenon of ceremonial gift-exchange in terms of both place (American northwest, Melanesia, Polynesia and Andaman Islands), and time. In this analysis he emphasises the common roots of the various gestures of gift-exchange and shows that they do not constitute a marginal phenomenon, but one of the fundamental aspects of life in traditional societies and a practice that still survives in modern societies. Mauss regards the gift as a perfect example of what he calls a total social phenomenon, since it involves legal, economic, moral, religious and aesthetic dimensions, which are all related to the construction of a community. He understands the gift as one of the archaic forms of the contract. The same can be said of Georges Davy, who, following also the footsteps of Durkheim, years before had published *La Foi jurée*, in which he attributed to the figure of gift the structural element of the contract.[37] Both authors focus on the circulation of objects in order to understand the contractual bond in the establishment of economic and legal relations. According to Mauss, the individuals and groups involved in the exchange of gifts are as important as the objects exchanged. Mauss considers that it is the circulation of the objects that makes communality. In fact, the gift in ancient times had two functions: first, it was the symbolic source of sociality and hierarchy; secondly, it was the means to circulate material goods. The main thesis of Mauss is that the given object, the gift (*mana*), had an originary impulse to recover its original place and for that reason it forced an exchange. Some ancient cultures presumed that the objects were endowed with energy, as if the objects themselves were alive. The objects were thought to embody something of the identity of the first owner and donor. Accepting the gift presupposed also accepting something of the donor. Zanardo speaks of a 'reserve of energy' of the given gift by reason of the 'transcendentality of the intention of the donor'.[38] The gift always returns to the donor, although later (at a temporal distance) and in a different form (through fluidity of passage).

Mauss' ideas can be seen as a good explanation of the economic interchange, but could they also be an explanation of power as a communal relation? Is power a circulating object and therefore interchangeable? Or is power more related to that '*sacra*' which are excluded from the ceremonial exchange? Contemporary philosophy has largely read and interpreted Mauss' *The Gift* in what appears to be an attempt to escape from economic determinism.[39]

In particular, Jacques Derrida has discussed Mauss' thesis by introducing the element of time in the argument. Derrida's main concern with Mauss' central thesis is the assumption of the return of the gift to the prior position. Something worthy of being called gift cannot return to the donor, not even over the long term.[40] Derrida stresses the idea that all one gives is given within time. It is not possible to give something without at the same time giving one's time. However, we cannot make time visible except through the contents that occur in time, given that time is a pure form. Time and gift share the condition of non-returnability.

In opposition to Mauss, he recovers Seneca's position in *De Beneficiis*. A gift should always be wasteful and for that reason can be thought of as a figure of the sacred. As Seneca explicitly states, pure giving is, above all, a divine privilege (*De Beneficiis*, 4.9). The gift cannot be thought of as having the economic rationality of the exchange, as Mauss does. In the presence of a counter-gift, the gift as such loses its reality and begins to be merchandise, that is, it begins to be governed by another type of relationship: purchase and sale. 'Return, exchange, counter gift, or debt'[41] are incompatible with the idea of a gift. In fact, the time of the gift cannot be a circular one, but an instant or at least a breaking of time, in any case irreversible.[42] However, this instant, or that effraction, in Derrida's words, is not extra-chronological. It is not even a now that should be concatenated with a past and a future in a temporal synthesis; however, it is not 'outside' time. The gift is 'external' to the economic calculation and, at the same time, it is within time: 'It is this exteriority that sets the circle going.'[43]

Another condition of the gift that happens in conjunction with its non-returnability is that it is not to be acknowledged. In fact, the condition of non-returnability of the material good must be accompanied by the non-recognition of the donor. Certainly, recognition is a symbolic good that could be considered in some cases as a kind of return. Therefore, Derrida insists that in the presence of recognition, the gift is cancelled. The mere identification of the gift as such seems to destroy it. The two conditions under which this non-recognition may occur are oblivion and fortune. Both can deactivate consciousness and intention in a way that allows the gift as such to happen. Unlike the case of the figure of the oath, in which the aim is to make memory happen, the gift is possible only if the act of giving and the giving self are forgotten.[44] Derrida speaks of an 'absolute oblivion' and not of an oblivion of something.[45]

The second possible condition is labelled by Derrida as occasion or fortune: something encounters me by chance that makes me a donor. What makes the gift an event is its unpredictability, that is, the impossibility of being contextualised in an horizon of expectation. It is random, or at least it cannot be chained in between causes and consequences. The factor that may impede intentionality is the irruption of an occasion: 'the event of the gift must always keep its status of incalculable or unforeseeable exception (without general rule, without program, and even without concept)'.[46]

It is just at this point that Jean-Luc Marion continues the discussion of Derrida with Mauss. His correction of Derrida is that the gift must be separated from exchange, by letting its natural meaning be reduced to givenness.[47] And to do so he applies a triple bracketing or, in phenomenological jargon, a triple reduction. In effect, the gift reaches its accomplishment by cancelling each one of the three terms of exchange: without a giver (*donateur*); without a recipient (*donataire*) – thus freeing itself from reciprocity; and even without a thing given (*don*) – thus freeing itself from a logic of equality.[48] Understood in this way, the gift always remains free to self-perform unconditionally.

The first aporia arises when the given gift appears. At this moment the consistency of the thing occupies the centre of the phenomenical stage and conceals the fact that it has been given. But the problem from the phenomenological point of view is that a gift with any relation to a giver no longer bears the mark of any process of givenness. The question that Marion then tries to solve is how the phenomenical character of the gift can be grasped.[49] How can the process of giving make its appearance while ensuring that the gift preserves the mark of having been given? Marion's response is that the character of gift can be granted only by the one who receives the gift, insofar as he is willing to offer it as something that has been given to him as a gift. It is this complicated logic that makes possible a gift that escapes exchange and emerges as the figure of a power that gives beyond economic calculation. This is in Marion's view the figure of sacrifice.[50] Sacrifice is not destruction, but privation of a good for the sake of experiencing myself as beyond things. The gesture of sacrifice, as much as that of gift, does not allow us to confuse giving with a simple exchange.[51] At issue is not the idea of counter-gift, since there is a wasting, but the possibility of the recognition of a gift as such. The interpretation of Abraham's sacrifice changes completely in this light: what God asked of Abraham is not the destruction of the beloved son; and Abraham knew it. He knew, in his response 'God will provide' that God did not want the destruction of Isaac. The idea and practice of human sacrifices, are alien to the religion of Israel. God just wanted Abraham to experience what it meant to be the donor of a gift.[52] Sacrifice destroys – or seems to destroy, as in the case of Abraham – the given in order to uncover that which made it visible and possible – the advance of givenness itself. The same could be said of Christ's sacrifice.[53] The non-taking place of the sacrifice of Isaac prefigured in an existential way the taking place of Christ's sacrifice as the only personal sacrifice made in the name of the Christian God.

In the figure of sacrifice, declares Derrida, death appears as the condition of the authenticity of the gift. This means that the unconditional can appear only under the condition of its death. Through a reading of Patocka, Derrida places the *mysterium tremendum* of the sacrificial gift at the centre of Christianity:

> What is it that makes us tremble in the *mysterium tremendum*? It is the gift of infinite love, the dissymmetry that exists between the divine regard that sees me, and myself, who doesn't see what is looking at me; it is the gift and endurance of death that exist in the irreplaceable, the disproportion between the infinite gift and my finitude, responsibility as culpability, sin, salvation, repentance, and sacrifice.[54]

This idea echoes the Pauline maxim 'work out your own salvation with fear and trembling' (Philippians 2:12), well-known through Kierkegaard's commentaries. The ethical order remits to another realm, where a higher obedience reigns: the absolute form of responsibility appears in this sacrificial responsibility that should always remain in secret, as was the case of Abraham's sacrifice. In fact, Abraham manifested his disposition to accept the sacrifice, but he kept secret that he was following a divine ordeal, even when tempted. This 'secret' (*deus absconditus*), Derrida would say, does not mean that something is concealed or hidden, but simply encoded or encrypted: it does not refer to something visible that is removed from sight, but to the invisible absolute. The relationship between God and Abraham is dissymmetrical: 'this gaze that sees me without my seeing'.[55] He looks into me in secret and I cannot see him, even if I hear his voice. According to Derrida, what lies in this secret is Abraham's non-calculation. From an external point of view, the economic gaze could think that Abraham has made the best transaction: a sacrifice in order to recover other revenues. However, God knew that Abraham had exposed himself to a complete loss, that he had sacrificed economic calculation altogether, because He had looked into him.[56] Derrida calls this act of renunciation a '*sovereign* calculation that consists in no more calculating'.[57] Also, Agamben insists on this aspect of authentic giving when he says that gratuitousness manifests itself as an irreducible excess with regard to all obligatory service. Grace does not provide the foundation for exchange and social obligations; it allows for their interruption.[58] Power is beyond the economic calculus. Sacrifice is the name of 'another' paradigm of power: not the power to dominate, but the power of renunciation.[59]

Hans Urs von Balthasar also insisted on the idea that the power of God shows in His absolute love, which achieves its plenitude on the Christ's *kenosis*. God's sovereignty consists in the voluntary dispossession of historical power and the conferring of that power to others. The glory of the Lord is the epiphany of this self-emptying of God, this *kenosis* of the highest that reduces Himself to nothingness.[60] True and long-lasting 'effective' power follows paradoxically this structure of 'ineffectivity'. Christ changes the political paradigm of power and sovereignty, since his death on the cross is considered a triumph, a victory over death and evil. God cuts the chain of violence: no other sacrifice is required any more. No more scapegoats.[61] Pardon, forgiveness is the new form of every sacrifice; the highest gift and the theological form of effective power.

Martyrs are exceptional witnesses of Christ in places and at times in which His sacrifice is being negated or eclipsed. In an appropriation of semantic terms from the field of power, Sigrid Weigel sees in them an example of 'counter-sovereignty'.[62] In fact, as Antonio Cerella underlines early Christian martyrs, through their sacrifice, escaped power or Roman *potestas*. Indeed, 'they claimed the truth (*veritas*) of their faith against the sovereignty (*imperium*) of the Romans'.[63] Cerella shows the theological–political genealogy of sacrifice, from ancient cultures, through the institution of the *rex sacrorum*, to the Christian martyrs, whose figure he distinguishes very clearly from the kamikazes or the human immolations of Islam. In any case, Cerella's main thesis, which has also been argued here, is that 'there is a close, structural relationship between martyrdom and political power'.[64] And this relationship has nothing to do with the biopolitics of which Foucault speaks, since this is inaugurated only with the annulment of the transcendent dimension, something that occurs only in political modernity. Foucault himself, as we have analysed in the previous chapter, speaks of martyrs as counter-sovereignty, as the epitome of parrhesia.

As mentioned, the theological–political transference of the gift that appears in the form of sacrifice is well illuminated by Derrida when he speaks of 'sovereign calculation'. In using the term 'sovereign', he refers to the sphere of power. This 'sovereign calculation', that consists, in Derrida's words, in 'savoir calculer ce qui excède le calcul'.[65] In fact, the political decision, far from being an economic transaction, should be a liberation from calculation, an excess or an aporia that breaks the economic chain to the point of assuming the extreme of violent death. The reinscription of charismatic power in its theological place speaks of a power that is understood as self-emptying, as a renunciation, as offering, as voluntary holocaust.

Pardon as the Supreme Power

Derrida uses yet another theological–political transference: 'sovereign forgiveness', as the counterpart of the right to punish. Forgiveness is not a condition of the gift, as sacrifice is; it is the highest gift.

In the seminar of 1997–8 devoted to perjury and pardon, Derrida follows Jankélévitch in his book *Le pardon*;[66] of which some parts of the seminar are an extended commentary. He says that the example *par excellence* of 'the absolute and *sovereign* forgiveness'[67] as opposed to the right to punish, is the regalian right of grace. In fact, he attests that pardon – for-give-ness – is the manifestation of human power:

> As soon as there is forgiveness, if there is any, we enter a zone of divinity in the so-called human experience, it is the genesis of the divine, the holy or the sacred. This analogy is the very place of theological-political . . .; it is also what ensures political sovereignty.[68]

Antonio M. Hespanha indeed speaks of pardon as a common practice of late medieval corporate monarchy. The 'complacent regime of pardon' is explicable for at least two reasons, in his view: on the one hand, by the role that the theory of government attributed to clemency and, on the other hand, by the role that the theory of justice attributed to equity. Indeed, clemency is an essential quality of the king and goes hand in hand with his legitimacy. This is how Seneca himself described it in *De clementia*. The prince must be loved rather than feared. The king should rather ignore and forgive than punish, even if this is contrary to a rigorous application of the law. The dialectic of terror and clemency made the king both lord of justice and mediator of grace. God himself, unfolds in the figures of the just Father and the kind Son. These were consistent with the two attributes of royal power: *summum ius, summa clementia*.[69]

Derrida focuses, however, on Kant's amendment of this medieval logic in the *Metaphysics of Morals* when he speaks about the legal effects arising from the nature of civil union, in point E of this treatise, which is titled 'Criminal law and the law of mercy'. In opposing mercy, Kant defends *ius talionis*. His argument follows the line that there must be an equivalence between the crime and the punishment. Nevertheless, Kant's criminal justice never ignores the innate personality of the offender, and this protects him from being treated as a means in this transaction. Kant understands punishment as 'a suffering' or as 'a physical evil' that the offender has to suffer because of the crime he has committed. The logic of criminal justice, which is, according to its nature pure, strict and public, is that of equalisation. This logic must be followed unconditionally and without commotion. To abandon this path, 'to lean more to one side than to the other', would undoubtedly be a severe blow, not only against criminal justice, but also indirectly against distributive justice as the pillar of the civil legal state among men. However, Kant allows, within a very narrow margin, the exercise of grace. In fact, when Kant refers to the sovereign's right of grace to exempt a criminal from punishment, he states that the exercise of this right will be subject to practical considerations related to the safety of the people and the survival of the state. The sovereign may make use of this right when the crimes committed affect his majesty, but not when they go against the interests of his subjects; not even in the case that his majesty would be affected, 'if impunity could endanger the safety of the people' (§ 174).

Also, Hegel exhibits in his *Philosophy of Right* a striking scepticism about mercy, both in the form of judicial discretion and in the form of pardons. Nonetheless, in certain respects Hegel shows some degree of openness to mercy: in principle he approves both the practice of 'equity' as a departure from formal right for moral reasons (§ 223) and the idea of monarchical pardon (§ 282).

He also holds a clear version of progressive hope, hitherto given voice mainly in the utilitarian tradition, that social advances will ultimately result in milder overall punishments (§ 218; see further § 96). Yet Hegel insists that even if society as a whole finds a way to show more leniency in criminal sentencing, it nevertheless remains 'impossible for society to leave a crime unpunished – since the crime would then be posited as right' (§ 218). Thus, for Hegel, every exercise of judicial discretion not only threatens to be arbitrary but also potentially violates by its very nature the necessary respect for the criminal's agency and humanity (§ 132; see also § 211). Furthermore, the fact that Hegel associates the power of pardon directly with the 'sovereignty' and 'majesty' of the monarch sharply limits its practical applicability. Sovereignty, Hegel stresses, implies moments of particular decision, but this particularity must arise from the underlying universality that guides the constitution and the law (§ 275). The monarch's only direct relevance is to create that 'decisive moment' of specific individuality in the state's process of self-determination (§ 279). We should view the monarch as only being 'someone who says "yes" and who dots the "i's"' (§ 280). Nevertheless, when we turn to look more closely at Hegel's account of the pardoning power, it turns out that it draws liberally on the idea that the monarch's rationale for pardoning derives not from temporal considerations, but rather from the higher 'logic' of divine mercy. Thus, when Hegel locates the origin of the pardoning power in the monarch's sovereignty, he goes on to explain that 'only the sovereign is entitled to actualize the power of the spirit' – that is, the *Geist* that stands in for religious concepts throughout his larger philosophy – and that only this 'spirit' has the proper right to undo what has been done and to nullify crime by forgiving and forgetting (§ 282). Hegel's philosophy thus permits the higher religious rationale for divine forgiveness to be translated into an earthly context and folded into what would otherwise constitute an unjustifiable contravention of universality. Such arbitrary and absolute mastery is in the end a fundamental characteristic of the spirit rather than of earthly relations. In the temporal realm, by contrast, such absolute mastery 'is to be found only in the majesty [of the sovereign] and is the prerogative of [the sovereign's] ungrounded decision' (§ 282, bracketed insertions in the original). Even in the hands of the sovereign, however, pardon is precluded from being properly exercised in its own right, and instead can be applied in the temporal sphere only by borrowing its justification from an analogy with the divine.[70]

This superior kind of justice, beyond the law, is called power. Contrary to what Kant supposes, in the case of the right of grace, the law remains valid and its logic is kept, but it will not be applied in a particular case for the sake of a higher level of justice; not because the law cannot rule over a particular case that happens to be an exception as defined by Schmitt. An exception to the law presupposes the suspension of the law. It is in this case where the sovereignty emerges as a supreme power. Since the legal order has failed, a decision to restore order is urgent. In the modern construction of state power, the sovereign state has supremacy over the construction of order. The political theology of the sovereign, one of the theological–political analogies used by Schmitt to describe the character of the secularised modern state, refers principally to this political situation – a situation that was paradigmatic at the historical moment of the civil religious wars in Europe. At that time, the sovereign character of power was shown in its capacity to decide and settle a new legal order in a state or situation of exception. The sovereign power therefore decides in a similar way to God regarding miracles, said Schmitt, making the well-known political–theological analogy.[71] However, this is not the only idea that Schmitt reserves for the representation of power. Indeed, in the most important theological–political text that Schmitt wrote on the question of the representation of power, already cited here, *Roman Catholicism and Political Form*, the basis of legitimate representation comes not so much from the decision on the exception as from a symbolically generated formal superiority, that is, from an excess, from a hyper-rationality. It is not an exception to law, but a hyper-power.[72] Also, in the case under discussion, the right of grace mediates, because it represents the power/disempowerment of a forgiving God who, while going beyond retributive justice, nevertheless respects justice.

Pardon does not represent an exception to the law as Jankélévitch and Derrida think.[73] The logic of the law remains, but a specific unlawful action is freed from the consequences of the application of the law. It does not interrupt the law in the way that miracles interrupt natural laws. The charismatic authority that is able and has the force to pardon is not sovereign in the sense in which the magistrate of the modern state is sovereign. Pardon is a charismatic and authentic representative, in the sense described by Schmitt in *Roman Catholicism*, because its justice, while being beyond law, keeps the logic of law. Grace cannot be a right as such, since the very idea of a 'right' to be pardoned annuls the possibility of forgiveness.

If there is a duty to forgive, it cannot be a legal one. Hence, the right of mercy can never be an unconditional forgiveness.

In fact, as Jankélévitch underlines, forgiveness is composed of three main features: it is an event; it is a personal relationship; and it is a free gift.[74] It is an event, a 'dated event'.[75] Forgiveness comes from another time that interrupts the political and juridical time. Pardon has, as does the gift, a temporal signature. Memory and oblivion mix in the experience of forgiveness. If the time of the gift implies irreversibility, this is also the case of pardon as the highest gift. Pardon has no meaning without the fact that something has happened in the past that affects the present and, in this sense, has been archived. As Derrida says 'a seminar on pardon must be a seminar on the archive of evil'.[76] The irreversibility of time implies that the past cannot be erased: to go back to the past, to change the direction of time is forbidden. Hence, forgiveness cannot be other in this context than a new 'inscription' of that past event that changes its meaning. Confronted with the past, forgiveness is a transcendent present. Forgiveness is, therefore, related not only with evil, but also with time. Derrida speaks of this time of forgiveness within time as inspired by Benjamin's idea of the inscription of the time of the Last Judgement in historical time, as a time that interrupts calculation and even retribution and puts an end to time in time. Benjamin characterises it as 'the storm of forgiveness'. But forgiveness relates also to the future. It is the inscription of a transcendent present in the historical instant that discloses a future. Resentment, on the contrary, is the incapacity to liberate this future by remaining encapsulated in that unpardonable past.[77] The simple passage of time, however, never produces the effect of a pardon. Forgiving is a way of giving time, as Derrida assumed in reference to the gift.

The question of the time of forgiveness is essential in order to understand the reason for the omnipotence attributed to the forgiving God in Scriptures. In fact, we confess to God in part, says Derrida, because of the absence of our wrongdoing.[78] The consequences in the future of a past evil require an absolute time in order to see the size of the offence and to ask for pardon. No one who is affected by temporality has the capacity to erase an evil. Mercy is then the proper name of an omnipotent power. The omnipotence of God means mercy, says Derrida.[79] This omnipotent power transforms evil into hope: it heals. Jankélévitch puts a force of mutation into forgiveness, which cannot be a legal duty or a legal right. It constitutes a militant hope, not a fatalistic hope; it is an act of trust, not idle waiting.[80]

The theopolitical transference of the omnipotent God then is not the modern sovereign, but merciful power. Derrida exemplifies this idea by quoting Augustine's *City of God* (IX, 5), in a passage where Cicero praises Caesar for his mercy.[81] In any case, as Derrida points out, there is an infinite distance between divine forgiveness and sovereign grace, the same that exists between unconditionality and sovereignty.[82] Divine forgiveness implies a renunciation of power that is impossible to represent historically.[83] In a democratic context, for example, all we can experience is the politisation of forgiveness; at most it has the character of a festival of 'collectives' confessions and forgivenesses'.[84] In fact, human power tends to dominate, even in the exercise of forgiveness.

Along with Derrida, we can ask if pardon is a constant experience of every culture or whether there are cultures of pardon and cultures of non-pardon. He notes that it is necessary to distinguish between biblical cultures (Judaism, Christianity and Islam) and others, such as Greek culture, which have an approach more akin to the idea of the alibi or the excuse.[85] In fact, the idea of pardon is embedded in the Jewish and Christian traditions in a preponderant way. He even affirms that all Western literature is inscribed in the request for forgiveness: from Augustine and Rousseau's *Confessions* to Baudelaire's *Fleurs du Mal*, Kafka's *Lettre au père* or Proust's *Recherche du temp perdu*.[86] Here we find again a topic we dealt with when speaking about the oath as a precondition of the possibility of manifesting a sworn faith – that of confession. But here we stress a different aspect: the granting to others of the power to forgive. This sentence has meaning because no one can forgive him/herself. The gift of forgiveness always implies the vulnerability of confession. The kind of power that takes over the evil of the other and takes it upon itself is called mercy. Every expression of vulnerability and repentance appeals to mercy, the kind of power that is beyond justice. In fact, the Hebrew word for 'mercy' has the same root as grace (חן /רַחֲמִים), *charis*).[87] Also, in other languages for-give-ness and gift are part of the same semantic field. It is the case of English (*for-give-ness*), French (*par-don*) or Spanish (*per-don*).

The reinscription of charismatic power in its theological locus leads to another theological–political transference noted by Derrida: that of 'sovereign forgiveness', as the counterpart of the right to punish. Forgiveness is not a condition of the gift as is the case with sacrifice; it is the highest gift, one of the most important *charisma*s in Paul's taxonomy – that of healing. Forgiveness is the name of the omnipotent God. The right of grace is the consequent transference of that omnipotence into the political sphere. Only such a power can be praised, glorified and honoured. All more or less dominant human sovereignty can be legitimised by its analogy with the divine omnipotence that makes itself voluntarily impotent. To recognise that political power has the capacity to forgive is to accept that some political decisions are beyond the law.

Glory: The Form of Charismatic Power

One of the manifestations of charismatic power is glory, another theological concept used by Paul. Here we can again find many possibilities of theopolitical analogies, as Giorgio Agamben has shown once again by recovering the tradition of Ernst Kantorowicz, Hans Urs von Balthasar and Erik Peterson.

Following the language of Paul, we can understand *doxa* as the splendour and luminous aspect of God's power that results from its manifestation through His given life. God is He 'who inhabits an inaccessible light'.[88] A blazing light that conceals while at the same time discloses His name, His face, His person. This intense light is already Him. Glory – the weight of his radiance – is an inconceivable and sublime power (Romans 6:4; Ephesians 1:17; Colossians 1:11). In fact, etymologically, the term 'glory' refers to the Hebrew word *kabôd* and the Greek word *doxa* ($\delta \acute{o} \xi a$). The root of the word *kabôd* occurs 376 times in the Bible.[89] This fact reaffirms the importance of this concept in the context of the Judeo-Christian tradition, which is consolidated in Patristic writings.[90]

In theological tradition, Hans Urs von Balthasar described glory as the aesthetical dimension of God.[91] The core of Balthasar's thesis, developed in the course eight volumes, is that the visible form of God not only refers to a deep and invisible mystery, but also to its manifestation. The content is not behind the form, but within it. Whoever is unable to see and understand the form is also incapable of perceiving the content. And if the form does not illuminate the perceiver, the content will not provide him with any light either.

Manifestations of the glory of God for the Jews were conceived as having three parameters: messianism, apocalypticism and wisdom literature. Israel never became a partaker of the glory of God, except in the form of a great deprivation. The grandiose theophany in whose shadow the covenant was made is situated in a remote and irretrievable past. Israel's knowledge of the glory of God is always under threat and it is always elusive. It never becomes presence. The New Dispensation begins with the knowledge that the glory of God inhabits in Christ's human form. The incarnation constitutes the theological form *par excellence*.[92] It is the purest expression of the embodiment of God and this is because the figure of Christ is God Himself, who delights in showing the Father, in being a 'transparency' of Him. As Balthasar points out, Christ is a 'legible form' through His signs: the sacraments, particularly the Eucharist, Scripture and the Church. All forms of sacramental grace are based on Him in a concrete and immediate way; they are not derived from the sociological situations and circumstances of their reception, but from the ways in which Christ has granted salvation. These ways represent some episodes of His life as a man until His sacrifice. Glory is then the splendour of self-emptying and divestment, but also of resurrection. The resurrected Christ is the centre of revelation. The glory of God is the opposite of vainglory, which, like emptiness, is a *simulacrum* of glory.[93]

Following Balthasar's inspiration but in a critical way, Giorgio Agamben has advanced the theoeconomic paradigm of glory. He renders a genealogy of glory putting aside the aesthetic aspects and focusing on the governmental ones. He elaborates the opposite paradigm to that of Balthasar: the construction of glory in the absence of the body, of the being, of depth.[94] Agamben focuses on the idea of God as Trinity instead of as omnipotent power, as Schmitt seems to do with his theopolitical paradigm of sovereignty.[95] From the inoperativity of Trinity he deduces a 'political economy of grace', which is centred on liturgies instead of on decisions. Economy refers to what is merely 'administrative' and 'governmental'. Acclamations are the main example he gives for the liturgical analogy.[96] Acclamations, show in his view, that behind the action is emptiness: 'the glorification stems from the glory that, in truth, it founds'.[97] This idea of glory as 'glorification', corresponds to the idea of God as an inoperative Trinity.[98] Glorification conciliates the action with its empty origin. The inoperativity of glory is symbolised in the figure of the 'empty throne': 'the empty throne, the symbol of glory, is what we need to profane'.[99]

In his view, this is the democratic paradigm as opposed to the sovereign and autocratic paradigm. Agamben reinforces the dual opposition of democracy/sovereignty, instead of focusing on charismatic power, as proposed here. For Agamben, the empty throne is the symbol of glory because it represents the adoration and the acclamation of emptiness that is an arbitrary glorification of nothing enacted for the sake of the unknown. The empty throne has all the majesty proper to a king, but without the king.

The glory shown in contemporary spectacular democracies is anarchic and manifests the dissemination of glorification without a centre.[100] His proposal falls back into the economic circle from which Derrida wanted to wrest the gift. Power circulates in the liturgical practices that construct it and no one can escape it. This empty centre cannot dominate, but neither can it generate gifts, sacrifice or forgive.

Emptiness instead of *kenosis* at the centre of glory and glorification is the core of the economic paradigm of power. The theoeconomic agrees well with the constructivist perspective of charisma. However, another genealogy of glory and acclamations different from Agamben's is possible, as some historical cases of the theopolitical transferences related to liturgy and charisma show.

Theopolitical Figurations of *Charisma*: The Case of Acclamations

Historically, one of the ways of adhering to a charismatic political leader has always been to acclaim him. To acclaim is a way of showing his glory as a saviour, a benefactor. The double character of the acclamations, religious and political, makes them a perfect case for analysing the theopolitical figure of *charisma*. Whether it be in the ancient model of emperors, in the medieval model of kings or in the mass acclamations of modern democracy, we experience the glory of power in the context of the political community as much as in the acclamations to Christ within the liturgy in the Church. The possibility of transferring the acclamatory liturgy from the political to the religious sphere and vice versa, with a certain similarity, speaks of a close analogy between the power of Christ and that of the political ruler. The theological–political character and evolution of the practice of acclamations in the West comes from the East and shows that the line that divided the sacred from the secular has always been far from fixed. Instead, it was subject to fluctuation, to pressures from every side and to constant renegotiation.

In fact, acclamations were central in ancient times in the constitution of the political community to demonstrate the acceptance of the ruler, whether they took place in a republic, in assemblies or during the accession of an emperor. The Church adopted this imperial ceremonial style with the introduction of imperial *laudes*, accommodating it to its own needs. Modern times recovered the magic of acclamations in order to give space to the *vox populi* in the constitution of the political community.

'The imperial ceremonial of pagan Rome had been gradually transformed into a divine service.'[101] This sentence, found in Ernst Kantorowicz's *Laudes Regiae*, refers to the widely known Christian appropriation of Late Antiquity's cultural legacy, of which acclamations were a central part. The main monograph on acclamations in Antiquity, before Kantorowicz's rediscovery of the topic, remains Erik Peterson's *Heis Theos* (1926).[102] Peterson's study disinterred the concept of acclamation in Antiquity and described it as an exclamation of applause or triumph, of praise or reprobation proffered by a multitude.[103] He informs us that acclamations were practiced during the appearance of the caesar or of any governor, at processes where a decision had to be made, such as trials or as a response to miracles. Peterson also indicates just how widely used such acclamations were, with evidence of their use not just in Alexandria, but also in Persia and Israel. It seems that acclamations have a Semitic–Iranian origin and that they spread through Egypt into the West.[104]

Charlotte Roueché describes acclamations as manifestations of a divine impulse, as well as of public opinion, in order to validate the authority of leaders, both secular and ecclesiastical.[105] In fact, Oriental and Hellenistic–Roman cultures had a custom of receiving their rulers in a most solemn manner. In Rome, the emperor's *felix adventus* was transcendentalised through pagan cults.[106] In the West, according to Peterson, acclamations by the Senate go back to Trajan in the first century.[107] In Kantorowicz's words:

> the acclamation of the people, the army, and the senate was legally constitutive in the fourth century in both Rome and Byzantium, as well as in the Teutonic realms where people and soldiers, and later magnates, assented to the prince's accession by hailing him thrice and raising their hands.[108]

In fact, it was through acclamatory election that the *vox populi*, audible through whichever group was politically strongest at the time, elevated the new monarch or assented to the fact of his elevation – whether the throne had been achieved by election or blood-right, adoption or violence, and whatever the customary ceremonies of inauguration were at the time: 'To acclaim means to create a new ruler and to recognize him publicly in his new dignity.'[109]

Far for being just marks of devotion to the ruler, all these acclamations were originally theopolitical acts. Acclamations appeared initially as a pagan cult.[110] For example, in pre-Christian Rome, to hail the emperor was a priestly function, which can be seen in the example of the Arvalian Brotherhood in the third century.[111] This aspect of worship contains the idea that the acclamation of the people implies a kind of inspiration with legal implications. Sacred and juridical forms were related.[112]

Peterson researched of one form of acclamation in particular: that of *Heis Theos* – One God is a good example for exploring these ideas. Indeed, *Heis Theos* was a typically Christian formula in fourth- and fifth-century Syria. Despite the clear monotheistic content of the Hail, Peterson insists that it was an acclamation and not a particular profession of a monotheistic faith.[113] Since it was used alternatively for representing the Christian god, the Jewish god and the pagan sun god, it does not express a common monotheistic background, but rather shares theological–political characteristics with the cult of the emperor.[114] This Hail spread in the *adventus* because of its theopolitical ambivalence: since the emperor could not be characterised as a *rex* or as a *dominus*, he should act for the masses as a mythical god.[115]

The Church adopted this imperial ceremonial style and accommodated it to its own needs. In fact, the use of acclamations by the senate was transferred to Christian assemblies. Conciliar acclamations already mixed profane and religious expressions by the mid-fourth century. The Roman Senate's ancient custom of acclaiming the emperor was passed on to Christian synods, which represented the Church as if they were the senate.[116] Moreover, in the case of the East, Peter Brown points out the role of bishops in monitoring the population through poverty assistance measures at the end of the fourth century. This mediating role of bishops was useful for governors and for the people to such an extent that the people acclaimed them as they did an emperor or his governors.[117] This was the case of Cyril of Alexandria, through whom the people transmitted their voice to Emperor Theodosius.[118] According to Brown, Christian people learned how to take advantage of the power of acclamations and used it to exercise political pressure. Moreover, Charlotte Roueché has shown how chant, which had an aura of divine inspiration, was used to influence political and theological decisions during the fifth century. Through acclamations, the people demonstrated their collective confidence and supernatural certitude.[119]

For Peterson, the dual character of acclamations reflects a pertinent analogy between the polis and the Church, both understood as communitarian congregations related to public actions. Through the progressive institutionalisation of the Church, acclamations were analogically central to its public action *par excellence* – its liturgy. Indeed, Peterson, in his subsequent theological writings, has developed the ideas of *Heis Theos* in an ecclesiological direction.[120] In fact, liturgy and worship are the constituent acts of the Christian people. In *The Book on the Angels*, ecclesiastical liturgy is not presented as a mere human contingency because the angels and all the cosmos are part of it. Celestial songs correspond to terrestrial church songs.[121] In the end, the Eucharist is a public ceremony:

> The worship it celebrates is a public worship and not a celebration of the mysteries; it is an obligatory public work, a *leitourgia*, and not an initiation dependent on the voluntary judgment . . . True, the Church is not the Kingdom. But something of the Kingdom clings to the Church . . .[122]

In the Church's liturgy, the *Heis Kyrios* takes the place of the *Heis Theos*.[123] Christ is thus acclaimed in the Church from an escatological perspective as the king of the world to come. Acclamations are actualisations in the present of the future to come. Analogically, as mentioned, Peterson insists that the old *Heis Theos* was not a profession of faith, but rather a pneumatically inspired *exhomologese*, a performative confession.

As he affirms in *Christ as Emperor*, this theopolitical duality flowed first from the Roman state to the Church, with the introduction of imperial *laudes* into the Church, and later vice versa with the application of church litanies to kings and emperors.[124] This is what Kantorowicz confirms through the study of the genealogy of the *Laudes regiae* as a particular case in which acclamations were transferred to the liturgical realm of the Church from the pagan arena, configuring a theological–political mixture.[125]

Kantorowicz reinforces Peterson's thesis on the dual theological–political character of the acclamations by studying the *Laudes regiae*, a litany that was shaped during the eighth century in the Gallo-Frankish Church under Anglo-Irish and Roman influences. The oldest known *Caroligian laudes* form falls in the period between 783 and 787. Kantorowicz remarks, that that particular litany is an exception in the context of the Litany of the Saints in the *Missale romanum*, which is the most genuine expression of the penitential spirit within the Church. First, the litany that corresponds to the *Laudes regiae* begins with the 'Chistus vincit triad', which, instead of humble petitions, expresses jubilant *acclamations*.

Secondly, it does not involve private devotion like the litanies of the saints.[126] Thirdly, this liturgical chant yearns for liberation through the militant nature of the victorious Christ rather than through the mysterious forces of salvation.[127]

A short analysis of the *laudes* makes it obvious that most of their formulae can be traced back to Late Antiquity; the *laudes* are constructed with the *Vita*-acclaim, the temporal origin of which remains unknown, and the *Exaudi*-invocation, which is also pre-Christian. The origin of the *Christus vincit* triad hail can be traced to the imperial acclamations of later Rome, which can be found in the *Historia Augusta*. The literary genre of an 'Emperor Litany' emerged in the fourth century.[128] Kantorowicz refers to a litany that legionaries sang and dedicated to the henotheistic supreme deity in an age of transition; both pagan and Christian soldiers invoked this deity indiscriminately.[129] Every liturgical celebration of a monarch's *adventus* began reflecting the archetype of Christ's entrance in Jerusalem, which has always been depicted as following the model of an acclaimed imperial *adventus*.[130]

The *Laudes Regiae* represent a remarkable example of a hierarchical–theocratic tendency. In this composed chant, the secular and ecclesiastical dignitaries and the celestial intercessors 'reflect, and merge into each other'.[131] It attempts to display cosmic harmony between heaven, church and state, an alliance between earthly and heavenly powers. As Kantorowicz comments: '. . . the *laudes* are among the earliest Western political documents in which the attempt was made to establish in the secular–political, as well in the ecclesiastical, sphere a likeness of the City of God'.[132]

This tendency continues into the Middle Ages as a liturgical homage to the ruler and, as Kantorowicz suggests, we can safely call it the 'medieval ruler cult'.[133] In fact, the first coronation that clergy actively conducted or assisted in took place in the year 450 during the Byzantine coronation of Marcian. In the West, however, it was not until Pippin's anointment (751 and 754) that we see a shift in the royal inauguration towards the sacramental, or at least liturgical, sphere. This does not imply, however, that the people's acknowledgement of a new ruler was doomed to vanish entirely. In fact, it survived in the so-called *collaudatio* of the people, which was performed in the solemnity of the ecclesiastical inauguration, but took place before unction and coronation. It represented the will of the people, including that of the clergy.[134] The *laudes* were chanted after the consecration during the ensuing Mass. The Church's acclamations did not automatically make a king in Byzantium or in the West. The *laudes* acclamation should be considered as an act of recognition rather than of constitution, with the exception of Charlemagne's coronation in Rome (800). Nevertheless, the *laudes* were a decisive element because royal authority was strengthened through the Church's solemn assent.

If we follow Kantorowicz's study, we can see that the old acclamations, as a constitutive and legal act on the part of the people, were supplemented by an ecclesiastical–legal act, namely, by acclamation on the part of the Church. This was precisely the function of the *laudes* at the coronation – they represented the sanction and assent of the acclaiming church, both visible and invisible. Thus, the *collaudatio* of the people and the *laudes* of the Church were two instances (corresponding to two different jurisdictional spheres of power in Christianity) of what had originally been one single act, namely, the acclamatory legitimation of a new ruler. The *collaudatio* referred to the publicly elected prince, whereas the *laudes* referred to the anointed, and thus visibly chosen, king. As Kantorowicz says: 'The *laudes* thus appear as the ecclesiastical antitype of the secular acclamations.'[135] Occasionally these two acts were condensed and appeared almost as one. Kantorowicz states that even if the *laudes* were not a 'constitutional' act, it is true that the particular case of Charlemagne's coronation in Rome was a quasi-juridical–constitutional act.[136] In fact, Kantorowicz argues that, in the Carolingian age, liturgy was like an additional law appended to the constitution. With the liturgy in his hands, the ruler maintained public worship. We could almost speak of 'liturgical politics'.

Kantorowicz reports that in the thirteenth century, the image of Christ the emperor, king and commander began to fade away in the West as did the Crusades. The imperial image of Christ was dominant from the age of Constantine until the end of the Romanesque; the Gothic and Renaissance ages then established a new image of Christ that was more human and intimate, essentially distancing Christ from an imperial or royal representation. Thus, the triumphant phrases of *Christus vincit, Christus regnat, Christus imperat* lost their substance and became meaningless. As a consequence, the whole performance of singing the ancient *laudes* to the ruler was eventually discarded. Liturgical ruler-worship became unnecessary, and this has remained true, as Kantorowicz indicates, all the way up to modern times.[137]

The *Laudes Regiae* reappeared in Europe when modern dictators established a new ruler/leader cult and when the Church rejoined this cult by instituting the feast of Christ the king. As in Ancient times, the image of political leaders again began to shape the public image of Christ and worship of Him. At the end of 1925, Pius XI instituted the new feast of Christ the King. In Kantorowicz's view, this new feast was an outcome of the Liturgical Movement. The totalitarian aims of Italian fascism were crowned with the ideal of the Universal Empire of *Christus Rex* and the chant of *Christus vincit, Christus regnat, Christus imperat* became popular again. Kantorowicz actually remembered the benediction of Pius XII in March 1939, after his election as pontiff, which was accompanied by a chant of the *laudes*. Kantorowicz underlined that 'in Italy, once Palazzo Venezia and Vatican were reconciled, the *laudes* became an integral part of Fascist devotion. Political acclamations have been resuscitated systematically in the authoritarian countries.'[138] He mentions Peterson's *Heis Theos* saying:

> The acclamation of March 1938, following the occupation of Austria, was *Ein Reich, Ein Volk, Ein Führer*! The stemma of which leads via Barbarossa (*unus Deus, unus Papa, unus imperator*) to the *heis theos* acclamations so brilliantly discussed by Peterson.[139]

Carl Schmitt transferred Peterson's thesis in *Heis Theos* to the juridical and political sphere, justifying the procedures of direct democracies, in his 1927 text *Volkstenescheid und Volksbegehren*, where he quotes Peterson's book.[140] Schmitt himself recognises not just the significance of *Heis Theos*, but also of Peterson's tractate on the Church in respect of the theory of plebiscitary democracy.[141] While Peterson revealed the public aspect of ecclesiastical liturgy, Schmitt underlined that every political form has to include a moment of popular manifestation of the glory of a legitimised political power.[142]

Following Schmitt's political–theological line of argument, we could consider Kantorowicz's study a particular case of the analogy between the representation of liturgical aspects in the Church and in the state – something which Schmitt surprisingly did not mention as such. Certainly, in *Roman Catholicism and Political Form*, the essay in which he contested Sohm's idea of the charismatic church, as we have mentioned, he refers to the *ethos* of glory, prestige and honour of the church.[143] *Roman Catholicism* was published in 1923, two years before the new feast of Christ the King was instituted, and was clearly influenced by the spirit of the time in Germany. Schmitt, as I have just mentioned, highlights glory rather than liturgy to recognise that sphere of *charisma*.

Acclamations are present in the ancient world; Peterson portrayed them in the case of Roman emperors. They are also present in Carolingian political theology, as Kantorowicz described them in dealing with the *Laudes regiae*. Finally, acclamations are also modern events in caesarean or radical democracy, as Schmitt showed.[144] The meaning and function of acclamations has been continually transferred from the political to the sacred sphere; and from the sacred to the political sphere at very different times and in very different contexts.

Notes

1. Derrida, *Le parjure et le pardon II*, 162.
2. Clifford Geertz, 'Centers, Kings, and Charisma: Reflections on the Symbolics of Power', in *Local Knowledge: Further Essays in Interpretive Anthropology*, Clifford Geertz (ed.) (New York: Basic Books, 1983), 123, 143.
3. William Smith, *A Dictionary of Greek and Roman Biography and Mythology* (London: I. B. Tauris, 2007).
4. See Martino Rossi, 'On Body and Beauty of Soul between Late Antiquity and Middle Ages', in *Faces of Charisma. Image, Text, Object in Byzantium and the Medieval West*, Brigitte Miriam Bedos-Rezak and Martha Dana Rust (eds) (Leiden: Brill, 2018), 47–75. In Rossi's view, early Christian hagiographers took the Greek dualistic understanding of *charis* further: for them the radiance of *charis* originated neither in the body nor in the gifted soul, but rather in the soul's surrender to Christ. He asserts that, between the fifth and sixth centuries, literary portraits exalting the luminous beauty and grace of abbots, monks and bishops became quite common, both in the East and the West. That was a beauty was an anticipation of the perfection of the resurrected body, which was thought to display a full correspondence between inner and outer beauty. The attention to the morphological, somatic and behavioural details was typical of the physiognomic tradition. In Rossi's view, this tradition was combined with Platonic and Christian traditions – of much more elusive properties, such as inward beauty, grace, splendour or purity, which take on metaphysical and spiritual meanings fundamentally alien to the physiognomic. The medieval mind was inclined to connote as sensible what we would rather describe as spiritual realities. The saints appeared as 'luminous beings': the source and nature of this light was spiritual, but its manifestations and miraculous effects were no doubt conceived as material. Rossi details also, 'how indebted the representation of religious (particularly episcopal) power and authority were to the model of secular power: in both cases,

physical beauty, as a sign of moral nobility or purity, seemed to work both as demonstration and a justification of their political and social role'. Rossi, 'On Body and Beauty of Soul', 57.

5. See Norbert Baumert, *Charisma, Taufe, Geisttaufe, Band 1: Entflechtung einer semantischen Verwirrung* (Würzburg: Echter, 2001), 222.

6. See James R. Harrison, *Paul's Language of Grace in Its Graeco-Roman Context* (Tübingen: Mohr Siebeck, 2003), 2.

7. For a detailed account of Seneca's *De Beneficiis* in the context of a study of the gift, see Marcel Hénaff, *The Price of Truth: Gift, Money, and Philosophy* (Stanford, CA: Stanford University Press, 2010), 257–66.

8. See Alain Cignac, 'Charismes pauliniens et charisme wébérien, des "faux-amis"?' *Théologiques* 17(1) (2009): 139–62, 143; Enrique Nardoni, 'The Concept of Charisma in Paul', *Catholic Biblical Quarterly* 55 (1993): 68–80; Charles Perrot, 'Charisme et institution chez Saint Paul', *Recherches de science religieuse* 71 (1983): 81–92. Erik Peterson, *Theological Tractates* (Stanford, CA: Stanford University Press, 2011), in particular in the article about the Church, argues that the introduction of the term by Paul was in order to legitimate himself as an 'apostle', since he did not belong to the Twelve and could not claim historical legitimation.

9. This is the case of John Potts, *A History of Charisma* (Houndmills: Palgrave Macmillan, 2009), 23. In this book, which follows the adventures of the word *charisma*, Potts delineates a timeline according to which, although a notion of *charis* was present in Greek, Paul of Tarsus invented the word *charisma*, which emerged as central in the early Christian Church of the first century but was later eclipsed as a religious concept within the Church by the end of the third century; it lay submerged for many centuries, with intermittent appearances, and was finally rescued and reinvented by Max Weber. The idea of that eclipse, however, is debatable since the Fathers of the Church continued to concede importance to *charisma* in the fourth and fifth centuries, as is the case of John Chrysostom, Theodor of Mopsuestia, Theodoret of Cyrus or Cyril of Alexandria, as Adolf Martin Ritter attests in *Charisma im Verständis des Johannes Chysostomos und seiner Zeit* (Göttingen: Vandehoeck & Ruprecht, 1972). For a complete history of the use of the word *charisma* in the religious context of Christianity, see Baumert, *Charisma, Taufe, Geisttaufe*; Ulrich Brockhaus, *Charisma und Amt. Die paulinische Charismenlehre auf dem Hintergrung der frühchristlichen Gemeindefunktionen* (Wupertal: Brockhaus, 1972). Baumert underlines the role of Johannes Damascenus in the passage from the seventh to the eighth century and Thomas Aquinas in the thirteenth century in his analysis of the transformation of the meaning and use

of the word. According to these studies, the thesis of Potts cannot be confirmed.
10. Cignac, 'Charismes pauliniens et charisme wébérien, des "faux-amis"?' 145, sets out a table with the semantic extension of Paul's concept of *charisma* in the different occurrences, which includes a broad variety of gifts.
11. Adolf Martin Ritter, *Charisma und Caritas. Aufsätze zur Alten Kirche* (Göttingen: Vandenhoeck & Ruprecht, 1997), 197. Another study of the representation of charisma in Late Antiquity and the Middle Ages is that already quoted by Rossi, 'On Body and Beauty of Soul'.
12. Baumert, *Charisma, Taufe, Geisttaufe*, 222–4.
13. Peter Munzert, *Charisma, Amt und Kirche. Theologische, religions- und kulturwissenschaftliche Aspekte für ein zeitgemässes Verständnis von Charisma im Kontext von Amt und Kirche* (Berlin: Litt, 2016), 80–104.
14. Rudolph Sohm, *Kirchenrecht* (Berlin: Duncker & Humblot, 1970), 26–8.
15. Sohm, *Kirchenrecht*, 2: 'In der Hauptsache aber ist die protestantische und insbesondere die lutherische Verfassungsentwicklung durch die Überzeugung bestimmt worden, dass es kein "göttliches" Kirchenrecht gibt, das die Rechtsordnung del Kirche etwas zur Wahl Gestelltes, durch die geschichtliche Entwicklung frei bestimmtes, für das geistliche Wesen der Kirche Gleichgültiges sei.'
16. Adolf von Harnack, *Entstehung und Entwicklung der Kirchenverfassung und des Kirchenrechts in den zwei ersten Jahrhunderten* (Leipzig: Hinrich, 1910).
17. Munzert, *Charisma, Amt und Kirche*, 105–18.
18. Jürgen Moltmann, *Kirche in der Kraft des Geistes. Ein Beitrag zur messianischen Ekklesiologie* (Munich: Kaiser, 1975); Jürgen Moltmann, *Der Geist del Lebens. Eine ganzheitliche Pneumatologie* (Gütersloh: Verlag-Haus, 1991); Jürgen Moltmann *Die Quelle des Lebens. Der Heilige Geist und die Theologie des Lebens* (Gütersloh: Verlag-Haus, 1997). Munzert calls Moltmann's church model re-formed-congregational. See Munzert, *Charisma, Amt und Kirche*, 210.
19. Moltmann, *Der Geist del Lebens*, ch. 9.
20. Erik Peterson, taking a different view, understands the church of the martyrs, as distinct from the apostolic church, as the specifically charismatic church. A suffering church, a church that has been sacrificed. See 'Witness to the Truth', in *Theological Tractates*, 154–5.
21. This distance between the Weberian and the Pauline *charisma* has been underlined in James D. G. Dunn, *Jesus and the Spirit: A Study of the Religious and Charismatic Experience of Jesus and the First Christians as Reflected in the New Testament* (Grand Rapids, MI:

Westminster Press, 1975). Also in Cignac, 'Charismes pauliniens et charisme wébérien, des "faux-amis"?'; Enrique Nardoni, 'Charisma in the Early Church since Rudolph Sohm: An Ecumenical Challenge', *Theological Studies* 53 (1992): 646–62.

22. See Bengt Holmberg, *Paul and Power: The Structure of Authority in the Primitive Church as Reflected in the Pauline Epistles*, New Testament series (Lund: CWK Gleerup Coniectanea biblica, 1978; re-edited Eugene: Wipf & Stock, 1978).
23. Max Weber, *Economy and Society* (Los Angeles: University of California Press, 1978), 1112.
24. In fact, Max Weber cites Rudof Sohm several times in *Economy and Society*, 216, 772, 1112.
25. This authoritarian turn can also be seen in Charles Lindholm's interpretation of Weber. The *charisma* is a personal self-referred quality, completely secular and purely authoritarian; that is, a self-referential power without limitations. See Charles Lindholm, *The Anthropology of Religious Charisma: Ecstasies and Institutions* (New York: Palgrave Macmillan, 2013), 10.
26. Carl Schmitt, *Roman Catholicism and Political Form*, trans. G. L. Ulmen (Westport, CT: Greenwood, 1996), 19.
27. Carl Schmitt, *Politische Theologie II* (Berlin: Duncker & Humblot, 1996), 42: 'Politische Theologie ist für Peterson erledigt. Auch die große Bedeutung, die seine eigenen Forschungsergebnisse des Buches *Heis Theos* für Max Webers Soziologie der charismatischen Legitimität haben (weil die Akklamation typisch dem charismatischen Führer zuteil wird), hat ihn nicht beschäftigt. Schließlich ist sie ja nur rein Derivat säkularisierter protestantischer (von Rudolf Sohm stammender) Theologie.'
28. Edward Shils, 'Charisma, Order, Status', *American Sociological Review* 30(2) (1965): 199–213, 203.
29. Geertz, 'Centers, Kings, and Charisma', 122.
30. Geertz, 'Centers, Kings, and Charisma', 122.
31. Geertz, 'Centers, Kings, and Charisma', 143.
32. Particularly important was Vincent Lloyd, *In Defense of Charisma* (New York: Columbia University Press, 2018). Lloyd's account of *charisma* is not descriptive or genealogical, like that of Potts, but normative. He identifies the two possible paradigms that we can find in our time, which he labels as authoritarian and democratic, the first being negative and the second positive in respect of normative categories: 'If charisma just names extraordinary gifts, the morality of charisma would depend on the use of those gifts.' Lloyd, *In Defense of Charisma*, 6. He describes the authoritarian as being immediate, fulfilling audience desires, accentuating the extraordinary, naturalising injustice; and the democratic as highlighting mediation, praising the ordinary and increasing justice. Moses is praised in the

book as a figure of what first appeared to be authoritarian charisma but turned out to be democratic charisma.
33. Among sociologists, such as Guy Debord and Malte Lenze, who speak of pseudo-*charisma*s, that is, *simulacra*, in the post-modern contexts instead of proper *charisma*s. Guy Debord, *La société du spectacle* (Paris: Buchet/Chastel, 1969); Malte Lenze, *Postmodernes Charisma. Marken und Stars statt Religion und Vernunft* (Wiesbaden: Springer, 2002). It is also the case of the historians Stephen Jaeger, *Enchantment: On Charisma and the Sublime in the Arts of the West* (Philadelphia: University of Pennsylvania Press, 2012) and Katherine L. Jansen and Miri Rubin, *Charisma and Religious Authority: Jewish, Christian, and Muslim Preaching 1200–1500* (Turnhout: Berpols, 2010). Bedos-Rezak speaks of the 'social construction of the charisma school' – Robert C. Tucker, Peter Worsley and Pierre Bordieu – as the new, post-Weberian trend on *charisma*. See Brigitte Miriam Bedos-Rezak, 'Faces of Charisma: An Introductory Essay', in *Faces of Charisma: Image, Text, Object in Byzantium and the Medieval West*, Brigitte Miriam Bedos-Rezak and Martha Dana Rust (eds) (Leiden: Brill, 2018), 9–12.
34. Particularly interesting is the genealogy followed by Robert Yelle arising from the distinction between the *potentia dei absoluta* and *potentia ordinata* up to Weber's theory of *charisma* and its routinisation, in Robert Yelle, *Sovereignty and the Sacred: Secularism and the Political Economy of Religion* (Chicago: University of Chicago Press, 2019), 37–74. In particular, Yelle, *Sovereignty and the Sacred*, 13: 'not only those institutions that are part of and that reinforce the social order, but also individual and collective acts that protest, dissent from, attack, or dissolve and remake that order. Indeed, the history of religions could be written in terms of such acts of transgression: the starving Buddha, crucified Christ, paralyzed Socrates (possessed by his *daimon*); Tantric libertines, orgiastic rites . . .'
35. See the very useful summary that Lloyd adds to his book, Lloyd, *In Defense of Charisma*, 177–90.
36. Marcel Mauss, *The Gift: The Form and Reason for Exchange in Archaic Societies* (New York: W. W. Norton, 2000).
37. Georges Davy, *La Foi jurée. Etude sociologique du problème du contrat. La formation du lien contractuel* (Paris: Librairie Félix Alcan, 1922). On the relationship between both, see Carlo Ginzburg, 'Lectures de Mauss', *Annales HSS* 6 (2010): 1303–20.
38. Susy Zanardo, *Il legame del dono* (Milan: Vita e Pensiero, 2007), 7.
39. There are also other views, such as that of Elettra Stimilli, who argues that it is impossible to move away from the paradigm of economic determinism when interpreting the gift, and she also does so from a theological–political perspective. In fact, she has traced a genealogy of the Christian religious practice that understands

capitalism as a 'parasitic' derivation from Christianity identified by Weber even before Benjamin, and taken to its extreme consequences by Foucault. See Elettra Stimilli, *Debt and Guilt: A Political Philosophy* (London: Bloomsbury, 2019).

40. Jacques Derrida, *Given Time: Counterfeit Money* (Chicago: University of Chicago Press, 1992), 40: 'For him (Mauss), it is a matter of thinking the economic rationality of credit on the basis of the gift and not the reverse. The gift would be originary. It would be the true producer of value, being in itself the value of values. As Valery says of spirit, the gift would be at once a value and the – priceless – origin of all value. For Mauss's discourse is oriented by an ethics and a politics that tend to valorize the generosity of the giving-being. They oppose a liberal socialism to the inhuman coldness of economism, of those two economisms that would be capitalist mercantilism and Marxist communism.' For Derrida the gift as such is the structure of reality because it is connected intrinsically with the problematic of the trace and consequently with that of dissemination. Dissemination means exactly the non-returnability of the gift. In fact, for Derrida this question is related with the problem of the death of the donor agency. Derrida, *Given Time*, 102: 'The death of the donor agency (and here we are calling death the fatality that destines a gift not to return to the donor agency) is not a natural accident external to the donor agency; it is only thinkable on the basis of, setting out from [*partir du*] the gift. This does not mean simply that only death or the dead can give. No, only a "life" can give, but a life in which this economy of death presents itself and lets itself be exceeded. Neither death nor immortal life can ever give anything, only a singular surviving can give. This is the element of this problematic.' Hénaff, *The Price of Truth* also discusses Mauss in his reading of *The Gift*, insisting on the non-returnability of the gift in coherence with Seneca's position. He shows that the ultimate motion of the engine of the interchange is neither the economical nor the moral necessity of acknowledgement, but a communitarian foundational motive: symmetric in the case of two equals or asymmetric in the case of statutory relations. In fact, a generous exchange generates a social bound and obligation. There is not a moral necessity of reciprocation. The gift escapes the economic relationship. The gift is not merely a functional reality but also a symbolic whole that integrates functions, values and representations: and for that reason it has the ceremonial aspect. Hénaff, *The Price of Truth*, 121–33. Stimilli, criticises Derrida's position in this attempt to overcome the economic aspect of the gift. See Elettra Stimilli, *La deuda del viviente. Ascesis y capitalismo* (Valencia: Pre-textos, 2021), 40–1.

41. Derrida, *Given Time*, 12.

42. Derrida, *Given Time*, 9: 'That wherever there is time, wherever time predominates or conditions experience in general, wherever time as circle (a "vulgar" concept, Heidegger would therefore say) is predominant, the gift is impossible. A gift could be possible, there could be a gift only at the instant an effraction in the circle will have taken place, at the instant all circulation will have been interrupted and on the condition of this instant.'
43. Derrida, *Given Time*, 30–1: 'the overrunning of the circle by the gift, if there is any, does not lead to a simple, ineffable exteriority that would be transcendent and without relation. It is this exteriority that sets the circle going, it is this exteriority that puts the economy in motion. It is this exteriority that engages in the circle and makes it turn. If one must render an account (to science, to reason, to philosophy, to the economy of meaning) of the circle effects in which a gift gets annulled, this account-rendering requires that one take into account that which, while not simply belonging to the circle, engages in it and sets off its motion.'
44. Derrida, *Given Time*, 18: 'forgetting would be in the condition of the gift and the gift in the condition of forgetting ... Forgetting and gift would therefore be each in the condition of the other.'
45. Jean-Louis Chrétien, however, insists that the mere possibility of an original oblivion is contradictory. If the oblivion were first, we would need to accept the 'absolute immemorial'. Jean-Louis Chrétien, *L'inoubliable et l'inespéré* (Paris: Desclée De Brouwer, 2014), 15–16.
46. Derrida, *Given Time*, 131. The gift without conditions is the gift itself, which is a figure of the unconditional. Therefore, the structure of the gift is as impossible as that of being. Derrida, *Given Time*, 29: 'the gift is another name of the impossible ... The gift itself – we dare not say the gift in itself – will never be confused with the presence of its phenomenon ... we still think it, we name it, we desire it. We intend it. And this even if or because or to the extent that we never encounter it, we never know it, we never verify it, we never experience it in its present existence or in its phenomenon.'
47. Jean-Luc Marion, *Being Given: Toward a Phenomenology of Givenness* (Standford, CA: Stanford University Press, 2002), 81: 'the gift can never again be envisaged within the system of exchange, the reciprocity of which connects giver and givee and freezes it in presence'. For Marion givenness is the internal structure of every event. The gift is the organising element of the proper being in the world: the gift is the unfolding of the donation and donation is thought of as the origin untouched by negativity. See Jean-Luc Marion, *The Reason of the Gift* (Charlottesville: University of Virginia Press, 2011), where he insists against his critics on the fact that his point of view is not an ontic one, in the sense that givenness

could be understood as a tacit substitution of creation. He confirms the strictly phenomenological status of givenness and therefore a mode of phenomenality and not as an ontic given. For a comparative analysis of Derrida and Marion, see Robyn Horner, 'Aporia or Excess? Two Strategies for Thinking r/Revelation', in *Derrida and Religion: Other Testaments*, Yvonne Sherwood and Kevin Hart (eds) (London: Routledge, 2005), 325–36.
48. Marion, *Being Given*, 85–113.
49. To solve this question, he let Heidegger help him: 'The latter [es gibt] withdraws in favour of the gift which It gives . . . A giving [Geben] which gives only its gift [nur seine Gabe gibt], but in the giving holds itself back and withdraws, such a giving we call sending [das Schicken].' Martin Heidegger, *On Time and Being* (New York: Harper & Row, 1972), 8.
50. Marion, *Being Given*, 119–20. The three marks of the phenomenon as given.
51. Marion, *The Reason of the Gift*, 83: 'Sacrifice does not separate itself from the gift but dwells in it totally. It manifests this by returning to the gift its givenness because it repeats the gift on the basis of its origin. The formula that perfectly captures the conditions of possibility of the gift is found in a verse from the Septuagint, ὅτι σὰ τὰ πάντα καὶ ἐκ τῶν σῶν δεδώκαμέν σοι – "all things are yours and it is by taking from among what is yours that we have given you gifts" (1 Chron. 29:14). To make a gift by taking from among gifts already given in order to re-give it; to "second" a gift from the first gift itself, to make a gift by reversing the first gift toward the one who gives it, and thus to make it appear through and through as a given arising from elsewhere – this is what accurately defines sacrifice, which consists in making visible the gift as given according to the coming-over of givenness.'
52. For Marion's interpretation of the sacrifice of Abraham, see *The Reason of the Gift*, 84–9.
53. Marion, *The Reason of the Gift*, 112: 'The death of the Christ accomplishes a sacrifice in this sense (more than in the common sense): by returning his spirit to the Father, who gives it to him, Jesus prompts the veil of the Temple (which separates God from men and makes him invisible to them) to be torn, and at once appears himself as "truly the son of God" (Matt. 27:51, 54), thus making appear not himself, but the invisible Father. The gift given thus allows both the giver and the process (here Trinitarian) of givenness to be seen.' And he quotes Josef Ratzinger in this passage: 'Christian sacrifice does not consist in a giving of what God would not have without us but in our becoming totally receptive and letting ourselves be completely taken over by him. Letting God act on us – that is Christian sacrifice . . . In this form of worship human achievements are not

placed before God; on the contrary, it consists in man's letting himself be endowed with gifts.' *Introduction to Christianity*, trans. J. R. Foster (San Francisco, CA: Ignatius Press, 1990, 2004), 283.

54. Jacques Derrida, *The Gift of Death* (Chicago: University of Chicago Press, 1995), 55–6. Derrida in *The Gift of Death*, tries to reinscribe in this theological locus the intertwining relation between gift and sacrifice. In fact, the title of the book responds to the connection between gift, sacrifice (death), secret (of death and sacrifice) and responsibility (to death and sacrifice).

55. Derrida, *The Gift of Death*, 91.

56. Derrida, *The Gift of Death*, 97: 'It is finally in renouncing life, the life of his son that one has every reason to think is as precious as his own, that Abraham gains or wins. He risks winning; more precisely, having renounced winning, expecting neither response nor recompense, expecting nothing that can be given back to him, nothing that will come back to him (when we once defined dissemination as "that which doesn't come back to the father" we might as well have been describing the instant of Abraham's renunciation), he sees that God gives back to him in the instant of absolute renunciation, the very thing that he had already, in the same instant, decided to sacrifice. In it given back to him because he renounced calculation.'

57. Derrida, *The Gift of Death*, 97: 'Demystifiers of this superior or *sovereign* calculation that consists in no more calculating might say that he played his cards well. Through the law of the father economy reappropriates the aneconomy of the gift as gift of life or, what amounts to the same thing, a gift of death.'

58. Agamben, *The Time that Remains*, 124: 'Nevertheless, in a different way than in Mauss, (in Paul) gratuitousness does not provide the grounds for obligatory service. Instead, it manifests itself as an irreducible excess with regard to all obligatory service. Grace does not provide the foundation for exchange and social obligations; it makes for their interruption. The messianic gesture does not found, it fulfils.'

59. Derrida, *The Gift of Death*, 68: 'In enter into a relation with the absolute other, my absolute singularity enters into relation with his on the level of obligation and duty. I am responsible to the other as other . . . But, of course what binds me thus in my singularity to the absolute singularity of the other, immedately propels me into the space or risk of absolute sacrifice . . . Every other (one) is every (bit) other *(tout autre este tout autre)*, everyone else is completely or wholly other.' There are many ways to interprete this sentence. The Christian one could be put under the rubric: God is the infinitely other as a wholly other; at the same time, every other, each one of the others, is God inasmuch as he or she is a wholly other. This is, I would say, the tremendous substitution. Derrida notes

that the 'place' where the sacrifice of Abraham occurred is the place where Salomon constructed the temple, also where the Mosque of Jerusalem stood and where Muhammed mounted his horse on his way to paradise before his death. The sacrifice of Isaac remains in a ritual and an existential way, and not only in memory, but as a figure.

60. Balthasar, *The Glory of the Lord*, I, 82.
61. The economic circle of the gift criticised by Derrida seems to be present in ancient theories of sacrifice. In fact, for anthropologists, such as Edward Burnett Tylor, James George Frazer, William Robertson Smith and Marcel Mauss, sacrifices prior to the Christian era, are offerings made by peoples to supernatural beings in order to ingratiate themselves with them. When the kinship between men and beast ceased to be plausible, human sacrifice replaced animal sacrifice, and anthropophagy took root in some primitive communities. This is how Marvin Harris, for example, describes the totemic practices of the Aztecs. Marcel Mauss, however, does not accept that totemism is at the origin of all sacrificial rites; among other reasons, it could be traced to only a few isolated tribes. He thinks that sacrifices are religious acts, which, by the consecration of a victim, modify the moral state of the person who performs them or of certain objects in which that person is interested. Some elements appear to be repeated in these descriptions of sacrifice: the victim, the moral modification of those who participate in it, that is, the fact that it allows for a differentiation between the sacred and the profane; and the encounter with the divinity, modulated by different motives, most notably, purification and expiation, but also communal healing. Sacrifice remains at the foundation of the community as a form of covenant with the gods. It is a sacred action. Durkheim insists on the essentially social construction of sacrifice. In his view, sacrifice is simply an instrument of social cohesion, which can be used in very different ways. See William Robertson Smith, *Lectures on the Religion of the Semites* (London: Black, 1894); James George Frazer, *The Golden Bough: A Study in Magic and Religion* (London: Macmillan, 1940); Edward Burnett Tylor, *Primitive Culture* (New York: Harper & Row, 1958); Alfred Loysi, *Essai historique sur le sacrifice* (Paris: Émile Nourry, 1920); Marvin Harris, *Cannibals and Kings: Origins of Cultures* (New York: Vintage, 1991); Marcel Mauss and Henri Hubert, *Sacrifice: Its Nature and Functions* (Chicago: University of Chicago Press, 1981); René Girard, *La violence et le sacré* (Paris: Fayard/Pluriel, 2011). The book by Ivan Strenski, *Theology and the First Theory of Sacrifice* (Leiden: Brill, 2003), contrasting with the structuralist rejection of the moral and religious character of sacrifice, offers a narrative of religious constructions of sacrifice of the nineteenth and twentieth centuries as 'objective historical facts of

the religious imagination', 7. In particular, he considers the dispute between the French liberal Protestants, who hold a religious view of sacrifice, and the Durkheimians, who hold a naturalist view. He distinguishes then between a theology of sacrifice and a theory of sacrifice. René Girard's reading of sacrifice follows this social constructivist path. He attests sacrifice not as a gift or as expiation, which is the restitution of a fault, but as a communitarian alibi to justify some fault or crime. The community looks for an undifferentiated victim and subjects the victim to a violence which, if applied to the community, would bring about its destruction. Hence, sacrifice is associated with power and sovereignty, since it is the sovereigns who mediate between the people and their gods. Indeed, in Girard's view, sacrifices function in favour of the instituted power in order to protect the entire community from its own violence by projecting it towards an outsider. An innocent person must always pay the price and be the 'scapegoat'. The sacrifice spreads violence and generates victims by making it circulate. But as Cerella argues: 'the perspective opened by René Girard in his *Violence and the Sacred* is not comprehensive enough and needs to be complemented. For in Girard's work sacrifice is always conceived of as an expiatory practice; even the crucifixion is, for him, a universal form of expiation – that is, the unveiling of the mechanism of the sacred. Sacrifice is a foundational practice because it discharges the tensions that cross human desires. And yet, as I will try to show, early Christian martyrdom is foundational precisely because it represents the fulcrum upon which the dialectical relationship between the visible and the invisible rests. Martyrdom is thought of as a short-circuit between these two worlds that makes possible, and exemplifies, *repraesentatio*. More importantly, it is because the martyr is innocent that she or he is sanctified and, consequently, able to open a sacral space and give life to a new political community. In other words, it is precisely through their innocent sacrifice that martyrs can become the "columns" upon which Christian civilization is to be established.' Antonio Cerella, *Genealogies of Political Modernity* (London: Bloomsbury, 2020), 237. For this topic, see also Robert Spaemann, 'The Rückehr des Erinnyen. Zur Theorie des Opfers', in *Life and the Sacred*, Carmelo Vigna and Rafael Alvira (eds) (Hildesheim: Olms, 2012), 101–13; Montserrat Herrero, 'El sacrificio ritual y lo sagrado', in *Life and the Sacred*, Carmelo Vigna and Rafael Alvira (eds) (Hildesheim: Olms, 2012), 115–27.

62. See Sigrid Weigel, *Märtyrer-Porträts. Von Opfertod, Blutzeugen und heiligen Kriegern* (Munich: Fink, 2007).
63. Cerella, *Genealogies*, 178.
64. Cerella, *Genealogies*, 179.

65. Derrida, *Le parjure et le pardon II*, 162: 'Il faut savoir calculer ce qui excède le calcul . . .'
66. Vladimir Jankélévitch, *Le pardon* (Paris: Aubier-Montaigne, 1967). See also Vladimir Jankélévitch, *L'Imprescriptible. Pardonner? Dans l'honneur et la dignité* (Paris Seuil: 1986).
67. Derrida, *Le parjure et le pardon I*, 46. My translation and my italics.
68. The complete French text is: 'dès qu'il y a pardon, s'il y en a, on accède dans l'expérience dite humaine a une zone de divinité, c'est la genèse du divin, du saint ou du sacre . . . Cette analogie est le lieu même du théologique-politique, du trait d'union entre le théologique et le politique; c'est aussi ce qui assure la souveraineté politique, l'incarnation chrétienne du corps de Dieu (ou du Christ) dans le corps du roi (Kantorowicz et Marin, Pascal et Port Royal). Cette articulation analogique et chrétienne entre les deux pouvoirs (divin et royal, céleste et terrestre) en tant qu'elle passe ici para la souveraineté du pardon et du droit de grâce . . .' Derrida, *Le parjure et le pardon I*, 98 (the translation is mine).
69. Antonio M. Hespanha, *La gracia del derecho. Economía de la cultura en la Edad Moderna* (Madrid: Centro de Estudios Políticos y Constitucionales, 1993), 229–33. Hespanha points to one of the most complete treatises in Portugal on what could be called a 'regimen of forgiveness', that of Domingos Antunes Portugal, *Tractatus de donationibus iurium et bonorum regiae coronae*, published in Lisbon between 1673 and 1675. In order to arrive at these observations on clemency, he presupposes that the gift, that is, the relationship of gratuitousness, being based on inequality, legitimises power relations between free men. Unlike commercial relationships, which are always equitable, no one is left in debt or subjugated. Therefore, in his opinion, the cliché of unequal friendship inspires all cultured ways of imagining patronage and clientele relationships from the Middle Ages to the present day. It is Christianity that most insists on the selfless character of liberality. But in any case, as Hespanha points out, this giving or this gift of power also comes to be regulated by law, to the extent that law understands grace as a field of action exempt from any discretionary power. To such an extent that the legal current which brings the *debitum morale* closer to the *debitum legale* triumphs. Hespanha, *La gracia del derecho*, 154: 'Acts that are by nature gratuitous make up a meticulous and precise normative universe, in which spontaneity has no place, while at the same time greasing the chains of other good deeds that end up being . . . an important agency for structuring political relations (both when they act on their own and when they dedicate themselves to reinforcing the law and other sources of normativity and power).'
70. As Derrida comments at length in *Le parjure at le pardon II*, forgiveness and reconciliation are very Hegelian topics in another

important sense: history as reconciliation. Even for Hegel this reconciliation has a theological connotation, since only an absolute spirit can heal every rupture, every injustice by pardoning.
71. Schmitt, *Political Theology*, 36.
72. I have argued extensively on this idea in Montserrat Herrero, 'Teología política y representación en el pensamiento de Carl Schmitt', *Aurora* 29(47) (2017): 377–403.
73. Jankélévitch, *Le pardon*, 16: 'Sans doute, en réglementant l'amnistie, la prescription et l'exercice même du "droit de grâce", la loi, s'efforce-t-elle de fixer dans ces délais et limites la généreuse illégalité.' Derrida, *Le parjure et le pardon II*, 72–3: 'un lieu (le droit de grâce accordé au souverain, la grâce accordé par le souverain) où s'unissaient le théologique et le politique, le divin et l'humain, le céleste et le terrestre, un lieu d'autant plus remarquable qu'il situait à la fois une exception absolue, l'inscription du non-juridique dans le juridique, de l'au-delà de la loi dans la loi, la transcendance dans l'immanence, et, du même coup, une exception qui fonde l'unité du corps social et de l'État nation, eh bien, de même aujourd'hui, cela reste vrai, bien sûr, partout où le droit de grâce demeure, mais aussi à travers la notion même d'imprescriptibilité.'
74. Jankélévitch, *Le pardon*, 12.
75. Jankélévitch, *Le pardon*, 12.
76. Derrida, *Le parjure et le pardon I*, 341.
77. Jankélévitch, *Le pardon*, 24: 'Le pardon aide le devenir à devenir, mais le devenir aide le pardon à pardonner.'
78. Derrida, *Le parjure et le pardon I*, 68.
79. Derrida, *Le parjure et le pardon I*, 187: 'Ce mouvement autorise l'identification de Dieu, de l'être, et de l'être à venir et de la promesse d'être de Dieu comme miséricorde. La miséricorde n'est pas un attribut parmi d'autres de Dieu: Dieu est et sera miséricorde, il est devant être miséricorde, son être, est, au futur, la promesse de l'Alliance comme Miséricorde comme grâce miséricordieuse.'
80. Jankélévitch, *Le pardon*, 144–5.
81. Augustine of Hypo, *City of God* (Cambridge: Cambridge University Press, 1988), IX, 5.
82. Derrida, *Le parjure et le pardon II*, 259.
83. Derrida explains the idea of power as impotence following Augustine's *City of God* in chapter XXI, where he speaks of God's omnipotence in terms of what God cannot do. He cannot lie: truthfulness, faithfulness, sincerity, forgiveness name Him. He cannot lie, says Augustine in Book XXII, chapter XV. In God who is the impossible, the non-power is not the experience of a limit, Derrida will say, but a superpower, a hyperbolic power. Derrida, *Le parjure et le pardon II*, 148.
84. Derrida in his address to the Jewish francophone intellectual community in 2001, realises that all over the world there is a

theatricalisation of confession. Jacques Derrida, Leçon', in *Comment vivre ensemble? Actes du XXXVIIe Colloque des intellectuels juifs de langue française*, Jean Halpérin et Nelly Hansson (ed.) (Paris: Albin Michel, 2001), 200–1: 'Débordant largement le territoire de l'État ou de la Nation, toutes ces scènes d'aveu et de réexamen de crimes passés en appellent au témoignage, voire au jugement d'une communauté, donc d'une modalité du vivre-ensemble, virtuellement universelle mais aussi virtuellement instituée en tribunal infini ou en confessionnal mondial.' See also Derrida, *Le parjure et le pardon II*.

85. Derrida, *Le parjure et le pardon I*, 198, 228.
86. Derrida, *Le parjure et le pardon I*, 161.
87. As Derrida notes, even if mercy is beyond the sphere of the law, in a trial repentance is considered as extenuating the guilt and mitigating the penalty, in such a way that we can say that the right of grace, exceptional in itself, also acts in some way in the normal course of legal life. Derrida, *Le parjure et le pardon I*, 210.
88. See Heinrich Schlier, *Grundzüge einer Paulinischen Theologie* (Freiburg: Herder, 1978).
89. See R. L. Harris, G. L. Archer, and B. K. Waltke, 'Kābēd', in *Theological Wordbook of the Old Testament* (Chicago: Moody, 1980).
90. Origen, *Contra Celsum*, VI, 5, V, 60; or Irenaeus of Lyon, *Against Heresies* (Createspace Independent Publishing Platform, 2012), para. 20.7: 'the glory of God is the living man – vivens homo – and the life of man consists in the vision of God'.
91. Balthasar, *The Glory of the Lord*.
92. Balthasar, *The Glory of the Lord* I, 155: 'In Jesus' finitude, and everything that is given with and which pertains to his form, we hold the infinite. As we pass through Jesus' finitude and enter into its depths we encounter and find the Infinite, or rather, we are transported and found by the Infinite'; see at I, 29: 'God's Incarnation perfects the whole ontology and aesthetics of created Being.'
93. Balthasar, *The Glory of the Lord*, I, 578. See also Derrida, *The Gift of Death*, 61: '*simulacra*, money without value – devalued or counterfeit – that is, without gold reserves or without the correspondent accrediting value.'
94. Agamben, *The Kingdom and the Glory*, 198.
95. Another approach that is close to Agamben's inspiration is that of Nicholas Heron. He discusses one of the main theses of Carl Schmitt's political theology in *Liturgical Power: Between Economic and Political Theology* (New York: Fordham University Press, 2018). He tries to show that, unlike Schmitt's view, it is depoliticisation instead of politicisation that has theological origins. He considers Christian theology to be the paradigm of depoliticisation and as such closer to the economical paradigm of power. He centres on

the legacy of Erik Peterson's research on celestial liturgy, which can be seen as epiphenomenal to the politics of this world. The view he deduces from this kind of paradigmatical power is akin to what we understand as charismatic power.

96. Agamben, *The Kingdom and the Glory*, 194: (The glory) 'constitutes, in this sense, the secret point of contact through which theology and politics continuously communicate and exchange parts with one another'.
97. Agamben, *The Kingdom and the Glory*, 199.
98. Agamben, *The Kingdom and the Glory*, 226: 'Perhaps glorification is not only that which best fits the glory of God but is itself, as effective rite, what produces glory; and if glory is the very substance of God and the true sense of his economy, then it depends upon glorification in an essential manner and, therefore, has good reason to demand it through reproaches and injunctions.' Already Karl Barth, when speaking of divine glory, asked about the glorification of God by his creatures and refuses to separate the two dimensions, as if there could be no glory without glorification. See Barth, *Kirchliche Dogmatik*, II, Part 1.
99. Agamben, *The Kingdom and the Glory*, xiii, also, 242: 'the centre of the governmental apparatus, the threshold at which Kingdom and Government ceaselessly communicate and ceaselessly distinguish themselves from one another is, in reality, empty; it is only the Sabbath and *katapausis* – and, nevertheless, this inoperativity is so essential for the machine that it must at all costs be adopted and maintained at its center in the form of glory'.
100. Agamben, *The Kingdom and the Glory*, 258: 'What our investigation has shown is that the holistic state, founded on the immediate presence of the acclaiming people, and the neutralized state that resolves itself in the communicative forms without subject, are opposed only in appearance. They are nothing but two sides of the same glorious apparatus in its two forms: the immediate and subjective glory of the acclaiming people and the mediatic and objective glory of social communication. As should be evident today, people-nation and people-communication, despite the differences in behaviour and figure, are the two faces of the *doxa* that, as such, ceaselessly interweave and separate themselves in contemporary society.'
101. Ernst H. Kantorowicz, *Laudes Regiae: A Study in Liturgical Acclamations and Medieval Ruler Worship* (Berkeley: University of California Press, [1946] 1958), viii, 65.
102. Erik Peterson, *Heis Theos. Epigraphische, formgeschichtliche und religionsgeschichtliche Untersuchungen zur antiken Ein-Gott-Akklamation* (Würzburg: Echter, 2012). There is not much literature on the political–theological consequences of Peterson's book except

Barbara Nichtweiss, 'Nachtwort zur Entstehung und Bedeutung von Heis Theos', in Peterson, *Heis Theos*, 583–642; Giancarlo Caronello, 'La critica del monoteismo nel primo Peterson', in *Il dio mortale. Teologie politiche tra antico e contemporaneo*, Paolo Bettiolo-Gionanni Filoramo (ed.) (Brescia: Morcelliana, 2002), 349–96; Uwe Hebekus, 'Enthusiasmus und Recht. Figurationen der Akklamation bei Ernst H. Kantorowicz, Erik Peterson und Carl Schmitt', in *Politische Theologie. Formen und Funktionen im 20. Jahrhundert*, Jürgen Brokoff and Jürgen Fohrmann (eds) (Paderborn: Schöningh, 2003), 97–113; Agamben, *The Kingdom and the Glory*. See also Büttgen and Rauwel, *Théologie politique et sciences sociales*.
103. Peterson, *Heis Theos*, 141.
104. See Tomas Kruse, 'The Magistrate and the Ocean: Acclamations and Ritualized Communication in Town Gatherings', in *Ritual and Communication in the Graeco-Roman World*, Eftychia Stavrianopoulous (ed.) (Liège: Presses universitaires de Liège, 2006), 297–315, 300: he asserts that protocols of the meetings of the city councils of Egyptian *nome metropoleis* from the third century list such acclamations before Constantine.
105. Charlotte Roueché, 'Acclamations in the Later Roman Empire: New Evidence from Aphrodisias', *Journal of Roman Studies* 74 (1984): 181–99, 188.
106. Mommsen has already related how acclamations played a legal role in Roman history. In fact, the principality was an institution that existed through the direct expression of the will of the people (usually in the form of an army's acclamation of its commanding officer) and that it lasted as long as the people's will remained unchanged. There was no continuity in the principality, therefore, because the emperor's power, although otherwise virtually limitless, did not allow him to circumvent a new appeal to the people when it came to the matter of selecting a successor. Theodor Mommsen, *Römisches Staatsrecht* (Leipzig: S. Hirzel, 1871–88), 2.842, on imperial succession in the principality: 'The transition of the Principate, in its essence, that is in the imperium, although not an act of the free self-determination of the individual citizen, is nonetheless an act that may be based either on the decree of the senate or on the acclamation of any random group of soldiers, so that, in actuality, every soldier [jeder bewaffnete Mann] has the right to make any other man, though not himself, an emperor' (the translation is mine). This is confirmed by Jan Burian, 'Die Kaiserliche Akklamation in Der Spätantike: Ein Beitrag Zur Untersuchung der Historia Augusta', *Eirene* 17 (1980): 17–42. Henry J. W. Tillyard, 'The Acclamation of Emperors in Byzantine Ritual', *Annual of the British School at Athens* 18 (1911): 239–60; Gregory S. Aldrete, *Gestures and Acclamations in Ancient*

Rome (Baltimore, MD: Johns Hopkins University Press, 1999); Hans-Ulrich Wiemer, 'Akklamationen im spätrömischen Reich. Zur Typologie und Funktion eines Kommunikationsrituals', *Archiv für Kulturgeschichte* 86 (2004): 55–73; Kruse, 'The Magistrate and the Ocean', 297–315.

107. Peterson, *Heis Theos*, 141. Roueché, 'Acclamations in the Later Roman Empire', 182, indicates that: 'It has in the past been argued that, during the second century, the Senate came increasingly to indicate assent by acclamation; but it has recently been demonstrated that there is very little solid evidence for such a development up to the mid third century. After that date there is very little reliable evidence for senatorial procedure; but the *Gesta Senatus* of 438 record the approval of the Theodosian Code by the Roman Senate with cries of *Placet* as well as more complex acclamations.' Kruse, 'The Magistrate and the Ocean', 301: 'the high dignity, which from the time of Constantine was bestowed upon the acclamations through imperial authority, was certainly partly responsible for the usual practice of inscriptional recording of acclamations'.

108. Kantorowicz, *Laudes Regiae*, 77, 83. A closely related topic of that of acclamations is the *triumphus*, which could also be explored in relationship with the theopolitical figure of *charisma*. On *triumphus*, Hendrik Simon Versnel, *Triumphus: An Inquiry into the Origin Development and Meaning of the Roman Triumph* (Leiden: Brill, 1970). I owe this reference to Robert Yelle. In the account of Versnel, acclamations as such did not appear as a part of the proper *triumphus*.

109. Kantorowicz, *Laudes Regiae*, 76. Roueché, 'Acclamations in the Later Roman Empire', 182: 'The most widely attested function of acclamations, which can be derived partly from religious and partly from legislative practice, is that properly described as acclamation – the honouring of an individual.' And ibid: 'Above all, such acclamations were used to honour rulers; and acclamation increased steadily in importance as part of the ceremonial surrounding Roman emperors. It is clear that by the first century A.D. the practice was already well and widely established.'

110. Peterson, *Heis Theos*, 144, 304.

111. In fact, Tertullian's polemic against Roman celebrations condemns performances of the *fratres Arvales*. This was around the year 300.

112. Peterson, *Heis Theos*, 301. In any case, there were many kinds of acclamations. Kruse, 'The Magistrate and the Ocean', 301.

113. Peterson, *Heis Theos*, 302.

114. Peterson, *Heis Theos*, 308. Caronello, 'La critica del monoteismo nel primo Peterson', 368: Caronello guesses that the use of this kind of acclamation speaks of the Christian metaphysical and cosmological reconstruction of the *pax augusta*.

115. Not only Peterson, but Peter Brown has also described the use of acclamations in Antiquity, see Peter Brown, *Power and Persuasion in Late Antiquity: Towards a Christian Empire* (Wisconsin: University of Wisconsin Press, 1992), 15. Brown also indicates that the *adventus principis* ceremony, *used* for receiving Roman governors in the eastern provinces, emerged around 438. Acclamations accompanied the associated discourse. In Antioch, people acclaimed governors in the theatre to make their acceptance known. On the contrary, extended silence meant unpopularity.
116. Kantorowicz, *Laudes Regiae*, 68. See Roueché, 'Acclamations in the Later Roman Empire', 182: 'By the mid fourth century it appears to be established practice for church councils to approve proposals by acclamation; thus, for example, several canons of the Council of Serdica of 343 are put forward with the final phrase, "Si hoc omnibus placet", followed by the response, "Synodus respondit: Placet".'
117. Brown, *Power and Persuasion*, 96–7.
118. Brown, *Power and Persuasion*, 149.
119. Roueché, 'Acclamations in the Later Roman Empire', 181: 'The earliest acclamations attested, throughout the ancient Near East, are religious: those shouted in honour of a deity by his worshippers, and the cries which had an essential function in certain religious and ritual ceremonies.' Also 188: 'The idea that unanimous acclamations are more than just an expression of opinion, but have a divinely inspired authority, is ancient, and may relate to the use of acclamations in religious ceremonies.'
120. Hence, Peterson's first monograph cannot be separated from his other books such as *The Book on the Angels: Their Place and Meaning in the Liturgy* (1935) and *Christ as Emperor* (1936). In Erik Peterson, *Theological Tractates*, ed. and trans., and with an introduction by Michael J. Hollerich (Stanford, CA: Stanford University Press, 2011). See Nichtweiss, 'Nachtwort zur Entstehung und Bedeutung von Heis Theos', 620. She quotes part of a letter to Carl Schmitt (17 March 1925): '*Das dignum et justum resp. Vere dignum et justum*, das auch die römische Messe kennt, ist eine vom Volk und Priester gesprochene Akklamation, die die rechtliche Gültigkeit der öffentlichen Leistung der Gottes Dienstes (*leitourgia*) um Ausdruck bringt.' Nichtweiss, *Erik Peterson*, 'Nachtwort', 622.
121. Peterson, *Theological Tractates*, 142: 'The angels demonstrate that the Church's worship is public worship offered to God, and through them the Church's worship also acquires a necessary relationship to the political sphere, because the angels possess a relationship to the religio-political world in heaven.'
122. The sentence continues, 'both of the political desire of the Jews for the Kingdom of God, as well as of the claim to sovereignty of "the Twelve" in the Kingdom of God'. Peterson, *Theological Tractates*, 38.

123. Caronello, 'La critica del monoteismo nel primo Peterson', 376, speaks of the Christological *caesura*, a numinous ideology concretised in the liturgical–sacramental sphere – from abstract spirituality to concrete liturgical praxis. Through this change Peterson manifests the liturgical praxis of the ancient church.
124. Erik Peterson, 'Christ as Imperator', in *Theological Tractates* (Stanford, CA: Stanford University Press, 2011).
125. Kantorowicz, *Laudes Regiae*, 65: 'It was in the surroundings of the Frankish court that the simple Roman *vita*-acclamation had been fitted together with the Litany of the Saints and with the militant cry *Christus vincit, Christus regnat, Christus imperat*. But it was in Rome that people were always conscious of the legal and constitutive character inherent in every acclamation, ecclesiastical or secular. And it was in Rome that the Frankish *laudes* disclosed their import as a legal act.' In any case he clarifies that it is always difficult to affirm whether the ceremonies and feasts of the Church are remnants of the pagan past or were constituted by other elements.
126. Kantorowicz, *Laudes Regiae*, 13.
127. Kantorowicz, *Laudes Regiae*, 14: 'In short, this chant is not directed to the suffering God. The *laudes* invoke the conquering God – Christ the victor, ruler and commander – and *acclaim* in him; with him or through him, his imperial or royal vicars on earth along with all the other power conquering, ruling, commanding, and safeguarding the order of this present world: the pope and the bishops, the ruler's house, the clergy, the princes, the judges, and the army. The *correlations* of the two worlds, the present and the transcendental, and the *dissolving of the one in the other* become manifest on closer inspection of the text of this chant.'
128. Kantorowicz, *Laudes Regiae*, 20.
129. Lactantius transmits this text in *De mortibus persecutorum* (XLVI, 6).
130. Kantorowicz, *Laudes Regiae*, 71: this was seen as early as in the letters of St. Paul, who applied the technical term of the imperial reception to the eschatological return of Christ. Kantorowicz offers more examples following Peterson's 'Die Einholung des Kyrios'.
131. Kantorowicz, *Laudes Regiae*, 62.
132. Kantorowicz, *Laudes Regiae*, 62.
133. Kantorowicz, *Laudes Regiae*, 63.
134. Kantorowicz, *Laudes Regiae*, 79.
135. Kantorowicz, *Laudes Regiae*, 81.
136. Kantorowicz, *Laudes Regiae*, 60.
137. Kantorowicz, *Laudes Regiae*, 145, 180.
138. Kantorowicz, *Laudes Regiae*, 185.
139. Kantorowicz, *Laudes Regiae*, 185.

140. Carl Schmitt, *Volksentscheid und Volksbegehren. Ein Beitrag zur Auslegung der Weimarer Verfassung und zur Lehre von der unmittelbaren Demokratie* (Berlin: de Gruyter 1927; new edn Berlin: Duncker & Humblot, 2014), 52. Barbara Nichtweiss points out that Erik Peterson's *Heis Theos* (1920) influenced Schmitt in relation to the topic acclamation. Barbara Nichtweiss, *Erik Peterson: Neue Sicht auf Leben und Werk* (Freiburg: Herder, 1992), 740.
141. Carl Schmitt, *Politische Theologie II. Legende von der Erledigung jeder Politischen Theologie* (Berlin, Duncker & Humblot, 1970), 42, 49. He quotes Erik Peterson, 'The Church', in *Theological Tractates*.
142. On the relationship between Schmitt and Kantorowicz, see Herrero, 'On Political Theology: The Hidden Dialogue between C. Schmitt and Ernst H. Kantorowicz'. Schmitt dealt with the topic of acclamations not just in *Volksentscheid und Volksbegehren*, but also afterwards in Carl Schmitt, *Verfassungslehre* (Munich: Duncker & Humblot, 1928). In any case, we cannot separate his reflection on acclamation in those books from the political theology of representation developed in his earlier writings, including Carl Schmitt, 'Die Sichtbarkeit der Kirche. Eine scholastische Erwägung', *Summa. Eine Vierteljahresschrift* 2 (1917): 71–80; Carl Schmitt, *Römischer Katholizismus und politische Form* (Hellerau: Jakob Hegner, 1923). In these writings, the transferences of meanings between the political leader's image and the image of Christ include a particular concept of political representation.
143. Schmitt, *Roman Catholicism and Political Form*, 31: 'In the proud history of the Roman Church, the ethos of its own power stands side by side with the ethos of justice. It is even enhanced by the Church's prestige, glory, and honor. The Church commands recognition as the Bride of Christ; it represents Christ reigning, ruling and conquering. Its claim to prestige and honour rests on the eminent idea of representation; it engenders the eternal opposition of justice and beauty.'
144. An interesting account that distinguishes between three types of acclamation in Western democracies following Schmitt's analysis in the context of Agamben and Kantorowicz's research is that of Mitchell Dean. Mitchell Dean, 'Three Forms of Democratic Political Acclamation', *Telos* 179 (2017): 9–32. In his conclusion, he writes: 'One of a direct democracy or, more accurately, authoritarian rule, can be imagined by the assemblies of the 1930s before the Pope in Piazza San Pietro or before the Duce a couple of miles away in Piazza Venezia. We have however illustrated its persistence as a central form in contemporary liberal or representative democracy. A second, of public opinion, is most clearly witnessed in the representations of the press and the technologies of mass media of twentieth-century liberal democracies. The third form of acclamation as

public mood is instanced by the social media "likes" made on the smartphones in our pockets and other devices. However, these three forms are less successive ideal types of political acclamation and more communicative and political machines for the capture and regulation of acclamation. If Schmitt is correct to pose the identification of governed and governor as the defining character of democracy, then these are the machines of the production of that identification. And in contemporary liberal democracies, they are all extant.' (30)

Chapter 5

Hospitality or the Limits of the Political Community

What have you done? Listen!
Your brother's blood cries out to me from the ground.[1]

Under the name of hospitality, we understand the generous opening of our space and time to another who is in principle a stranger. This willingness to welcome the other, both stranger and fellow, is an unconditional duty for anyone who wishes to live as a human being. Levinas and Derrida have written eloquently on this idea.[2] But this is an old 'Christian trope'. In fact, as Derrida notes in *The Gift of Death*, the *mysterium tremendum* of dying for the other is the secret of the historic and political responsibility that engulfs the future of European politics.[3] The 'weakness' of a God who dies for the fellow other makes hospitality imaginable in a political context marked by the idea of a community with borders.

Derrida arrives at the idea of hospitality via the ideas of fraternity and friendship. In fact, in *Politics of Friendship*, Derrida undertakes the deconstruction of several political texts in which the idea of a political community is associated with that of proximity, as if it were an extension of the idea of the brotherhood proper to the family. His aim is to situate the political beyond fraternity and consequently beyond the family schema. The political deals with the distant other who arrives to my side; not with the one who is in my genealogy. Separation is the condition of possibility, and at the same time of impossibility, of the political friend, he says, echoing Schmitt's political concept of the political as friend–enemy relationship.

Indeed, one of the Christian tropes that Derrida takes most seriously is the Judeo-Christian ethos of 'brotherhood'.[4] He speaks of the Christian semantics of fraternity, specifically of a 'christianization of fraternization'.[5] In fact, brotherhood was a Christian appropriation of the classical Greco-Latin trope: 'brother or sister in religion'.[6] According to Derrida, Kant's statement that 'all men represent themselves as brothers under a universal father' remains rooted in the need for natural fraternity, and thus refers to the anthropological schema of the family. By deconstructing the elements of 'natural' and 'spatial contiguity', generally attributed to fraternity, Derrida tries to decentre the Christian trope of fraternity.

Derrida's intervention in this scenario involves insisting that what is at stake with the principle of hospitality is how to found a politics of separation far removed from the old trope of fraternity: 'It would be a matter of thinking an alterity without a hierarchical difference at the root of democracy . . . this democracy would free a certain interpretation of equality by removing it from the phallogocentric schema of fraternity.'[7] The true friend is the distant and separated one, the one who is constituted in a relationship without relationship and who can, consequently, irrupt into one's life. The politics of hospitality is not based on an *ordo amoris*, organised in concentric circles, as is the case of Augustine of Hippo's ethical and political view; it is based on a hyperbolic ethic of the most extreme case, that of the one who comes from the furthest away. The historical conditions in which we find ourselves undoubtedly lead us to this understanding of the political community as always opening up to the distant that becomes unexpectedly close to us. The ethical task in this historical condition is the acceptance of the obligation imposed by the absent other. If hospitality is a central issue of ethics, every human has an unconditional duty towards hospitality. The politics of hospitality is based on this ethical duty. The great frustration, however, comes when we try to put that duty into practice and we find it is impossible because of the circumstantial limits imposed on it. In fact, every specific form of hospitality denies, in its logic, absolute hospitality, which seems to be the only acceptable ethical position. Therefore, any form of conditional hospitality can be considered a form of violence.

Is there any possibility of resolving that aporia in which the French philosopher leaves us immersed and which leads our action to the responsibility of an always unsatisfactory decision? What solution does the Christian trope of hospitality offer if we reinscribe it in its theological place?

The Christian Trope of the Neighbour

Unfortunately, Derrida does not delve deeper into the specifically Christian aspects of the trope of brotherhood and its already decentred spatial and temporal proximity. Indeed, in the religion of Israel, the brother is the one who is part of God's chosen people; outside this circle are the heathens. This idea generates a double ethos: the behaviour towards one's 'neighbour' is not the same as towards others. Despite this dual character, based on the idea of natural brotherhood, hospitality in the religion of Israel is not dualistic, as it was in the Greek world or in the religions around Israel. Dualism is overcome by the idea of the unity of the human race and even in the idea of a cosmos understood as God's creation. Concerning humans, Genesis inaugurates what we could call the 'theology of the two brothers'.[8] Thus, in Genesis 4:1–15, 25, to Cain's question after killing his brother – Am I my brother's keeper? – the Lord answers that his brother's blood cries out to Him from the earth. There is no doubt that between humans there is a deep mutual responsibility, the rupture of which was, in the case of Abel, repaired by a gift. In fact, Seth came to 'replace' Abel, though not properly to substitute him. Adam slept with his wife, who gave birth to a son and called him Seth, for he said: 'God has given me another descendant in place of Abel, killed by Cain.' Indeed, there is a mystery of solidarity and substitution in every true ethical and religious position. However, the faces are not interchangeable.

Christianity will produce a new spatial and temporal decentring of hospitality. In Paul's political theology, to which Derrida refers in *Cosmopolites*, pneumatic reference replaces spatial and temporal proximity. The decentring of fraternity – temporal and spatial – produced by Christianity has nothing to do with any philosophical precedent, but with the symbolically communitarian configuration of the body of Christ in the Church. And yet the Church does not renounce exclusion. Not everyone is part of Christ's body, but they are called to be. This communal body is a hospitable structure of which all are called to be a part. The Church is always fulfilled and, at the same time, always to come. Its spiritual boundaries, while delimiting the community, form a hospitable structure beyond spatial–temporal categories. Matthew 25:31–46 and Luke 10:25–37 in the Parable of the Good Samaritan, speak of the neighbour as the one in need who presents himself to me. Alongside this figure of the neighbour, there is the figure of the brother, as the one who shares his faith with me and with my community. In fact, in Romans 9:3,

Paul uses the word brother to refer to the Christian, that is, to the brother in faith. Christianity works with a double ethos that marks the character of its pneumatic hospitality. This double ethos contrasts to the natural familial ethos of antiquity, with the enlightened universal fraternity of Kant as an undifferentiable hospitality, and also with Derrida's hospitable democracy. In Christianity there is a pre-existing community that opens itself to the other and that indeed exists 'for another' on a messianic horizon; that is, it already implies the reality of replacement. This pre-existing community, however, is not a territorial space – a *dominium*. Its power is not political or juridical. Both Jean-Louis Chrétien and Giorgio Agamben help us to understand the ethos of Christian hospitality as being far removed from domination and exclusion.

For Chrétien, hospitality is the encounter with the other in the form of listening to the inaudible. Of all the other forms of hospitality, this is, from his point of view, the original one. Indeed, only in listening to what has not yet been said and even seems impossible to say can the word that brings me and the other together emerge. To listen to the other is not only to listen to what he says, but also to listen to the world or to other worlds to which his word responds; it implies listening to that which also calls the other, requires him, threatens him or terrifies him. Listening to the other is therefore listening with the other to a polyphony that is beyond both selves. It is clear that any encounter calls into question not only one's own identity, but also that of the other who arrives.[9] Listen, not name. Indeed, Adam names the other, whether animals or plants, and, by the very act of naming, he gains mastery over them. How is it possible to forgo this domination? Chrétien turns the argument on its head by stressing that the one who names, in fact, already inhabits the world and in naming is himself also at the same time named. There is no identity without the other. His humanity is named at the same time by his relation to God and to all that inhabits the world. Dominion is not a juridical act, indifferent from the one who dominates, but an act which presupposes looking and listening. This is where hospitality begins.

On the other hand, Agamben's interpretation of the Pauline 'remainder' helps to shed light on the double ethos of a brotherhood beyond dominion: Israel's position is neither the whole nor the part; rather, it speaks of the impossibility for the whole and the part to fully coincide. At the decisive moment the chosen people necessarily constitute themselves as a remainder, as a not-all.[10] This idea, which is applied to Israel in the Old Testament, is appropriated by

Paul for the nascent Christian church. In Ephesians 2:19 he says: 'So then, you are no longer strangers and sojourners, but fellow citizens of the saints and members of the household of God.' Paul declares that the peace that Christ has established implies that every man who participates in the faith is no longer a foreigner. However, it is not possible to interpret Paul as a universalist without nuances, as Badiou does.[11] Following Agamben, it could be argued that Paul does not consider the universal as a transcendent principle from which to contemplate differences; instead, he considers it the operational principle that divides the 'nomistic' divisions themselves and renders them inoperative without achieving a single ultimate term. Ultimately, there is no universal person in Jewish or Greek thought, either as a beginning or an end, but only a remainder; there is only the impossibility for the Jew or the Greek to coincide.[12] An ethic of hospitality is already implicit in the idea of the remainder.

The Gaze on the Other

Already in his first critical writings of Husserl's transcendental phenomenology, Derrida addresses the question of alterity as the experience of the other as other, insofar as it is irreducible to oneself. Derrida criticises Husserl's aim to methodically reduce empirical language to the transparency of its univocal and translatable elements and to establish otherness as the basis of the notion of presence – and the linguistic impoverishment that such a reduction entails.[13] But the experience of otherness is the experience of an original absence. As we have already pointed out in Chapter 1, Scripture or the Unconditional Character of Justice, the very idea of 'trace' implies a deep, real structure of mediation, which does not allow for a centred origin, a definitive foundation or a definitive *Aufhebung*. We now encounter the structure of the trace in hospitality in the form of otherness, as we encountered it in scripture insofar as every sign is related to other signs. The absence of the other is constitutively 'present' as the very possibility of the other in me, as a constitutive opening of my world, as a dislocation of all presence. I can never find myself without the other in me. This perspective raises the problem of the impossibility of the proper name and, therefore, of identity. It is impossible to access an original nucleus of meaning and the presence of consciousness itself, which would be the 'I'.

Ethical rectitude is structurally linked then to reception. Hospitality has the character of an unexpected visit. Hence, the first decision that hospitality requires is a 'passive' waiting as opposed to any active thematisation of the other.[14] Hospitality is waiting for the possibility of someone becoming present, constituting himself as a face. Hospitality is the name of what opens up to that face. The welcome is an opening to the unexpected and unpredictable other. So, the character of that opening depends on what is to come. It has the character of a visitation, as Derrida says, commenting on Levinas.[15] When Derrida thinks of the other, he is not thinking, as in the case of Levinas, about another human being, *autrui*; but everything else, be it human, divine, animal or whatever. Indeed, the figures of the other that he contemplates are friendship, hospitality, democracy, religion or the messianic. The very possibility of the other opens an uncertain future and, therefore, the possibility of the 'event', as the unpredictable, unproducible and unreproducible. In fact, Derrida understands intentional openness as an openness to any event, to any phenomenon of any kind, even one that is beyond the limits of the senses, which delimit the space of the empirical. Hence, hospitality must be a figure of the attitude implicit in the messianic event, in order for it to be ethically upright, to be an absolute event.[16] Hospitality is, therefore, the name of the expectant attitude that deconstructs the future as understood by teleology, as we saw in Chapter 2, Prophecy or the Deconstruction of Historical Expectation. It is the attitude proper to temporality. This is the decisive factor in understanding hospitality as Levinas and Derrida do, despite their differences.[17] Messianism is a waiting that is always waiting. It does not pretend to find a specific content, because doing so would break the very structure of the act of waiting. In this sense, hospitality requires an indefinite as well as an infinite waiting.[18] Hospitality as the welcoming response to the irruption of a visitation is the figure of a structural or *a priori* messianicity.

The ethics of hospitality, therefore, are configured on the basis of the idea of a receiving that is beyond the relationship between an 'I' and a 'you'. In fact, some kind of community precedes it.[19] The foreigner or the stranger is not the absolute other, who destroys the order of coexistence that makes my life possible as I welcome him, but the one who enters my living space from outside its borders, be they the family or the political community. Only the house, the home, makes hospitality possible. Hence, an appropriation precedes any form of hospitality. Certainly, the element of property belongs to the order of conditions and, for that reason, can be easily perverted: the precedence of appropriation frequently transforms hospitality into a power of exclusion and violence to the extent that it changes its logic towards a logic of sovereignty. Hospitality is not free from being totally perverted, even to the point of dominion. The politics of hospitality becomes a politics of sovereignty when the relation to the guest is somehow paternalistic.[20]

This is what Levinas calls the presence of the third party. He differentiates this 'third party' from the neighbour as the limit of responsibility. In contrast to the fidelity to the other implied by ethical hospitality, which could be understood as an oath 'in advance', a debt prior to a contract, the attitude towards the third party, justice, which opens up the possibility of a specific right, in fact implies perjury. Hospitality is beyond justice. The 'welcome' is that which constitutes the house; and not the house that makes welcoming possible, as happens in the perversion of hospitality. Reception presupposes withdrawal. For Derrida, the politics of hospitality is at the heart of making justice happen. However, for him justice itself is beyond the mechanical–grammatological positivity of law.[21] In *Force of Law* he points to a trans-legal, trans-graphological foundation of law, which vindicates the true character of the political: having to decide.

However, when it comes to deciding on hospitality, that is, when it comes to establishing a hospitality policy, a problem arises: being hospitable towards someone excludes hospitality towards another, for one can be hospitable only 'at the very moment' of being hospitable. Derrida points out the significance of the 'at the very moment' to show how the principle of contradiction rules in hospitality and in all unconditional events. Certainly, on the one hand, an absolute imperative must exist that prompts the welcome of the other. But on the other, we are once again faced with the aporia that affects all phenomena that touch on the divine: the aporia of origin.[22] It is an injunction that is impossible to follow. A specific existence makes the absoluteness of the unconditional impossible and places limits to that welcome. No relation can be drawn between the regime of the unconditional, as expressed by Derrida and Levinas' ethics, on the one hand, and the regime of the conditional, as described in Kant's cosmopolitanism, on the other. They represent two antinomic logics, both mediated by a responsible decision that, however, always remains frustrated.[23] What Derrida experiences is the impossibility of deducing and founding a decision that explains an ethical hospitality. There is a hiatus between ethics, on the one hand, and law or politics, on the other. In any case, a decision for a specific case should be taken, even if the decision remains alien to any form of calculation. The beyond of the political, Derrida will say glossing on Levinas, does not point to something non-political, but towards messianic politics, towards the state of David.[24]

Substitution as Hyperbolic Hospitality

Faced with the reception of the other, a new aporia arises: how to welcome him, while letting him at the same time retain his otherness. How can we resolve this new aspect of the aporia? Glossing the expression of Hent de Vries, Derrida places the thought of substitution, another 'old Judeo-Christian trope', at the centre of his reflection on hospitality.[25] It is an old theological theme in Christianity. Indeed, absolute hospitality has already happened in the Christ event, says Agamben.[26]

Also, Foucault mentions the example found in Clement of Alexandria when he speaks of the spiritual director as an alter ego, a representative, a witness, a guarantor, a surety before God and with respect to God. Foucault will say that this alter ego is a 'sacrificial substitute' according to the Christological model.[27] Substitution would be the hyperbolic mode of hospitality, insofar as it is a mode of welcoming the other to the point of losing oneself.

But, it was Levinas who first echoed this idea in *Totality and Infinity*, in *Substitution* and in *Otherwise than Being*.[28] Substitution is one of the names expressing the asymmetric relation between the Other and me. The idea of substitution appears in proposing a challenge to the concept of modern identity as a hypertrophy of self-consciousness, self-possession and sovereignty.[29] 'Being in-itself, backed up against the self, to the point of being substituted for all that drives you into this non-Place, is the way in which the ego is in-itself, or "beyond essence".'[30] For Levinas, substitution belongs to the logic of the subject's evasion from himself, evasion from the evil of identity. In a crescendo of that flight from self, Levinas draws figures such as obsession, expiation, persecution, substitution, guilt, precisely to prevent self-control of the ontological subjectivity.[31] As pure alterity, subjectivity must be stripped of all ontological predicates. Substitution is understood not as the act of substituting oneself for another as if something like a constituted self could ever happen, but as the sacrifice of one's own substantiality of self by others.[32] It is not only that the self is challenged by the wholly other to the point of obsession, but that the self is another. Substitution for Levinas is not properly an act, but passivity.

Derrida recovers this Levinasian topic and interprets it in terms of an absolute hospitality.[33] Substitution is for him 'a matter of an absolutely singular and irreplaceable existence that, in a free act, substitutes itself for another, makes itself responsible for another, expiates for another, sacrifices itself for another outside of any homogeneous series'.³⁴ Here he addresses the question of the replaceability–irreplaceability of the other.³⁵ In his messianic logic, this implies even waiting for the other in a time that is continuously displaced. There is always another who has not arrived. All authentic hospitality presents the other to us in his distance, states Derrida. The other must be welcomed before asking for his name, before knowing who he is and how he thinks, before any question. The authenticity of my hospitable disposition demands that this other can be anyone. The welcome of each one raises the problem of substituting one face for another.³⁶

Derrida suggests 'another thinking of substitution'³⁷ that does not belong to the Jewish but to the Christian tradition.³⁸ This is Louis Massignon's perspective on substitution; Massignon is an author who does not seem to have been known to Levinas and who is heir to the Christian mystical tradition of Léon Bloy, Paul Claudel and Charles de Foucauld. Through Massignon, Derrida opens the door to the meditation on hospitality at the core of Islamic culture. Indeed, Massignon, together with Charles de Foucauld, were pioneers in the dialogue of Christianity with Islam and in the possibilities of hospitality embedded in both Islamic and Christian cultures. This is possible if the starting point is the common root of Abraham. Abraham is the figure of the absolute guest (*hôte*), insofar as his existence consists of an endless pilgrimage. But also, as Genesis (18:1–33) points out, Abraham receives God as an unexpected visitor who bursts in like an apparition; and he announces the arrival of other visitors, who will be his guests.³⁹ It is these visitors who bring God's promise to him. In them Abraham receives the absolute host as if he were a host in his condition of pilgrim and guest. And that visit transforms his life, which is indicated by the change of his name. From that moment on, Abraham's paternity is instituted. For Massignon, this pact between God and Abraham implies the birth of the three monotheistic religions and the experience of 'sacred hospitality':⁴⁰ 'With hospitality we find the sacred at the center of the mystery of our destiny, as a furtive and divine favor.'⁴¹ And further on: 'This mystery touches the very bottom of the mystery of the Trinity, where God is both the guest (*Hôte*), the host (*Hospitalier*) and the home (*Foyer*).'⁴²

Abraham's three prayers motivated by visits from the divine – the prayer for Sodom, the prayer for the exile of Ishmael and the prayer for the sacrifice of Isaac – all assume the possibility of 'substitution'; one offered for another or for all. This idea is central to Al-Badaliya, the association that Massignon founded in 1934 in

Damiette to 'consummate and realize, in all its providential truth, the vocation of Christians in the East, of race or of Arabic language, which the Muslim conquest had confined to being a small group'.[43] It is above all a union of prayers whose purpose is the manifestation of Christ in Islam through the Christians living in Islam, who are to complete the passion of Christ in the Muslim world. This idea translates into a will to become hostages of Muslims and to pay with their own lives for the lives of their takers, as Christ did with every sinner. It is, therefore, a commitment of the Christians of the East towards their Muslim brothers in the midst of whom they live. These Christians, therefore, have a providential mission that is already present in Matthew 5:4 and Romans 5:10. This 'substitution' implies an inverted hospitality. Whoever wants to be hospitable has to become a guest or a hostage. Massignon seems to be permeated with the Christian spiritualities of reparation that connect with the mystical tradition of Islam through Huysmans.[44] Expiation for others is nothing other than the mystical law of substitution.[45] In substitution, Massignon establishes a common element to Christian and Muslim mysticism.[46] Undoubtedly, this idea has Jewish roots: the doctrine of the thirty-six righteous through whom salvation would come to the world and the image of the just sufferer announced by Isaiah (Isaiah 53). Again, the figure of the 'the remainder' reappears. The first, especially the firstborn, are the most precious substitutes for the whole. This is the Pauline doctrine on solidarity in Jesus Christ. Massignon takes the Pauline argument to the extreme. By substitution, Massignon understands 'to respond in the place of another'.[47] The substitution that Massignon is talking about has to do with a physical and spiritual expatriation. Only then does the metaphor of hospitality make sense: 'It is a spiritual expatriation to offer hospitality to those other souls in all humility, modesty and faith.'[48]

Derrida re-read these texts by Massignon. The distant other meets me: I am his hostage.[49] We are hostages of others, whom we welcome into our lives to the point of suffering what they have to suffer: 'these souls for which we wish to substitute ourselves "fil badaliya", by paying a ransom for them at our expense, is a replacement, say the Statues of the Badaliya, where the word "hostages" is written in bold letters: "we offer and we commit our lives, beginning now, as hostages".'[50] Ultimately, it is about "putting oneself in the place of another', 'to be one at the place of the other, the hostage and the hôte'.[51] The relevant question is what it means 'to give on behalf of another', that is, to perform a vicarious action.

Derrida proposes a displacement in reading Massignon: I can forget my name, but only in the name of another.[52] This is ultimately what is meant by love: an experience in which one abandons oneself to the other. It is not simply to give something; it is to give yourself. To think about this, he makes a detour and gives some examples taken from Littré that clarify the impossibility of substitution taken to its ultimate consequences. The first is the idea of replacing a child: changing your child for another. From the point of view of absolute hospitality, this example would be the purest extreme. He takes the second example from Rousseau, specifically from *Emile*, where the following sentence appears: 'there is no substitute for a mother's love'.[53] The same man who says this, notes in the *Nouvelle Héloïse* that life is something that one possesses on the condition of passing it on, of substituting it for another. Here the substitution appears in the context of genealogy, of generation: one living being is substituted by another. The third example is legal or political representation. The possibility of substitution of the people by a magistrate institutes community. The possibility of replacing a person by his or her representative makes legal and political representation possible.[54]

In fact, when we speak of absolute hospitality, what we have in mind are things that in themselves are not substitutable, because they cannot be part of a homogeneous series. When Levinas and Massignon speak of substitution, they refer to these singular and irreplaceable existences, which, however, as a consequence of a free act are substituted by others, who become responsible for them. In Derrida's view none of this occurs in the three cases mentioned above. The substitution is ethical, not an arithmetical. It is necessary not only for the irreplaceable to be replaced – that is, for the impossible to be made possible – but also for the irreplaceable to be aware of itself as such, and therefore to be a self that is capable of relating to itself. This self-awareness is the condition of ethical substitution understood as compassion or sacrifice.

Paul, however, did not formulate a radical substitution theology when he spoke about the absolute hospitality of Christ; he merely said that Christ was crucified for us (υπερ or περι), for our sake: for sinners, for all men. But he did not say that Christ died in our place (αντι), which would have dispensed us from dying.[55] Hence, Pauline theology since Anselm of Canterbury speaks more of a vicarious satisfaction than of a vicarious substitution, which was at the centre of the soteriology of the early reformers.[56] Faced with the question of the non-substitutive satisfaction of the absolutely hospitable divine mercy, Thomas Aquinas invokes a principle of mystical solidarity: 'the head and the limbs form like a mystical person. Consequently, the satisfaction of Christ belongs to all the faithful as to their members.'[57] In this case, instead of speaking of a mystical substitution, he speaks of a mystical solidarity that seeks the participation of the actions of some in others without eliminating any of the members of that united body. This is the 'Kafkaesque universe of grace' to which Agamben refers in his commentary on Paul's letter to the Romans: the Pauline *charis*.[58] Here we return again, as if in a circle, to the question of charismatic power. Indeed, we can now better understand that only from a solidarity-based substitution, an existential representation, can hospitality take place in the political community. Charismatic power, in fact, manifests itself as hospitality and not as dominion. The relationship between charismatic power, sacrifice and hospitality is thus highlighted.

Symbolic Representation

The unconditional–ethical and the conditional–political regimes derive nothing from each other, says Derrida. There is an antinomic logic between ethics and politics.[59] The possibility of a gradual approach to this problem, as would be reasonable following a model of Kantian logic, which could prescribe absolute hospitality as a regulative idea, is lacking too. This hiatus must be overcome by a decision that will be at the same time necessarily responsible and frustrated. And yet such an action is unavoidable in order to determine a political order. The decision, Derrida says, 'remains heterogeneous to the calculations, knowledge, science, and consciousness that nonetheless condition it'.[60]

Despite establishing a 'thought of hospitality', Derrida's 'hyperbolic' ethics give us a bad or guilty conscience. No one can be sufficiently hospitable. It is an ethic of infinite responsibility that can only apply properly to God.[61] Hospitality cannot be understood without reference to faith and what lies beyond reason. It is always aporetical. It is the world in its structure and not the moral subject that is at stake in this impossibility. But Derrida's position does not stop at inaction: political civilisation is always better than barbarism.[62] Somehow civilisation has no way of not being unfair and, in that sense, the best policy always remains absolutely undecidable. For this reason, as de Vries points out, 'there are structural reasons why a good conscience, but also radical idealism and sober or cynical pragmatism, are ipso facto signs of bad faith and perhaps not even possible in full rigour'.[63]

Faced with this dilemma, Kakoliris points out that Derrida makes us believe that there is an alternative where perhaps there is not.[64] The philosopher who has identified himself with the 'disclosure' and the deconstruction of the hierarchical binary logic of the opposites of Western metaphysics seems to have founded a binary logic of his own. The first element of opposition, unconditionality, is identified with purity, truth and the absolute. The second, the field of conditionality, is identified with those elements that threaten or contaminate purity. Moreover, Derrida uses terms like truth, purity, absolute – that is, the very terms which he criticises as an inheritance of a metaphysics of presence.[65]

However, in my opinion, Derrida is right when he shows that every ethical perspective always has to do with the absolute and the unconditional, and that this is beyond the realm of any condition. Nevertheless, they are not opposite, but indissociable. Rather than the contradiction of opposites, we must speak of the *complexio oppositorum* of unconditionality–conditionality, absolute–relative. For an ethical hospitality to take place, unconditionality has to be preserved in some way in every instance–instantiation. How can this happen? How can the logic of hospitality be stated in such a way that the character of the absolute is retained in every concrete gesture of hospitality?

To describe the Derridean hospitality de Vries uses the expression: it is first of all a pure intentional structure.[66] And at the same time, for de Vries, the irreducibility of the theological–political is marked less by systemic structures than by singular historical instantiations that refer to that intentionality, even if they cannot represent the unconditional as such.[67] He illustrates this with the example of the plurality of monotheistic religions, which are historical instantiations of the unconditionality of the divine. In his terms, the question is: what comes first? The ideal, the transcendental, the pure condition of possibility of the religious, that is, a concept of God, that we could call mystical, as the foundation of any possible attribution? Or their supposedly empirical or ontic instantiations, such as the historical revelations, positive religions and their rituals, practices and doctrines, which are always conditioned?[68] De Vries asserts that when Derrida works with topics such as hospitality, he tries to 'turn religion around', by folding the transcendental into the empirical and the historical. But again, how can the unconditional be preserved in every historical instantiation? It has to be if hospitality is to be preserved from the economic calculus, that is, from the exchange of negotiation. This commodification would represent a dehumanisation; however, in many cases hospitality must always negotiate with particular and changing circumstances. How can we consider hospitality so that the unconditioned remains represented in any condition?

Following Kant, de Vries explains this 'between' the unconditioned and the conditioned as the recourse to an infinite series of 'intermediate schemata', which mediate (not dialectically or hermeneutically) the singular instance. With the idea of transcendental schematism, Kant tries to imagine under what conditions the application of transcendental categories to empirical multiplicity is possible. Indeed, empirical multiplicity is presented as a non-unified set of sensible elements independent of each other in space and successive in time. The application of a concept to an intuitive multiplicity presupposes that the content of the former can be found in each element of that multiplicity. These are synthesising procedures of the imagination. Hence, de Vries, following Derrida's Kantian appropriation, attributes a symbolic character to the schemes of the imagination; he uses it in a sense similar to the one to which we have referred here of symbolic representation to account for the theological trope of solidary substitution. De Vries points to brotherhood as an example of 'symbolic presentation' of openness to the other, as democracy might also be.[69] Hence, the central notion that 'all men are represented as brothers under a universal father' can receive an infinite variety of non-synonymous substitutions. Thus, the appropriate place for the brother or for the universal brotherhood is 'there', so to speak, only to 'receive' the host of the different 'inscriptions' in which 'the brother' can be substituted by whoever arrives.[70] This logic of 'symbolic representation' is what de Vries calls 'hospitable thinking', as a logic that underpins all possible specific instances of hospitality. As he points out, what might seem an unjustifiable restriction of friendship or fraternity can give way to the most hospitable of thoughts. In this sense, hospitality is more than an ethical or political concept in Derrida: it is the very structure of thought that is revealed in considering hospitality. More generally, but in the same vein, Michael Naas reminds us that the best description of deconstruction is hospitality. This is Derrida's legacy: thought is hospitality.[71] Indeed, this logic differs from the logic of presupposition that Derrida criticises in *Aporias*. The relation is not one of subordination or justification in which the unconditioned makes the conditioned possible. Following classical and modern logic, one order has to precede the other, because they cannot be coextensive or co-originary, insofar as one makes the other possible. On the contrary, the logic that Derrida had already glimpsed in Levinas leaves the 'coming first' in abeyance.[72]

But is there another possibility of considering the co-implication of the conditioned and the unconditional different from Kant's schematism? Indeed, another possibility is to think of 'symbolic representation' as the inhabitation of the unconditional in every condition. First, we could point out that the truly unconditioned cannot by definition be diluted when entering into the negotiation of conditions. If it were, we would have mistaken its unconditioned character. This sentence is the one that Derrida cannot say without breaking with his metaphysical plot of the trace.[73] Secondly, in contrast to the undecidable logic of the possible–impossible, the logic of symbolic representation puts an end from an ethical – though not political – point of view to the 'infinite demand' that always goes beyond the apparently justified restrictions and conditions to which the course of history, and to some extent political action, are condemned.

When we reinscribe hospitality in its theological locus, it can be experienced, following the logic of symbolic representation, that absolute openness to the other can be present in its purity in the reception of any other, as in the vicarious action of Christ. Each other is every other. This becomes possible through the institution of figures of hospitality, that is, of instituted practices representing all possible welcomes. Indeed, if we apply the 'reverse implication' that de Vries speaks of as the heart of Derridian logic – the folding of the trascendental into the particular – then we can interpret unconditional solidarity as being fully executed in every instituted structure of hospitality. In other words, Kantian transcendental schematism is transformed into a historical instantiation that is open by its own institutional constitution to any possible reception. In this symbolic representative logic, each concrete substitution refers completely to every other substitution. Each act of hospitality is a remainder. Despite the consciousness of one's own limitations that ethical responsibility usually bears, hope can be glimpsed in any present political order by inaugurating symbolic figures of hospitality therein.

Utopias of Hospitality

Derrida himself seems to propose this last logic, since the idea of the city, understood as a 'welcoming structure', is central to his idea of hospitality. The hospitality of cities proposed by Derrida would be possible through the conception of cities as 'free places'.[74] This idea is in contrast to the unlimited intervention of police power in modern states. Indeed, where control grows, free spaces disappear. Traditionally, spaces free from control were places of hospitality such as the house, the family home, which implies not only a dignified material home, but also a kind of relationship on the outskirts of civil relations. Churches have also been such a space. We cannot forget the 'immunity' of the churches converted into cities or the space of immunity reserved for certain lordly estates. The experience of hospitality is forged on the margins of civil law, in those spaces open to a different kind of freedom.

Moreover, in the city there are some elements that are hospitable in themselves, such as what Derrida calls the 'threat of ruin', which represents the possible incursion from the outside and denotes a porous border. The idea of ruin corresponds to the experience of non-saturation: the city is always an incomplete reality that is under permanent construction and reconstruction. And this is precisely what opens it to future generations and, therefore, to every other. This congenital impossibility of completion is figured in the Tower of Babel.[75]

Another image that indicates a suitable kind of place for hospitality is that of the desert. The desert is the most anarchic place possible. It is prior to any social or political determination, to any intersubjectivity. Cities of refuge, which pretend not to be a utopia at all, but rather publicise themselves as a plan of action, operate according to the schematism of ruin, unsaturation and desert.[76]

Indeed, Derrida proposes refuge cities as a possible solution to the problem of migrations and all kinds of exodus.[77] Levinas and Daniel Payot had already dedicated a number of pages to refuge cities.[78] With this idea Derrida evokes the command to Moses himself in Numbers 35. The purpose at that time was the protection of the involuntary murderer. This theopolitical figure of hospitality also appears in 1 Chronicles 6:42, 52 and in Joshua 20:1–9. Derrida imagines them as independent cities of established political communities, distributed throughout the world and with a form of solidarity between them still to be invented.[79] They would welcome the foreigner in general: the immigrant, the exile, the refugee, the deported, the stateless person, the displaced person. They would constitute a new space of belonging that could be a critical counterpoint to modern states and oblige them to revise their model of citizenship. Subverting territorial sovereignty is the only horizon of hope for the establishment of a correct policy of hospitality, in Derrida's opinion. The victims of sovereignty are many and generally anonymous. Derrida dreams of contravening what modernity understood as the main guarantee of peace within a limited territory and which is, according to Weber, the essence of the modern state – the monopoly of violence. Not only because it causes many to flee, but also because today it is not capable of guaranteeing peace, and is likewise impotent in the face of global threats. Derrida refers to Arendt's reflections on 'stateless peoples' and 'minority nations'. In fact, in *The Origins of Totalitarianism* she denounces the progressive irrelevance of the right of asylum, as well as of the mechanisms of repatriation or nationalisation.

Derrida asserts that the figure of the city of refuge belongs to the context of a 'democracy to come'.[80] He not only demands that the right of asylum be extended, but also that the motivation for the application of this right be 'ethical' and not simply economic or even political, that is, as a manoeuvre to gain social recognition.[81]

Something of Greek Stoicism and Pauline Christianity, in Derrida's view, is present in the Enlightenment tradition developed by Kant through his idea of cosmopolitanism, which insists that universal hospitality is a natural right. In his *Perpetual Peace*, he addresses the idea that cosmopolitanism must abide by the conditions of universal hospitality. And those conditions are: first of all, a common use of universal land. Therefore, no one can legitimately appropriate the surface of the Earth to the extent of preventing access by others. However, whatever is erected or built on this land must no longer be unconditionally accessible to all. Two limitations follow from this distinction: first, that hospitality is limited to the right of visitation, but not to the right of residence.[82] Secondly, Kant makes hospitality dependent on the sovereignty of the state, since both public and private hospitality are dependent on and controlled by the law and the police. Precisely by claiming to ensure its application, this legal–political regulation makes hospitality impossible.

As can be seen, the possibilities that Derrida wants to open up for political hospitality are more in line with the Hebrew and medieval experience than with the Enlightenment hypothesis outlined by Kant, which has inspired contemporary international politics. Certainly, the Hebrew tradition preserved the right of asylum for those who were the object of revenge. Furthermore, the European medieval tradition saw a significant growth of hospitality.

Theopolitical Figurations of Hospitality: The Case of Hospitaller Malta

As Brugère and le Blanc point out, however, Derrida never speaks of hospitals as a structure of hospitality which remain beyond the political sphere of statehood and domination. In fact, the hospital was one of the first welcome structures or instituted practices of hospitality in the world.[83]

In his book on feudalism, George Duby wrote that from the ninth century onwards, Haymon of Auxerre formulated the classic composition of society in three elements, dividing it into those who pray, those who fight, command or lead, and those who work.[84] In fact, already Plato's *Republic* had argued that only the differentiation of the members of the *polis* make the generation of strong unity possible: those who are different need mutual assistance. Solidarity and differentiation go hand in hand. This was also the conviction of medieval society. The association of several of these functions in promoting hospitality was truly exceptional. This promotion began to evolve in the context of the pilgrimages to Jerusalem and particularly during the Crusades, which launched in 1095 as armed pilgrimages to liberate Jerusalem.

Indeed, after the Arab conquest in 638, pilgrimages to Jerusalem were at the mercy of the political situation in the Muslim world, which meant that pilgrims were increasingly grouped together. They encountered favourable conditions from the ninth century onwards, thanks to Charlemagne's protection of the Holy sites. There was, however, serious alarm during the caliphate of al-Hakim (996–1021). In fact, this caliph broke with a long tradition of hospitality to pilgrims and vehemently persecuted Jews and Christians. Shrines were destroyed and pilgrimages were interrupted for ten years (1004–14). Hakim himself put an end to this persecution; by proclaiming himself divine, he in fact sought allies among Christians and Jews against the Muslims. Western pilgrimages resumed and the whole of the eleventh century was a golden age of peregrinations. In 1027, an agreement between the Byzantine emperor Constantine VIII and the Fatimid caliph allowed restoration of the churches destroyed in the time of al-Hakim. These reconstructions produced a large influx of people. Trade between Constantinople and Palestinian Syria was active and Byzantium's Italian allies, the Amalafi merchants, were also based in Jerusalem. It was they who built the first hospital in the vicinity of the Holy Sepulchre.

This took place between 1048 and 1063.⁸⁵ The generosity of the faithful or the protection of a prince had previously built hospitals or hospices (*xenodochium*). The first hospital gave way to a larger one, which, after the capture of Jerusalem, came to be governed from Rome. In fact, in a papal bull of 15 February 1113, Paschal II recognised the hospital as an independent establishment directly protected by the pope; it was made an international order and was affiliated to the hospices created in Europe. The Hospitallers (the brothers working in those charitable activities) abandoned the rule of St. Benedict to adopt that of St. Augustine, and, finally, became integrated into the rule of Raymond of Le Puy, the true ruler of the Order. In 1113, the Hospital was recognised as an international charitable order, independent of the Benedictines. The Hospital of Jerusalem was the head of the order from that moment onwards. It was by no means a military order. Nevertheless, the brothers of the hospital not only provided shelter for pilgrims, but also accompanied them on the roads and defended them with their weapons.

It was then that the idea of a military order was born. In fact, taking advantage of the appeal for help from the Byzantine emperor Alexius I Comnenus, who was in conflict with the Seljuk Turks, in 1095 Pope Urban II called on various Christian countries of Western Europe to reconquer the so-called Holy Land. The crusade combined the penitential value of the pilgrim with the ideology of a peace movement and intensified the process of the sacralisation of war. The crusader is a pilgrim who leaves his homeland, a migrant who, on his way to Jerusalem, becomes Christ's soldier, *miles Christi*. Jerusalem is the place that attracts this new institution of the military orders. At first, they existed only to protect the pilgrimages of the faithful to the Holy Land which might be attacked during the journey, but over time they became warlike institutions, much frowned upon even within the Church itself. Indeed, many Christians were against the crusades and the pacifist movement in Christendom ran its course, as Martin Aurell has shown.⁸⁶ Hence, as Alain Demurger points out, this pacifist movement gives credibility to a hypothesis first proposed by the anthropological school of historians – that of a Christian appropriation of the Muslim concept of holy war and of the influence of the Islamic institution *ribat* on the reaction of the military order.⁸⁷

A crucial event occurred at the Council of Triyes in 1129: it recognised the legitimacy of the order of the Temple to associate the two functions of praying and fighting. There arose a context of great bellicosity in which knights abounded and generated violence in favour of particular interests. However, the tenth century was a century of great pacifism within the Church. There was at least a desire to distinguish sanctioned from unsanctioned violence, to use a contemporary expression. In that sense, self-defence and defence against unjust attacks were considered a work of charity. But, in any event, the justice of such sanctioned violence and the interpretation of the cases in which it could be used were always an open question.

Fighting against violence and banditry was the aim of the Templars, and was not only understood as lawful within Christendom but also began to spread further afield. Much has been written about the atrocities of these behaviours, to the point of considering them as an actual perversion of hospitality. Before the order was established, two entities were active in protecting pilgrims: along with the Hospitallers, there were the canons of the Holy Sepulchre, who were dedicated to liturgy rather than to charity. But within the Holy Sepulchre there were also armed forces, a kind of lay brotherhood associated with the canons. It was not a military order; they were knights at the service of the Holy Sepulchre to defend it from attack. It is possible that the first Templars were recruited from among them. Indeed, a group of them separated themselves from both the canons and those who served at the hospital. These knights consolidated themselves as a group of laymen who were subject to the monastic vows of obedience, chastity and poverty. Their aim was to protect pilgrims and to maintain armed defence of the Holy Land.

In any case, it was inevitable that the foundation of the Knights Templar led to the militarisation of the Hospitallers. It took nine years, from 1120 to 1129, for this type of association to be recognised as a military order that combined the functions of prayer and charity with defensive warfare. St. Bernard, one of the major religious authorities in Christendom at the time, was extremely circumspect. The essentially charitable order of the Hospital seems to have become a military order around 1129 in Muslim lands. However, in the kingdom of Aragon, the Hospital was not considered a military order until 1149, unlike the Temple which, from the 1130s, had been involved in the struggle against Islamic imperialism in the Iberian Peninsula. The militarisation of the Hospital is mentioned only belatedly in official texts. We have to wait for the statutes of Rigelius de Moulins in 1182. The military structures of the order were described for the first time in the statutes of Margat in 1203–6. Nevertheless, twice, in 1168–70 and 1178–80, Pope Alexander III reminded the Hospitallers to respect their original mission: the care of pilgrims. He also asked them not to take part in military missions except when the king of Jerusalem summoned them, like other citizens, in the defence of the kingdom.[88] That this was the case indicates the extent to which many of the Hospitallers' interventions were dubious from the point of view of charity.[89]

It would be inappropriate to forget that, if the crusade triggered a movement of enthusiasm in its beginnings, it soon came to be criticised by the clergy. In 1187, the taking of Saladin's Jerusalem stirred trouble in Western consciousness. Radulphus Niger (c. 1140–c. 1217), canon of Lincoln, wrote a Latin opuscule to condemn the expedition by means of which the most prominent kings were preparing to recover the city. He asserted the superiority of the inward journey towards the heavenly Jerusalem over the outward conquest of the city, criticising the massacre of Muslims who, even if they were heathens, were still human beings. He who seeks to propagate faith through violence, he said, transgresses the commandments of that faith itself.[90] Opposition to military orders was becoming more intense. The notion of the monk-knight seems to be incompatible with the *Gratien Decree* of 1140: the laity on one side, the tonsured on the other. In Canon law, in fact, the shedding of blood is a stain that is incompatible with the clerical state. This is why the Praise of Bernard speaks ironically of his Cistercian brother Isaac de l'Étoile († 1178): 'He was born the new monster of the new chivalry!'[91] Increasing criticism within the Church, but also the plot by the king of France, forced the dissolution of the order of the Knights Templar by Clement V in 1312.[92]

However, as Demurger clearly points out, the action of the constituted military orders was not limited to the warlike aspects that the chroniclers of the time and certain contemporary historiographers have mythologised in excess. The primary aim of Hugo de Payns, the founder of the Temple, in defending pilgrims, even by force, was charity. The military orders were born at a time when in the West there was a proliferation of houses of God and hospitals devoted to the poor and the excluded, as well as to pilgrims passing through, who could be either one or the other. These institutions and the military orders, particularly in the case of the Hospitallers, had much in common: both were foundations with a majority of lay people and were governed by lay 'masters'.[93]

In the Holy Land, only the Temple was born as a military order. The others, particularly the Hospital, but also the Teutonic Order and the Order of St. Lazarus, were always charitable, although they were considered as military orders in the ecclesiastical taxonomy. In actual fact, the Teutonic Order makes it clear that it had a hospital before it had knights. The Temple, on the other hand, also had the duty of charity and almsgiving. But while the Templars performed these activities out of religious obligation, the Hospitallers did so as the specific mission of their order.[94]

The physical protection of pilgrims on their way to the Holy Land was also a charitable action. It was also practiced on other routes such as those to Santiago de Compostela, Toulouse and Puente la Reina. Gregory IX, for example, strongly reminded the Templars to protect pilgrimages to the Holy Land. Although Jerusalem was then in Christian hands, pilgrims were often ambushed by Muslims. The pope ordered them to re-establish security on this route.

The Hospitallers were primarily entrusted with the task of welcoming people. This is why they developed large hospital structures, which gradually became infirmaries. According to some manuscripts of the time, they were to receive pilgrims, the poor, women and men, women in childbirth, abandoned children and all the sick, regardless of their denomination: Christians, Jews and Muslims. The Order of St. Lazarus had been created, on the other hand, to attend to lepers. In Rhodes, the charitable action of the Hospitallers also manifested itself in the sending of emergency aid in case of natural disasters. Over time, the Hospitallers opened up to the outside world, becoming both a hospice and a hospital in the modern sense of the term.[95]

None of these activities would have been possible without a patrimony. The patrimonial policy of the military orders was always similar. A hospital was founded wherever there were sufficient donations. The foundation phase therefore depended on donations, on the generosity of private individuals; then came a phase of consolidation and organisation in which exchanges and purchases increased; and, finally, a phase of stabilisation and administration. From the end of the thirteenth century, the possessions and men of the military orders were subject to the king's taxation, from which they always tried to be relieved.

By the fourteenth and fifteenth centuries, the Hospitallers were already established in Rhodes and Cyprus, where they had retreated with many other refugees in 1291 after being expelled from Syria-Palestine. From 1530, the order was established in Malta: it is for this reason that they are known today as the Order of Malta.[96] The Order was finally transferred to Rome in 1798. While still in Malta they began their activities with an infirmary, but they were defensively equipped with new walls against a possible attack by the Turks. In fact, the Turks did attack the island during the

Grand Siege from 18 May to 8 September 1565, but were defeated by the knights under the command of Grand Master Jean de La Vallette; this event marks the beginning of the decline of Ottoman naval power. The Order's navy became one of the most powerful in the Mediterranean and took part in the final destruction of the Ottoman navy at the Battle of Lepanto in 1571. Once Napoleon decreed that the Order had to leave Malta, it first moved to Russia and then to Rome. The hospital in Malta was still used as such for more than 136,000 soldiers during the First World War; by the end of which Malta was internationally known as the 'Nurse of the Mediterranean'.

The aim of the Hospitallers has been so crucial for all communities that it still has an important meaning in our societies. Today it has 13,500 members (called knights and dames), 25,000 employees and 80,000 volunteers worldwide. The funds for its projects come mainly from donations and agreements with countries. Its leaders are all laymen, although they take vows of poverty, chastity and obedience before the pope. The Order of Malta is present today in most countries of the world and is involved in medical, social and humanitarian projects. The Order again has a hospital in Bethlehem.

The institution has the characteristics of a quasi-sovereign entity, even if it is not a state. It maintains diplomatic relations with more than a hundred states and the European Union, and maintains permanent observer status at the United Nations. It has its own legal system and issues its own stamps, passports and vehicle registration plates. Its insignia is an eight-pointed or octagonal cross, called the Maltese Cross. This small sovereignty of a few people without territory united by a hospitable action in any part of the world, which has been mobilising resources for the poor and needy since the twelfth century is a figure of hospitality; it is the first one with this name and with a physical structure to welcome the pilgrim and the homeless.

Notes

1. Genesis 4:10.
2. Levinas devoted the whole of his work to this topic in one way or another. Initially Derrida developed his ideas on hospitality in a monograph in the seminars at l'École des Hautes Études between 1995 and 1997. Some of those seminars were published. Two of them, dated 16 and 17 January 1996 were part of *De l'hospitalité* (1997), published in English as *Of Hospitality* (Stanford, CA: Stanford

University Press, 2000). Another four, dated 18 January, 12 February, 5 March and 7 May 1997 were collected in *Acts of Religion* (New York: Routledge, 2002). At about the same time that he gave the seminars, he published a commentary on the work of Emmanuel Levinas titled *Adieu à Emmanuel Lévinas* (1997), published as *Adieu to Emmanuel Lévinas* (Stanford, CA: Stanford University Press, 1999); and *Cosmpolites de tous les pays, encore un effort* (1996), which was originally an intervention sent to a meeting of the writers' parliament that he had not been able to attend. New references are found in *Paper Machine* (Stanford, CA: Stanford University Press, 2005). All these texts appeared after *Politics of Friendship* (New York: Verso, 1997). Other publications on the topic are 'Abrahan, the Other', in *Religion: Beyond a Concept*, Hent de Vries (ed.) (New York: Fordham University Press, 2008); *On Cosmopolitanism and Forgiveness*.
3. Derrida, *The Gift of Death*.
4. Derrida, *Politics of Friendship*, 117.
5. Derrida, *Politics of Friendship*, 117.
6. Derrida, *Politics of Friendship*, 118.
7. Derrida, *Politics of Friendship*, 232.
8. Joseph Ratzinger, *Die christliche Brüderlichkeit* (Munich: Kösel, 1960).
9. Chrétien, *L'arche de la parole*.
10. Agamben, *The Time that Remains*, 44–58.
11. Badiou, *Saint Paul*. A critical account of Badiou's interpretation of universalism can be found in Troels Engberg-Pedersen, 'Paul and Universalism', in *Paul and the Philosophers*, Ward Blanton and Hent de Vries (eds) (New York: Fordham University Press, 2013), 87–105.
12. See Agamben, *The Time that Remains*, 44–58.
13. See Jacques Derrida, 'Introduction' to Edmund Husserl, *L'origine de la géométrie* (Paris: PUF, 1974), 104. Also in *Metaphysics and Violence* (1964), in Jacques Derrida, *L'écriture et la différence* (Paris: Éditions du Seuil, 1967). The relationship between otherness and concept is also developed in *La voix et le phénomène* (1967).
14. Derrida, *Adieu*, 22. Levinas calls this passivity 'liturgy', which he equals to ethics itself. See Emmanuel Levinas, 'The Trace of the Other', in *Deconstruction in Context. Literature and Philosophy*, M. C. Taylor (ed.) (Chicago: University of Chicago Press, 1986), 345–59, 350.
15. Derrida, *Adieu*, 63: 'Does not hospitality follow, even if just by a second of secondariness, the unforeseeable and irresistible irruption of a visitation? And will not this inverse translation find its limit, the limit of the liminal itself, there where it is necessary to arrive, that is, at the place where, as past visitation, the trace of the other passes or has already passed the threshold, awaiting neither invitation nor hospitality nor welcome? This visit is not a response to an invitation; it exceeds every dialogical relation between host and guest. It must,

from all time, have exceeded them. Its traumatizing effraction must have preceded what is so easily called hospitality – even, as disturbing and pervertible as they already appear, the laws of hospitality.'

16. Derrida, 'Hospitality', in *Acts of Religion*, 362: 'To wait without waiting, awaiting absolute surprise, the unexpected visitor, awaited without a horizon of expectation: this is indeed about the Messiah as hôte, about the messianic as hospitality, the messianic that introduces deconstructive disruption or madness in the concept of hospitality, the madness of hospitality, even the madness of the concept of hospitality.'
17. For Levinas there is a distinction between the infinite otherness of God and that of any human, while for Derrida, as he insists in *Donner la mort*, everything else can be the other.
18. Derrida, 'Hospitality', in *Acts of Religion*, 359: 'the question of hospitality is also the question of waiting and of waiting beyond time'.
19. In fact, contrary to this, Derrida does not hesitate to point out his reservations about the concept of community, in 'Eating Well, or the Calculation of the Subject: An Interview with Jacques Derrida', in E. Cadava, P. Connor and J-L. Nancy (eds), *Who Comes After the Subject?* (New York: Routledge, 1991) or in *Politics of Friendship* (New York: Verso, 1997). Derrida makes an interesting exegesis of how the Internet has forced a new interpretation of borders in which the public has become private and vice versa in Jacques Derrida, 'Foreigner Question', in *Of Hospitality*, 25–9, 43.
20. Jacques Derrida, 'Pas d'hospitalité', in *Of Hospitality*, 135, 149. Derrida, *Adieu*, 15, 98. He speaks of 'androcentric politics' in Derrida, *Politics of Friendship*, Foreword, viii.
21. Jacques Derrida, *Force de loi. Le fundament mystique de l'autorité* (1994) and *Politiques de l'amitié* (1994), addresses this topic. If the first question is from the 1960s and 1970s, this is from the 1990s. Finally, in 1997 he will claim a politics of hospitality as a corollary of these two philosophical paths.
22. Jacques Derrida, 'No Hospitality', in *Of Hospitality*, 75–7: 'It is as though hospitality were the impossible: as though the law of hospitality defined this very impossibility, as if it were only possible to transgress it, as though the law of absolute, unconditional, hyperbolical hospitality, as though the categorical imperative of hospitality commanded that we transgress all the laws (in the plural) of hospitality, namely, the conditions, the norms, the rights and the duties that are imposed on hosts and hostesses, on the men or women who give a welcome as well as the men or women who receive it. And vice versa, it is as though the laws (plural) of hospitality, in marking limits, powers, rights, and duties, consisted in challenging and transgressing the law of hospitality, the one that would command that the "new arrival" will offered an unconditional welcome.'

23. Jacques Derrida, 'The Principle of Hospitality', in *Paper Machine* (Stanford, CA: Stanford University Press, 2005), 66–9, 67. See also Derrida, 'No Hospitality', 135. Derrida, 20: 'Let us assume, *concesso non dato*, that there is no assured passage, following the order of a foundation, according to a hierarchy of founding and founded, of principial originarity and derivation, between an ethics or a first philosophy of hospitality, on the one hand, and a law or politics of hospitality, on the other.'
24. Derrida, *Adieu*, 74.
25. Hent de Vries, 'Hospitable Thought: Before and Beyond Cosmopolitanism', in Hent de Vries, *Religion and Violence: Philosophical Perspectives from Kant to Derrida* (Baltimore, MD: Johns Hopkins University Press, 2001), 293–398, 367, in particular 303.
26. Agamben, *The Time that Remains*, 62–3.
27. Michel Foucault, *Du gouvernement des vivants* (Paris: Seuil, 2012), 250–1.
28. 'Substitution' is a lecture presented by Levinas in 1967 that can be thought the most important part of *Otherwise than Being*. Indeed, in an expanded version, that lecture came to constitute chapter 4 of that book. On the complicated relationship between the texts of Levinas and Derrida, see the lucid article by Emmanuel Biset, 'Jacques Derrida, between Violence and Hospitality', *Daimon* 40 (2007): 131–43. The author points out how in his early days Derrida deconstructively distances himself from Levinas and, nevertheless, in his later days he approaches the idea of Levinasian hospitality as the place to begin thinking about ethics.
29. Emmanuel Levinas, 'Substitution', in *Basic Philosophical Writings*, Adrian Peperzak, Simon Critchley and Robert Bernasconi (eds) (Bloomington: Indiana University Press, 1996), 80.
30. Levinas, 'Substitution', 90.
31. See Egli Bonan, *Soggetto ed Essere. Indagini sul pensiero di Emmanuel Levinas* (Treviso: Piazza Editore, 2002), 324.
32. Levinas, 'Substitution', 91: 'The ego is not a being which is capable of expiating for others; it is this original expiation which is involuntary because prior to the initiative of the will.' And also, ibid., 94: 'Modern antihumanism . . . makes a place for subjectivity positing itself in abnegation, in sacrifice, and in substitution. Its great intuition is to have abandoned the idea of person as an end in itself. The Other (*Autrui*) is the end, and me, I am a hostage.'
33. As Hent de Vries points out in 'Hospitable Thought', 302, Derrida in *Adieu à Emmanuel Levinas* reorganises his position vis-à-vis Levinas in the relationship between ethics, politics and religion in terms of the theme of hospitality. In some way it tells us that hospitality is 'the topic' behind *Totality and Infinity*. Hospitality is an instantiation of ethics, insofar as it is an instantiation of the relationship with

the other. The Levinasian other inaugurates a 'relationship without relation' and thus defines a 'religion for adults', which departs both from the philosophies of identity and from the mysticisms of the totality that encapsulate the self in the other. Derrida, for his part, when dealing with the theme of hospitality, makes a supplement to *Politics of Friendship* and *Specters of Marx*. In fact, the theme of arch-friendship as an overcoming of the politics of fraternity is reoriented towards the question of hospitality.

34. The complete text is Jacques Derrida, 'Hospitality', in *Acts of Religion*, 417: 'When they speak of substitution, it is a matter of an absolutely singular and irreplaceable existence that, in a free act, substitutes itself for another makes itself responsible for another, expiates for another, sacrifices itself for another outside of any homogenous series. Substitution is not indifferent replacement of an equal thing by an equal or identical thing . . . No, the Abrahamic substitution implicates exceptional, elected existences that make themselves or expose themselves of themselves, in their absolutely singularity and as absolutely responsible, the gift or the sacrifice of themselves. That they would be implicated, that they would give themselves as pledge does not mean that substitution would be a free and voluntary act. It is also a grace and a certain passivity, a reception or a visitation, but in any case, it is not the passivity of an effect to which an inert thing would be submitted.'

35. Derrida, *Adieu*, 70: 'this thinking of substitution leads us toward a logic that is hardly thinkable, almost unsayable, that of the possible-impossible, the iterability and replaceability of the unique in the very experience of unicity as such'.

36. Derrida, *Adieu*, 110: 'It is as if the unicity of the face were, in its absolute and irrecusable singularity, plural *a priori*. As we have insisted, Levinas already takes this into account, so to speak, in *Totality and Infinity*, well before the "logic" of substitution, already sketched out in 1961, gets developed in *Otherwise than Being*. The most general possibility of substitution, a simultaneous condition, a paradoxical reciprocity (the condition of i-reciprocity) of the unique and of its replacement, a place that is at once untenable and assigned, the placement of the singular as replaceable, the irrecusable place of the neighbour and of the third-is not all this the first affection of the subject in its ipseity?'

37. Derrida, *Adieu*, 70.

38. Hent de Vries sees in this unification of traditions around the praxis of hospitality more than a kind of Judeo-Christian–Islamic consensus. It refers to a common heritage with structural similarities and language and national dissimilarities. De Vries, 'Hospitable Thought', 318. This coincidence is what he calls 'reverse implication': the folding of the universal into the particular.

39. Derrida, 'Hospitality', in *Acts of Religion*, 372: 'This is indeed hospitality *par excellence* in which the visitor radically overwhelms the self of the "visited" and the *chez-soi* of the hôte (host).' An exegesis of Abraham in Jacques Derrida, 'Abrahan, the Other', in *Religion: Beyond a Concept*, Hent de Vries (ed.) (New York: Fordham University Press, 2008), 311–38.
40. Some fragments of the correspondence between Massignon and Mary Kahil were published in Louis Massignon, *L'hospitalité sacrée* (Paris: Nouvelle Cité, 1987).
41. Louis Massignon, *Opera minora III, Textes recueillis, classés et présentés par Y. Moubarac* (Paris: Presses universitaires de France 1969), 350.
42. Louis Massignon, *Covocation de la Badaliya*, 2 February 1962.
43. Massignon, *L'hospitalité sacrée*, 388.
44. In a letter dated 13 March 1900, Huysmans describes the mystical substitution as follows: 'Humanity is governed by two laws which in its carelessness it ignores: the law of solidarity in evil, the law of reversibility in good; solidarity in Adam, reversibility in Our Lord. In other words, each one is to some extent responsible for the faults of the others and must also atone for them; and each one can also attribute the merits that he possesses or that he has acquired to those who do not possess any or cannot acquire them. God is the first to be submissive to these laws, insofar as he has applied them in the person of his Son . . . He wanted Jesus to give the first example of mystical substitution, of the substitution of one who owes nothing for another who owes everything, and Jesus wants that when certain souls touch Him, they will inherit the benefits of His sacrifice and complete what is lacking in His Passion, as Saint Paul says . . . but there are few saints and contemplative orders and the poor Lord is obliged to turn to us, who are not holy, to make the exact amount. Hence the penalties and illnesses. They probably prevent catastrophes.' Quoted in Christian Destremau and Jean Moncelon, *Louis Massignon, le Cheikh admirable* (Paris: Plon, 1994), 23 (the translation is mine).
45. Massignon, *L'hospitalité sacrée*, 389.
46. Louis Massignon, *Essai sur les origines du lexique technique de la mystique musulmane* (Paris: Vrin, 1954), 132.
47. Massignon, *L'hospitalité sacrée*, 395: 'In order to respond in someone else's place, to speak on their behalf, it is necessary, if not to be the same, at least "be one of their own". The Latin Catholic cannot substitute his Muslim brother through a Latin response: he must respond as an Oriental who opens himself to the word of God. We leave our spiritual and cultural world to put ourselves in the axis of our brother's own vocation.'
48. Massignon, 'La Badaliya du Caire, 1964', in *L'hospitalité sacrée*, 382.

49. Derrida, *Adieu*, 57; Derrida, *Acts of Religion*, 377.
50. Derrida, *Adieu*, 146.
51. Derrida, 'Hospitality', in *Acts of Religion*, 387: 'therefore the subject of the other, subject to the other, there, where not only cannot places be exchanged – insofar as they remain unexchangable and where everything withdraws from a logic of exchange – but where this unicity, this irreplaceability of the non-exchange poses itself, affirms itself, tests and suffers itself, in substitution. I am like the other, there where I cannot be, and could never be like him, in his resemblance, his identification or in his place.'
52. Derrida, 'Hospitality', 386: 'Perhaps one should think about the substitution from those limit experiences, possible-impossible, the impossible of the possible, which is the decision, the gift, forgiveness.'
53. For a reading of Derridean hospitality in terms of motherhood, see Cleo McNelli Kearns, 'Mary, Maternity, and Abrahamic Hospitality in Derrida's Reading of Massignon', in *Derrida and Religion: Other Testaments*, Yvonne Sherwood and Kevin Hart (eds) (London: Routledge, 2005), 73–93.
54. The question of the 'double' in theological–political terms is treated magnificently in Cerella, *Genealogies*, ch. 1. He connects this political representation with the self-founding sacrificial figure of the *rex sacrorum*.
55. Ferdinand Prat, *La teología de San Pablo*, II (Cartoné, México: Jus, 1947), 289–90.
56. The thought that Christ is punished in our place is at the centre of the soteriology of the early Reformers. The idea of 'penal substitution' implies the vindictive justice of an angry God that would have fallen on an innocent Christ, who would have substituted sinful humanity to expiate their penalties. See Martin Luther, *Epistolam S. Pauli ad Galatas Commentarius* in *Werke. Weimarer Ausgabe* (Munich: Metzler, 2000–7), 40/I, 436, 24. 29. In that case, both justice and sin seem to be able to be imputed to man from outside and they seem to belong to a fateful order of the universe. Paul's idea of the vicarious satisfaction of Christ implies that Christ does not satisfy instead of men, but as their head. That is, not from the outside, but from a personal relationship with each men or women. There are no anonymous faces, no strangers. It is more about intimate solidarity.
57. Tomas Aquinas, *STh* III, q. 48, a. 3, ad 1.
58. Agamben, *The Time that Remains*, 123.
59. Derrida, 'Pas d'hospitalité', in *Of Hospitality*, 135.
60. Derrida, *Adieu*, 116.
61. Gerasimos Kakoliris, 'Jacques Derrida on the Ethics of Hospitality', in *The Ethics of Subjectivity: Perspectives since the Dawn of Modernity*, Elvis Imafidon (ed.) (New York: Palgrave Macmillan, 2015), 152.
62. Derrida, *Of Hospitality*, 147.

63. de Vries, 'Hospitable Thought', 348.
64. Kakoliris, 'Jacques Derrida on the Ethics of Hospitality', 144–56.
65. Kakoliris, 'Jacques Derrida on the Ethics of Hospitality', 150.
66. de Vries, 'Hospitable Thought', 349.
67. de Vries, 'Hospitable Thought', 353. The irreducibility of the theological–political is: 'no mere obscurity, nor the consequence of a formal approach or of identifying all legal indeterminacy with the theological. On the contrary, its irreducibility is determined less by general or systemic structures than by singular instances and instantiations, whose events and proper names punctuate history at every juncture.'
68. de Vries, 'Hospitable Thought', 297, 344, 398: 'As Kant already knew, respect for the best has no existence – no chance, no necessity – outside or independent of the many multifaceted institutional, that is to say, political and cultural, forms that punctuate the path of humankind on its postulated progression toward the better and the best. Of this, I have suggested, the history of religion forms the most salient example. In this history, in order to mitigate the propensity toward radical evil, that other curvature in the order of things, one must run the risk of indispensable yet disposable errors, that is to say, idolatries and blasphemies. To risk less is to risk the worst. What's more, to risk less than the worst is to risk the worst of the worst, the evil of evil, more radical than radical evil: the indifference of indecision or, worse still, the complacency of good conscience.'
69. de Vries, 'Hospitable Thought', 349, 370.
70. Certainly, in *Politics of Friendship*, Derrida highlights the Kantian version of the representation of universal brotherhood under the same father, which 'on ne peut ni ne doit s'en passer', 293.
71. Following the same affirmation of Derrida in 'Hospitality': 'Hospitality – this is a name or an example of deconstruction', *Acts of Religion*, 364. See Michael Naas, '"Alors, qui est-vous" Jacques Derrida and the Question of Hospitality', *SubStance* 34(106) (2005): 6–16, 11. Another interpretation, with a similar orientation is that of Scott Huelin, who underlines the identity between hospitality and deconstruction, saying that deconstruction is an hermeneutic of hospitality. Scott Huelin, 'Peregrination, Hermeneutics, Hospitality: On the Way to a Theologically Informed General Hermeneutics', *Literature and Theology* 22(2) (2008): 223–36.
72. de Vries, 'Hospitable Thought', 307. A logic that, in de Vries' view, seeks to subvert the relationship of priority or supremacy between Judaism and Christianity. Rather, it is a move towards unity that is generated by mutual exclusion. Choosing between one or the other mode of hospitality requires the same decision or suspension of decision as choosing one or the other religion.
73. However, Derrida is not so far away from saying it. Speaking on forgiveness Derrida says: 'These two poles, the unconditional and the

conditional, are absolutely heterogeneous, and must remain irreducible to one another. They are nonetheless indissociable . . . that all (concrete actions) of that refers to a certain idea of pure and unconditional forgiveness, without which this discourse would not have the least meaning.' Derrida, *On Cosmopolitanism*, 45.
74. Derrida, *On Cosmopolitanism*, 9: 'If the name and the identity of something like the city still has a meaning, could it, when dealing with the related questions of hospitality and refuge, elevate itself above nation-states or at least free itself from them (*s'affranchir*), in order to become, to coin a phrase in a new and novel way, a free city (*une ville franche*)? Under the exemption itself (*en général*), the statutes of immunity or exemption occasionally had attached to them, as in the case of the right to asylum, certain places (diplomatic or religious) to which one could retreat in order to escape from the threat of injustice.'
75. Jacques Derrida, 'Des Tours de Babel', in *Difference in Translation*, Joseph F. Graham (ed. and trans.) (New York: Cornell University Press, 1985), 165–207.
76. See Puspa Damai, 'Messianic-City: Ruins, Refuge and Hospitality in Derrida', *Discourse* 27(3) (2005): 68–94. The article is critical of Derrida's Eurocentrism, as we can see in the following paragraph, 92: 'The address to the other, therefore, must involve inventing new norms, new idioms and new languages. Derrida at once seems to infinitize the possibilities of that address to occur, but at the same time assuming the diction of a certain Europe.'
77. Derrida, *Adieu*, 107–8; Derrida, *On Cosmopolitanism*. To what extent this proposal can lead to a renewal of international law has been commented on in several books on cosmopolitanism, as is the case of Oliver Kozlarek (ed.), *Entre cosmopolitismo y conciencia del mundo. Hacia una crítica del pensamiento atópico* (Madrid: Siglo XXI, 1997).
78. Emmanuel Levinas, 'Les villes-refuges', in *Au delà du verset* (Paris: Minuit, 1982), 51. Daniel Payot, *Des villes-refuges. Temoignage et espacement* (Paris: L'Aube, 1992), 65.
79. Derrida, *On Cosmopolitanism*, 4.
80. Much has been written about the meaning of the Derridian position on democracy, for example, John D. Caputo, 'Who is Derrida's Zarathustra? Of Fraternity, Friendship, and a Democracy to Come', *Research in Phenomenology* 29 (1999): 184–98; Matthias Fritsch, 'Derrida's Democracy To Come', *Constellations: An International Journal of Critical and Democratic Theory* 9(4) (2002): 574–97; Alex Thomson, 'What's to Become of "Democracy to Come"?' *Postmodern Culture* 15(3) (2005); Andrew Kaufmann, '"Democracy to Come" in the Political Thought of Jacques Derrida', PhD dissertation, Catholic University of America (2014).

81. Derrida, *On Cosmopolitanism*, 10.
82. Interesting reflections concerning this point are to be found in Angelo Cicatello, 'Il diritto di visita entro i limiti della semplice ragione. Note a margine del cosmopolitismo di Kant', *Estudos Kantianos* 3(2) (2015): 73–90. On Derrida, particularly, 76.
83. Fabienne Brugère and Guillaume le Blanc, *La fin de l'hospitalité* (Paris: Flammarion, 2018), 196: 'Il y a hospitalité quand il y a invention d'un hôpital pour les vulnérables, les pauvres, les sans-abri, les étrangers, les n'importe qui en faisant la demande . . . Le réalisme de l'hospitalité plaide pour la nécessité de tels lieux. À l'hôpital, celui qui vient n'est pas rejeté. Nul ne demande s'il a de quoi payer. Du moins en France. On le laisse entrer et on le soigne. L'hôpital n'est pas l'hôtel.'
84. George Duby, *Les Trois Ordres ou l'imaginaire du feodalisme* (Paris: Gallimard, 1978).
85. Benjamin Kedar, 'A Note on Jerusalem's Bimaristan and Jerusalem's Hospital', in *The Hospitallers, the Mediterranean and Europe Festschrift for Anthony Luttrell*, Karl Borchardt; Nicholas Jaspert and Helen J. Nicholson (eds) (London: Ashgate, 2007), 7–11; Benjamin Kedar, 'A Twelfth-century Description of the Jerusalem Hospital', in *The Military Orders: Fighting for the Faith and Caring for the Sick*, vol. 2, H. Nicholson (ed.) (London: Ashgate, 1998); Anthony T. Luttrell, 'The Earliest Hospitallers', in *Montjoie: Studies in Crusade History in Honour of Hans Eberhard Mayer*, Benjamin Kedar, Jonathan Riley-Smith and Rudolf Hiestand (eds) (London: Variorum, 2007); Anthony T. Luttrell, 'The Hospitallers' Early Written Records', in *The Crusades and their Sources: Essays Presented to Bernard Hamilton*, John France and William G. Zajac (eds) (London: Routledge, 1998), 135–54.
86. Martin Aurell, *Des chrétiens contre les croisades: XIIe–XIIIe siècle* (Paris: Fayard, D.L. 2013); Martin Aurell and Catalina Girbea, *Chevalerie et christianisme aux XIIe et XIIIe siècles* (Rennes: Presses universitaires de Rennes, 2019).
87. Alain Demurger, *Chevaliers du Christ. Les ordres religieux-militaires au Moyen Age (XIe–XVIe siècle)* (Paris: Le Seuil, 2015).
88. Alain Beltjens, *Aux Origines de l'Ordre de Malte. De la fondation de l'Hôpital de Jérusalem à sa transformation en ordre militaire* (Brussels: A. Beltjens, 1995), 350–1.
89. It can clearly be said that the Hospitallers overstepped their functions in the framework of the crusades, which were themselves an inadequate instrument of protection of the faith. However, it is not the purpose of this section to discuss the historical atrocities of the crusades, but to show a step in the historical genealogy of hospitality, certainly never entirely pure and often mixed with domination and power. For the history of the crusades, see Steven Runciman,

The First Crusade (Cambridge: Cambridge University Press, 2004). For a historical–critical judgement on the crusades that seems to me to be accurate, see Aurell, *Des chrétiens contre les croisades*.

90. Aurell, *Des chrétiens contre les croisades*, 139–58.
91. Martin Aurell and Catalina Girbea, 'Introduction', in *Chevalerie et christianisme aux XIIe et XIIIe siècles* (Rennes: Presses universitaires de Rennes, 2019), 23. See also Aurell, *Des chrétiens contre les croisades*, 97.
92. In effect, the pope was trapped by the play of King Philip IV of France, who had made ignominious accusations against the Templars in order to get his hands on their gold. The result was that the Templars had covered themselves in infamy, despite the fact that the bull *Vox in excelso*, issued by Pope Clement V, dissolving the order of the Templars, states that 'from the processes carried out against the order, a sentence condemning it could not in law be pronounced'. On 18 March 1314, however, Jacques de Molay, Grand Master of the Temple, who had been imprisoned for seven years as a result of a trial rigged by the king of France, was burned at the stake. See Alain Demurger, *The Persecution of the Templars: Scandal, Torture, Trial* (London: Profile, 2018).
93. Demurger, *Chevaliers du Christ*, 169.
94. Demurger, *Chevaliers du Christ*, 171. As Demurger points out, every religious order had to practice almsgiving to the poor on all occasions, but especially on the great solemnities of the liturgical calendar. For example, the rule of the Temple included the feeding of a poor person for forty days after the death of a brother, and encouraged leaving a tenth of the bread for the poor in the same circumstance to leave. The Hospitallers did the same.
95. The statutes of the hospital order denounced certain abuses in the nursing services: there were fake patients, convalescences that went on forever, good food and entertainment. The General Chapter of 20 November 1440 made a survey of the nursing teams and instituted a control of expenditure.
96. For this last historical journey of the Hospitallers, see Helen Nicholson, *The Knights Hospitaller* (Woodbridge: Boydell, 2001), 116–46.

Epilogue

The complex relationship between the post-secular and the theological turn in philosophy and political theology is the backdrop that inspired the main theme of in this book: to what extent the centrality of theological discourse in originating meanings, symbols and realities has been, and continues to be, relevant in shaping instituted practices in the political realm.

This relevance has historically been shown in the conceptual transfers and mutual borrowings of terms and meanings from one field to another: from the theological to the political and vice versa. Through this hybridisation of theological and political vocabulary, it is shown that some divine traces could be considered embedded in institutionalised political practices. Throughout the various chapters, we have tried to discover the divine marks, the theological signatures or, as we have characterised them here, the figures of the divine embedded in certain instituted political practices. These figures speak of God. In a way, they reveal God by saying something about Him or by representing Him. The five theopolitical figures examined in this book are other names of God found in the political realm. Following the tradition of the apophatic theology, they name God in a negative and symbolic way: in particular, He is the written revelation (scripture); He is the to come (prophecy); He is truthful and faithful (oath); He is mercy and forgiving (charisma); and He is the absolute host (hospitality). These figures refer to symbolic meanings which happen as historical events representing the divine in a negative way. In fact, these theopolitical figures appear in the form of a paradox: while being the necessary conditions for the constitution of any possible community, they always remain unconditional and impossible in their absolute happening.

Hence, this book is intended to be a contribution to the theological turn in political philosophy. It reinscribes contemporary political concepts and experiences in the 'theological locus' from which they supposedly come and at the same time looks for alternative semantic derivations for the political theory and practice. The discursive trajectory of the book has engaged with the discussions of different continental philosophers of the twentieth century, including Walter Benjamin, Jacques Derrida, Jean-Louis Chrétien, Michel Foucault, Giorgio Agamben, Jean-Luc Nancy, John Caputo, Jean-Luc Marion and Vladimir Jankélévitch among others. It also engages, on the one hand, with the theological literature of Tertullian, Augustine of Hypo, Oscar Cullmann, James Barr, Karl Barth, Louis Massignon, Henry de Lubac, Josef Ratzinger, Hans Urs von Balthasar and Erik Peterson among others, and, on the other hand, with the work of historians such as Ernst H. Kantorowicz, Philippe Buc, Paolo Prodi, Walter Ullmann, Reinhart Koselleck, Peter Brown or Robert Markus.

We have considered five theopolitical figures: scripture, prophecy, oath, *charisma* and hospitality. Scripture occurs as the figure of the divine par excellence insofar as it is the voice of God that endures in historical time with an unalterable presence in the absence of a visible God. The very structure of scripture contains what this book identifies as the figurative character of some theopolitical instituted practices, according to which meaning occurs historically through the reiteration of certain events. Indeed, this unique feature of scripture inaugurates what we have called prophetic time – a conception of time oriented to a promise; scripture also occurs as a very specific instance of giving one's word – it is in itself an oath; it gives an account of power as gift; and, finally, its word unfolds by founding political community.

But what are the political meanings associated with scriptures? Sacred Scriptures have never been alien to the political. The possibility of being translated, interpreted or deconstructed resides in the special character of the Scriptures as written texts. As scriptures, they share the destiny ascribed to the written word by post-structuralist philosophy. As sacred, they stand as a point of non-replaceability, and consequently a point of orientation for an entire system of signification. Or in Benjamin's expression, every sacred text is the archival receptacles of pure language – that has for him the character of a disturbance. Scripture as a theopolitical figure never disappears over the course of historical time; it is and always will be disputed. The figurative force of scriptures is always disruptive. Indeed, as a figure, they occur over and over again in all epochs. As Gadamer suggests, everything that is not immediately situated in a context, such as the spiritual creations of the past, is estranged from its original meaning and depends on the unlocking and mediating spirit of every epoch. In the same vein, scriptures considered as sacred texts are situated at the centre of political disputes, shaping the way in which political power has been conceived. The legitimisation of power through scriptural interpretation has been an iterated theological–political practice, as can be seen in a number of cases concerning the political practices of the West. In fact, at the end of the Chapter 1, the book explores, by way of example, the interpretative vicissitudes of the Scriptures in the transition from the Middle Ages to the Enlightenment, and shows how crucial the theological–political dilemma is in this interpretation.

But beyond that, the destiny of every core text of a community is associated with that of scriptures: it is to be read, to be translated, to be interpreted, to be misinterpreted and to be deconstructed. This applies particularly to the text of the law. In fact, legal dogmatics is in itself a figure of scripture, and occurs when scripture itself loses its dogmatic place in the political arena. In Derrida's words, justice is never contained in the law, in the same way that God is absent from the Scriptures. Each position of law is a betrayal of justice, just as any interpretation is the betrayal of a given text, but it speaks of justice in the negative way of the negative theology.

Concerning historical time, the figure of prophecy, which is at the heart of scripture, speaks of alternative representations of time, other than linear. The prophetic narratives representing God's voice in their principal task of achieving meaning for history speak of a future–present, which is committed neither to the notion of progress nor to the model of linear time. Indeed, prophetic time comes to birth within a narrative in which a certain interpretation of the present is related to the past, but fundamentally to a future destiny. That future destiny is not imaginable, or foreseeable or calculable, but remains a given destiny in the form of a divine trace in the course of history. This divine trace is a judgement that has already taken place in the perspective of meaning, but which will become fully effective at the end of time. Consequently, that judgement is a promise.

Historical action has been driven by different horizons of expectation: auspices and divinations, astrology, messianism, prophetism and apocalypticism, and, finally, the rise of statistical prediction of every kind. Every age has to interpret history according to its own expectations, which may even include attempts to avoid any destiny whatsoever. Moreover, we are not in a post-prophetic period. We are forced to recognise that our time is situated within a prophetic word and cannot relinquish the kind of temporality that emerges from this word. We are part of a promise of a future to come. The Jewish people have a historical sense based on Old Testament prophecies: the occupation of the promised land, the coming of the Messiah and the definitive reconstruction of the temple at Jerusalem. Muslims also interpret history within a prophetic time; after Mohammed, there will be a reorganisation of the religious community. Christians await the second coming of Christ and the institution of Christ's kingdom. These are prophetic futures that still pervade our present and past representations of time as an 'absolute future' that is not and never will be a consequence of past and present times, or, in other words, something that can be achieved through human action, prevision or calculation alone.

What consequences does this prophetical temporality have for our historical representations and political decisions? In the manner of a negative theology, it speaks to us of what is not. First, it warns us that we are not the ultimate builders of our future. Time comes from an unexpected future rather than from a constructed past. Secondly, prophetical time shows that we live in multiple representations of time and not just in linear time. In fact, by recovering the scriptural characterisation of time in the discussion between Barr, Cullmann and Peterson, we have seen how the Christian narrative speaks of very different ways of qualifying time as cyclical, linear and other mixed forms such as occasion, age, season, etc. One of them is prophetic time, which translocates future, present and past in the logic of the 'already and not yet'. Thirdly, prophetic time instructs us that we have to be prepared to accept the unknowable event to come that can visit us at any moment. From the political perspective, this kind of temporality favours the possible achievement of justice through 'conviction' – in Weberian terms – and avoids consequentialist politics centred on the efficacy of our own action and on a precise calculation of consequences in order to achieve a mandatory progressivism. And, finally, prophetic time avoids the false delusions of utopia. Utopia calls for political actions and forces, while the prophetic requires only one quality, that of actively awaiting the promise, which is found in the content of the prophecy itself. The unexpected future thus appears as an incision of the divine in historical time, which is always figuratively, albeit discontinuously, present in history through the extraordinary. The disruptive event always recalls the prophetic force of the apocalypse, as the book shows through the examination of the historical case of the 1755 Lisbon Earthquake, which was widely commented upon and interpreted by both Enlightenment philosophy and prophetic literature.

Contemporary philosophy has tried to recover other ways of interpreting historical time from a theological perspective which imply new political consequences. This is the case of the recovery of the idea of messianic time, most particularly in Benjamin, Derrida and Agamben, who in their writings all allow for theological–political transfer. Indeed, Benjamin thinks of the messianic as a past that triggers our responsibility to liberate history. To do justice to the oppressed past becomes the most relevant political action. While considering our debt to the past, Derrida emphasises the radical futurity of justice, democracy and equality, the promise of emancipation that is an index of the indeterminate structure of the messianic itself. Both refrain from speaking of a future–present for two related reasons: such a conception commits us to a false notion of progress – the idea that the present moves towards a determined future – and this in turn commits us to the model of objective, linear time.

Considering scriptures as the figure of a given word, we have explored the theopolitical character of the oath. In fact, in view of the experience of the fallibility of the human word, the rite of the oath functions as a stabilising device for the word given. Hence, it has been considered a fundamental element in any *testimonium* that forms part of a judicial process and in the foundation of any kind of promise. Through fear of the punishment for perjury, God was the guarantor of the faithfulness to and truthfulness of the word given, either as a promise or as a testimony. The efficacy of the ritual falls on and transforms the subject who carries it out. By assuring a truthful and faithful subjectivity, oaths were a central practice in the constitution of the political community. The practice of the oath can be attested from time immemorial.

Christianity transformed the meaning of the oath in a particular way, not only because it transferred it to the specifically sacramental sphere of the church, but also because it established the prohibition of swearing in the name of God. In fact, the command of Christ himself resounds: thou shalt not swear. Foucault was more aware than any other philosopher of this incision of Christianity in the history of the oath. He pointed out that the experience of false conversions led the Church to emphasise a new sacramental praxis, that of confession. The guarantee of truthfulness and faithfulness that resided in the external witness was then transferred to subjectivity. Both oath and confession are rituals of veridiction, but while in the former God acts as an external witness, in confession his gaze is directed to the interior of the subject and binds truthfulness from within. Without this second kind of veridiction of the subject, the oath is not reliable even if the name of God is pronounced in the rite, whether it be baptism in the profession of faith, the testimonial practices in a judicial system, or the social covenant in the form of submission to the law. Two internal dispositions must exist in the person in order to be able to swear: truthfulness and faithfulness. These two attitudes are a figure of the divine in the absence of the divine name in the oath, and, as rituals of veridiction, constitute the possibility of not swearing falsely.

Just as Prodi has showed that oath, insofar as it uses God as an external witness, has sustained the constitutional history of the West, Foucault points out that the rituals of subjective veridiction sustain the juridical practice of modern states, in which the very name of God seems to have been eclipsed in juridical institutions. In this case, a new theological–political transfer of meaning takes place: the transference from an economy of salvation – a canonical system with penalties for every fault – to a juridical system of civil penalties. Indeed, according to Foucault, the imperative 'tell me who you are', which originated in Christianity, is the fundamental imperative of contemporary Western civilisation, just as the oath was for centuries a metapolitical guarantor of the political bond. Indeed, apart from the inscription of the name of God in the formula of oaths, the divine is present in the structural form of every civil juridical system. Or, to put it another way, every given word, whether testimonial or promissory, is a 'figure of the divine' or it betrays itself. Whoever promises or gives testimony follows the internal logic of God's oath: the absolute efficacy of the word, even if, as Derrida and Chrétien say, for humans that is impossible. The divine logic persists analogically in the theopolitical aspects disclosed in the giving of one's word, again in the negative way of the *theologia negativa*, since nobody can really make their own promises truly happen, except God. But in any case, God is ceaselessly invoked in every human act of giving the word through the very structure of language and the law. There is a strange and complex relationship in this kind of pronouncement, which includes the act of giving the word, language and the divine. What is said and promised cannot be undone. Hence, even if God is not invoked, He is already present in the very possibilities offered by language. The book has tried to show this with the particular case of the theological–political transfers of meaning that take place in the word *sacramentum*, which moves from the civil–military sphere to the strictly theological and ecclesiastical one. In both cases as a performative ritual that ensures truthfulness and loyalty.

To speak truthfully is a liminal practice of society. It allows for its constitution or for its deconstruction, as we have tried to show in the description of the Foucauldian analysis of the two figures who speak truthfully about themselves: the confessing subject and the parrhesiast. Only the first allows for the constitution of a truth–power *dispositif*. Not, however, the second, who represents the exception to the rule. Both are completely reliable and therefore both can swear authentically. The memory of a political community is founded on the structure of a faithful promise embedded in the law. The terms of political coexistence, or, to put it in another way, the possibility of governmentality, depend on the form of a truthful and faithful subjectivity, which can give its word and be considered reliable.

Charisma as a theopolitical figure invokes the sacred character of power. The invocation of this figure was intended to call into question the legitimacy of political power. Through reflection on the trajectories of meaning of the term *charisma* in theology and politics, we have sought to challenge the reflection on legitimate power that is usually enclosed in the dichotomies democracy–autocracy, political theology–economical theology, governmental paradigm–sovereignty paradigm. Our effort has been to elucidate what idea of political power is hidden behind the idea of *charisma* when we appropriate it from Weberian sociology and reinscribe it into its theological place. Weber transferred the theological concept of *charisma* to the political sphere, but at the same time gave it an authoritarian nuance that it lacked in Paul's appropriation of the term: so much so in fact, that the concept of charismatic power was always aligned with totalitarian, irrational and dangerous autocracies. This is not, however, the ultimate meaning of a charismatic political theology, as we have tried to show by reinterpreting the idea of power as gift, which corresponds to Paul's idea of *charisma* much more than to the charismatic legitimacy as proposed by Weber. In this itinerary, we have engaged in dialogue with Mauss, Derrida, Marion, Patocka and Jankélévitch among others, who, far from any economical exchange and *simulacra*, have seriously considered the centrality of gift in the founding of the political community, and not only in economical exchange. We have also considered Agamben's defence of an economical paradigm of power, which avoids a political theology based on the Schmittian concept of sovereignty, which in turn derived from the idea of a sovereign God.

In opposition to the idea of the gift as a circulating object, Derrida along with Marion, interprets the authentic gift as non-circulating. In fact, the Pauline theopolitical character of power appears as a kind of salvation from every 'economical' power. In particular, Derrida uses the felicitous expression '*sovereign* calculation' to express the attitude of going beyond calculation that must be characteristic of power as opposed to the economic attitude. Sacrifice is the historical condition of power as gift, and the exceptional gift is pardon. In fact, Derrida also speaks of a *sovereign* and absolute forgiveness. Modifying Schmitt's well-known definition, we could say that the sovereign is he who can make the *sovereign* calculation of not calculating at all. People acclaim those sovereigns whom they recognise as saviours and in this sense every authentic politics has something of a messianic character. Nevertheless, *charismata* can be produced authentically or as *simulacra*: that is, as if it were devalued or counterfeit money, without gold reserves, as Derrida would say.

What we have found in this search is: first, that the theological–political idea of power that is symbolised in the figure of charisma transcends the abovementioned opposition between democracy–autocracy insofar as it can be applied to either of the two poles of the opposition; secondly, that in the language of Paul, *charisma* means mainly a gift for the community. In fact, the original hallmark of the theopolitical transfer is contrary to the Weberian authoritarian turn. Indeed, the theopolitical legitimation of power comes from a consideration of power as gift. However, the only possibility of the occurrence of an unconditional gift is sacrifice. The supreme gift given in sacrifice is forgiveness. The theological–political figure of power moves in this triad: sacrifice is the condition of any gift, of which forgiveness is the highest expression. Here, too, however, the theological–political figure illuminates in the manner of a negative theology, from the impossibility of such a sacrifice or such a forgiveness happening in its purity outside the Christ event.

Historically, there are many specific examples that could be analysed. We have focused on acclamations, which are an example of the *pathos* of glory in which both divine power and political power participate. As we have seen in the historical case of acclamations, from the beginning, the ruler cult served as a model for Christians to glorify Christ; in fact, many of the characters of pagan political power were transferred into the imagery of God's government. But we could have taken other historical figures, such as the power of relics, which 'sanctify' political power by their connection with salvation or resurrection, or the figure of the thaumaturgical kings, which exemplify the interest that miracles aroused in political theory, as, for example, in the case of Hobbes and Spinoza.

Finally, hospitable action is at the heart of the configuration of any community, since defining what the community consists of has to do with defining welcoming and belonging as much as with defining exclusion. Every community presupposes at least a certain limit, albeit a porous one, since openness without limits blurs the borders of community and renders any welcome impossible. But if a community wants to be human in the highest sense of the word, it cannot close itself off indifferently to the fellow human being who approaches it. This ethical duty to welcome the other, which urges political action not to completely close the political community, is based on an idea of human solidarity which has theological roots. We have tried to reinscribe the figure of hospitality in its theological locus, in this case by understanding why there is an unconditional duty to welcome the other and how this unconditionality cannot disappear whatever the specific conditions of the welcome might be.

When this duty, which the Enlightenment simply interpreted as a cosmopolitan duty, is reinscribed in its Jewish and Christian existential root, two aspects appear without which it would not make sense: the thought of substitution and the idea of symbolic representation. Both have been addressed by Derrida, albeit from the viewpoint of the aporetic logic that defines all phenomena that somehow relate to the origin. In fact, Levinas, Derrida and Chrétien are among the foremost who have inspired a politics of hospitality in the twentieth century. It is by reading them that we have attempted to find another way of considering substitution and another alternative way of contemplating the conditional unconditionality which will allow us to escape the *aporia* in which Levinas and particularly Derrida leave us immersed.

The first question addresses the possibility of accessing the other as such without subjugating him as soon as he approaches. This problem is at the heart of the possibility of doing justice to the other; moreover, it opens up the question of the possibility of substitution of the other, which is a traditionally theological question. For Levinas, substitution belongs to the logic of the subject's evasion from himself, the evasion from the evil of identity. For him, substitution is not to be understood as the act of substituting oneself for another as if something like a constituted self could ever happen; it should be understood as the sacrifice of the own substantiality of self by others. Derrida recovers this Levinasian topic in a theological way, by addressing the question of the replaceability–irreplaceability of the other in terms of their salvation. By reading Massignon, Derrida offers impossible substitution as an example of authentic hospitality: he refers to singular and irreplaceable existences that, as the consequence of a free act, however, are substituted by others, who become responsible for them. Absolute hospitality depends then on an existential expatriation.

To reinscribe this Christian trope in its theological locus leads us again to Paul. Christ did not die in our place (αντι), because this would have dispensed us from dying. Hence, Pauline theology speaks more of a vicarious satisfaction than of a vicarious substitution. Rather than of a 'mystical substitution', in this case it is necessary to speak of a 'mystical solidarity'. Such a solidarity illuminates the possibility of undertaking actions from which others can benefit without subjugating them: it allows for the participation in the actions of some members by other members in need without eliminating either of the two. Such a form of solidarity can be called 'mystical' insofar as it belongs only to 'mystical bodies'.

The second aporetic question is that of the cancellation of ethical hospitality in any specific hospitable action; that is, the impossibility of reconciling the unconditionality and the conditions in every hospitable action. This question is related to the closeness or remoteness of the other. We also find here the theological locus. How can we consider hospitality so that the unconditioned remains represented in any condition? The truly unconditioned is not conditioned when dealing with conditions. If it were, we would have mistaken its unconditioned character.

In contrast to the undecidable logic of the possible–impossible, we offer the logic of symbolic representation. This kind of logic puts an end from an ethical – though not political – point of view to the 'infinite demand' that always goes beyond the apparently justified restrictions and conditions to which the course of history, and to some extent political action, are condemned. When we reinscribe hospitality in its theological locus, absolute hospitality is possible in a symbolic way by following the logic of the representation of the whole in the part. Each other is every other. This is possible only by considering the mystical solidarity we have just mentioned. We could then interpret unconditional solidarity as being fully executed in every empirically verifiable act of hospitality. Despite the consciousness of one's own limitations that ethical responsibility usually bears, hope can be glimpsed in any present political order by inaugurating symbolic figures – that is, instituted structures – of hospitality therein. In the Pauline sense of the term, each act of hospitality is a 'remainder': each concrete substitution is waiting for any other substitution it refers to. The end of the chapter on hospitality draws attention to a specific historical figure of hospitality, namely, the practice of the Knights Hospitaller.

* * *

The analysis of the above figures, which has been the immediate aim of the book, has led to some other conclusions of a more general scope, related to what was defined as the backdrop at the beginning of the book. As for the secularisation thesis, the different chapters have shown that when a concept comes from the Christian vocabulary and is introduced into the political sphere, it retains the mark of its original domain, that is, ultimately, the mark of God himself. Thus, through these concepts, meanings or ideas coming from the theological realm, a trace of God is introduced into the political theory and practice; to such an extent that a complete secularisation would be an infinite task, never fully achieved. Therefore, a completely secular political realm is not possible when it operates with words, ideas and meanings coming from theology, such as those analysed in the book.

But, moreover, in relation to the traffic between theological and political ideas and meanings, one of the main arguments of the book is that throughout the history of ideas there has been no single pattern. Sometimes the political sphere takes on theological concepts, as Schmitt pointed out, but often the opposite is true, with theology drawing on political concepts, as in the case of the *sacramentum*; and sometimes the concepts remain indistinct. In any case, neither always in antiquity are theological concepts sacralised political concepts, as Assmann says; nor in the modern world, as Schmitt says, is it the other way around; nor can we say, as Agamben points out, that we have entered a moment of indistinction. Rather, we could argue for every epoch what Kantorowicz attests for the Middle Ages, that there is much borrowing in both directions and that in the course of this borrowing ideas are nuanced, transformed and enriched in their meaning.

In the case of the proposed figures, the book has tried precisely to recover their theological meaning in order to re-mark them theologically and thus to bring them out of the indistinction in which the history of ideas has been able to derive them in some cases. To do so, the book has followed the methodology proposed by Carl Schmitt's political theology, consisting in searching for the radical conceptualisation of juridical and political concepts. But far from his work, he has focused on theological–political concepts that had not been dealt with by him in more than a cursory manner – since his political theology is more centred on the idea of representation, sovereignty and constituent power. In this sense, the book aims to expand the political–theological archive.

In addition, the book has added to these theses, a new one beyond the way Schmitt, Kantorowicz, Assmann and Agamben practice political theology, and that is that it calls these concepts figures, inspired at this point by Auerbach's studies. In other words, he assumes and shows that they reveal something of God, albeit in the manner of a negative theology. The reflection of the book is not about how political actions are legitimised in theological concepts, but about how the meanings acquired by theological–political figures can affect political praxis and theory. The book's proposal, therefore, is that a reinscription of these figures in their theological place can heal political practice from harmful theological–political distortions. It is thus a discourse critical of many of the theological–political derivations of past history and seeks to open the way to new transfers that can be hopeful for political experience.

* * *

Some central issues for contemporary societies are discernible in the symbolic meaning of the theopolitical figures referred to. These include the endurance of the law and the unconditional character of justice, the unfeasibility of historical expectation, the stability of the given word, the way political power is legitimised, and the openness to the coming other as a political–ethical imperative. Through the description of these figures we have addressed at the same time the implicit question of whether or not society has always to be thought of as being at the same time both sacred and civil. The sacred and the civil appear to be two sides of the same coin, even if we consider them separate and autonomous spheres from the jurisdictional point of view.

Bibliography

Adam, Armin, *Rekonstruktion des Politischen, Carl Schmitt und die Krise der Staatlichkeit 1912–1933* (Weinheim, VCH–Acta Humaniora, 1992).
Adorno, Theodor W., *Negative Dialectics* (London: Routledge, 1990).
Adorno, Theodor W., *The Meaning of Time in the Moral World, Gesammelte Schriften in 20 Bänden* (Frankfurt: Suhrkamp, 2017).
Agamben, Giorgio, *The Time that Remains: A Commentary on the Letter to the Romans* (Stanford, CA: Stanford University Press, 2005).
Agamben, Giorgio, *Profanations* (New York: Zone Books, 2007).
Agamben, Giorgio, *The Kingdom and the Glory: For a Theological Genealogy of Economy and Government* (Standford, CA: Stanford University Press, 2011).
Agamben, Giorgio, *The Sacrament of Language* (Sandford, CA: Standford University Press, 2011).
Aldrete, Gregory S., *Gestures and Acclamations in Ancient Rome* (Baltimore, MA: Johns Hopkins University Press, 1999).
Alexis-Baker, Andy, 'Spinoza's Political Theology: Theocracy, Democracy and Monism', *Journal of Church and State* 54(3) (2012): 426–44.
Althoff, Gerd, '*Conventiculum, conspiratio, coniuratio*: The Political Power of Sworn Associations in 10th and 11th Century Germany', in *Le Sacré et la Parole. Le Serment au Moyen Age*, Martin Aurell, Jaume Aurell and Montserrat Herrero (eds) (Paris: Classiques Garnier, 2018), 57–69.
Altizer, Thomas J. J., 'Theology and the Death of God', *Centennial Review* 8 (1964): 129–46.
Altizer, Thomas J. J. and William Hamilton, *Radical Theology and the Death of God* (New York: Bobbs-Merrill, 1966).
Anders, Günther, *Die Antiquiertheit des Menschen. 1, Über die Seele im Zeitalter der zweiten industriellen Revolution* (Munich: Beck, 1961).

Anders, Günther, *Endzeit und Zeitsende. Gedanke über die atomare Situation* (Munich: Beck, 1972).
Aroney, Nicholas, 'Faith in Public Office: The Meaning, Persistence and Importance of Oaths', paper in Conference Faith in Public Office, Centre for the Study of Science, Religion and Society, Emmanuel College, University of Queensland, 3 September 2015, published on ABC *Religion and Ethics* website.
Asad, Talal, *Formations of the Secular: Christianity, Islam, Modernity* (Standford, CA: Stanford University Press, 2003).
Assmann, Jan, *Herrschaft und Heil* (Munich: Carl Hauser, 2000).
Assmann, Jan, *Politische Theologie zwischen Ägypten und Israel* (Munich: Carl Friedrich von Siemens, 2006).
Assmann, Jan, *Exodus. Die Revolution der Alten Welt* (Munich: Beck, 2015).
Auerbach, Eric, *Mimesis: The Representation of Reality in Western Literature* (Princeton, NJ: Princeton University Press, 1953).
Auerbach, Eric, 'Figura', in *Scenes from the Drama of European Literature*, Eric Auerbach (ed.) (Minneapolis: University of Minnesota Press, 1984).
Augustine of Hypo, *De dilectica* V (PL 32, 1410).
Augustine of Hypo, *The City of God* (Cambridge: Cambridge University Press, 1988).
Aurell, Jaume, *Medieval Self-Coronations: The History and Symbolism of a Ritual* (Cambridge: Cambridge University Press, 2020).
Aurell, Martin, *Des chrétiens contre les croisades. XIIe–XIIIe siècle* (Paris: Fayard, D.L. 2013).
Aurell, Martin, Jaume Aurell and Montserrat Herrero (eds), *Le Sacré et la Parole. Le Serment au Moyen Age* (Paris: Classiques Garnier, 2018).
Aurell, Martin and Catalina Girbea, *Chevalerie et christianisme aux XIIe et XIIIe siècles* (Rennes: Presses universitaires de Rennes, 2019).
Auzépy, Marie-France et al. (eds), *Oralité et lien social au Moyen Age (Occident, Byzance, Islam)* (Paris: ACHCByz, 2008).
Backer, Émile, 'Tertullien', in *Pour l'histoire du mot 'sacramentum'. Les Anténicéans*, Joseph de Ghellinck (ed.) (Paris: Honoré Champion, 1924).
Badiou, Alain, *Saint Paul: The Foundation of Universalism* (Stanford, CA: Stanford University Press, 2003).
Baêta Neves, Luiz Felipe, 'Profetismo e Iluminismo no Terremoto de Lisboa de 1755', *Revista Convergência Lusiada* 24 (2007): 145–56.
Baker, Herschel C., *The Wars of Truth: Studies in the Decay of Christian Humanism in the Earlier Seventeenth Century* (Cambridge, MA: Harvard University Press, 1952).
Balthasar, Hans Urs von, *The Glory of the Lord: A Theological Aesthetics*, vol. 1 (San Francisco, CA: Ignatius Press, 1989).
Barr, James, *Biblical Words for Time* (London: SCM Press, 1962).
Barth, Karl, *Kirchliche Dogmatik*, II, Part 1 (Zurich: Theologische, 1940).

Bassnett, Susan, 'Seismic Aftershocks: Responses to the Great Lisbon Earthquake of 1755', in *Sites of Exchange: European Crossroads and Faultlines,* Maurizio Ascari and Adriana Corrado (eds) (Amsterdam: Rodopi, 2006), 177–87.

Bates, David, 'The Political Theology of Entropy: A Katechon for the Cybernetic Age', *History of the Human Sciences* 33(1) (2020): 109–27.

Baumert, Norbert, *Charisma, Taufe, Geisttaufe, Band 1: Entflechtung einer semantischen Verwirrung* (Würzburg: Echter, 2001).

Bedos-Rezak, Brigitte Miriam and Martha Dana Rust (eds), *Faces of Charisma: Image, Text, Object in Byzantium and the Medieval West* (Leiden: Brill, 2018).

Beltjens, Alain, *Aux Origines de l'Ordre de Malte. De la fondation de l'Hôpital de Jérusalem à sa transformation en ordre militaire* (Brussels: A. Beltjens, 1995).

Bell, Catherine, *Ritual Theory, Ritual Practice* (Oxford: Oxford University Press, 1992).

Bell, Catherine, *Ritual: Perspectives and Dimensions* (Oxford: Oxford University Press, 1997).

Bell, Daniel M. Jr, *Liberation Theology After the End of History: The Refusal to Cease Suffering* (London: Routledge, 2001).

Benjamin, Walter, 'Theses on the Philosophy of History', in *Illuminations* (New York: Schocken, 1969).

Benjamin, Walter, 'Theologisch-politisches Fragment', in *Illuminationen: Ausgewahlte Schriften* (Frankfurt am Main: Suhrkamp, 1977).

Benjamin, Walter, 'Theologico-Political Fragment', in *Reflections: Essays, Aphorisms, Autobiographical Writings* (New York: Schocken, 1978).

Benjamin, Walter, *Das Passagen-Werk* (Frankfurt am Main: Suhrkamp, 1982).

Benjamin, Walter, *Gesammelte Schriften* (Frankfurt am Main: Suhrkamp, 1991).

Benjamin, Walter, *The Origin of German Tragic Drama* (London: Verso, 1998).

Benjamin, Walter, *The Arcades Project* (Cambridge, MA: Belknap Press of Harvard University, 1999).

Benjamin, Walter, 'The Lisbon Earthquake', in *Selected Writings,* vol. 2, Michael W. Jennings, Howard Eiland and Gary Smith (eds) (Cambridge, MA: Harvard University Press, 1999), 536–40.

Benjamin, Walter, *On Language as Such and on the Language of Man,* in *Selected Writings, vol. 1: 1913–1926,* Marcus Bullock and Michael W. Jennings (eds) (Cambridge, MA: Harvard University Press, 2002), 62–74.

Benjamin, Walter, *Selected Writings* (Cambridge, MA: Harvard University Press, 2002).

Benjamin, Walter, *The Task of the Translator,* in *Selected Writings, vol. 1: 1913–1926,* Marcus Bullock and Michael W. Jennings (eds) (Cambridge, MA: Harvard University Press, 2002), 253–63.

Bento, Antonio, 'Machiavelli's Treatment of *congiure* and the Modern Oath', in *Le Sacré et la Parole. Le Serment au Moyen Age*, Martin Aurell, Jaume Aurell and Montserrat Herrero (eds) (Paris: Classiques Garnier, 2018), 267–97.

Benveniste, Émile, *Vocabulaire des institutions indo-européennes*, vol. 2 (Paris: Les Editions de Minuit, 1969).

Benveniste, Émile, *Problèmes de linguistique générale II* (Paris: Gallimard, 1974).

Bengtson, Josef, *Explorations in Post-Secular Metaphysics* (New York: Palgrave Macmillan, 2015).

Benson, Bruce E. and Norman Wirzba, *Words of Life: New Theological Turns in French Phenomenology* (New York: Fordham University Press, 2010).

Berger, Peter (ed.), *The Desecularization of the World: A Global Overview* (Grand Rapids, MI: Eerdmans, 2005).

Berick, Francis H. and John Couch, *The Fulfilment of Prophecy, Or, A Prophetic History of the World, Including a Few Suggestions on the Probable Termini of the Chronological Periods* (Lowell: S. J. Varney, 1852).

Bertman, Martin A., 'Hobbes on Language and Reality', *Revue Internationale de Philosophie* 32 (1978): 536–50.

Betz, Otto, 'Der Katechon', *New Testament Studies* 9(3) (1963): 276–91.

Bickerman, Élias Joseph, 'Les deux erreurs du prophète Jonas', *Revue d'histoire et de philosophie religieuses* 45 (1965): 232–64.

Bielik-Robson, Agata, *Jewish Cryptotheologies of Late Modernity: Philosophical Marranos* (London: Routledge, 2014).

Bielik-Robson, Agata, 'The Messiah and the Great Architect: On the Difference between the Messianic and the Utopian', *Utopian Studies* 29(2) (2018): 133–58.

Biset, Emmanuel, 'Jacques Derrida, between Violence and Hospitality', *Daimon* 40 (2007): 131–43.

Blanton, Ward and Hent de Vries (eds), *Paul and the Philosophers* (New York: Fordham University Press, 2013).

Blanton, Ward, Noelle Vahanian, Jeffrey W. Robbins and Clayton Crockett, *An Insurrectionist Manifesto: Four New Gospels for a Radical Politics* (New York: Columbia University Press, 2016).

Blumenberg, Hans, *Die Legitimität der Neuzeit* (Frankfurt am Main: Suhrkamp, 1966).

Blumenberg, Hans, *Begriffe in Geschichten* (Frankfurt am Main: Suhrkamp, 1998).

Bohrer, Karl-Heinz, *Nach der Natur. Über Politik und Ästhetik* (Munich: Hanser, 1988).

Boll, Franz and Carl Bezold, *Le Stelle. Credenza e interpretazione* (Turin: Bollati Boringhieri, 2011).

Boman, Thorleif, *Das hebräische Denken im Vergleich mit dem griechischen* (Göttingen: Vandenhoeck & Ruprecht, 1965).

Bonan, Egli, *Soggetto ed Essere. Indagini sul pensiero di Emmanuel Levinas* (Treviso: Piazza Editore, 2002).
Bourgeois, Daniel, *Être et signifier* (Paris: Vrin, 2016).
Bouton, Christophe, *Faire l'histoire* (Paris: Cerf, 2013).
Boyarin, Daniel, *Border Lines: The Partition of Judaeo Christianity* (Philadelphia: University of Pennsylvania Press, 2004).
Brand, Chad, Charles W. Draper and Archie England (eds), *Holman Bible Dictionary* (Nashville, TN: Holman Bible Publishers, 2003).
Bradley, Arthur, 'Derrida's God: A Genealogy of the Theological Turn', *Paragraph* 29 (2006): 21–42.
Bradley, Arthur, *Derrida's Of Grammatology: An Edinburgh Philosophical Guide* (Edinburgh: Edinburgh University Press, 2008).
Bradley, Arthur, *Unbearable Life* (New York: Columbia University Press, 2019).
Braun, Theodore E. D. and John B. Radner (eds), *The Lisbon Earthquake of 1755: Representations and Reactions* (Oxford: Voltaire Foundation, 2005).
Breidert, Wolfgang (ed.), *Die Erschütterung der vollkommenen Welt. Die Wirkung des Erdbebens von Lissabon im Spiegel europäischer Zeitgenossen* (Darmstadt: Wissenschaftliche Buchgesellschaft, 1994).
Briese, Olaf, *Die Macht der Metaphern. Blitz, Erdbeben, Kometen im Gefüge der Aufklärung* (Stuttgart: Metzler, 1998).
Brighi, Elisabetta and Antonio Cerella, *The Sacred and the Political: Explorations on Mimesis, Violence and Religion* (London: Bloomsbury, 2016).
Britt, Brian, *Walter Benjamin and the Bible* (New York: Continuum, 1996).
Britt, Brian, 'The Schmittian Messiah in Agamben's The Time That Remains', *Critical Inquiry* 36 (2010): 262–87.
Brockhaus, Ulrich, *Charisma und Amt. Die paulinische Charismenlehre auf dem Hintergrung der frühchristlichen Gemeindefunktionen* (Wupertal: Brockhaus, 1972).
Broecke, Steven van den, 'Astrology and Politics', in *A Companion to Astrology in the Renaissance*, Brendan Dooley (ed.) (Leuven: Brill, 2014), 193–232.
Brown, Norman O., 'Philosophy and Prophecy: Spinoza's Hermeneutics', *Political Theory* 14(2) (1986): 195–213.
Brown, Peter, *Power and Persuasion in Late Antiquity: Towards a Christian Empire* (Madison: University of Wisconsin Press, 1992).
Brugère, Fabienne and Guillaume le Blanc, *La fin de l'hospitalité* (Paris: Flammarion, 2018).
Brunner, Otto, *Sozialgeschichte Europas in Mittelalter* (Göttingen: Vandenhoeck & Ruprecht, 1978).
Buc, Philippe, *L'ambigüité du Livre. Prince, pouvoir et peuple dans les commentaires de la Bible au Moyen Age* (Paris: Beauchesnes, 1994).

Buc, Philippe, 'Martyre et ritualité dans l'Antiquité tardive. Horizons de l'écriture médiévale des rituels', *Annales. Histoire, Sciences Sociales* 48(1) (1997): 63–92.

Buc, Philippe, 'Ritual and Interpretation: The Early Medieval Case', *Early Medieval Europe* 9(2) (2000): 183–210.

Buc, Philippe, *The Dangers of Ritual: Between Early Medieval Texts and Social Scientific Theory* (Princeton, NJ: Princeton University Press, 2001).

Burian, Jan, 'Die Kaiserliche Akklamation in Der Spätantike: Ein Beitrag Zur Untersuchung der Historia Augusta', *Eirene* 17 (1980): 17–42.

Burke, Peter, 'The Repudiation of Ritual in Early Modern Europe', in *The Historical Anthropology of Early Modern Italy*, Peter Burke (ed.) (Cambridge: Cambridge University Press, 1987).

Büttgen, Philippe, 'Eschatologie et temps présent chez Martin Luther', in *Metamorphosen der Zeit*, Éric Alliez, Gerhart Schröder, Barbara Cassin, Gisela Febel and Michel Narcy (eds) (Munich: Wilhelm Fink, 1999), 343–61.

Büttgen, Philippe and Alain Rauwel, *Théologie politique et sciences sociales. Autour d'Erik Peterson* (Paris: EHESS, 2019).

Bryden, Mary, *Deleuze and Religion* (London: Routledge, 2000).

Cadav, Eduardo, Peter Connor and Jean-Luc Nancy (eds), *Who Comes After the Subject?* (New York: Routledge, 1991).

Camby, Cristophe, 'Le serment dans la société franque. Innovation germanique ou continuité romaine?' in *Le Sacré et la Parole. Le Serment au Moyen Age*, M. Aurell, J. Aurell and M. Herrero (eds) (Paris: Classiques Garnier, 2018), 17–33.

Caputo, John D., *The Prayers and Tears of Jacques Derrida: Religion without Religion* (Bloomington: Indiana University Press, 1997).

Caputo, John D., *Radical Hermeneutics: Repetition, Deconstruction, and the Hermeneutic Project* (Bloomington: Indiana University Press, 1998).

Caputo, John D., 'Who is Derrida's Zarathustra? Of Fraternity, Friendship, and a Democracy to Come', *Research in Phenomenology* 29 (1999): 184–98.

Caputo, John D., 'Philosophy and Prophetic Postmodernism: Toward a Catholic Postmodernism', *American Catholic Philosophical Quarterly* LXXIV (2000): 549–67.

Caputo, John D., *The Weakness of God: A Theology of the Event* (Bloomington: Indiana University Press, 2006).

Caputo, John D., Gianni Vattimo and Jeffrey W. Robbins, *After the Death of God* (New York: Columbia University Press, 2007).

Caronello, Giancarlo, '"La critica del monoteismo nel primo Peterson"', in *Il dio mortale. Teologie politiche tra antico e contemporáneo*, Paolo Bettiolo-Gionanni Filoramo (ed.) (Brescia: Morcelliana, 2002), 349–96.

Carrette, Jeremy R., *Foucault and Religion: Spiritual Corporality and Political Spirituality* (London: Routledge, 2000).
Caspary, Gerard E., *Politics and Exegesis: Origen and the Two Swords* (Berkeley: University of California Press, 1979).
Castro, João de, *Paráfrase e Concordância de Algumas Profecías de Bandarra*, João Carlos Gonçalves Serafim (ed.) (Porto: University of Porto Press, 2018).
Cavanaugh, William T., *Theopolitical Imagination: Discovering the Liturgy as a Political Act in an Age of Global Consumerism* (London: T & T Clark, 2002).
Cavanaugh, William T., *Migrations of the Holy* (Grand Rapids, MI: Eerdmans, 2011).
Cavanaugh, William T. and P. Scott, *The Blackwell Companion to Political Theology* (Oxford: Blackwell, 2004).
Cerella, Antonio, *Genealogies of Political Modernity* (London: Bloomsbury, 2020).
Certeau, Michel de, *L'absent de l' histoire* (Liège: Mame, 1973).
Certeau, Michel de, 'The Gaze of Nicholas of Cusa', *Diacritics* 17(3) (1987): 2–38.
Chevalier, Philippe, *Michel Foucault et le christianisme* (Lyon: ENS Editions, 2011).
Chrétien, Jean-Louis, *La voix nue. Phénomenologie de la promesse* (Paris: Les Éditions de Minuit, 1990).
Chrétien, Jean-Louis, *L'arche de la parole* (Paris: PUF, 1998).
Chrétien, Jean-Louis, *L'inoubliable et l'inespéré* (Paris: Desclée De Brouwer, 2014).
Cicatello, Angelo, 'Il diritto di visita entro i limiti della semplice ragione. Note a margine del cosmopolitismo di Kant', *Estudos Kantianos* 3 (2015): 73–90.
Cicero, Marcus Tullius, *De Officiis*, trans. with Introduction and Notes Andrew P. Peabody (Boston, MA: Little, Brown, 1887).
Cignac, Alain, 'Charismes pauliniens et charisme wébérien, des "faux-amis"?' *Théologiques* 17(1) (2009): 139–62.
Cohn, Norman, *Cosmos, Chaos and the World to Come* (New Haven, CT: Yale University Press, 1993).
Condren, Conal, *Argument and Authority in Early Modern England: The Presupposition of Oaths and Offices* (Cambridge: Cambridge University Press, 2006).
Contenau, Georges, *La Divination chez les Assyriens et les Babyloniens* (Paris: Payot, 1940).
Cox, Harvey, *The Secular City. Secularization and Urbanization in Theological Perspective* (New York: Macmillan, 1966).
Critchley, Simon, *The Faith of the Faithless* (New York: Verso, 2012).
Crockett, Clayton, *Radical Political Theology: Religion and Politics after Liberalism* (New York: Columbia University Press, 2011).

Cuesta, José Mª, 'Erich Auerbach: una poética de la historia', in *Figura*, Erich Auerbach (ed.) (Madrid: Trotta, 1998), 9–40.
Cullmann, Oscar, *Christ and Time: The Primitive Christian Conception of Time and History* (London: SCM Press, 1962).
Cumont, Franz, *Astrology and Religion among the Greeks and Romans* (New York: Dover, 1960).
Cunningham, Conor, *Genealogy of Nihilism: Philosophies of Nothing and the Difference of Theology* (London: Routledge, 2002).
Curley, Edwin (ed. and trans.), 'Introduction to the *Ethics*', *The Collected Works of Spinoza* (Princeton, NJ: Princeton University Press, 1985).
Curley, Edwin, *Behind the Geometrical Method* (Princeton, NJ: Princeton University Press, 1988).
Cusa, Nicolas de, *Nicholas of Cusa on God as Not-Other: A Translation and Appraisal of De Li Non Aliud*, trans. Jasper Hopkins (Minneapolis, MN: Arthur J. Baning Press, 2001).
Damai, Puspa, 'Messianic-City: Ruins, Refuge and Hospitality in Derrida', *Discourse* 27(2/3) (2005): 68–94.
Danielou, Jean, *Origen* (New York: Sheed & Ward, 1955).
Davis, Kathleen, *Periodization and Sovereignty: How Ideas of Feudalism and Sovereignty Govern the Politics of Time* (Philadelphia: Pennsylvania University Press, 2008).
Davy, Georges, *La Foi jurée. Etude sociologique du problème du contrat. La formation du lien contractuel* (Paris: Librairie Félix Alcan, 1922).
Dawson, Hannah, 'Locke on Language and (Civil) Society', *History of Political Thought* 26(3) (2005): 397–425.
Dawson, Hannah, *Locke, Language and Early-Modern Philosophy* (Cambridge: Cambridge University Press, 2007).
Dean, Mitchell, 'Three Forms of Democratic Political Acclamation', *Telos* 179 (2017): 9–32.
Dean, Mitchell, 'Oath and Office', *Telos* 185 (2018): 67–91.
Dean, Mitchell, 'What is Economic Theology? A New Governmental-Political Paradigm?' *Theory, Culture and Society* 36(3) (2019): 3–26.
Debord, Guy, *La société du spectacle* (Paris: Buchet/Chastel, 1969).
Delouis, Olivier, 'Eglise et serment à Byzance: norme et pratique', in *Oralité et lien social au Moyen Age*, Marie-France Auzépy (ed.) (Paris: Association des amis du Centre d'histoire et civilisation de Byzance, 2008), 211–46.
Demurger, Alain, *Chevaliers du Christ. Les ordres religieux-militaires au Moyen Age (XIe–XVIe siècle)* (Paris: Le Seuil, 2015).
Demurger, Alain, *The Persecution of the Templars: Scandal, Torture, Trial* (London: Profiles, 2018).
Depreux, Philippe, 'Les carolingiens et le serment', in *Oralité et lien social au Moyen Age (Occident, Byzance, Islam)* Marie-France Auzépy et al. (eds) (Paris: ACHCByz, 2008), 63–80.
Derrida, Jacques, *L'écriture et la différence* (Paris: Éditions du Seuil, 1967).

Derrida, Jacques, 'Introduction' to Edmund Husserl, *L'origine de la géométrie* (Paris: PUF, 1974).
Derrida, Jacques, *Writing and Difference* (Chicago: University of Chicago Press, 1978).
Derrida, Jacques, 'Des Tours de Babel', in *Difference in Translation*, Joseph F. Graham (ed. and trans.) (New York: Cornell University Press, 1985), 165–207.
Derrida, Jacques, *Limited Inc.* (Evanston, IL: Northwestern University Press, 1988).
Derrida, Jacques, 'Force of Law: "The Mystical Foundation of Authority"', in *Deconstruction and the Possibility of Justice*, Drucilla Cornell and Michael Rosenfeld (eds) (New York: Routledge, 1992).
Derrida, Jacques, *Given Time: Counterfeit Money* (Chicago: University of Chicago Press, 1992).
Derrida, Jacques, *Specters of Marx: The State of the Debt, the Work of Mourning and the New International* (New York: Routledge, 1993).
Derrida, Jacques, *The Gift of Death* (Chicago: University of Chicago Press, 1995).
Derrida, Jacques, 'How to Avoid Speaking: Denials', in *Languages of the Unsayable: The Play of Negativity in Literature and Literary Theory*, Sanford Budick and Wolfgang Iser (eds) (Stanford, CA: Stanford University Press, 1996), 3–70.
Derrida, Jacques, *Of Grammatology* (Baltimore, MD: Johns Hopkins University Press, 1997).
Derrida, Jacques, *Politics of Friendship* (New York: Verso, 1997).
Derrida, Jacques, *Adieu to Emmanuel Levinas* (Stanford, CA: Stanford University Press, 1999).
Derrida, Jacques, *Of Hospitality* (Stanford, CA: Stanford University Press, 2000).
Derrida, Jacques, 'Leçon', in *Comment vivre ensemble? Actes du XXXVIIe Colloque des intellectuels juifs de langue française*, Jean Halpérin and Nelly Hansson (eds) (Paris: Albin Michel, 2001), 200–1.
Derrida, Jacques, *On Cosmopolitanism and Forgiveness* (London: Routledge, 2001).
Derrida, Jacques, 'What Is a "Relevant" Translation?' *Critical Inquiry* 27(2) (2001): 174–200.
Derrida, Jacques, *Acts of Religion* (London: Routledge, 2002).
Derrida, Jacques, *Voyous. Deux essays sur la raison* (París: Galilée, 2003).
Derrida, Jacques, *On Touching-Jean Luc Nancy* (Stanford, CA: Stanford University Press, 2005).
Derrida, Jacques, *Paper Machine* (Stanford, CA: Stanford University Press, 2005).
Derrida, Jacques, 'A Certain Impossible Possibility of Saying the Event', *Critical Inquiry* 33(2) (2007): 441–61.

Derrida, Jacques, 'Abrahan, the Other', in *Religion: Beyond a Concept*, Hent de Vries (ed.) (New York: Fordham University Press, 2008), 311–38.

Derrida, Jacques, 'Marx & Sons', in *Ghostly Demarcations: A Symposium on Jacques Derrida's 'Specters of Marx'*, Michael Sprinker (ed.) (London: Verso, 2008), 213–69.

Derrida, Jacques, *Le parjure et el pardon I* (Paris: Seuil, 2019).

Derrida, Jacques, *Le parjure et el pardon II* (Paris: Seuil, 2020).

Derrida, Jacques, *Donner le Temps II* (Paris: Seuil, 2021).

Derrida, Jacques and Bernard Stiegler, *Echographies of Television* (New York: Polity, 2002).

Derrida, Jacques and John Caputo, *Deconstruction in a Nutshell* (New York: Fordham University Press, 1997).

Destremau, Christian and Jean Moncelon, *Louis Massignon, le Cheikh admirable* (Paris: Plon, 1994).

Dickinson, Colby, *Between the Canon and the Messiah: The Structure of Faith in Contemporary Continental Thought* (London: Bloomsbury, 2013).

Dillon, Michael, '"Specters of Biopolitics: Finitude, Eschaton, and Katechon',' *South Atlantic Quarterly* 1 (2011): 780–92.

Dobschütz, Ernst von, 'Zeit und Raum im Denken des Urchristentums', *Journal of Biblical Literature* (1922): 212–23.

Duby, George, *Les Trois Ordres ou l'imaginaire du feodalisme* (Paris: Gallimard, 1978).

Dunn, James D. G., *Jesus and the Spirit: A Study of the Religious and Charismatic Experience of Jesus and the First Christians as Reflected in the New Testament* (Grand Rapids, MI: Westminster Press, 1975).

Dunn, John, *The Political Thought of John Locke* (Cambridge: Cambridge University Press, 1969).

Dynes, Russell, 'The Dialogue between Voltaire and Rousseau on the Lisbon Earthquake: The Emergence of a Social Science View', *International Journal of Mass Emergencies and Disasters* 18(1) (2000): 97–115.

Engberg-Pedersen, Troels, 'Paul and Universalism', in *Paul and the Philosophers*, Ward Blanton and Hent de Vries (eds) (New York: Fordham University Press, 2013), 87–105.

Esders, Stefan, 'Les origines militaires du serment dans les royaumes barbares (V–VII siècles)', in Marie-France Auzépy et al (eds) (Paris: Association des amis du Centre d'histoire et civilisation de Byzance, 2008), 19–27.

Esposito, Roberto, 'Chair et corps dans la déconstruction du christianisme', in *Sens en tous sens. Autour de travaux de Jean-Luc Nancy*, Francis Guibal and Jean-Clet Martin (eds) (Paris: Galilée, 2004), 153–64.

Farneti, Roberto, 'A Political Theology of the Empty Tomb: Christianity and the Return of the Sacred', *Theoria: A Journal of Social and Political Theory* 116 (2008): 22–44.

Fergusson, David, *The Providence of God: A Polyphonic Approach* (Cambridge: Cambridge University Press, 2018).
Finkelde, Dominik, *Politische Eschatologie nach Paulus. Badiou, Agamben, Zizek, Santner* (Vienna: Turia, 2007).
Fiori, Roberto, *Homo sacer. La dinámica político-constituzionale di una sanzione giuridico-religiosa* (Naples: Jovene Editori, 1996).
Fishbane, Michael, *Biblical Interpretation in Ancient Israel* (New York: Oxford University Press, 1985).
Fofget, Philippe (ed.), *Text und Interpretation. Eine deutsch-franzosische Debatte* mit Beiträgen von Jacques Derrida (Munich: Wilhelm Fink, 1984).
Fohrer, Georg, 'Prophetie und Geschichte', *Theologische Literaturzeitung* 89 (1964): 481–500.
Foster, Theodore B., '*Mysterium* and *Sacramentum* in the Vulgate and Old Latin Versions', *American Journal of Theology* 19 (1915): 402–15.
Foucault, Michel, *Dits et Écrits* IV (Paris: Gallimard, 1994).
Foucault, Michel, *L'herménéutique du sujet* (Paris: Gallimard/Seuil, 2001).
Foucault, Michel, *The Courage of the Truth: The Government of Self and Others, vol. II: Lectures at the Collège de France 1983–1984* (New York: Palgrave Macmillan, 2011).
Foucault, Michel, *Du gouvernement des vivants* (Paris: Gallimard/Seuil, 2012).
Foucault, Michel, *Mal faire, dire vrai. Fonction de l'Aveu en Justice. Course de Louvain, 1981* (Louvain: Presses universitaires de Louvain/ University of Chicago Press, 2012).
Foucault, Michel, *Lectures on the Will to Know: Lectures at the Collège de France 1970–1971* (New York: Palgrave Macmillan, 2013).
Foucault, Michel, *Confessions of the Flesh: The History of Sexuality*, 4 (New York: Penguin, 2021).
Fraenkel, Carlos, *Philosophical Religions from Plato to Spinoza* (Cambridge: Cambridge University Press, 2012).
Franck, Didier, *Nietzsche et l'ombre de Dieu* (Paris: PUF, 2014).
Franke, William, *A Philosophy of the Unsayable* (Notre Dame, IN: Notre Dame University Press, 2014).
Franke, William, *On What Cannot be Said: Apophatic Discourses in Philosophy, Religion, Literature, and the Arts*, 2 vols (Notre Dame, IN: Notre Dame University Press, 2014).
Franke, William, *Secular Scriptures: Modern Theological Poetics in the Wake of Dante* (Columbus: Ohio University Press, 2016).
Franke, William, *The Universality of What is Not: The Apophatic Turn in Critical Thinking* (Notre Dame, IN: Notre Dame University Press, 2020).
Frazer, James George, *The Golden Bough: A Study in Magic and Religion* (London: Macmillan, 1940).

Frick, Peter (ed.), *Paul in the Grip of the Philosophers: The Apostle and Contemporary Continental Philosophy* (Minneapolis, MN: Fortress Press, 2013).

Friesenhahn, Ernst, *Der politische Eid* (Bonn: L. Röhrscheid, 1928).

Fritsch, Matthias, 'Derrida's Democracy to Come', *Constellations: An International Journal of Critical and Democratic Theory* 9(4) (2002): 574–97.

Fustel de Coulanges, Numa Denis, *The Ancient City: A Study on the Religion, Laws, and Institutions of Greece and Rome* (Kitchener: Batoche, 2001).

Gadamer, Hans-Georg, 'The Continuity of History and the Existential Moment', *Philosophy Today* 16(3) (1972): 230–40.

Gadamer, Hans-Georg, *Truth and Method* (New York: Continuum, 2006).

Gauchet, Marcel, *Le désenchantement du monde. Une histoire politique de la religion* (Paris: Gallimard, 1985).

Geertz, Clifford, *The Interpretation of Culture* (New York: Basic Books, 1973).

Geertz, Clifford, 'Centers, Kings, and Charisma: Reflections on the Symbolics of Power', in *Local Knowledge: Further Essays in Interpretive Anthropology*, Clifford Geertz (ed.) (New York: Basic Books, 1983).

Gennep, Arnold van, *Rites of Passage* (London: Routledge, 1960).

Ginzburg, Carlo, 'Lectures de Mauss', *Annales HSS* 6 (2010): 1303–20.

Girard, René, *La violence et le sacré* (Paris: Fayard/Pluriel, 2011).

Goethe, Johann Wolfgang von, *From My Life: Poetry and Truth* (Princeton, NJ: Princeton University Press, 1994).

Goldenberg, Naomi R., 'The Category of Religion in the Technology of Governance: An Argument for Understanding Religions as Vestigial States', in *Religion as a Category of Governance and Sovereignty*, Trevor Stack, Naomi R. Goldenberg and Timothy Fitzgerald (eds) (Leiden: Brill, 2015), 280–93.

Gregory of Nazianz, Oration 25 in Saint Gregory of Nazianzus, *Select Orations* (Washington, DC: Catholic University of America Press, 2003).

Gröne, Valentine de, *'Sacramentum' oder Begriff und Bedeutung von Sakrament in der alten Kirche bis zur Scholastik* (Soest: Nasse in Comm, 1853).

Gros, Frédéric, 'Course Context', in Michel Foucault, *The Government of Self and Others*, Lectures at the College of France 1982–1983 (New York: Palgrave Macmillan, 2011), 377–8.

Grossheutschi, Felix, *Carl Schmitt und die Lehre vom Katechon* (Berlin: Duncker & Humblot, 1996).

Guibert, María, 'La memoire et l'oubli chez Nietzsche. Une approche à partir de la Généalogie de la moral', PhD dissertation, Université Sorbonne/Universidad de Navarra, 2021.

Guindon, Bernard, *Le Serment. Son histoire, son caractère sacré* (Ottawa: Éditions de l'Université, Ottawa, 1957).

Günther, Horst, *Das Erdbeben von Lissabon erschüttert die Meinungen und setzt das Denken in Bewegung* (Berlin: Wagenbach, 1994).
Günther, Horst, *Das Erdbeben von Lissabon und die Erschütterung des aufgeklärten Europa* (Frankfurt: Fischer, 2005).
Habermas, Jürgen, *Glauben und Wissen* (Frankfurt: Suhrkamp, 2001).
Habermas, Jürgen, *Zwischen Naturalismus und Religion* (Frankfurt: Suhrkamp, 2005).
Hahn, Scott W. and Benjamin Wiker, *Politicizing the Bible: The Roots of Historical Criticism and the Secularization of Scripture 1300–1700* (New York: Crossroads, 2013).
Hamann, Johann Georg, *Kleeblatt Hellenistischer Briefe* (Frankfurt: Peter Lang, 1994).
Hamblyn, Richard, 'Notes from the Underground: Lisbon after the Earthquake', *Romanticism* 14(2) (2008): 108–18.
Hamill, Graham and Julia R. Lupton, *Political Theology and Early Modernity* (Chicago: Chicago University Press, 2012).
Harnack, Adolf von, *Entstehung und Entwicklung der Kirchenverfassung und des Kirchenrechts in den zwei ersten Jahrhunderten* (Leipzig: Hinrich, 1910).
Harnack, Adolf von, *Militia Christi. Die Christliche Religion und der Soldatenstand in den ersten Drei Jahrhunderten* (Darmstadt: Wissenschaftliche Buchgesellschaft, 1963).
Harris, Marvin, *Cannibals and Kings: Origins of Cultures* (New York: Vintage, 1991).
Harris, R. Laird, Gleason L. Archer and Bruce K. Waltke, 'Kābēd', in *Theological Wordbook of the Old Testament* (Chicago, IL: Moody, 1980).
Harrison, James R., *Paul's Language of Grace in Its Graeco-Roman Context* (Tübingen: Mohr Siebeck, 2003).
Hebekus, Uwe, 'Enthusiasmus und Recht. Figurationen der Akklamation bei Ernst H. Kantorowicz, Erik Peterson und Carl Schmitt', in *Politische Theologie. Formen und Funktionen im 20. Jahrhundert*, Jürgen Brokoff and Jürgen Fohrmann (eds) (Paderborn: Schöningh, 2003), 97–113.
Heidegger, Martin, *On Time and Being* (New York: Harper & Row, 1972).
Heidegger, Martin, *Einführung in die phänomenologische Forschung*, Gesamtausgabe Abt. 2 Vorlesungen Bd. 17 (Frankfurt am Main: Vittorio Klosterman, 2006).
Hell, Julia, 'Katechon: Carl Schmitt's Imperial Theology and the Ruins of the Future', *Germanic Review: Literature, Culture, Theory* 84(4) (2009): 283–326.
Hemming, Laurence P., *Heidegger's Atheism: The Refusal of a Theological Voice* (Notre Dame, IN: Notre Dame University Press, 2002).
Hempel, Johannes, *Geschichten und Geschichte im Alten Testament* (Giltersloh: Gerd Mohn, 1964).

Hénaff, Marcel, *The Price of Truth: Gift, Money, and Philosophy* (Stanford, CA: Stanford University Press, 2010).
Heron, Nicholas, *Liturgical Power: Between Economic and Political Theology* (New York: Fordham University Press, 2018).
Herrero, Montserrat, *Carl Schmitt und Álvaro d'Ors Briefwechsel* (Berlin: Duncker & Humblot, 2004).
Herrero, Montserrat, 'El sacrificio ritual y lo sagrado', in *Life and the Sacred*, Carmelo Vigna and Rafael Alvira (eds) (Hildesheim: Olms, 2012), 115–27.
Herrero, Montserrat, *Ficciones políticas. El eco de Thomas Hobbes en el ocaso de la modernidad* (Buenos Aires: Katz, 2012).
Herrero, Montserrat, *La política revolucionaria de John Locke* (Madrid: Tecnos, 2015).
Herrero, Montserrat, 'On Political Theology: The Hidden Dialogue between C. Schmitt and Ernst H. Kantorowicz in The King's Two Bodies', *History of European Ideas* 41(8) (2015): 1164–77.
Herrero, Montserrat, *The Political Discourse of Carl Schmitt* (Lanham, MD: Rowman & Littlefield, 2015).
Herrero, Montserrat, 'Teología política y representación en el pensamiento de Carl Schmitt', *Aurora* 29(47) (2017): 377–403.
Herrero, Montserrat, 'The Quest for Locke's Political Theology', *Ethics & Politics* 18 (2016): 83–109.
Herrero, Montserrat, 'The Early Modern "Philosophical Bible" and the Supposedly Secular Modern State', *European Legacy* 22(1) (2017): 31–49.
Herrero, Montserrat, 'Sacrament and Oath: A Theological–Political Displacement', *Political Theology* 19(1) (2018): 35–49.
Herrero, Montserrat, 'Variaciones hegelianas de la crítica bíblica ilustrada: el espíritu frente a la letra', *Scripta Theologica* 50 (2018): 275–302.
Herrero, Montserrat, 'Political Theologies Surrounding the Nietzschean "Death of God's Trope"', *Nietzsche-Studien. Internationales Jahrbuch fur die Nietzsche-Forschung* 49 (2020): 125–49.
Herrero, Montserrat, 'Sacred Anarchy Instead of Divine Democracy', *Political Theology* 23(3) (2022): 243–51.
Herrero, Montserrat, Jaume Aurell and Angela Miceli, *Political Theology in Medieval and Early Modern Europe: Discourses, Rites and Representations* (Turnhout: Brepols, 2017), 23–43.
Hespanha, António Manuel, *La gracia del derecho. Economía de la cultura en la Edad Moderna* (Madrid: Centro de Estudios Políticos y Constitucionales, 1993).
Hirzel, Rudolf, *Der Eid. Ein Beitrag zu seiner Geschichte* (Aalen: Sciencia, 1966).
Hobbes, Thomas, *On the Body: The English Works of Thomas Hobbes of Malmesbury* (Aalen: Scientia, 1966).
Hobbes, Thomas, *De Homine* (Paris: Albert Blanchard, 1974).

Hobbes, Thomas, *Man and Citizen* (De Homine and De Cive) (Indianapolis, IN: Hackett, 1991).
Hobbes, Thomas, *The Elements of Law Natural and Politic* (Oxford: Oxford University Press, 1994).
Hobbes, Thomas, *Leviathan* (Oxford: Oxford University Press, 1998).
Hofmann, Johann Christian K., *Weissagung und Erfüllung im alten und im neuen Testamente* (Nördlingen: C. H. Beck, 1841–4).
Holmberg, Bengt, *Paul and Power: The Structure of Authority in the Primitive Church as Reflected in the Pauline Epistles*, New Testament series (Lund: CWK Gleerup Coniectanea biblica, 1978; re-edited Eugene: Wipf & Stock, 1978).
Hoppe, Heinrich, *Syntax und Stil des Tertullians* (Leipzig: Teubner, 1903).
Horner, Robyn, 'Aporia or Excess? Two Strategies for Thinking r/Revelation', in *Derrida and Religion: Other Testaments*, Yvonne Sherwood and Kevin Hart (eds) (London: Routledge, 2005), 325–36.
Horst, Friedrich and Hans Walter Wolff, *Gottes Recht. Gesammelte Studien zu dem Recht im Alten Testament* (Munich: Kaiser, 1961).
Hübner, Wolfgang, 'The Culture of Astrology from Ancient to Renaissance', in *A Companion to Astrology in the Renaissance*, Brendan Dooley (ed.) (Leuven: Brill, 2014), 17–58.
Huelin, Scott, 'Peregrination, Hermeneutics, Hospitality: On the Way to a Theologically Informed General Hermeneutics', *Literature and Theology* 22(2) (2008): 223–36.
Inge, John, *A Christian Theology of Place* (Abingdon: Routledge, 2016).
Irenaeus of Lyon, *Against Heresies* (Createspace Independent Publishing Platform, 2012).
Israel, Jonathan, *Radical Enlightenment: Philosophy and the Making of Modernity 1650–1750* (Oxford: Oxford University Press, 2002).
Israel, Jonathan, *The Democratic Enlightenment: Philosophy, Revolution and Human Rights 1750–1790* (Oxford: Oxford University Press, 2011).
Jaeger, Stephen, *Enchantment: On Charisma and the Sublime in the Arts of the West* (Philadelphia: University of Pennsylvania Press, 2012).
James, Ian, 'Incarnation and Infinity', in *Re-treating Religion: Deconstructing Christianity with Jean-Luc Nancy*, Alena Alexandrova (ed.) (New York: Fordham University Press, 2012), 246–60.
Jankélévitch, Vladimir, *Le pardon* (Paris: Aubier-Montaigne, 1967).
Jankélévitch, Vladimir, *L'Imprescriptible. Pardonner? Dans l'honneur et la dignité* (Paris Seuil: 1986).
Jansen, Katherine L. and Miri Rubin, *Charisma and Religious Authority: Jewish, Christian, and Muslim Preaching 1200–1500* (Turnhout: Berpols, 2010).
Jenni, Ernst and Claus Westermann, *Theological Lexicon of the Old Testament* (Peabody, MA: Hendrickson, 1994).
Jonkers, Peter and Rund Welten, *God in France: Eight Contemporary French Thinkers on God* (Leuven: Peeters, 2005).

Kahn, Paul W., *Political Theology. Four New Chapters on the Concept of Sovereignty* (New York: Columbia University Press, 2011).

Kahn, Victoria, *The Future of Illusion: Political Theology and Early Modern Texts* (Chicago: University of Chicago Press, 2014).

Kakoliris, Gerasimos, 'Jacques Derrida on the Ethics of Hospitality', in *The Ethics of Subjectivity: Perspectives since the Dawn of Modernity*, Elvis Imafidon (ed.) (New York: Palgrave Macmillan, 2015), 144–56.

Kalyvas, Andreas, *Democracy and the Politics of the Extraordinary: Max Weber, Carl Schmitt, and Hannah Arendt* (New York: Cambridge University Press, 2008).

Kantorowicz, Ernst H., *Laudes Regiae: A Study in Liturgical Acclamations and Medieval Ruler Worship* (Berkeley: University of California Press, 1958).

Kantorowicz, Ernst H., *The King's Two Bodies: A Study in Medieval Political Theology* (Princeton, NJ: Princeton University Press, 1997).

Käsermann, Ernst, *An die Römer* (Tübingen: Mohr, 1980).

Kaufmann, Andrew, '"Democracy to Come" in the Political Thought of Jacques Derrida', PhD dissertation, Catholic University of America (2014).

Kearney, Richard, *The God Who May Be: A Hermeneutics of Religion* (Bloomington: Indiana University Press, 2001).

Kedar, Benjamin, 'A Twelfth-century Description of the Jerusalem Hospital', in *The Military Orders: Fighting for the Faith and Caring for the Sick*, Helen J. Nicholson (ed.) (London: Ashgate, 1998).

Kedar, Benjamin, 'A Note on Jerusalem's Bimaristan and Jerusalem's Hospital', in *The Hospitallers, the Mediterranean and Europe Festschrift for Anthony Luttrell*, Karl Borchardt, Nicholas Jaspert and Helen J. Nicholson (eds) (London: Ashgate, 2007), 7–11.

Keller, Katherine, *Face of the Deep: A Theology of Becoming* (Abingdon: Routledge, 2003).

Keller, Katherine, *Political Theology of the Earth: Our Planetary Emergency and the Struggle for a New Public* (New York: Columbia University Press, 2018).

Kendrick, Thomas Dawning, *The Lisbon Earthquake* (London: Methuen, 1956).

Klever, Wim, 'Locke's Disguised Spinozism', *Conatus* 11 (2012): 61–82.

Koselleck, Reinhart, 'Krise', in *Geschichtliche Grundbegriffe. Historisches Lexikon zur politisch-sozialen Sprache in Deutschland*, 8 vols, O. Brunner, W. Conze and R. Koselleck (eds) (Stuttgart: Klett-Cotta, 1972–97, vol. 3, 1982), 617–50.

Koselleck, Reinhart, *Zeitschichten. Studien zur Historik* (Frankfurt: Suhrkamp, 2000).

Koselleck, Reinhart, *The Practice of Conceptual History: Timing History, Spacing Concepts* (Stanford: Stanford University Press, 2002).

Koselleck, Reinhart, *Futures Past* (New York: Columbia University Press, 2004).
Kosky, Jeffrey, *Levinas and the Philosophy of Religion* (Bloomington: Indiana University Press, 2001).
Kozák, Jan T., Victor S. Moreira and David R. Oldroyd, *Iconography of the 1755 Lisbon Earthquake* (Prague: Geophysical Institute of the Academy of Sciences of the Czech Republic, 2005).
Kozlarek, Oliver (ed.), *Entre cosmopolitismo y conciencia del mundo. Hacia una crítica del pensamiento atópico* (Madrid: Siglo XXI, 1997).
Kramme, Rüdiger, *Helmuth Plessner und Carl Schmitt. Eine historische Fallstudie zum Verhältnis von Anthropologie und Politik in der deutschen Philosophie der zwanziger Jahre* (Berlin: Duncker & Humblot, 1989).
Kreck, Walter, *Die Zukunft des Gekommenens* (Berlin: Evangelische Verlagsanstalt, 1968).
Kroeker, Travis, 'Messianic Ethics? Paul as Political Theorist', *Journal of the Society of Christian Ethics* 25(2) (2005): 37–58.
Kruse, Tomas, 'The Magistrate and the Ocean: Acclamations and Ritualized Communication in Town Gatherings', in *Ritual and Communication in the Graeco-Roman World*, Eftychia Stavrianopoulous (ed.) (Liège: Presses universitaires de Liège, 2006), 297–315.
Kümmel, Werner G., *Promise and Fulfilment* (London: SCM Press, 1957).
Laborde, Cecile, *Liberalism's Religion* (Cambridge, MA: Harvard University Press, 2017).
Laerke, Mogens, 'Jus Circa Sacra. Elements of Theological Politics in 17th Century Rationalism: From Hobbes and Spinoza to Leibniz', *Distinktion: Scandinavian Journal of Social Theory* 6(1) (2005): 41–64.
Laska, Bernd A., '*Katechon*' und '*Anarch*'. *Carl Schmitts und Ernst Jüngers Reaktionen auf Max Stirner* (Nürnberg: LSR, 1997).
Lefort, Claude, 'The Permanence of the Theologico-Political?' in Claude Lefort, *Democracy and Political Theory* (Cambridge: Polity, 1988), 213–55.
Lemm, Vanessa, 'The Embodiment of the Truth and the Politics of Community: Foucault and the Cynics', in *The Government of Life: Foucault, Biopolitics, and Neoliberalism*, Vanessa Lemm and Miguel Vatter (eds) (New York: Fordham University Press, 2014), 208–223.
Lenze, Malte, *Postmodernes Charisma. Marken und Stars statt Religion und Vernunft* (Wiesbaden: Springer, 2002).
Levinas, Emmanuel, *Au delà du verset* (Paris: Minuit, 1982).
Levinas, Emmanuel, 'The Trace of the Other', in *Deconstruction in Context: Literature and Philosophy*, Mark C. Taylor (ed.) (Chicago: University of Chicago Press, 1986), 345–59.
Levinas, Emmanuel, 'Substitution'" in *Basic Philosophical Writings*, Adrian Peperzak, Simon Critchley and Robert Bernasconi (eds) (Bloomington: Indiana University Press, 1996), 79–97.

Levy-Bruhl, Henri, 'Reflexions sur le serment', *Études d'histoire du droit privé offertes à Pierre Petot* (Paris: Dalloz, 1959).
Lima, Renato Samuel, *Revolta e esperança. A Guerra do Contestado e o messianismo portugués* (Lisbon: Gramma, 2018).
Lindholm, Charles, *The Anthropology of Religious Charisma: Ecstasies and Institutions* (New York: Palgrave Macmillan, 2013).
Lloyd, Vincent, *In Defense of Charisma* (New York: Columbia University Press, 2018).
Lobrichon, Guy, 'Une nouveauté, les gloses de la Bible', in *Le Moyen Age et la Bible*, Pierre Riche and Guy Lobrichon (eds) (Paris: Beauchesne, 1984).
Locke, John, *A Letter on Toleration* (Oxford: Oxford University Press, 1968).
Locke, John, *The Second Treatise of Civil Government* (Indianapolis, IN: Hackett, 1980).
Locke, John, *An Essay concerning Human Understanding* (Stansted: Wordsworth Editions, 1998).
Long, Stephen, *Divine Economy: Theology and the Market* (London: Routledge, 2000).
Löwith, Karl, *Weltgeschichte und Heilsgeschehen. Die theologischen Voraussetzungen der Geschichtsphilosophie* (Stuttgart: Kohlhammer, 1953; Munich: Metzler, 2004).
Loysi, Alfred, *Essai historique sur le sacrifice* (Paris: Émile Nourry, 1920).
Lubac, Henri de, *Medieval Exegesis: The Four Senses of Scripture* (Grand Rapids, MI: Eerdmans, 1998).
Lukac de Stier, María L., 'Potentia Dei: De Tomás de Aquino a Hobbes', *Intus-Legere Filosofía* 7 (2013): 43–57.
Luther, Martin, *Epistolam S. Pauli ad Galatas Commentarius*, in *Werke. Weimarer Ausgabe* (Munich: Metzler, 2000–7).
Luttrell, Anthony T., 'The Hospitallers' Early Written Records', in *The Crusades and their Sources: Essays Presented to Bernard Hamilton*, John France and William G. Zajac (eds) (London: Routledge, 1998), 135–54.
Luttrell, Anthony T., 'The Earliest Hospitallers', in *Montjoie: Studies in Crusade History in Honour of Hans Eberhard Mayer*, Benjamin Kedar, Jonathan Riley-Smith and Rudolf Hiestand (eds) (London: Variorum, 2007).
Macaulay, Rose, *They Went to Portugal* (London: Cape, 1946).
Malcolm, Noel, 'Hobbes and Spinoza', in *Aspects of Hobbes* (Oxford: Oxford University Press, 2004).
Malpas, Jeff, *The Ethics of Place* (Abingdon: Routledge, 2021).
Maraviglia, Massimo, *La penultima guerra. Il 'katéchon' nella dottrina dell'ordine politico di Carl Schmitt* (Milan: LED, 2006).
Marion, Jean-Luc, *Being Given: Toward a Phenomenology of Givenness* (Standford, CA: Stanford University Press, 2002).

Marion, Jean-Luc, *The Reason of the Gift* (Charlottesville: University of Virginia Press, 2011).
Markus, Robert A., 'St. Augustine on Signs', *Phronesis* 2(1) (1957): 60–83.
Markus, Robert A., *Signs and Meanings: World and Text in Ancient Christianity* (Liverpool: Liverpool University Press, 1996).
Marsh, John, *The Fullness of Time* (London: Nisbet, 1952).
Martel, James, *Divine Violence: Walter Benjamin and the Eschatology of Sovereignty* (New York: Routledge, 2012).
Mason, Mark, 'Exploring the Impossible: Jacques Derrida, John Caputo and the Philosophy of History', *Rethinking History* 10(4) (2016): 501–22.
Massignon, Louis, *Essai sur les origines du lexique technique de la mystique musulmane* (Paris: Vrin, 1954).
Massignon, Louis, *Opera minora III, Textes recueillis, classés et présentés par Y. Moubarac* (Paris: Presses universitaires de France 1969).
Massignon, Louis, *L'hospitalité sacrée* (Paris: Nouvelle Cité, 1987).
Mauss, Marcel, *The Gift: The Form and Reason for Exchange in Archaic Societies* (New York: W. W. Norton, 2000).
Mauss, Marcel and Henri Hubert, *Sacrifice: Its Nature and Functions* (Chicago: University of Chicago Press, 1981).
McNelli Kearns, Cleo, 'Mary, Maternity, and Abrahamic Hospitality in Derrida's Reading of Massignon', in *Derrida and Religion: Other Testaments*, Yvonne Sherwood and Kevin Hart (eds) (London: Routledge, 2005), 73–93.
McQueen Grant, Robert, *The Earliest Lives of Jesus* (London: SPCK, 1961).
Meier, Heinrich, *The Lesson of Carl Schmitt: Four Chapters on the Distinction between Political Theology and Political Philosophy*, expanded edn (Chicago: Chicago University Press, 2011).
Metzger, Paul, *Katechon: II Thess 2, 1-12 im Horizont apokalyptischen Denkens* (Berlin: De Gruyter, 2005).
Meuter, Günter, *Der Katechon. Zu Carl Schmitts fundamentalistischer Kritik der Zeit* (Berlin: Duncker & Humblot, 1994).
Milbank, John, *Being Reconciled: Ontology and Pardon* (London: Routledge, 2003).
Milbank, John and Simon Oliver (eds), *The Radical Orthodoxy Reader* (London: Routledge, 2009).
Milbank, John and Catherine Pickstock, *Truth in Aquinas* (London: Routledge, 2000).
Milbank, John, Catherine Pickstock and Graham Ward (eds), *Radical Orthodoxy: A New Theology* (London: Routledge, 1999).
Minois, Georges, *Histoire de l'avenir. Des prophètes à la prospective* (Paris: Fayard, 2014).
Moltmann, Jürgen, *Kirche in der Kraft des Geistes. Ein Beitrag zur messianischen Ekklesiologie* (Munich: Kaiser, 1975).

Moltmann, Jürgen, *Der Geist del Lebens. Eine ganzheitliche Pneumatologie* (Gütersloh: Verlag-Haus, 1991).

Moltmann, Jürgen, *Die Quelle des Lebens. Der Heilige Geist und die Theologie des Lebens* (Gütersloh: Verlag-Haus, 1997).

Momigliano, Arnaldo, 'Time in Ancient Historiography', *History and Theory*, Supplement 6: *History and the Concept of Time* 6 (1966): 1–23.

Mommsen, Theodor, *Römisches Staatsrecht* (Leipzig: S. Hirzel, 1871–88).

Mommsen, Theodor, *The History of Rome under the Emperors* (London: Routledge, 1999).

Mondot, Jean (ed.), *Lisbonne 1755. Un tremblement de terre et de ciel* (Bordeaux: Presses universitaires de Bordeaux, 2005).

Moreau, Pierre-François, *Spinoza. L'experience de l'etérnité* (Paris: PUF, 1994).

Morris, Colin, *The Discovery of the Individual, 1050–1200* (Toronto: University of Toronto Press, 1987).

Morrow, Jeffrey L., 'The Bible in Captivity: Hobbes, Spinoza, and the Politics of Defining Religion', *Pro Ecclesia* 19 (2010): 285–99.

Moses, Stéphane, 'The Theological–Political Model of History in the Thought of Walter Benjamin', *History and Memory* 1 (1989): 5–33.

Motschenbacher, Alfons, *Katechon oder Grossinquisitor? Eine Studie zu Inhalt und Struktur der Politischen Theologie Carl Schmit* (Marburg: Tectum, 2000).

Mowinckel, Sigmund, 'Israelite Historiography', *Annals of the Swedish Theological Institute* 2 (1963): 4–26.

Munzert, Peter, *Charisma, Amt und Kirche. Theologische, religions- und kulturwissenschaftliche Aspekte für ein zeitgemässes Verständnis von Charisma im Kontext von Amt und Kirche* (Berlin: Litt, 2016).

Murchadha, Felix Ó, *A Phenomenology of Christian Life: Glory and Night* (Bloomington: Indiana Univerity Press, 2013).

Naas, Michael, '"Alors, qui est-vous" Jacques Derrida and the Question of Hospitality', *SubStance* 34(106) (2005): 6–16.

Nadler, Steven, *A Book Forged in Hell* (Princeton, NJ: Princeton University Press, 2011).

Naishtat, Francisco, 'Benjamin's Profane Uses of Theology: The Invisible Organon', *Religions* 10(93) (2019): 1–16.

Nancy, Jean-Luc, *Sense of the World* (Minneapolis: University of Minnesota Press, 1997).

Nancy, Jean-Luc, *The Ground of the Image* (New York: Fordham University Press, 2005).

Nancy, Jean-Luc, *Dis-enclosure: The Deconstruction of Christianity* (New York: Fordham University Press, 2007).

Nancy, Jean-Luc, *Corpus* (New York: Fordham University Press, 2008).

Nancy, Jean-Luc, *L'Adoration. Déconstruction du christianisme II* (Paris: Galilée, 2010).

Nancy, Jean-Luc, 'In the Midst of the World; or, Why Deconstruct Christianity?' in *Re-treating Religion: Deconstructing Christianity with Jean-Luc Nancy*, Alena Alexandrova (ed.) (New York: Fordham University Press, 2012), 1–22.

Nancy, Jean-Luc, *Adoration: The Deconstruction of Christianity II* (New York: Fordham University Press, 2013).

Nardoni, Enrique, 'Charisma in the Early Church since Rudolph Sohm: An Ecumenical Challenge', *Theological Studies* 53 (1992): 646–62.

Nardoni, Enrique, 'The Concept of Charisma in Paul', *Catholic Biblical Quarterly* 55 (1993): 68–80.

Neiman, Susan, *Evil in Modern Thought: An Alternative History of Philosophy* (Princeton, NJ: Princeton University Press, 2002).

Nicholson, Helen, *The Knights Hospitaller* (Woodbridge: Boydell, 2001).

Nichtweiss, Barbara, *Erik Peterson. Neue Sicht auf Leben und Werk* (Freiburg: Herder, 1992).

Nichtweiss, Barbara, 'Nachtwort zur Entstehung und Bedeutung von Heis Theos', in *Heis Theos. Epigraphische, formgeschichtliche und religionsgeschichtliche Untersuchungen zur antiken Ein-Gott-Akklamation*, Erik Peterson (ed.) (Würzburg: Echter, 2012), 583–642.

Nietzsche, Friedrich, *Nachgelassene Fragmente, Kritische Gesamtausgabe*, Giorgio Colli and Mazzino Montinari (eds) (Berlin: de Gruyter, 1977).

Nietzsche, Friedrich, *Posthumous Fragments 1884 25 [406], Kritische Gesamtausgabe*, Giorgio Colli and Mazzino Montinari (eds) (Berlin: de Gruyter, 1977).

Nietzsche, Friedrich, *On the Use and Abuse of History for Life* (Indianapolis, IN: Hackett, 1980).

Nietzsche, Friedrich, *Daybreak: Thoughts on the Prejudices of Morality* (Cambridge: Cambridge University Press, 1997).

Noze, Judite (ed.), *The Lisbon Earthquake of 1755: British Accounts* (Lisbon: British Historical Society of Portugal and Lisóptima, 1990).

Nuovo, Victor, *Christianity, Antiquity, and Enlightenment* (Dordrecht: Springer, 2011).

Oakley, Francis, 'The Absolute and Ordained Power of God and King in the Sixteenth and Seventeenth', *Journal of the History of Ideas* 59 (1998): 669–90.

Ojakangas, Mika, 'Potentia absoluta et potentia ordinata Dei: On the Theological Origins of Carl Schmitt's Theory of Constitution', *Continental Philosophy Review* 45 (2012): 505–17.

Origen, *Contra Celsum* (Leiden: Brill, 2001).

Origen, *De Principiis* (Lausanne: Université de Lausanne, 2008).

d'Ors, Álvaro, *De la Guerra y de la Paz* (Madrid: Rialp, 1954).

d'Ors, Álvaro, *Ensayos de teoría política* (Pamplona: Eunsa, 1979).

d'Ors, Álvaro, *Derecho privado romano* (Pamplona: Eunsa, 1997).

Ott, Walter R., *Locke's Philosophy of Language* (Cambridge: Cambridge University Press, 2003).

Otto, Rudolf, *The Kingdom of God and the Son of Man: A Study in the History of Religion* (Eugene, OR: Wipf & Stock, 2009).

Paipais, Vassilios, '"Already/Not Yet": St. Paul's Eschatology and the Modern Critique of Historicism', *Philosophy and Social Criticism* 44(9) (2018): 1015–38.

Payot, Daniel, *Des villes-refuges. Temoignage et espacement* (Paris: L'Aube, 1992).

Perrot, Charles, 'Charisme et institution chez Saint Paul', *Recherches de science religieuse* 71 (1983): 81–92.

Peterson, Erik, 'Christ as Imperator', in *Theological Tractates* (Stanford, CA: Stanford University Press, 2011).

Peterson, Erik, *Theological Tractates* (Stanford, CA: Stanford University Press, 2011).

Peterson, Erik, *Heis Theos. Epigraphische, formgeschichtliche und religionsgeschichtliche Untersuchungen zur antiken Ein-Gott-Akklamation* (Würzburg: Echter, 2012).

Pettit, Philippe, *Made with Words: Hobbes on Language, Mind, and Politics* (Princeton, NJ: Princeton University Press, 2008).

Potts, John, *A History of Charisma* (Houndmills: Palgrave Macmillan, 2009).

Prat, Ferdinand, *La teología de San Pablo*, II (Cartoné, México: Jus, 1947).

Price, Ira M., 'The Oath in Court Procedure in Early Babylonia and the Old Testament', *Journal of the American Oriental Society* 49 (1929): 22–9.

Prodi, Paolo, *Il sacramento del potere. Il giuramento político nella storia constituzionale dell' Occidente* (Bologna: Il Mulino, 1992).

Prozorov, Sergei, 'The Katechon in the Age of Biopolitical Nihilism', *Continental Philosophy Review* 45 (2012): 483–503.

Przywara, Erich, *Lessons sur Dieu* (Paris: Cerf, 2011).

Purcell, Michael, 'Beyond the Limit and Limiting the Beyond', *International Journal for Philosophy of Religion* 68 (2010): 121–38.

Quenet, Grégory, *Les tremblements de terre aux XVIIe et XVIIIe siècles. La naissanced'un risqué* (Seyssel: Champ Vallon, 2005).

Ranke, Leopold V., *Über die Epoche der neuern Geschichte* (Munich: Duncker & Humblot, 1917).

Raschke, Carl A., *The End of Theology* (Aurora, CO: Davies, 2000).

Raschke, Carl A., *Force of God: Political Theology and the Crisis of Liberal Democracy* (New York: Columbia University Press, 2015).

Ratmoko, David, *On Spectrality: Fantasies of Redemption in the Western Canon* (New York: Peter Lang, 2006).

Ratzinger, Josef, *Die christliche Brüderlichkeit* (Munich: Kösel, 1960).

Ratzinger, Josef, *The Theology of History in St. Bonaventure* (Chicago: Franciscan Herald Press, 1971).

Ratzinger, Josef, *Eucharistie, Mitte der Kirche* (Munich: Sankt Ulrich, 1978).

Ratzinger, Josef, *Introduction to Christianity* (San Francisco, CA: Ignatius Press, [1990] 2004).

Ratzinger, Josef, 'Discurso en la Investidura de Doctor Honoris Causa del Cardenal Joseph Ratzinger en la Universidad de Navarra', *Scripta Theologica* 30 (1998): 390–2.

Ratzinger, Josef, as Benedict XVI, *Post-synodal Apostolic Exhortation Verbum Domini* (Vatican: Libreria Editrice Vaticana, 2010).

Ratzinger, Josef, as Benedict XVI, *Jesus of Nazareth* (London: Bloomsbury, 2007).

Ray, Gene, 'Reading the Lisbon Earthquake: Adorno, Lyotard, and the Contemporary Sublime', *Yale Journal of Criticism* 17(1) (2004): 1–18.

Reedy, Gerard, *The Bible and Reason: Anglicans and Scripture in Late Seventeenth-Century England* (Philadelphia: University of Pennsylvania Press, 1985).

Regier, Alexander, *Fracture and Fragmentation in British Romanticism* (Cambridge: Cambridge University Press, 2010).

Reinach, Adolf, *Zur Phänomenologie des Rechts. Die apriorischen Grundlagen des bürgerlichen Rechts*, in *Sämtliche Werke. Textkritische Ausgabe in 2 Bänden* (Munich: Philosophia, 1989).

Reventlow, Henning Graf, *The Authority of the Bible and the Rise of the Modern World* (London: SCM Press, 1984).

Ricoeur, Paul, 'The Sacred Text and the Community', in *The Critical Study of Sacred Texts*, Wendy D. O'Flaherty (ed.) (Berkeley, CA: Berkeley Religious Studies Series, 1979).

Riedel, Manfred, *Vorspiele zur Ewigen Wiederkunft. Nietzsches Grundlehre* (Vienna: Böhlau, 2012).

Ritter, Adolf Martin, *Charisma im Verständis des Johannes Chysostomos und seiner Zeit* (Göttingen: Vandehoeck & Ruprecht, 1972).

Ritter, Adolf Martin, *Charisma und Caritas. Aufsätze zur Alten Kirche* (Göttingen: Vandenhoeck & Ruprecht, 1997).

Robinson, John A. T., *In the End, God: A Study of the Christian Doctrine of the Last Things* (London: James Clarke, 1950).

Robinson, John A. T., *Honest to God* (Philadelphia, PA: Westminster Press, 1972).

Robbins, Jeffrey, *Radical Democracy and Political Theology* (New York: Columbia University Press, 2011).

Rossi, Martino, 'On Body and Beauty of Soul between Late Antiquity and Middle Ages', in *Faces of Charisma. Image, Text, Object in Byzantium and the Medieval West*, Brigitte Miriam Bedos-Rezak and Martha Dana Rust (eds) (Leiden: Brill, 2018), 47–75.

Roszak, Piotr, 'Language, Metaphysics and the Bible: The Philosophical Background of Aquinas's Exegesis of Sacred Scripture', *European Journal of Science and Theology* 14 (2018): 123–35.

Roueché, Charlotte, 'Acclamations in the Later Roman Empire: New Evidence from Aphrodisias', *Journal of Roman Studies* 74 (1984): 181–99.

Rousseau, Jean Jacques, *The Social Contract and Other Political Essays* (Cambridge: Cambridge University Press, 1997).

Ruffini, Eliseo and Enzo Lodi, *Mysterion e Sacramentum. La sacramentalità negli scritti dei Padri e nei testi liturgici primitive* (Bologna: Centro Editoriale Dehoniano, 1987).
Runciman, Steven, *The First Crusade* (Cambridge: Cambridge University Press, 2004).
Ryan, Fáinche, *Formation in Holiness: Thomas Aquinas on Sacra doctrina* (Leuven: Peeters, 2007).
Saint Victor, Hugh of, *On the Sacraments of the Christian Faith*, Roy J. Deferrari (ed.) (Cambridge, MA: Mediaeval Academy of America, 1951).
Santner, Eric, *The Psycotheology of Everyday Life: Reflections on Freud and Rosenzweig* (Chicago: University of Chicago Press, 2001).
Savan, David, 'Spinoza and Language', *Philosophical Review* 67 (1958): 212–25.
Schlier, Heinrich, *Grundzüge einer Paulinischen Theologie* (Freiburg: Herder, 1978).
Schmidt, Andreas, 'Wolken krachen, Berge zittern, und die ganze Erde weint'. *Zur kulturellen Vermittlung von Naturkatastrophen in Deutschland 1755 bis 1855* (Münster: Waxmann, 1999).
Schmidt, Hans-Joachim, 'The Papal and Imperial Concept of *plenitudo potestatis*: The Influence of Pope Innocent III on Emperor Frederick II', in *Pope Inocent III and his World*, J. C. Moore (ed.) (Aldershot: Ashgate, 1999), 305–14.
Schmitt, Carl, *Theodor Däublers 'Nordlicht'. Drei Studien über die Elemente, den Geist und die Aktualität des Werkes* (Munich: Georg Müller, 1916).
Schmitt, Carl, 'Die Sichtbarkeit der Kirche. Eine scholastische Erwägung', *Summa. Eine Vierteljahresschrift* 2 (1917): 71–80.
Schmitt, Carl, *Volksentscheid und Volksbegehren. Ein Beitrag zur Auslegung der Weimarer Verfassung und zur Lehre von der unmittelbaren Demokratie* (Berlin: de Gruyter 1927).
Schmitt, Carl, 'Der bürgerliche Rechtsstaat', *Abendland* 3 (1928): 202–3.
Schmitt, Carl, *Verfassungslehre* (Munich: Duncker & Humblot, 1928).
Schmitt, Carl, 'Drei Stufen historischer Sinngebung', *Universitas. Zeitschrift für Wissenschaft, Kunst und Literatur* 5(8) (1950): 927–31.
Schmitt, Carl, *Ex Captivitate Salus: Erfahrungen der Zeit 1945–1947* (Cologne: Greven, 1950).
Schmitt, Carl, *La Unidad del Mundo* (Madrid: Ateneo, 1951).
Schmitt, Carl, 'Tres posibilidades de una visión cristiana de la historia', *Arbor* 62 (1951): 237–41.
Schmitt, Carl, 'Coloquio sobre el poder y el acceso al poderoso', *Revista de Estudios Políticos* 52(78) (1954): 3–20.
Schmitt, Carl, *Die Lage der europäischen Rechtswissenschaft*, in *Verfassungsrechtliche Aufsätze*, Carl Schmitt (ed.) (Berlin: Duncker & Humblot, 1958), 386–430.

Schmitt, Carl, *Ex Captivitate Salus. Experiencias de los años 1945–1947*, trans. A. Schmitt (Santiago de Compostela: Porto y Cia., 1960).
Schmitt, Carl, 'Die vollendete Reformation: Bemerkungen und Hinweise zu neuen Leviathan Interpretationen', *Der Staat* 4 (1965): 51–69.
Schmitt, Carl, *Politische Theologie II. Legende von der Erledigung jeder Politischen Theologie* (Berlin, Duncker & Humblot, 1970).
Schmitt, Carl, *Römischer Katholizismus und politische Form* (Hellerau: Jakob Hegner, 1923).
Schmitt, Carl, *Der Begriff des Politischen. Text von 1932 mit einem Vorwort und drei Corollarien* (Berlin: Duncker & Humblot, 1979).
Schmitt, Carl, 'The Legal World Revolution', *Telos* 72 (1987): 73–89.
Schmitt, Carl, 'The Plight of European Jurisprudence', *Telos* 83 (1990): 35–70.
Schmitt, Carl, *Glossarium. Aufzeichnungen der Jahre 1947–1951* (Berlin: Duncker & Humblot, 1991).
Schmitt, Carl, *Politische Theologie II* (Berlin: Duncker & Humblot, 1996).
Schmitt, Carl, *Roman Catholicism and Political Form* (Westport, CT: Greenwood, 1996).
Schmitt, Carl, *Land and Sea* (Washington, DC: Plutarch, 1997).
Schmitt, Carl, *The Crisis of Parliamentary Democracy*, trans. E. Kennedy (Cambridge, MA: MIT Press, 2000).
Schmitt, Carl, *The Nomos of the Earth in the International Law of the Jus Publicum Europaeum* (New York: Telos, 2003).
Schmitt, Carl, *Political Theology: Four Chapters on the Concept of Sovereignty* (Chicago: University of Chicago Press, 2005).
Schmitt, Carl, *Constitutional Theory* (Durham, NC: Duke University Press, 2008).
Schmitt, Carl, *Political Theology II: The Myth of the Closure of Any Political Theology* (Cambridge: Polity, 2008).
Schmitz, Alexander and Martin Lepper (eds), *Hans Blumenberg. Carl Schmitt. Briefwechsel* (Frankfurt: Suhrkamp, 2007).
Schramm, Percy E., *Herrschaftszeichen und Staatssymbolik. Beiträge zu Ihrer Geschichte vom Dritten bis zum Sechzehnten Jahrhundert*, Monumenta Germaniae historica, Schriften, XIII/1 (Stuttgart: Hiersemann, 1954).
Schweidler, Walter (ed.), *Postsäkulare Gesellschaft. Perspektiven interdisziplinärer Forschung* (Munich: Alber, 2007).
Sherlock, Richard, 'The Theology of Toleration: A Reading of Locke's The Reasonableness of Christianity', *Jewish Political Studies Review* 9 (1997): 19–49.
Shils, Edward, 'Charisma, Order, Status', *American Sociological Review* 30(2) (1965): 199–213.
Simmons, J. Aaron, *God and the Other: Ethics and Politics after the Theological Turn* (Bloomington: Indiana University Press, 2011).

Simonutti, Luisa, *Locke and Biblical Hermeneutics: Conscience and Scripture* (Cham: Springer, 2019).
Smith, James K. A., 'Liberating Religion from Theology: Marion and Heidegger on the Possibility of a Phenomenology of Religion', *International Journal for Philosophy of Religion* 46 (1999): 17–33.
Smith, James K. A., *Speech and Theology: Language and the Logic of Incarnation* (London: Routledge, 2002).
Smith, Jonathan Z., *To Take Place: Toward Theory in Ritual* (Chicago: University of Chicago Press, 1987).
Smith, William, *A Dictionary of Greek and Roman Biography and Mythology* (London: I. B. Tauris, 2007).
Smith, William Robertson, *Lectures on the Religion of the Semites* (London: Black, 1894).
Soden, Hans von, *Das Lateinische Neue Testament in Afrika zur Zeit Cyprians* (Leipzig: J. C. Hinrichs, 1909).
Soden, Hans von, 'Μυστήριον und *sacramentum* in den ersten drei Jahrhunderten der Kirche', *Zeitschrift für den neutestamentarische Wissenschaft* 12 (1911): 188–227.
Sohm, Rudolph, *Kirchenrecht* (Berlin: Duncker & Humblot, 1970).
Spaemann, Robert, 'Lo ritual y lo moral', *Anuario Filosófico* 34 (2001): 655–72.
Spaemann, Robert, 'The Rückehr des Erinnyen. Zur Theorie des Opfers', in *Life and the Sacred*, Carmelo Vigna and Rafael Alvira (eds) (Hildesheim: Olms, 2012), 101–13.
Spinoza, Baruch, *Theological-Political Treatise*, Jonathan Israel (ed.) (Cambridge: Cambridge University Press, 2007).
Spurr, John, 'A Profane History of Early Modern Oaths', *Transactions of the Royal Historical Society* 11 (2001): 37–63.
Stack, Trevor, 'Introduction', in *Religion as a Category of Governance and Sovereignty*, Trevor Stack, Naomi R. Goldenberg and Timothy Fitzgerald (eds) (Leiden: Brill, 2015), 1–21.
Stiegler, Bernard, *La technique et le temps* (Paris: Galilée, 1994).
Stimilli, Elettra, *Debt and Guilt: A Political Philosophy* (London: Bloomsbury, 2019).
Stimilli, Elettra, *La deuda del viviente. Ascesis y capitalismo* (Valencia: Pre-textos, 2021).
Strenski, Ivan, *Theology and the First Theory of Sacrifice* (Leiden: Brill, 2003).
Taeger, Fritz, *Charisma. Studien zur Geschichte des Antiken Herrscherkultes* in 2 Bände (Sttutgart: Kohlhammer, 1957).
Taubes, Jacob (ed.), *Der Fürst dieser Welt. Carl Schmitt und die Folgen* (Munich/Paderborn: Finck/Schöningh, 1983).
Taubes, Jacob, *The Political Theology of Paul* (Stanford, CA: Stanford University Press, 2003).

Taubes, Jacob, *From Cult to Culture: Fragments toward a Critique of Historical Reason* (Stanford, CA: Stanford University Press, 2009).
Taubes, Jacob, *Occidental Eschatology* (Stanford, CA: Stanford University Press, 2009).
Taylor, Charles, *A Secular Age* (Cambridge, MA: Belknap Press of Harvard University Press, 2007).
Taylor, Mark C., *Erring: A Postmodern A/theology* (Chicago: University of Chicago Press, 1984).
Thomas Aquinas, *Summa Theologiae* (Cambridge: Cambridge University Press, 2006).
Thomson, Alex, 'What's to Become of "Democracy to Come"?' *Postmodern Culture* 15(3) (2005), doi:10.1353/pmc.2005.0028.
Tillyard, Henry J. W., 'The Acclamation of Emperors in Byzantine Ritual', *Annual of the British School at Athens* 18 (1911): 239–60.
Tondo, Salvatore, 'Il "sacramentum militiae" nell' ambiente culturale romano-italico', *Studia et documenta historiae iuris* 29 (1963): 1–123.
Tosel, André, 'Démocratie du commun et religion civile', in *L'actualité du Tractatus de Spinoza et la question théologico-politique*, Quentin Landenne and Tristan Storme (eds) (Bruxelles: Edition de l'Université de Bruxelles, 2014), 165–89.
Turner, Victor, *Celebration: Studies in Festivity and Ritual* (Washington, DC: Smithsonian Institution Press, originally published University of Michigan, 1982).
Tylor, Edward Burnett, *Primitive Culture* (New York: Harper & Row, 1958).
Udías, Agustín, 'Earthquakes as God's Punishment in 17th- and 18th-century Spain', in *Geology and Religion: A History of Harmony and Hostility*, Martina Kölbl-Ebert (ed.) (London: Geological Society, 2009), 41–8.
Ullmann, Walter, 'The Bible and the Principles of Government in the Middle Ages', in *La Bibbia nell'alto medioevo* (Spoleto: Settimane di Studio del Centro italiano di studi sull'alto medioevo 10, 1963), 181–227.
Ullmann, Walter, 'Der Souveranitätsgedanke in der mittelalterlichen Krönungsordines', in *Festschrift für Percy Ernst Schramm*, Peter Classen and Peter Scheibert (eds) (Wiesbaden: Franz Steiner, 1964), 72–89.
Uríbarri, Gabino, 'La reserva escatológica: un concepto originario de Erik Peterson (1890–1960)', *Estudios Eclesiásticos* 78 (2003): 29–105.
Uríbarri, Gabino, *La vivencia cristiana del tiempo* (Madrid: BAC, 2020).
Vahanian, Gabriel, *The Death of God: The Culture of Our Post-Christian Era* (New York: George Braziller, 1961).
Valadier, Paul, *Nietzsche et la critique du christianisme* (Paris: Ed. du Cerf, 1974).
Vatter, Miguel, *Divine Democracy: Political Theology after Carl Schmitt* (Oxford: Oxford University Press, 2021).

Vattimo, Gianni, *Dopo la cristianità. Per un cristianesimo non religioso* (Milan: Garzanti Libri, 2002).

Vattimo, Gianni and Jeffrey W. Robbins, *After the Death of God* (New York: Columbia University Press, 2007).

Venard, Olivier-Thomas, 'Is There a Thomist Hermeneutic?' in *Redeeming Truth: Considering Faith and Reason*, Susan F. Parsons and Laurence-Paul Hemming (eds) (London: SCM Press, 2007).

Versnel, Hendrik Simon, *Triumphus: An Inquiry into the Origin Development and Meaning of the Roman Triumph* (Leiden: Brill, 1970).

Vries, Hent de, *Philosophy and the Turn to Religion* (Baltimore, MD: Johns Hopkins University Press, 1999).

Vries, Hent de, *Paul and the Philosophers* (New York: Fordham University Press, 2001).

Vries, Hent de, *Religion and Violence: Philosophical Perspectives from Kant to Derrida* (Baltimore, MD: Johns Hopkins University Press, 2001).

Vries, Hent de, 'Hospitable Thought: Before and Beyond Cosmopolitanism', in Hent de Vries, *Religion and Violence: Philosophical Perspectives from Kant to Derrida* (Baltimore, MD: Johns Hopkins University Press, 2001), 293–398.

Vries, Hent de (ed.), *Religion: Beyond a Concept. The Future of the Religious Past* (New York: Fordham University Press, 2008).

Vries, Hent de and Lawrence E. Sullivan, *Political Theologies: Public Religions in a Post-Secular World* (New York: Fordham University Press, 2006).

Walzer, Michael, Menachem Lorberbaum and Noam J. Zohar (eds), *The Jewish Political Tradition*, vol. 1 (New Haven, CT: Yale University Press, 2000).

Ward, Graham, *Cities of God* (London: Routledge, 2000).

Ware, Owen, 'Dialectic of the Past/Disjuncture of the Future: Derrida and Benjamin on the Concept of Messianism', *Journal for Cultural and Religious Theory* 5(2) (2004): 99–114.

Weber, Max, *Economy and Society* (Los Angeles: University of California Press, 1978).

Weber, Max, 'Zwischenbetrachtung. Theorie der Stufen und Richtungen religiöser Weltablehnung', in *Die Wirtschaftsethik der Wertreligionen. Konfuzianismus und Taoismus* (Tübingen: JCB Mohr, 1989).

Weigel, Sigrid, *Märtyrer-Porträts. Von Opfertod, Blutzeugen und heiligen Kriegern* (Munich: Fink, 2007).

Weinrich, Harald, 'Literaturgeschichte eines Weltereignisses. Das Erdbeben von Lissabon', *Literatur für Leser. Essays und Aufsätze zur Literaturwissenschaft* (Stuttgart: Kohlhammer, 1971), 64–76.

Weiser, Artur, *Glaube und Geschichte im Alten Testament* (Stuttgart: W. Kothlhammer, 1931; reprinted Göttingen, 1961).

Wesley, John, *Serious Thoughts Occasioned by the Late Earthquake at Lisbon, 1755*, in *The Works of John Wesley, vol. II: Thoughts, Addresses, Prayers, Letters* (Grand Rapids, MI: Baker Books, 1996).
Westphal, Merold, *Overcoming Onto-theology: Toward a Postmodern Christian Faith* (New York: Fordham University Press, 2001).
White, Hayden, *Figural Realism: Studies in the Mimesis Effect* (Baltimore, MD: Johns Hopkins University Press, 1999).
Wiemer, Hans-Ulrich, 'Akklamationen im spätrömischen Reich. Zur Typologie und Funktion eines Kommunikationsrituals', *Archiv für Kulturgeschichte* 86 (2004): 55–73.
Winquist, Charles E., *Epiphanies of Darkness* (Minneapolis, MN: Fortress Press, 1986).
Wolff, Hans Walter, 'Das Geschichtsverstindnis der alt-testamentlichen Prophetie', *Gesammelte Studien zum Alten Testament* (Munich: Kaiser, 1964), 289–307.
Yelle, Robert, *Semiotics of Religion: Signs of the Sacred in History* (New York: Bloomsbury, 2013).
Yelle, Robert, *Sovereignty and the Sacred: Secularism and the Political Economy of Religion* (Chicago: University of Chicago Press, 2019).
Zahn, Theodor, *Geschichte des neutestamentlichen Kanons* (Hildesheim: Georg Olms, 1975).
Zanardo, Susy, *Il legame del dono* (Milan: Vita e Pensiero, 2007).
Zizek, Slavoj, *The Fragile Absolute: Or, Why is the Christian Legacy Worth Fighting For?* (New York: Verso, 2009).
Zourabichvili, François, *Spinoza. Une physique de la pensée* (Paris: PUF, 2002).

Index

Abraham, 168–9, 214–15
absolutism, 53
acclamation
   in Antiquity, 179–81, 182, 185
   in Church liturgy, 181, 182
   in democracy, 184, 185
   dual theological–political character of, 179–82
   Heis Theos – One God, 180–1, 184
   the *Laudes regiae* litany, 181–4, 185
   theopolitical transference of, 178–9
Agamben, Giorgio, 5
   absolute hospitality, 213
   on authentic giving, 169
   economical–political paradigm, 7–8, 240
   the ethos of Christian hospitality, 209–10
   messianic time, 88–9, 242
   Pauline *charis*, 217
   on promissory oaths, 123
   signature concept, 10
   theoeconomic paradigm of glory, 177–8, 245
Althoff, Gerd, 151 n.75
Altizer, Thomas J. J., 23 n.15, 24 n.16

Ambrose, 50–1
Ancient Greece and Rome
   acclamations in Antiquity, 179–81, 182, 185
   charis, 158
   culture of pardon, 175
   gnostic idea of perfection, 148 n.61
   Greek and Hebrew historiography contrasted, 75–7, 96 n.6
   military oaths, 132–3, 134, 135
   rituals of giving and receiving, 158–9
   sacramentum, 118, 131–3
   sacred-civil character of oaths, 118
Anders, Günther, 85
apophatic theology
   apophatic discourse, 13–14
   avoidance of idolatry, 11
   the divine in, 5–6, 11–12, 239–40
   figures, 19–20
   God as Not-other, 16
   the Names of God, 12–16, 239
   silence, 15
   the symbolic, 17–18
Aquinas, Thomas, 48, 122, 160, 217

INDEX | 281

Arendt, Hannah, 222
art, 12–13
Asad, Talal, 1
Assmann, Jan, 6, 7, 145 n.50, 249, 250
Auerbach, Erich, 19, 20, 250
Augustine of Hypo, 17, 19, 66 n. 54, 82, 83, 175, 240
Aurell, Jaume, 26 n.26, 68 n.79, 138 n.13, 151 n.75, 154 n.85
Aurell, Martin, 138 n.13, 151 n.75, 154 n.85, 224, 237 n.89, 237 n.90, 237 n.91

Backer, Émile, 132, 133, 134
Balthasar, Hans Urs von, 169, 176, 177, 240
Bandarra, António Gonçalves de, 93, 94
Barr, James, 76–7, 240
Barth, Karl, 76, 199 n.98, 240
Benjamin, Walter
  historical time, 86–7, 174, 243
  on language, 40, 43, 62 n. 36, 240
  messianic time, 242
Berick, Francis H., 94
Bible, the, 46, 75–8
Bielik-Robson, Agata, 95 n.4, 111 n.65
Blumenberg, Hans, 3, 8
Bradley, Arthur, 23 n.11, 58 n.7, 59 n.14, 84, 88, 103 n.35, 103 n.37, 110 n.62, 112 n.69, 112 n.72, 143 n.39
bricolage, 60 n. 22
brotherhood ethos, 206–7, 208, 219
Brown, Peter, 180, 202 n.115, 240
Buc, Philippe, 48–9, 52–3, 125, 146 n.52, 240

Caputo, John, 5, 12, 24 n.21, 240
Caspary, Gerhard E., 17
Cavanaugh, William T., 8–9

Cerella, Antonio, 169–70
Certeau, Michel de, 10, 17
charis/charites, 158
charisma
  acclamation's theopolitical transference, 178–85, 246–7
  charismatic power, 157, 164, 170, 175–6, 245
  definition, 157
  genealogy of the meaning of, 157–64
  the gift of *charismas*, 159–60, 161, 164–5
  as a 'gift of grace', 162
  glory as charismatic power, 176–8
  the glory of God, 176–7
  in the institution of the Church, 160–2, 163
  the legitimacy of political power, 157, 160, 162, 163–4, 245, 246
  the Names of God, 239
  Paul's conception of, 157, 159–60, 162, 164, 245, 246
  as a theopolitical figure, 157, 240, 245
Chrétien, Jean-Louis, 14–15, 209, 240, 244
Christianity
  affirmative political theology, 8–9
  alterity in, 12–13
  charisma as a 'gift of grace', 162
  the Crusades, 223, 224, 226
  decentering of hospitality, 208–9
  the *mysterium tremendum*, 168
  parrhesiastic figures, 130–1, 245
  pilgrimage to Jerusalem, 223–4, 226
  prophetic time, 242
  rituals of veridiction, 127–9, 243–4
  role of the oath, 121–2, 127, 242–3

Christianity (*cont.*)
  the Templars, 224–8
  temporality of, 81, 85
  tradition of hospitality, 214–15
  the vocabulary of Christian
    theology, 10, 49, 133, 162, 249
Chrysostom, John, 160
Cicero, 90, 123, 175
Clement of Alexandria, 213
Cohn, Norman, 89, 90
community
  brotherhood ethos, 206–7, 208, 219
  charismas as a gift to the community, 158–61, 162, 164–5
  Christian trope of the neighbour, 208–10
  communal body of Christ, 208
  communal gift exchanges, 160–1, 164–5
  hospitality and, 211, 247
  Scriptural interpretation and, 45–8
Couch, John, 94
Crusades, the, 223, 224, 226
Cullmann, Oscar, 76, 77, 78, 240
Cynics, 130–1, 151 n. 73, 151 n. 74, 152 n. 76

Davis, Kathleen, 3
Dean, Mitchell, 28 n.36
Derrida, Jacques
  on alterity, 210
  the *aporia* of origin, 87, 88, 207, 212–13, 247
  différance, 41–2
  on gift-giving, 166–7, 168–9, 170, 245
  on hospitality, 206, 220–1
  justice and the law, 241
  justice and the politics of hospitality, 212
  language as the first type of perjury, 123–4
  the logic of supplement, 42
  merciful power, 175
  messianic time, 87–8, 242
  on negative theology, 14
  on the priority of writing, 40–3, 45, 46–7
  problematic nature of oaths, 126–7, 243–4
  role of the oath, 242–3
  Scripture as a figure of the divine, 39
  the sign and divinity, 40–1
  sovereign forgiveness, 170–1, 173, 174, 245
  substitution and hospitality, 213–14, 215–16, 247, 248
  on symbolic speech, 17
  the theological turn, 4, 5, 10, 240
  topolitology, 20
  unconditional–ethical, 217–18
Dionysius the Aeropagite, 11, 16–17, 20, 53
divinity
  within a democratic discursive framework, 9
  the divine witness to oaths, 120–2, 126–7
  imagination of the divine, 5–6
  marks of in secularisation, 9–11
  the sign and, 40–1
  see also God
dogma, 89
Duby, George, 223
Durkheim, Emile, 165

Enlightenment
  cosmopolitanism, 222
  impact of the Lisbon earthquake, 91–3
  the post-secular age, 3–4
  prophetic time and political action, 90
  Scriptural interpretation, 54–5
  theodicy literature and, 93
  the theological–political Bible, 57

eschatological time, 79–81
ethics
   of hospitality, 207, 217–18, 247
   the unconditional–ethical, 217–18
exegesis
   the gloss, 51–2
   Luke 22:38, 49–51

faithfulness
   promissory oaths, 123–5
   and pronounced oaths, 118
figures
   figural temporality, 20
   historical–theological concept of, 19–20
   pahrresiasts, 129–31, 245
   topolitology, 20
   see also theopolitical figures
Foster, Theodore B., 132, 133, 135
Foucauld, Charles de, 214
Foucault, Michel, 240
   on the Cynics, 151 n. 74, 152 n. 76
   history of sexuality, 146 n.56
   the juridical system of civil penalties, 128–9, 244
   on oaths, 121
   on parrhesia, 129–31, 245
   substitution and hospitality, 213
   on truth regimes, 127–9
Franck, Didier, 10
Franke, William, 5–6, 9–10, 13
fraternity, 206–7, 208–10
friendship, 206–7

Gadamer, Hans-Georg, 18, 40, 44–5, 46–7, 80, 81, 241
Geertz, Clifford, 144 n.48, 157, 163
gifts
   Christ's *kenosis*, 169, 178
   communal gift exchanges, 160–1, 164–5
   the condition of non-returnability, 166–7, 245
   as a form of social contract, 165–6
   the gift of *charismas*, 159–60, 161, 162, 164–5
   Greco-Roman gift-giving and receiving, 158–9
   the non-recognition of the donor, 166–7
   the sacrificial gift, 168–9, 170
   sovereign forgiveness, 170–6
   supernatural gifts, 161–2
   temporality of, 166
   within the terms of exchange, 165–8
Giles of Rome, 53
Girard, René, 194 n.61
glory
   glory as charismatic power, 176–8
   the glory of God, 176–7
   theoeconomic paradigm of glory, 177–8, 245
God
   as the divine witness to oaths, 120–2, 126–7
   the forgiving God, 174–5
   God's power (*doxa*), 176
   God's sovereignty, 169–70
   Heis Theos – One God acclamations, 180–1, 184
   images of, 18
   the Names of God, 11–17, 239
   natural law, 91
   symbolic speech for, 17–18
   theological philosophies on the death of God, 4–5, 9
   see also divinity
Goethe, Johann Wolfgang von, 35 n.99, 95

Habermas, Jürgen, 3
Harnack, Adolf von, 160–1, 162
Hegel, Georg Wilhelm Friedrich, 171–2

Heidegger, Martin, 10, 40
hermeneutics
  Christian hermeneutics, 19, 47
  literary hermeneutics, 13
  theological hermeneutics, 45
Heron, Nicholas, 198 n.95
Hespanha, Antonio M., 196 n.69
Hippolytus, 50–1
history
  the cosmovision of ancient civilisations, 89–90
  eschatological time, 79–81
  Greek and Hebrew historiography contrasted, 75–7, 96 n.6
  historical time, 73, 75–8, 86–7, 174, 241–2, 243
  historical-theological concept of figures, 19–20
  the Last Judgement, 80–1, 174
  messianic time, 85–6
  prophetic thought and historical events, 90–1
  time in prophetic narratives, 73–82, 211
  Voltaire's histories, 92
Hobbes, Thomas, 49, 54–5, 57, 119
Höfling, Johann Wilhelm Friedrich, 160
Homer, 158
hospitality
  absolute hospitality, 207, 213–14, 216–17, 248
  the *aporia* of origin and, 207, 212–13, 247
  of cities, 220–2
  the community and, 211, 247
  concept, 206
  conditional hospitality, 207
  ethical hospitality, 207, 217–18, 247
  the ethos of Christian hospitality, 208–10, 216, 248
  fraternity and, 206–7
  the Hospitaller Malta, 223–8
  in hospitals, 223, 226
  in Islam, 214–15
  justice and the politics of hospitality, 212
  the Names of God, 239
  the reception of the other, 207, 210–12, 248
  sacred hospitality, 214
  substitution as hyperbolic hospitality, 213–17, 247–8
  symbolic representation, 217–20, 247, 248–9
  as a theopolitical figure, 240
  the third party, 212
  towards pilgrims in the Middle East, 223–4, 226
Hugh of Saint Victor, 135–6
Husserl, Edmund, 210

immanence, 3, 10
Islam
  holy war concept, 224
  hospitality, 214–15
  prophetic time, 242

Janicaud, Dominique, 4
Jankélévitch, Vladimir, 170, 173, 174, 240
Jerome, 46, 53
Judaism
  Abraham's sacrifice, 168–9
  brotherhood ethos, 206–7, 208, 210
  Covenant of Sinai, 121
  culture of pardon, 175
  the glory of God, 176–7
  prophetic time, 242
  prophetism, 74–5
  role of the oath, 120–1
justice
  the Last Judgement, 79, 80–1, 174
  mercy and the logic of criminal justice, 171–3

messianicity, 87–8
oaths as judicial procedure, 122–3
and the politics of hospitality, 212
temporality and, 87
see also law

Kant, Immanuel, 92–3, 171, 207, 222
Kantorowicz, Ernst, 6–7, 176, 179, 181–4, 240
Koselleck, Reinhart, 79, 80–1, 84, 85, 240
Kümmel, Werner G., 79

Laborde, Cecile, 22 n.8
language
    biblical language of temporality, 76–8
    différance, 41–2
    as the first type of perjury, 123–4
    linguistic turn, 40
    relationship to the written text, 45
    the sign, 18, 40–1
    the vocabulary of Christian theology, 10, 49, 133, 162, 239, 249
    see also writing
Last Judgement, 79, 80–1, 174
law
    exceptions to the law, 173, 241
    the juridical system of civil penalties, 128–9
    mercy and the logic of criminal justice, 171–3
    oaths as judicial procedure, 122–3
    sovereign power, 173
    sworn promises of the legal system, 124–5
    see also justice
Lefort, Claude, 7
Leibniz, Gottfried Wilhelm, 92, 93

Levinas, Emmanuel, 87, 206, 211, 212, 213, 216, 221, 247–8
Levi-Strauss, Claude, 60 n. 22
Lisbon earthquake, 90–5
liturgy, 178, 181, 182, 183–4
Lloyd, Vincent, 188 n.32
Locke, John, 3, 49, 54–7, 119
lordship, 53
Löwith, Karl, 2–3, 85
Lubac, Henry de, 240
Luther, Martin, 65 n.47, 83, 84, 105 n.48, 160

Malagrida, Gabriele, 93
Marion, Jean-Luc, 167–8, 240
Markus, Robert, 17, 240
martyrs, 169–70
Massignon, Louis, 214–16, 240, 248
Mauss, Marcel, 165–6, 167
messianism
    justice and, 87–8
    messianic time, 85–9, 211, 242
    Pauline *hos me*, 88–9
    prophecy and, 74–5
Middle Ages
    private and public oaths, 119
    promotion of hospitality, 223
    regime of pardon, 170–1
    sacred kingship concept, 53
    social structure, 223
    superioritas concept, 53
    theopolitical transference of ideas and concepts, 6–7, 49
Moltmann, Jürgen, 8, 161
Momigliano, Arnaldo, 75–6
Mommsen, Theodor, 200 n.106
monarchism
    interpretations of Luke 22:38, 52
    the *laudes* at the coronation, 182–4
    regal pardon and clemency, 170–2
    sacred kingship concept, 53

Ó Murchadha, Felix, 89, 97 n.13, 113 n.80
mystery, 134–5
mysticism, 11, 79–81

Nancy, Jean-Luc, 5, 12–13, 240
nation state
    oaths of office and allegiance, 117–18
    religion in definition to, 1
    scriptural interpretation in Modern State theory, 54–6
    separation between Church and State, 49–50, 53–4, 56–7, 119–20
Nicholas of Cusa, 11, 15–17
Nietzsche, Friedrich, 5, 9, 73, 81

oaths
    the baptismal oath, 122, 127–8, 132–3, 134
    the Christian Mysteries, 134–5
    confession in Christianity, 127–8, 245
    covenants, 119, 121
    the divine witness to, 120–2, 126–7
    and mystery, 133
    the Names of God, 239
    in the New Testament, 121
    parrhesia, 129–31, 245
    perjury, 120, 123–4
    as a political institution, 117–18
    as promissory, 122, 123–5, 133, 136
    as rituals of veridiction, 125–6, 127–8, 131, 243–4
    Roman military oaths, 132–3
    the Roman *sacramentum*, 118, 131–4
    the sacrament-oath, 119, 126, 128, 132–6, 245
    as sacred rituals, 126, 131–2
    sacred-civil character of, 118–20
    separation between Church and State, 119–20
    sworn promises of the legal system, 124–5
    temporality of, 122, 123–4
    as testimony, 122–3, 133, 136
    theological–political transfers of the truth, 117–18, 127–9, 131–6, 244–5
    as a theopolitical figure, 240, 242
    verification of subjectivity, 127
Origen of Alexandria, 19, 49–51, 132, 159
Ors, Álvaro d', 84, 106 n.53, 106 n.54, 113 n.83, 138 n.12, 154 n.87, 156 n.107

Parousia, the, 148 n.62
Paul of Tarsus
    charis, 217
    the ethos of Christian hospitality, 208–10, 216, 248
    glory as charismatic power, 176
    the *hos me*, 88–9
    idea of *charisma*, 157, 159–60, 162, 164, 245, 246
    katechon, 82–5
    Pauline political theology, 5
Peterson, Erik
    acclamations in Antiquity, 179–81
    dogma, 113 n.80
    Heis Theos – One God, 180–1, 184
    scriptural characterisation of time, 79, 80, 242
philosophy
    theological philosophies on the death of God, 4–5, 9
    the theological turn in, 4–6, 10–11, 239–40
philosophy of history, 2–3, 8
pilgrims, 223–4, 226

Plato, 158, 223
political community
  acclamation's theopolitical transference, 178–9
  core literary texts, 39–40
  proximity and, 206
  sacred-civil character of oaths, 118–20, 121, 125, 126–7
  Scriptural interpretation and, 48–57
political power
  charisma and the legitimisation of, 157, 160, 162, 163–4, 245, 246
  and the deinstitutionalisation of religion, 56–7
  the oath and, 117–18
  reason and political freedom, 56
  Scriptural interpretation and, 48–9, 240
political theology
  affirmative political theology, 8–9
  economical–political paradigm, 7–8
  radical political theology, 9
  structural analogy between the political and the theological, 6, 7–8
  definition, 6
  transference of meanings, 6–7, 10
Pope, Alexander, 91
post-secular, 2
Potts, John, 186 n.9, 188 n.32
power
  acclamation's theopolitical transference, 178–85, 246–7
  charismatic power, 157, 164, 170, 175–6, 245, 246
  as a circulating object, 166
  culture of pardon, 175
  the glory of God, 176–7
  God's sovereignty, 169–70
  merciful power, 175
  sacrifice as a paradigm of power, 168–70
  sovereign forgiveness, 170–6
  in spaces of hospitality, 221
  theopolitical character of political power, 157
Proclus, 15
Prodi, Paolo, 117, 121, 129, 131, 240, 244
prophecy
  ancient traditions of, 74–5, 90
  by Bandarra, 93–4
  the cosmovision of ancient civilisations, 89–90
  impact of the Lisbon earthquake, 93–4
  interpretation of historical events, 74–5, 211
  the Names of God, 239
  in the New Testament, 75, 82–3
  Pauline *katechon*, 82–5
  the prophetic event as written word, 47–8
  prophetic thought and historical events, 90–1
  prophetic time, 73–82, 89, 123, 211, 240, 241–3
  the prophetic word in Scriptures, 47–8, 73
  revelations in prophetic literature, 47–8, 73–5
  theological-political prophetic literature, 93–4
  as a theopolitical figure, 240
  the working of miracles, 55
prophetism, 74–5

radical political theology, 9
radical theology, 4–5, 9
Raschke, Carl A., 5, 26 n.26
Ratzinger, Josef, 65 n.49, 99 n.21, 192 n.53, 240
Reformation, the, 1

religion
  continued place in modern
    society, 3–4
  semiotics, 6
  definition, 1
revelation
  literature's role in, 5–6
  monotheistic, 11
  in prophetic literature, 47–8,
    73–5
  in relation to secularisation,
    9–10
Riedel, Manfred, 102 n.33
Rossi, Martino, 185 n.4
Roueché, Charlotte, 179, 180, 202 n.119
Rousseau, Jean Jacques, 92, 94, 120, 175, 216

sacrifice
  Christ's *kenosis*, 169, 178
  dying for the other, 206
  early Christian martyrs, 169–70
  as a paradigm of power, 168–70
  of the pre-Christian era, 194 n.61
  the sacrificial gift, 168–9, 170
Saussure, Ferdinand de, 18, 40
Schiller, Friedrich, 80
Schmitt, Carl
  the charismatic character of the
    Church, 162–3
  on direct democracy, 184
  the friend-enemy relationship of
    the political, 206
  on oaths, 117, 120, 124
  on the Pauline *katechon*, 82, 83–4
  political theology, 6, 8
  theopolitical paradigm of
    sovereignty, 172, 177
Scriptures
  as both text and event, 46–8
  the dialectic between *ustitia* and *misericordia*, 52–3
  as a figure of the divine, 39
  the forgiving God, 174
  the fulfilment of, 47
  the gloss, 51–2
  as God's speech, 39
  historical-political impacts of, 49–57
  as the inscription of an absence, 43, 210
  interpretation of and political power, 48–9, 240
  interpretation/re-interpretation of, 44, 52, 241
  Luke 22:38, 49–51
  the Names of God, 239
  performativity of, 47–8
  plurality of, 46
  political, 39–40
  as prophetic word, 47–8, 73
  as sacred texts, 43–4, 240–1
  scriptural concept of time, 76–7
  scriptural interpretation in
    Modern State theory, 54–6
  the scriptural turn, 40–6
  as a theopolitical figure, 240–1
secularisation
  divine marks of origin in, 9–11
  in modernity, 3–4, 8, 10
  the radical inscription of God in
    the world, 10
  in relation to revelation, 9–10
secularisation thesis, 2–4, 8
semiotics, 6, 18, 40–1
Seneca, 159, 166, 171
Shils, Edward, 163
Sohm, Rudolph, 160, 161, 162, 184
sovereignty
  covenants, 119
  economical–political paradigm, 7–8
  God's sovereignty, 169–70
  the medieval *superioritas*
    concept and, 53

the monarchical sovereign
    pardon, 170–2
  scriptural interpretation in
    Modern State theory, 55–6
  separation between Church and
    State, 53–4, 56–7
  sovereign forgiveness, 170–6,
    245
  theopolitical paradigm of
    sovereignty, 172, 177
Spinoza, Baruch, 49, 54–5, 56,
  57
Stack, Trevor, 1
Stahl, Julius Friedrich, 160
state *see* nation state
Stimilli, Elettra, 189 n.39
symbolism
  in apophatic theology, 17–18
  oaths as rituals, 125–6
  symbolic representation of
    hospitality, 217–20, 248–9

Taubes, Jacob, 5, 95 n.4
Templars, the, 224–8
Tertullian, 19, 46, 50–1, 82,
  132–4, 135, 159, 240
testimony, 122–3, 133, 136
Teutonic Order, the, 226–7
theological, the
  Pauline political theology, 5
  radical theology, 4–5, 9
  definition, 1–2
  the theological turn in
    philosophy, 4–6, 239–40,
    249–50
theopolitical figures, concept, 11,
  20–1, 249–50
time
  absolute limit, 79–81
  aeon, 76–7
  the *aporia* of origin, 87, 88
  chronos, 77, 88
  the end of time, 75, 79–80,
    82–5
  eschatological time, 79–81

historical time, 73, 75–8, 86–7,
  174, 241–2, 243
kairos, 77, 88
messianic time, 85–9, 211, 242
Nietzschean temporal
  perspectivism, 81
the *parousia*, 78–9, 82, 84, 88
Pauline *hos me*, 88–9
Pauline *katechon*, 82–5
prophetic thought and historical
  events, 90–1
prophetic time, 73–82, 89, 123,
  211, 240, 241–3
sovereign forgiveness, 174
temporality of oaths, 122,
  123–4
tragic time, 86
topolitology, 20
truthfulness
  confession in Christianity,
    127–8, 245
  oaths as rituals of veridiction,
    125–6, 127–8, 131, 243–4
  parrhesia, 129–31, 245
  theological-political transfers
    of the truth, 117–18, 127–9,
    131–6, 244–5

Ullmann, Walter, 49, 53, 54, 240

Voltaire, 91–2
Vries, Hent de, 2, 4, 11, 38 n.110,
  213, 217–19, 231 n.33, 232
  n.38

Weber, Max, 2, 157, 162, 163,
  164, 222, 245
Wesley, John, 93–4
writing/written texts
  as both text and event, 46–8
  historical narratives, 73
  language's relation to the written
    text, 45
  the priority of the written word,
    40–3, 45, 46–7

writing/written texts (*cont.*)
   reader interpretation of, 44–5
   sacred texts, 43–4, 240–1
   the Scriptures as prophetic word, 47–8, 73
   as a theological question, 45–6
   translatability of the written text, 43–4, 46
   see also Scriptures

Yelle, Robert, 164, 189 n.34

Zoroastro, 89–90

EU representative:
Easy Access System Europe
Mustamäe tee 50, 10621 Tallinn, Estonia
Gpsr.requests@easproject.com